# THE
# HISTORY OF
# ADVERTISING
## 40
## MAJOR BOOKS
## IN FACSIMILE

Edited by
HENRY ASSAEL
C. SAMUEL CRAIG
New York University

A
GARLAND
SERIES

# ADVERTISING
## PROCEDURE

OTTO KLEPPNER

GARLAND PUBLISHING, INC.
NEW YORK & LONDON
1985

$(LT)$
HF
5823
.K45
1985

For a complete list of the titles in this series
see the final pages of this volume.

This facsimile has been made from a copy in
the Yale University Library.


**Library of Congress Cataloging in Publication Data**

Kleppner, Otto, 1899–
  Advertising procedure.
  (The History of advertising)
  Reprint. Originally published: New York : Prentice-
Hall, 1925.
  Bibliography: p.
  Includes index.
  1. Advertising.  I. Title.  II. Series.
HF5823.K45  1985    659.1    84-46040
ISBN 0-8240-6734-7 (alk. paper)


*Design by Donna Montalbano*

The volumes in this series are printed on
acid-free, 250-year-life paper.

Printed in the United States of America

# ADVERTISING PROCEDURE

### THE RAW PRODUCT

**1** A piece of asbestos. What shall we do with it?

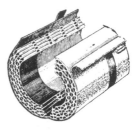

### THE TRANSFORMING IDEA

**2** Make pipe insulation of the asbestos, embodying an improved design.

*Have you a Cinderella in your cellar?*

### THE COPY AND VISUALIZING IDEA

**3** "Is your furnace with its pipes neglected? Cover them with this insulation."

### THE COMPLETED ADVERTISEMENT

**4** based on the above. (*See also page* 181.)

THE EVOLUTION OF AN ADVERTISING IDEA

# ADVERTISING PROCEDURE

BY

## OTTO KLEPPNER, M.C.S.

ADVERTISING MANAGER, PRENTICE-HALL, INC.

New York
PRENTICE-HALL, Inc.
1925

LONDON
SIR ISAAC PITMAN & SONS, LTD.
PARKER STREET, KINGSWAY, W.C.2

# PREFACE

This book was written to show in a simple manner the inception of advertising ideas and their development, and to trace the course of the advertisement through each of its many steps. The methods described for planning and preparing advertisements are based upon practices actually followed in advertising offices. The principles offered for use in creating ideas may appear new, but will be recognized as underlying all effective advertisements.

Ideas, as Matthew Arnold said in his essay on Criticism, are the element with which the creative power works. Ideas are the element with which advertising builds. It was the idea of making clothing conform to a dependable standard, and of identifying it with a label, that first brought Hart-Schaffner & Marx advertising its success; it was the idea of making a fashionable suiting of a cloth which heretofore had been used for workmen's trousers, that enabled the advertising of Palm Beach Clothing to be so effective. The variety of uses to which oil could be employed was the idea which gave to 3-in-1 Oil advertising its significance, while the success of Gargoyle advertising was based on its chart, listing the grades of oil best suited to the various makes of cars. Back of each advertising success there is an idea, born of a definite reason.

In giving emphasis to the creation of ideas, the book holds of no less importance the methods of expressing those thoughts, or the practical details of the work. The fact that the text is supported throughout by the experiences of advertisers may commend it as being sound and useful. But the book endeavors to do more than bring experiences together, however notable they might have been. It seeks an approach to advertising easy to comprehend and capable of being immediately applied. Whether or not it succeeds in doing so, the reader best can judge.

The writing of this book was inspired by Ralph M. Leseritz, whose decease, April 29, 1920, called from advertising one of

ix

its energetic, constructive influences. Those men are fortunate who possess a discernment so fine, an expression so lucid, and who find in their calling a pleasure so genuine. His unflagging devotion to his work, though he had been weakened by the war, brought a wholesome career to an early close.

The author is indebted to his friend, Richard B. Franken, for the generous collaboration on the chapter dealing with Packages and on the chapter dealing with Research. William Paul Langreich helped in formulating the chapters dealing with Visualizing and Layouts. That the section on Dealer Displays is a useful one is due to Joseph N. Leigh. Robert Ash, Member of the Bar, Supreme Court of the United States, served as legal consultant on questions dealing with trademarks. Throughout this work, Fred Weeks gave liberally of his sound judgment and opportune aid.

In order that the book might be as comprehensive as possible within the confines set for it, various chapters were submitted for review to men well known in their respective fields. For their painstaking care in this work, also for the graciousness with which they undertook it, thanks are particularly due to H. Frank Smith, L. A. Wollner, H. Belding Joseph, Edward Kramer and F. R. Barnard. The writer also appreciates the courtesy of his associates in advertising who placed the facilities of their organizations at his disposal. In charming spirit and with unbounded patience, the author's sister, Vilma, handled completely the actual preparation of the manuscript.

George L. Hollrock designed and prepared the special illustrations which appear here, and gave much of his time in arranging the make-up of the book.

OTTO KLEPPNER

# TABLE OF CONTENTS

## Part I

### THE PURPOSES OF ADVERTISING

## Part II

### PREPARATION OF ADVERTISEMENTS

xi

# CONTENTS

# PART I

# THE PURPOSES OF ADVERTISING

CHAPTER I

# THE ADVERTISING SPIRAL

SHORTLY after the Radiola made its appearance, one of
its advertisements dwelt upon the fact that the owner of
this instrument would now be able to enjoy hearing the actual
concerts by the finest orchestras; the advertisement then went
on to explain that the loud-speaker had reached a point of
development which enabled sound to be reproduced in all its
original richness of tone. Just two decades prior to the appearance of that advertisement, another one was published
which read: "The Improved Victor Talking Machine now
brings the living voices of the greatest opera singers to your
home for the first time in the history of the world. The
tapering arm gives the vibrations gradually more room to
grow, round out and develop the full richness and volume of
tone that makes the charm of a fine voice or instrument."

Great progress had been made in advertising during the
years which elapsed between the appearance of the two advertisements. Certainly the man who created the radio advertisement had little occasion to borrow any thoughts from the
phonograph advertisement of bygone days. What is it, then,
which causes the similarity in the ideas of these two advertisements?

The same question is raised by the similarity between the
recent airplane advertising and that of automobiles of 1902
and thereabouts. In the early days of the automobile, the
Jackson Automobile advertisement said that no hill was too
steep, no sand too deep, for the motor car. A Riker Electric
Vehicle advertisement declared that up-hill, down-dale, rough
roads and smooth were now all alike. How interesting it is to
compare these statements with those of a Martin Airplane
advertisement, appearing twenty years later—"The airplane
knows no barriers. The world's airways go on forever. There

3

is no valley too deep, no mountain too high for the airplane to vault with ease. There is no desert so broad, no forest so dense over which the airplane cannot ply its way." The similarity becomes all the more striking when it is realized that innumerable advertisements made their appearance in the interval which elapsed between these two advertisements; each of the twenty years brought forth new developments in advertising, each of these developments served quickly to antiquate previous conceptions of advertising. But despite all these reasons for expecting a complete departure in airplane advertising from the early automobile advertising, the identical presentation of arguments is found still to exist.

What has caused advertising history to repeat itself to a phrase? Before endeavoring to find an answer, it may be interesting to make still another comparison between an advertisement of the Ucan Hair Cutter appearing 16 years after a Gillette Safety Razor advertisement of 1907. In this manner were men enfranchised from the barber:

UCAN SAFETY HAIR CUTTER

Now I can cut my own hair. Regularly, every Sunday and Wednesday I spend five minutes with my Ucan. Keeps my hair neat and trim around the ears and down the sides and back. Cutting hair with Ucan is easier than shaving—and quicker. Just as simple as combing your hair. Dampen the hair—and comb it with Ucan. That's all there's to it.

Business men, professional men, salesmen, army and navy officers—men to whom personal appearance is a definite asset, are regular users of Ucan. They cut their own hair not just once a month—they can't afford to look shaggy. They cut it twice a week.

The Ucan Safety Hair Cutter, complete with part for shaving

GILLETTE SAFETY RAZOR

If you are still depending upon the barber or old fashioned razor, you are in the same category as the man who climbs ten flights of stairs when there is an elevator in the building. You are not like him—losing time—which is money —but you are losing the benefits of a clean, comfortable home shave.

My idea was to shave smoothly without leaving stray hairs or rough patches of beard in the corners and places hard to get at. All these are accomplished by the Gillette Safety Razor.

With the Gillette, the most inexperienced man can remove, without cut or scratch, in three to five minutes, any beard that ever grew.

back of neck and sides of head. Now on sale at hardware, sporting goods, dry goods, and general stores everywhere. If you do not find Ucan Safety Hair Cutter at your local store, send me two dollars with name of your dealer and we will deliver Ucan to your home, parcel post.

Gives the best possible shave at home or away—saving you time, money, and endless inconvenience. Over two million men know how well I succeeded. At all jewelry, drug, hardware, and sporting goods dealers. Or write us at once for our booklet and free trial offer.

Both advertisements mention the few minutes required to use the respective instruments; both speak of the simplicity of operation, the ability to remove the hard-to-reach hairs, the convenience of cutting hair and of shaving at home, and the large number of men who are already users of these devices. Two advertisements so far removed from each other in point of time would never show such marked similarity, were it not for the fact that products themselves were passing through a similar advertising evolution.

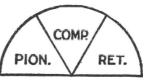

CHART A.—THE THREE STAGES

The advertising stages of a product.—The radio, the phonograph, the airplane, the automobile, the safety hair cutter, the safety razor, all underwent a typical advertising evolution—an evolution in which the attitude of the public toward the product was changed. This evolutionary process is one in which most products participate, and can be traced as it passes through three phases, the "pioneering" stage, the "competitive" stage, and the "retentive" stage. What the advertisements for any given product shall say depends largely upon the stage in which the product finds itself at that time.

The pioneering stage.—For many years an inventor may diligently be trying to develop some useful device. When he finally succeeds in perfecting his model, does the public arise in elation at the achievement? Not in most cases, because it never occurred to the people that they needed a device such as the one now offered. Until they do appreciate that fact,

# Every Home Can Now Own a Wireless Telephone

*Captures actual news, music and voices out of the air. Practically indestructible. Anyone can set it up. Full information at any one of our three stores.*

ON Saturday afternoon, November 26, thousands of people in New York and vicinity sat comfortably in the living rooms of their own homes, listening to the results of the great Army-Navy football game, play by play, just as they had listened to the results of other great games previously — the Yale-Harvard game, the Harvard-Princeton game, etc., etc.

Every night thousands of people are enjoying at home, dance music, popular songs, or concerts by leading vocal or instrumental artists—not through the medium of recorded sound, but direct from the artist to the home over the wireless telephone.

Every day, thousands of people are getting the news of the world right in their own home — several hours before the newspapers are on the street—reports of athletic events—football, baseball, boxing, etc., weather forecast, the correct time, etc., etc.

This new great pleasure and convenience is the result of the achieved success of the wireless telephone for receiving messages, as an actual practicable reality for every home.

### The Sensation of the Year

Few people even imagined that the wireless telephone would ever get beyond the stage where it served a worthy purpose for professional radio men and a plaything for boys with a technical turn of mind.

Few people even imagined that the wireless telephone would ever be available to every home; so easy to install that the most inexperienced layman can set it up; so inexpensive that it is available as low as $27.50, which initial cost is the final and only cost on this low-price set.

### What is the Wireless Telephone?

The wireless telephone for the home is generally confined to a receiving instrument only, which captures voices, music, news out of the air, and transmits it to your living-room for your entertainment and information. It is not an instrument for sending messages to your neighbors, nor does it compete in any way with the ordinary telephone. A central sending station provides a daily program that is carried through the air into every home equipped with this wireless receiving set.

This program is well planned. It includes opera music, dance music, concerts. For the children it sends out fairy stories. It gives weather forecasts. It gives local, national and international news every evening. It gives the results, play by play, of important athletic events. It transmits, word for word, the actual speeches of great men on great occasions. You receive the addresses almost immediately they are made. Only last week, Mr. Hiram Percy Maxim, famous scientist and inventor of the Maxim Silencer, delivered an address over the wireless telephone.

### Easily Installed by Anyone

To many people, the word "wireless" conjures up visions of danger, of electricity, of fire hazard, of complicated mechanisms.

A wonderful thing about the wireless telephone is its utter freedom from any danger of any kind.

The wireless telephone is a simple instrument. There is nothing intricate about it that requires technical knowledge; nothing that might involve anyone in the slightest danger.

Demonstrations of the wireless telephone are held daily from 9 A. M. to 5.30 P. M. at all three of the convenient stores of the Manhattan Electrical Supply Company. You are invited to visit any one of these stores and listen to the wireless 'phone yourself.

Even if you have no intention of purchasing you should at least know the new, delightful experience of hearing music and messages gathered from the air—inaudible except to the possessors of the wireless telephone.

The price range of the wireless phone enables the humblest home to afford one. A very satisfactory size can be obtained as low as $25.00 or $27.50 complete with wire to erect. Larger sizes up to $300. An unusual Christmas gift for year round entertainment.

* * *

In introducing the wireless telephone to the general public, the Manhattan Electrical Supply Company is simply adhering to the same policy of pioneering and progress which impelled it to open one of the earliest electrical stores in New York in 1890, one of the first wholesale distributing offices for electrical merchandise, and one of the first departments especially devoted to wireless supplies, in 1909. Each of the 3 New York stores is conveniently located, and each is a veritable department store of electrical merchandise and supplies of every variety.

*Come in and hear the wireless telephone today*

## Manhattan Electrical Supply Co., Inc.

*Downtown:* 17 Park Place
Near Broadway

*Times Square District:* 110 West 42nd Street
Between Sixth Ave. and Broadway

*Uptown:* 127 West 125th Street
Between Lenox and Seventh Aves.

### ARE THERE ADVERTISING STAGES?

Radio in the pioneering stage. The advertisement tells of the advantages provided by the "wireless telephone."

ARE THERE ADVERTISING STAGES?

Radio in the competitive stage four years later. The advertisement takes for granted that the reader contemplates buying a radio and shows why this particular make is preferable.

however, a product is in the first, a pioneering, stage. The advertising used in the first stage really introduces an idea which antiquates previous conceptions. Methods which were accepted as having been the only ones possible are now shown to have been improved; shortcomings tolerated as having been necessary are now demonstrated to have been overcome. The advertising for a product in the pioneering stage (or "pioneering advertising" as we may call it) has to do more than merely present a new product—it must implant a new custom, develop a new usage, cultivate new standards of living in order that there may be a demand for the goods offered. For generations the broom was accepted proverbially by the housewife as the proper tool for sweeping. To sell carpet-sweepers, it was necessary to show that a "dustless" sweeper was more sanitary and more thorough than a broom, and when vacuum cleaners were offered, the housewife had to be convinced that there was still too little dirt removed from the carpet and too much dust being raised by the old methods. As long as she felt satisfied with the dust which remained in the carpet, she was satisfied to use a carpet sweeper, but as soon as she was shown how much dirt really settled into her floor covering, and the ease with which it could be removed with an "air-suction cleaner," she was ready to consider vacuum cleaners.

There is another circumstance under which a product may be considered in the first stage. It may be that an inventor has been working on an idea which has long been wanted, but which has not been developed heretofore, as, for example, an inexpensive fuel to replace gasoline. Upon the appearance of such a product, people will not have to be shown why they need it, for that will be self-evident; rather, the public will have to be shown in a most convincing manner that the inventor's product can actually fulfil the requirements imposed upon it.

The purpose of pioneering advertising, reduced to its simplest terms, is to show either or both of the following:

1. That the reader has a need which he did not appreciate before, and in order to fill that need he must use a product.

2. (When the reader already recognizes his need for á product which was not available heretofore) That a product now exists actually capable of filling that need.

**Applying the idea.**—Pioneering advertising, as a rule, has to stress that which the product can do, offer or provide, which could not be done, offered or provided before. By way of illustration, we have the five following products in the pioneering stage. Alongside of each is summarized the outstanding idea around which their advertisements were developed. Whatever else was said in the respective advertisements merely amplified and substantiated these ideas.

| PRODUCT | IDEAS |
|---|---|
| Indoor Wireless Loop (*De Forest Radio*) | With the new DeForest indoor loop you can hear 3,000 miles. *You are saved the bother of raising an outdoor aerial.* |
| Steel Tennis Racquet (*Dayton*) | Moisture does not affect this racquet. which enables you to play earlier in the spring; you can play with it at the seashore for the racquet will not warp. *Do not accept the limitations imposed by the wooden racquets even though you have always taken these restrictions for granted.* |
| Corn Picker (*International*) | The McCormick Picker eliminates the drudgery of picking, husking and loading corn. It is not affected by the ordinary objections to hand-picking, such as frosty mornings, bad weather, down and tangled corn— *why should you continue to put up with the hardship of hand-picking?* |
| Oven Glass (*Pyrex*) | Oven glass withstands sudden changes in temperature. It bakes evenly and quickly. It insures fast, even baking and saves extra dishwashing. *You have always wished for these conveniences in cooking. Now you can secure them.* |

| PRODUCT (CONT.) | IDEAS (CONT.) |
| --- | --- |
| Cuticle Remover............................ | Liquid cuticle remover makes it pos- |
| (*Cutex*) | sible for you to have faultlessly mani- |
| | cured nails, without injurious cutting |
| | —*Cutting cuticles with scissors the* |
| | *way you have been doing, is ruinous* |
| | *to the charm of your hands.* |

Most other pioneering advertisements run the same way—concerning themselves more with an attempt to change people's habits and combat their acceptance of certain limitations, than with a portrayal of the product itself.

An interesting feature of pioneering advertisements is their reference to the time element: "Now you can do this" or "At last you can do that" will often be found in these advertisements. They also make frequent comparison with other products "as essential to your comfort as the electric light and telephone." That this method of presentation is not as original as it might be (and may be improved upon as will be shown) does not detract from the soundness of the ideas which the pioneering advertisements sought to express.

**The competitive stage.**—When a product in the first or pioneering stage comes into general acceptance, when people have learned to recognize their need for it, a new situation invariably arises. Others will appear on the scene, offering their own make of that product. The advertiser is no longer confronted with the task of inspiring appreciation for the product as such, but he is obliged to secure preference for his particular make over similar ones. In the pioneering stage, people do not want the product at all; in the second, or competitive stage, they merely inquire which of several competing brands is the best to buy. Among the many everyday products which are now largely in the competitive stage are shoes, hosiery, automobile tires, typewriters, cigarettes and a legion of other commodities whose use the public accepts, but brands of which many different firms offer. The problem of the individual advertiser is to have his brand chosen.

**Advertising in competitive stage.**—If the product in the competitive stage is to be chosen, it must stand above the host of others in its field. While pioneering advertising stresses what the product can do which could not be done before, competitive advertising (advertising of a product which is in the competitive stage) endeavors to show what that particular product offers which others similar to it do not provide. Competitive advertising seeks to impress upon the public the distinctive superiority of a particular brand, to earn for it the choice of purchase.

When the Eversharp pencil came before the public, its advertisements told of the advantages afforded by metallic pencils. "Always sharp, never sharpened" was the keynote of the message, emphasizing in good pioneering style the inconvenience of using the "old-fashioned" lead pencil as compared with the advantages of the neat refillable pencils. The public took to the idea quickly, as did other manufacturers of metallic pencils. The result was that the Eversharp soon found itself in the competitive stage. It had to show why people should buy an Eversharp, rather than any of the other makes offered. A series of well-conceived Eversharp advertisements appeared, featuring the rifled tip, the automatic lead index, the handy eraser under the cap, the balanced construction—each feature representing an advantage found only in the Eversharp pencil. Other metallic pencil manufacturers likewise rushed into the competitive arena with their advertisements—each dwelling upon the particular merits of his pencil. One had a non-slip finger grip, a hard rubber barrel, and extra long leads; another had a patented expansion block, ball clip, and bell-shaped cap; a third filled quickly through the point and was so constructed that leads would feed smoothly. The noteworthy fact is that the advertisements pitted one mechanical pencil against the other, not mechanical pencils as a class against wooden pencils, as was done in the pioneering stage.

Advertisements of shingles provide another typical illustration of products in the competitive stage. One shingle has a patented form which is featured; the superiority of another is proclaimed because it can be nailed right over the old shingle; a third seeks consideration because it will not curl, while a fourth invites purchase because it is mineral-surfaced. In this manner each shingle advertiser endeavors to show the superiority of his shingles in order that they may be chosen by those who contemplate buying.

**The retentive stage.**—There is still a third stage through which a product may pass. After having enjoyed great success in its competitive stage, a particular brand of goods may have become so well known that the advertiser sits back, satisfied merely to retain the clientele already established. Further mention of the product's superiority is held unnecessary. Neither by word, by illustration, by statement, nor by implication are people urged to buy. The article coasts along, content to maintain its current following on the strength of its past record.

Very few advertisers reach the point where they can consider their product in the retentive stage. Fewer still can afford to let their product remain in this stage, for reasons which will soon be evident. The retentive stage is worth knowing about, in order to understand the relationship between the various problems met by an advertiser, but in actual practice the pioneering stage and the competitive stage of a product require the most consideration and thought.

A fact which is interesting, if not significant, is that pioneering advertisements usually give greatest attention to the purpose of the product and secondary consideration to the features of the article; the name of the advertisers is quite incidental. In competitive advertising the purpose served by the product is mentioned less and less. Instead the features of the product are emphasized, and the name is accorded more prominence than heretofore. When a product reaches its retentive stage, the purpose of the product and its character are barely touched upon. Perhaps a single descriptive phrase is used; that is all; the name, trade-mark, or package is the dominant feature of the advertising.

**How stages are determined.**—*The stage of a product depends upon the attitude of the people towards it.* The advertising stage cannot be determined by examining the commodity itself, rather by learning the degree of acceptance which the product has earned among a particular group of prospective buyers. The pioneering stage lasts until the need or desire for an article, such as the one offered, is everywhere recognized.

A

**TIFFANY & CO.**

Gifts for Spring Weddings

The Tiffany Blue Book for 1909 contains more suggestions for wedding presents than any previous issue

Gifts purchased from Tiffany & Co. give permanent satisfaction to purchasers and recipients, because they embody the standards of quality of a well-known house whose reputation has been achieved by a rigid adherence to the best principles of manufacture and by the careful inspection of every object offered for sale

Tiffany & Co. always welcome a comparison of prices. The Tiffany Blue Book will greatly facilitate such comparison, and will be mailed upon request

**Fifth Avenue & 37th Street New York**

**TIFFANY & CO.** B

Fifth Avenue & 37th Street

**PEARLS**
**JEWELRY SILVERWARE**

ARE THERE ADVERTISING STAGES?

Even Tiffany's passed through the competitive stage, 1909, into a retentive stage several years later. While the first advertisement invites comparison, the second neither says nor implies anything about the desirability of the products, nor does it offer any reason why they should be bought from Tiffany.

Only when that point has been reached, and when alternative brands are being offered, does the competitive stage begin.

A pioneering product does not necessarily enter the competitive stage just because other manufacturers or producers offer their brands "in competition." The only way to determine whether a product should be regarded as pioneering or competitive, is to know just how any group of people regard it. Do they have to be educated to their *need* for the product? Then it is in the pioneering stage. Or do they already accept that fact, and await to be shown the superiority of that particular brand over others? In this case, the product has entered the competitive stage.

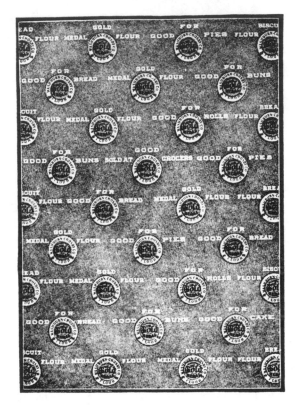

THE RETENTIVE STAGE
Gold Medal is here riding on its reputation (1909).

**Difference in policies.**—These facts may be determined readily enough, but two advertisers may follow different policies in heeding them. The first will recognize that there is still a large public which buys neither his article nor any like it; he will continue to do pioneering work among the people, bringing more customers into the field. The second advertiser will believe the time opportune to capitalize on the pioneering work which has already been done, and endeavor to secure the preference for his product; he engages in competitive work.

Since the pioneering advertiser is to stand the expense of educating the public and since he may reasonably expect others to follow in his wake, taking advantage of the work he has done in cultivating buyers, he may rightly ask what benefits, if any, there are to compensate him for the extra amount of work he has to do. Without question, pioneering advertising helps others besides the man who pays for the advertising. But he secures the greater benefit. If the selling process were to be divided into two parts—implanting the idea and selling the product to carry out the idea, it would be seen that the pioneering advertiser secures first choice for his own wares, since his make will be the first one which will come to the mind of the prospect in connection with the product. By securing a new user for that product, the pioneering advertiser has established himself as the leader in the field—thereby gaining an advantage others will have a hard task to overcome.

That pioneering work is more desirable under many circumstances than is competitive work, is affirmed by George L. Fowler, Advertising Manager of Colgate & Company, who in his speech before the Cleveland Advertising Club [1] said:

> "A period of years passes and we find ourselves in that position most pioneers must find themselves in. And after having educated a fair share of the public to use the new idea, then comes the question whether we should politically build our fences when attacked by competitors or whether we shall go on making converts to the habit rather than to advertise simply 'Use the stuff.' Well, we choose the former, and we are not so philanthropic in making that choice."

In other words, Colgate & Company are perfectly willing to concede that a competitive fray is going on for the business of those people who already use dentifrices, but they are also firm in their determination to go on "making converts to the habit." This policy is a sound one; there is no better idea for a competitive advertiser to follow than that of doing more pioneering work, thereby moving out of the class of the competitive advertisers, into a class by himself.

**Age of product no gauge.**—Very often a newly offered brand enters the competitive stage without pioneering work of any sort, such work having been performed previously.

---

[1] *Printer's Ink*, November 24, 1921, p. 60.

A new make of scouring soap, if offered now, would benefit by the pioneering work which has already been done, and would enter the arena fully in the competitive stage. A new brand of shoes, or of men's suits, would likewise embark upon competitive work the moment it arrived, for people do not have to be told why they ought to wear shoes and clothing. Every new brand thus enjoys whatever pioneering work has already been done for that article.

**Dual personalities of products.**—The advertising stage of a product is not determined so much by its recency of invention or of its discovery as by its novelty to the group of people for whom the product is intended. It often happens that a product has to do pioneering work among one part of the public while among other groups of people it is in the competitive stage. In large cities, tooth brushes are largely in the competitive stage, yet in the rural districts, where the use of dentifrices is limited, pioneering work is required. Adding machines are in the competitive stage as far as banks are concerned, but still in the pioneering stage among retailers. Products may be regarded as strictly in the competitive stage in the domestic field, but in the export market they may require strenuous pioneering work. As a result, pioneering and competitive advertising for a product will be often going on simultaneously. Similarly, most products may be regarded as pioneering with one group of people and competitive with another. *It is always absolutely necessary, therefore, to designate the group of people among whom the term holds true, in stating whether a product is in the pioneering stage or in the competitive stage.*

**Current advertising no gauge.**—When a new advertiser approaches an industry his most natural act is to jump into advertising similar in vein to that already appearing. Of course, his advertisements may be executed in a manner that somewhat distinguishes them from the others. But originality and distinctiveness in advertising are secondary to the soundness of the idea upon which the advertisements are built. Because others in the field are engaged in competitive advertising is no reason in itself for following suit. The fact that pioneering advertising is not appearing is little proof that

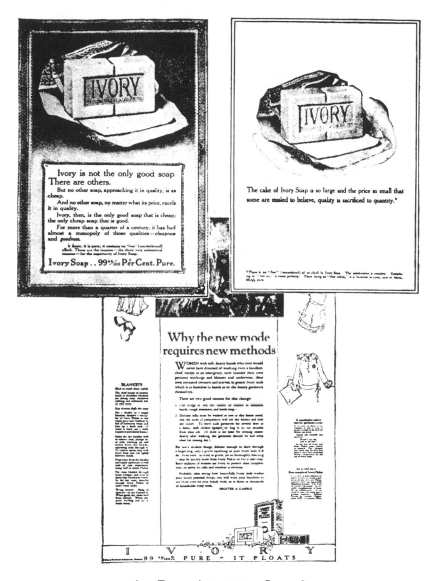

ARE THERE ADVERTISING STAGES?
Ivory Soap in a competitive stage, 1904; retentive stage, 1910; and, fifteen
years later, in a new pioneering stage.

IN A RETENTIVE STAGE    IN A NEW PIONEERING STAGE

extensive advertising of this nature will be necessary for the new product. The only principle to follow is that of securing an independent judgment showing how the article is regarded by the prospective buyers.

Advertising is but one of several forces influencing public opinion. There is the word-of-mouth recommendation of people. There are the editorial columns of newspapers and magazines. The motion picture has done much to influence people, particularly in habits of living and in matters of style. Furniture manufacturers credit the moving pictures with raising among people their standards of interior decorating.

Finally, there is. the influence exerted by the schools. "Give me a child until he is seven and you can have him afterwards," it has been said. In those years, the ideals of the people are being moulded; habits are being formed that are carried through many years, and spread through the families of those who attend the schools.

All these methods may have inculcated among people the need for an entirely new type of product before an advertiser comes upon the scene. When the advertiser does arrive under those circumstances, he usually finds a host of others likewise capitalizing on the opportunity; his first task will be competitive to secure the business that is being done at that time. This situation explains why the initial advertising of typewriters, bicycles, automobiles, phonographs in their day, and radio sets in more recent times was so intensely competitive in character, rather than pioneering as may have been expected. After the first competitive rush subsides, the real pioneering advertising makes its appearance.

A precaution.—There is always danger of underrating the amount of pioneering work necessary and of rushing into competitive advertising, with the result that the advertiser's message falls upon unhearing ears. The tendency is to assume that the people appreciate thoroughly the advantages they could enjoy with a product, when in fact they quite ignore its existence, or may not even know of it. Consequently the advertisements of such a product need not necessarily state or infer the advantages of one make over another. They should describe the desirability of the article as such, not by straining exclusively for individual advantage over another advertiser in the same line, but by explaining the usefulness of the article.

When an article in the competitive stage is provided with a new feature serving to individualize it, pioneering work may have to be planned to cause appreciation of that feature. The new principle or detail will consequently be given most prominence in the advertisements which are pioneering in nature as far as that detail is concerned, though the product as such is in a competitive stage. If a soap powder were to be offered in a newly patented sifter can, the advertising would concentrate on the value of that can, in true pioneering style.

**The sequence of the stages.**—The advertising stage of a product can be gauged only by the receptivity of people towards the product; as they change their minds, the product changes its stages. Since all people do not change their minds at the same time and do not definitely change their conception of a subject at one time, the transition from one stage to the next is gradual; the nature of the advertising changes in similar degrees.

The change may be represented graphically as in the accompanying charts. Assume that the semi-circle in Chart B is divided into the three stages through which a product may pass. For clearness, the light section of the graph indicates the stage in which the product is at the present time among a group of people; the shaded area representing the remaining stages.

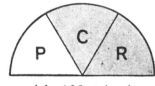

Chart B

Chart B represents an article 100% in the pioneering stage —an article such as commercial airplanes at the present writing let us say.

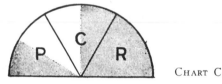

Chart C

Chart C represents an article which is passing out of the pioneering stage and into the competitive stage—50% pioneering and 50% competitive work. Such products might be hot water heaters for homes and vacuum cleaners. Half the efforts of their advertisers is to secure more users of the product and half the effort to selling their own make.

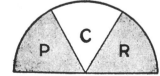

Chart D

Chart D represents a product which is entirely in a competitive field, as cigarettes, ties and men's clothing. This chart also visualizes the task of advertising a popular product which is adopted immediately by the public and produced by many manufacturers. Articles riding on the wave of a fad, or existing because of a passing style are likewise in this category; there is little time for pioneering work on the part of the advertiser, but an immediate need for competitive effort in abundance.

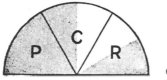

CHART E

Chart E shows a product in an advanced competitive stage, and early retentive stage. The advertiser is beginning to "ride on his name." Chart F represents an advertiser doing retentive advertising exclusively.

CHART F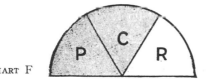

The course of any one product beginning in the pioneering stage may similarly be traced. The jump from one stage to the next would not be as abrupt as here indicated. The change might be as gradual and steady as the passing of an eclipse. But as the stages change, the proportion of pioneering and competitive and retentive work would likewise change.[2] Actually, there may be the difference of only a paragraph of text in advertisement. That is, the first advertisement may contain five paragraphs of pioneering and none competitive; the second four paragraphs of pioneering, with the final paragraph competitive; the third advertisement, three paragraphs pioneering, with the last two competitive; and so on until the

---

[2] For convenience in reference, a product which is more in the pioneering stage than in the competitive is spoken of as a "pioneering product," and vice versa. Similarly in the case of the competitive stage and the retentive stage.

change into the competitive stage and subsequently the retentive stage is completed. On the other hand the transition may be effected over a period of years.

After the retentive stage?—When a sailor in the days before Columbus consulted a map to see where he would fall off the earth, he undoubtedly got the same impression which comes to a person examining the chart of the advertising stages. After the retentive stage—what then?

It appears only logical that the life of a product does not cease when it reaches the retentive stage, for here it seems at the very height of its popularity. After great heights come great falls, however, and at the retentive stage—the stage in which the advertiser feels himself so well-known that he deems it necessary simply to announce the fact that his product is still on sale to secure all the orders he can accommodate— at this stage two pitfalls await him. One is his expectation that his past success will carry forward the sale of the product, unassisted by the advertising which contributed to that success. "Why should we advertise? We are so well known that we don't have to advertise any further. Everybody knows us," he argues. Or else, "We've sold all that can be sold—we have more orders than goods. Besides, we alone sell 80% of the goods that are sold all together in this field." The advertising appropriation is therefore to be curtailed. As a consequence of this reasoning, advertisers whose names were bywords of other years are now quite forgotten and their products likewise. Reputations which were regarded as good-will and valued at hundreds of thousands of dollars have atrophied until worthless. What happened to "Pearline" and "St. Jacob's Oil," and a host of other products of yesterday which have been so completely forgotten that they cannot even be cited? A retentive advertiser encounters his greatest danger if he forgets the principle which he himself has so well applied —the need for advertising consistently.

The second danger which confronts an advertiser whose product is in the retentive stage arises when he disregards the changing nature and habits of the people. Merely "keeping the name" before current buyers does not necessarily keep that public as customers. Advertising the name has a value only as

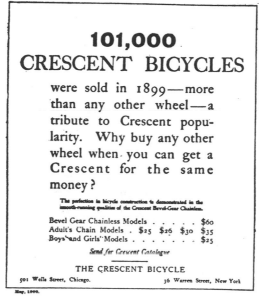

**A LESSON THE SPIRAL TEACHES**

Even the most complete success in business is no assurance of continued success, for products do not stand still.

long as the name means something to the reader. When the use of a product is discontinued, the significance of its name is forgotten and the mere repetition of that name becomes meaningless. Similarly, the fact that a certain brand of a product is used everywhere to-day does not prevent another advertiser from offering an improved device, nor does it keep the buying public, with its ever-changing habits, from dispensing with the article entirely. Where are the automobile goggles of yesterday? When advertising is successfully used at this point, it takes a strange turn: it shows the very people who are most familiar with the product how they can use more of it. ("Use Lux for lingerie, for laces, for dishes as well as for washing woolens.") To all intents and purposes, they are treated like a new group of buyers. Or else the product is offered to an entirely new group of people, who had never used an article like that before. It then reverts to a new pioneering stage and, in a large measure, runs through the three stages already explained:

1. Getting more people to require the product—*pioneering* (thus increasing the field of users for the product).
2. Getting more people to buy the advertised brand—*competitive* (when the buyer's chief question is, "Which make shall I purchase?").
3. Letting the existing prestige keep the old buyers as customers—*retentive*.

The product goes through a transition similar to the original one, in cyclic rotation. It does not actually return to the point at which it first started its career, however, but stretches out to include the additional buyers now embraced. After it

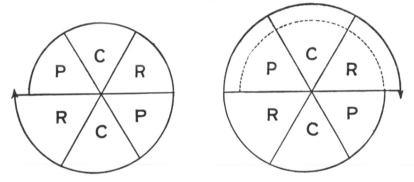

CHART G

has gone through the three stages in this field, the product again repeats the movement in another field, with every turn enlarging the total market of buyers. The whole process can be represented by a spiral (Chart G). Gold Medal Flour, Wrigley's Chewing Gum, Ivory Soap, all passed through their retentive stage, on to a new pioneering stage, in which they increased the uses or the number of users of their respective products. For many years Cream of Wheat engaged in purely retentive work, yet it likewise passed into a new pioneering stage, showing mothers the importance of good nutrition for their children. "There's a Reason" was the sum and substance of Postum advertising for many years. That phrase and the name represented the complete advertisement. But for those who did not know what Postum was, the slogan meant little, and the name meant less. Hence that too was chiefly retentive advertising, dependent upon the past experiences which the reader may associate with mention of the name. Surely enough, the product went into a new pioneering stage—showing men who did not particularly relish breakfast foods, the importance of the healthful nutrition to be obtained through Postum.

A product may hold its ground in one competitive field, while going after new markets with pioneering work among other people. Furthermore, a product does not necessarily move at equal speed through all its stages. It may go swiftly from a pioneering stage in one field to a new pioneering stage in another field. This action is a matter of feasibility. An advertiser may believe that he can secure more business at less cost by suggesting a new use for his product, thus entering a new pioneering field, than he could obtain by continuing to battle at a close margin of profit in a highly competitive market. A retentive advertiser may suddenly find his market slipping, and plunge directly into a new competitive fray, without endeavoring to do any new pioneering work. The individual judgment of the advertiser is taxed to determine the thoroughness with which he shall cover each field, and the rate of speed at which he shall travel. The spiral indicates direction and tendency only.

Every product has a spiral of its own. Before establishing a selling policy and endeavoring to create the necessary ideas the advertiser can use the spiral in answering the following important questions: In which stage is the product? Shall pioneering work be done, in an effort to add new converts to the users of the product in general, or shall the advertising be devoted to purely competitive work, in an attempt to show why this product deserves a preference over others in the field? Or else, What proportion of the advertising shall be pioneering, in character, what proportion competitive?

## Chapter II

# THE SPECIFIC PURPOSES OF ADVERTISING

EVERY once in a while an advertising man will satisfy his own curiosity and arouse that of others by compiling a list of the unusual things which advertising has sought to accomplish. In a broad sense, and in varying degrees, all advertisements endeavor to do pioneering work, competitive work, or retentive work. But an individual advertisement or a series of advertisements will further be designed to serve some specific purpose, the character of which will depend upon the nature of the task at hand. Of the scores of different purposes for which advertising has been used, a certain number underlie most of the campaigns which are in evidence, and provide "key" cases, which, being understood, enable a person to determine for himself exactly what his own advertising is to do.[1] We shall consider these.

**Increasing the use of a product.**—What prompts a man to purchase an article? A desire to possess it. Why does he want it? Because its use will be of a certain value to him, or will afford him a certain amount of satisfaction. It is the use of the object, not the object itself, which prompts the transaction. It follows logically that anything which will increase the use of a product will increase its desirability to prospective buyers. On this simple principle, the sales of a product have been increased with notable success by advertisers who enter a new pioneering stage, by showing why their product should be used more frequently, or else how their product may be used in more ways than the present one.

**Increasing frequency with which product is used.**—A family drinking coffee once a day, requiring two pounds of coffee

---

[1] The sequence of these purposes is an arbitrary one. In actual procedure one does not necessarily follow the other, nor do all enter into a given assignment.

# Eat More Wheat

## TOAST

### Here are many ways to enjoy it:

For Breakfast—hot, crunchy, brown, buttered toast made as you eat it and served with a cup of steaming, fragrant coffee.

For Luncheon—creamy milk toast or delicately browned French toast or spicy cinnamon toast.

For Dinner—tender buttered asparagus or other vegetables on toast.

For Sunday night supper—toothsome hg toast or rare old cheese on toast—an aristocratic club sandwich or maybe just toast and tea.

Every meal is more attractive, appetizing and healthful with toast as a part of the menu.

Toast—bread—flour—wheat—man's best and cheapest food.

Good baker's bread is best for toast.

The modern baker is giving service. We are striving to help him by making GOLD MEDAL FLOUR as perfect as possible.

### WASHBURN-CROSBY COMPANY

General Offices

MINNEAPOLIS, MINN.

*Eventually* **GOLD MEDAL** **FLOUR** Why Not Now?

### IN A NEW PIONEERING STAGE

Gold Medal Flour in a new pioneering stage, encouraging people to use more flour, after having passed through the retentive stage.

per week, would require an additional two pounds if it used coffee twice a day. Advertising is accordingly used to increase the volume of sales by encouraging present buyers of a product to use it oftener. The "Drink More Coffee," "Eat More Wheat," "Drink More Milk," "Eat More Bread" campaigns reveal their purpose very frankly. The same purpose has been served by increasing the length of the season during which the product is used, and by increasing the size of the unit in which the product is bought.

Increasing the length of the buying season.—For many generations, the walnut season was confined to the six weeks between Thanksgiving and New Year's Day. Walnuts were considered distinctly a holiday delicacy—to the detriment of the entire industry, yet they are equally as delicious in other months. Advertising created to encourage their consumption over a wider period of time has succeeded in extending their season of popularity from six weeks to over eight months. Similarly, manufacturers of men's athletic union suits have sought to have their garments worn four seasons of the year instead of in the summer only, beverage manufacturers have endeavored to make thirst last through the winter season, and automobile manufacturers have made notable headway in fostering an all-year-round use of cars.

The plan of lengthening the buying season has more advantages than has the plan of merely increasing the sales proper. With a short season, the work of an industry fluctuates widely from month to month. The height of the season and the dull times follow each other closely, thereby placing an undue strain on production, which in turn increases the cost of the product. Furthermore, the possibility of having unsold stock on hand at the end of the so-called "season" is a bugbear to the distributors. The industry is reduced to a highly speculative undertaking in which each manufacturer and dealer gambles heavily on the possible demand for the goods during the short season. Since an advertiser can only guess at the weather and popular fancy as they will exist several months off, his guesses will not always be correct. The advertisers lose heavily by having unsalable goods on hand when the buying spurt is over. Short seasons are truly the bane of business; long seasons the boon.

Advertising can be used to lengthen this buying season, provided the article can be used satisfactorily in a season other than the customary one. Foodstuffs, of course, have to be fresh when delivered to the consumer; if a crop is seasonal and cold storage or preserving is impracticable, it is naturally unwise to foster the use of the fruit out of season. The plan is advisable when the limited buying season is due to custom rather than to reason, as in the case of cranberries, which were regarded purely as a Thanksgiving commodity until advertising showed the possibility of using them as a relish regularly at dinner, or as a breakfast conserve throughout the year.

Lack of ability to manufacture or to provide the goods at a time other than the existing limited season, difficulty in keeping the product fresh, and obstinate adherence by the public to an unfavorable custom, may make an effort to lengthen a season difficult. Where the idea can be put into effect, however, the total buying span can best be lengthened by gradually stretching the present season.

**Increasing the units of purchase.**—The first plan we considered was that of increasing the frequency of a product's use by urging people to use more of it; the second was to increase the length of the buying season; the third plan, which we shall now consider, is to increase the size of the units in which the product is bought. For many years, electric light bulbs for automobiles were bought singly, whenever an automobilist happened to need one. He never knew just when he would require one, however, as a bulb is likely to break or burn out at any time. An advertiser conceived the idea of offering a box assortment of these bulbs, one for each of the various lamps on a car. Sets were then arranged for the different makes of cars. This practice enabled the dealers to sell six or twelve bulbs at a time, whereas they formerly sold only one. Advertising has been designed to show housewives the advisability of buying preserved fruits by the entire case, instead of by the single can, so that the larder may be well-stocked at all times. It has also encouraged securing toweling by the bolt instead of by the yard. As for sheets and linens— "the thrifty housewife keeps her shelves always well-stocked by buying sheets and pillow cases by the half-dozen or dozen at a time, and uses them in rotation." (*Wamsutta Mills.*)

The unit of purchase may furthermore be increased by making larger sized packages. Frequently the larger unit will be called the "Family Size," "Economy Size," or "Gift Size" to indicate its desirability. Still a third method of inviting customers to purchase in larger quantities is that of making sets or assortments of related products—as was done by placing Greenfield Taps and Dies of varying sizes into well-conceived "Utility Chests," and the Cutex products into "Manicuring Sets."

Where the difference in cost between a single unit and a completed set is large, the suggestion is often made that the reader begin with a small purchase and accumulate the set gradually. Advertisers of phonographs have suggested the purchase of entire concert selections rather than single numbers. A secondary suggestion is made, however, that the reader buy as many records as convenient now, and complete the set later, record by record. Silverware advertisers have likewise fostered the "get a set" idea—beginning with only half a dozen spoons, if need be. As the International Silver Company expresses it, "Perhaps you have been hindered many times in giving a luncheon, tea or dinner because you have not had enough silverware or the right kind of pieces. But such annoyance is unnecessary! You can add the pieces you lack, a few at a time and at reasonable cost."

The unit of purchase can best be increased under the following conditions:

1. *When a shortage does not exist in production.* It would be foolhardy to recommend that people buy more of a product when they cannot obtain even what they already want.

2. *When the purchaser is logically in a position to use the product in a larger quantity.* From an economical and social point of view, it is unsound to sell a person more than he can use within a reasonable length of time.

**3. *When enough advantage will accrue to the buyer to warrant the additional expenditure and the bother of having the goods on hand.*** The advantage may be the convenience of having enough of the article on hand to take care of all requirements and save embarrassment, or else the advantage may be the actual money saving. The former reason lends itself best to advertising presentation.

**Increasing the variety of a product's uses.**—Besides encouraging the people to use a product more often for the purpose they already employ it, the advertiser may increase the sale of the article by having it used for different purposes as well. 3-in-1 Oil received its name from the fact that it was an article of three uses, not merely one. Seventy-nine different uses for it were subsequently listed and as many hundred more have been suggested. Electric fans, many people believe, are made for cooling only. That fans are equally as useful for drying one's clothes and hair quickly, and for removing cooking odors, was the message of the Westinghouse Electric Company advertisement which went on to say that if a person did use the fan for cooling purposes, he should not fail to have it in the dining room to make the meal more comfortable; in the living room to make the evening more pleasant; and in the bedroom to make his slumber more restful.

To find a new application for an article, or a new occasion for its use, is to find a new sales outlet among the very people who already buy that article, thus increasing sales without increasing the territory over which the sales effort has to be extended. Another effect of increasing the use of an article is to decrease the initial cost of obtaining new business. Since the nature of the product is already well known, its new possibilities are all that need be presented to get the desired sales. This policy has a profound effect on the production side of a business. As Rogers, Brown & Company declare in their contest advertisement which was run to discover a new use for cast iron, "The danger in turning out only one type of casting is obvious. For instance, a foundry concentrating on the machine tool trade is shut down where there is no demand for machine tools, while the shop which caters to several non-associated industries is not so seriously affected when any one is in a slump."

As long as some one can find new uses for a product, there is little danger of a plant having to shut down. Increasing the use of a product plays such an important part in all advertising, that it may be well to digress at this point to examine the methods followed in presenting the new uses.

**Methods of advertising new uses.**—A new use for a product, or a new occasion for using it, may be recommended through:

1. Direct suggestion.
2. Indirect suggestion.
3. Altruistic suggestion.

**Increasing use by direct suggestion.**—By this method of securing acceptance of new uses for a product, the advertising merely expresses the idea, "Use this article for this new purpose, as well as in the regular way." True to its name, this plan makes direct and specific recommendations, giving instructions where necessary, and frequently illustrating the new applications as well.

The procedure for applying this plan of direct suggestion varies with the number of the uses and their nature. An entire campaign may be devoted to presenting just one new use— as was done in selling yeast as a tonic as well as for baking.

Again, instead of devoting the campaign to one use only, the advertising may concentrate upon each of several new uses. Linoleum manufacturers have followed this practice in introducing their covering for floors other than kitchen-floors. They have devoted one group of advertisements to hotels, another to schools, still another to offices. Tractors have likewise had their different uses presented to the respective industries, one at a time. This method is most desirable in making an intensive presentation of each of a number of new uses.

When the uses of a product are almost unlimited, as in the case of a mending tape, still another plan has been adopted— that of showing a variety of different possibilities, in one advertisement. This method suggests the versatility of a

## Needed Almost Daily
### and Ever-Ready

Tirro, the new and remarkable mender, makes a friend of each person who tries it. For it has countless uses and it is ever ready to save money and time. No need to throw things away —Tirro reclaims them.

Tirro is a super-strong tape. It is waterproofed. It sticks to *anything*—glass, wood, metal, china—and stays stuck.

In fact, Tirro becomes a part of the thing mended. It can be used for a permanent mend, or it can be used temporarily. It stops leaks. It binds split or weak handles. It mends torn things.

Tirro, once you use it, suggests its own many interesting uses. Hardly a day goes by but that you need it.

The Ideal Mending Tape

# Tirro

*Waterproofed*
*Extra Strong*

### For Sale at All Druggists

We picture here some of the multitudinous uses. Tirro is for tiny jobs as well as big. It can be cut to suit. Or in wrapping, it can be applied many ply to give added strength. Outdoors and indoors, wherever you go, whatever you do, Tirro helps in countless ways where nothing else would do. Troubles are made trifles by it.

### Free Trial Strip

Merely send us your name and address and we'll gladly mail you a strip of Tirro as a sample, together with our Book of a Thousand Uses. Once you try it you'll buy it from your druggist. Tirro comes in two sizes. Prices in the United States: ½ inch wide, 30c; 1½ inches wide, 50c.

**BAUER & BLACK**
Chicago,    New York    Toronto

*Makers of Sterile Surgical Dressings and Allied Products*

INCREASING USES OF A PRODUCT
BY DIRECT SUGGESTION

product. It awakens the reader's appreciation of its utility and arouses his resourcefulness in finding for himself new applications.

Increasing use by indirect suggestion.—In the methods just considered, the advertiser's suggestion involves solely the use of the product in question. By the adoption of indirect suggestion, however, the advertiser offers another idea which must be accepted before his product is brought into play. Electric light and power companies, for instance, increase the sale of current by selling electric irons, lamps, washing-machines, and other accessories; the use of these appliances automatically results in an increased consumption of electricity, their principal commodity.

By the indirect method it may not be necessary to undertake the sale of the additional product but it *is* necessary to sell an idea. Paper manufacturers advocate better printing and more of it—to sell more paper. Railroads advertise vacations to sell mileage; harvesting machine manufacturers encourage better farming to sell their implements; makers of filing cabinets show the advantage of accurate filing systems to sell their equipment.

Indirect suggestion can be used advantageously in cases where the indirect idea is of greater interest to the reader than a direct recommendation to use the main product. By its very nature, the indirect method requires an additional selling step, and depends for its effectiveness upon the aptness of the approach.

Increasing use by altruistic suggestion.—The third method for increasing the use of a product goes a step further than indirect suggestion does. It offers the reader some constructive idea which may help him without necessarily involving the use of the advertised product. "Study your silhouette" is the substance of an advertisement for women's hair shampoo (*Q-Ban*). "There is an ideal way to dress the hair for every type of face." Accompanying this suggestion is a series of silhouettes illustrating the coiffures for various profiles. As a part of this particular advertisement, the advertised shampoo is given emphasis. To act upon this suggestion, however, it was not necessary to use the advertised article. The woman who did study her silhouette was at perfect liberty to use the product of a competitor, if she so desired. She could even apply the idea without using any shampoo at all. Yet if a woman is critical in dressing her hair, she will desire to shampoo it more frequently, thus becoming a potential shampoo customer, and probably a buyer of the brand that brought the suggestion to her immediate attention.

The du Pont de Nemours Company has issued a superb pictorial booklet, "Game Birds," for distribution among sportsmen who may use its powder for shooting. The du Pont Company is neither in the business of selling picture booklets nor of selling ammunition to sportsmen, but of selling powder to the maker of the shells which sportsmen use. The company profited very remotely indeed, but profit no doubt it did. In banking circles the Irving National Bank, the Guaranty Trust Company, and the National City Bank have become internationally renowned for their work in cultivating foreign markets for domestic industries. They have prepared whole libraries of books dealing with these countries. Altruistic suggestion in its different forms may require only a few lines of the advertisement, or it may require the work of an entire "service department."

Its value lies in the helpfulness of the information to the reader. The suggestion may arouse greater appreciation either of an opportunity or of the product itself. It may bring about greater satisfaction in the use of the product, or it may merely heighten the reader's esteem for the advertiser.

This spirit of constructive altruism can be effectively introduced in advertising:

1. Where the opportunity for direct and indirect suggestion is limited (as in an intensely competitive market).

2. Where a helpful suggestion of interest to the customer can be offered. (It would seem best that it be in some manner allied to the sphere of the product.)

3. Where the good-will and support of the public are sought.

Advertising, if its history is studied, will be seen to have passed from the dark ages when mere announcements were run and everything was left to the reader's imagination, through the period of self-praise when every superlative in the language was used and nothing was left to the reader's imagination, to the era of helpfulness in which it is now discovering its true power. In keeping with its spirit of helping the reader in his tasks, advertising resorts more and more to methods of increasing the frequency and variety of a product's use.

Reaching the person who influences the purchaser.—There is still another method of increasing sales—that of addressing the person who influences the buyer. The plan will be recognized by any one who has observed the method followed by a retail clothing store salesman when a man and his wife enter to buy a suit—for the man. The salesman undoubtedly works on the rule, "Sell the woman on the suit." To her the suggestions are directed; upon her the salesman's attention is centered. Of course, the man may say, "Yes, I'll take that suit," but the chances are that the woman's nod is responsible for the verdict to buy. 'Twas ever thus, not only between man and wife in buying a suit, but between man and man in buying almost anything. The prospective buyer may lean heavily upon the judgment of another in placing the order; when the influence of others bears considerable weight in the sale of a product, and when those who constitute this influencing group can be segregated, advertising is often directed squarely at them. Farm machinery has been advertised to bankers, for it is their judgment which the farmer heeds when investing in equipment. In large industrial plants the purchasing agent orders all the material required, but the overalled engineer in the boiler room many floors below may have been the one to specify the product. Advertising is accordingly designed for him. Architects obviously are in a position to make their influence felt in the selection of material ordered for their clients, as are also machinery designers. Tarvia is advertised to the public at large for its influence, rather than its orders. As a community, it is interested in good roads, and if it be a public-spirited community, it will see that the road-building Commission uses good material in building roads. Advertisements of Grinnell sprinklers, as another example, show the public why they should demand that officials of public buildings install the sprinklers. Each plan aims to reach the person who influences the purchaser.

Early in any undertaking it is necessary to learn which personalities enter into the final buying decision. They may not be in a labelled class, or recognizable in their true capacity. If their opinion is influential, and if they can be reached, however, advertising can best secure their approval by showing how they will be better satisfied if the article is selected by the person who will place the order. Before advertising is used in this manner, it should, of course, be directed to the buyer himself.

**Linking one product with another.**—Advertising can go a step further in securing the approval of people who may influence the decision. It can at times enlist their active help, as the advertising of Lever Brothers did in the sale of Lux. When a sweater, or other woolen article is washed with ordinary soap, it is very apt to shrink, causing resentment against the manufacturer. Not so, however, when Lux is used in the washing. When the significance of this fact was brought to the attention of the knit-goods manufacturers, they not only recommended the use of Lux on all their products, but entered into an arrangement whereby instruction tickets which Lever Brothers supplied were attached to their garments, advising the purchaser to use Lux in washing.

The linking of two products in a sales-campaign affords an opportunity which is both constructive and profitable. It is first necessary to find the persons, ideas, or products naturally involved in the successful selling of an advertised article. The plan must be based upon an idea which will be helpful to the final purchaser and the plan must further be reciprocal in its advantages to the advertisers so joining forces. It must not antagonize those who are not invited to participate. If a tooth brush manufacturer worked together with a dentifrice manufacturer he might find that the salesmen for other dentifrices would lose no occasion to knock him, along with the

RETAIL ADVERTISEMENT

The advertising of a retail store usually stresses the economy and convenience of purchasing needed goods at that store. No effort is made, in above advertisement, to explain the need for the various products nor the merits of the particular brands. That has already been done by the manufacturers.

product of his association. Linking two products in this manner should not be confused with securing the testimonial of one advertiser of a product made by a second. Co-operation of this nature involves active participation by both advertisers.

**Securing the support of the trade.**—Much is said about the "marketing channels" through which goods travel from the time 'they are made until the time they are used. In the very beginning, *A*, the maker of the goods, sold them in person to *C*, the consumer. Afterwards *A* became so occupied in making the goods that he found it difficult to get around to all his customers. A number of other producers found themselves in the same predicament as *A*. Then along came a man named *B*, who said, "I am going to open a stand in the public market to which all buyers may come. I shall buy from each of you producers, of whom *A* is one, enough to provide my clientele with all they need." From that beginning the retail store established itself as a convenient distributing post. Today there are over a million retail stores in the United States and Canada. These stores represent the final link between the manufacturers and the purchasers of the goods; to secure their acceptance of a product constitutes the task of "trade" advertising. The purpose of advertising to the trade is first to encourage its members to buy enough of the product for the immediate demand of their clientele; second, and of more importance, to encourage their support of that article so that, in selling their present stock, they will make way for another shipment and still another, ad infinitum. Advertising to the trade is done generally in conjunction with advertising to the consumer.

**Retail advertising.**—In every community the energy of the retail advertisers is very much in evidence. The local merchant advertises to sell the wares he offers; he advertises either to sell a definite article, or else to invite purchasers to do their shopping in his store. The standing of a tradesman in a community depends upon his ability to buy merchandise which is satisfactory in fashion, wear and price, and to afford his customers the conveniences, courtesies, and extra services which they expect. Most retail advertisements, consequently, devote their attention to opportune offers of merchandise, and feature either one item at a time, one department at a time, or the wares of several of the departments. Combined in these advertisements may be the advertisement of the "house" itself.

Retail advertising differs essentially from manufacturers' (or "national") advertising in that the burden of the latter is to create 'a demand for a product, whereas the retailer's advertising is in large measure occupied with telling people that in a particular store they can obtain the merchandise they wish. The manufacturer sells the need for the product and its advantages; the retailer sells the convenience, economy and satisfaction of buying the product at his store. A merchant may feature a passing vogue and further popularize the use of a new product. More often, his advertising will confine itself to well-known merchandise in a manner commensurate with the character of the store and sufficiently virile literally to bring the purchasers to his doors.

**Securing acceptance for subordinate product.**—What can be done by the maker of a product which is such an incidental part of another's product that it is entirely overlooked by the final purchaser? Take, for instance, the case of equipment which is required in the making of automobiles—equipment such as bearings, axles, and speedometers. The manufacturers of the cars are the actual buyers of the equipment. Obviously advertising should be addressed to them. But the number of automobile manufacturers is comparatively small, the equipment field is crowded, and the competition among the equipment manufacturers to sell their products to the car makers is exceptionally keen. This situation has been responsible for another strategy in advertising—that of directing public attention to the importance of the "subordinate parts," thus prompting purchasers of cars to appreciate the inclusion of a particular brand of equipment. The "parts" manufacturer really advertises to the public to look for his equipment whenever they buy the product in which it is included.

To the consumer the advantages of this plan lie in the fact

that he gets a unit whose character he can recognize. Also, the manufacturer of the finished product is able to sell more of his own line because the advertised part is included. As a consequence, the advertiser of the secondary product increases his sale to the manufacturers who already use his article. He also sells more to the additional manufacturers who now see fit to use the advertised part. The net result is that the secondary article is removed from its highly competitive, nondescript status, dependent for its sales upon the acceptance of a small but very influential group of manufacturers. This plan makes the fraction as important as the whole.

In adopting this policy of advertising, however, it is necessary to overcome three outstanding disadvantages. The prorata cost of reaching possible prospects is excessive. In order to reach one person who may be interested in buying the finished product, the advertising usually blankets a large circulation of disinterested readers.

The effect of the actual sale is weakened by the indirect manner in which the plan operates. Before a consumer will even look for the finished product, the advertiser must expend a great amount of energy to call his attention to it; and before the manufacturer recognizes this demand from consumers, once it has been created, the advertising cost mounts further. When the part is finally installed, advertising must start in afresh to push the sale of the completed product, by saying "Be sure to get the car with this equipment," or, "Be sure to get the product made of this material."

The third obstacle met in using the "straddling tactics" is that of difficult identification. How is the consumer to recognize the advertised part in the final product? Trade-marking may be a simple matter for a speedometer and for bearings (even here it may be obscure), but when the advertised commodity is a raw material, such as metal which is recast, or a fabric which is recut, the task becomes still more difficult. In these circumstances an advertiser may furnish the manufacturers who use his material with a trade-mark die. The manufacturer, in turn, can then stamp his products with the mark. Then again, the advertiser may provide labels for use on all products in which his material is used. This plan of telling a buyer to look for the subordinated product when he buys the major article requires the ability to invest the advertising appropriation over a long period of time before the profits are realized.

**To bring a family of products together.**—A "family" of products is a group of associated articles produced by one organization—such as shingles, roofing, insulating, building papers, and cement waterproofing; harvester-threshers, reapers, shockers, and knife grinders; scouring powder, soap flakes, toilet soap, shaving soap, talcum powder, and perfumes; or automobile tires, rubber gloves, rubbers, rubber heels, rubber-soled shoes, hot-water bags, and other medical rubber articles. Viewed from the aspect of production, it is often desirable to make products in "families" because of the saving in the cost of manufacture. In order to make rubber tires, a firm must establish buying connections for getting its raw material as well as introduce special equipment for handling the rubber. Once this has been done, the equipment may of course be used in manufacturing other rubber articles. A "family" is thus created to take advantage of manufacturing facilities, and to absorb the by-products used in making the major commodity. From the sales standpoint, the "family" gives the salesman a greater variety of articles to sell, each of which articles may enjoy some of the reputation established by the others. If the products are used in limited seasons throughout the year, the family arrangement may keep at least one product to the fore all-year-round. If a new member is to be added to the family, it may borrow heavily on the prestige already created for the line as a whole. An article difficult to identify by a trade-mark may become known by the family name. Finally, the cost of selling a number of items, when a part of the cost is allocated to each item, permits of more extensive advertising in behalf of all, whereas one member alone would not justify the expenditure.

It is not unusual, however, to find cases in which two or more articles are produced by one house which purposely avoids identifying them as a family because one cannot help sell the others. If an advertiser known for his disinfectant were to obtain financial control over a factory making per-

# Once upon a time

We were all kids, wide eyed we stared at the marvels that absorbed grownups and if we happened to be little girls, sometimes fairies and elphin creatures transformed us into grand ladies that haughty shop-keepers scraped and bowed before—other times we wondered why shopkeepers paid so much attention to the desires of grownups and so little to those of we smaller folks; surely, we liked pretty things just as well as mother or big sister.

The girl of to-day is the woman of to-morrow and the milliner who has made no special effort to develop the Juvenile Trade of her community has waiting for her a treasure chest unopened.

Dorothy Keith Hats for Girls and the Merchandising Plan behind them will open this treasure chest for you.

*Investigate Now*

It is the biggest forward step in mer-chandising that has been taken in years.

### *Edson Keith & Company*
### CHICAGO, ILL.

TO ATTRACT THE YOUNGER GENERATION

The advantage of selling to a rising generation as told by a manufacturer to retailers.

fume, or if he were to have one of his own departments branch off into that field, he would not help sales by proclaiming the family relationship. Whether or not a family should be grouped depends largely upon the effect knowledge of the relationship will have upon the public and upon the dealers.

**To attract the new generation.**—Between the time an article first attained popularity and the present day, an entire new generation of prospects may have grown up. The reputation of the firm may have been strongly established among the older folks, while in the estimation of the people who were in swaddling clothes when the name of the product was a household word, it may stand no higher than does the name of any other concern; accordingly advertising can be designated to reach the rising generations. The Equitable Trust Company purposely invites young men to open their accounts at that institution. The deposits of men just set out in the financial world, in comparison with those of commercial and fiduciary accounts, are indeed small. In themselves, they may hardly defray the expense of handling them. Yet the institution, recognizing that these accounts will grow as rapidly as the young depositors themselves grow, advertises for their patronage. Similarly, Procter and Gamble stress teaching the use of their soap to "the little miss." "Teach her," they say in their advertisement, "that it is the frequent, regular use of Ivory Soap which gives her the lustrous hair and the spotless garments which she innocently admires. It is easy to imbue a child with that love of cleanliness which is the basis of all-enduring charm." Though the amount of soap used by a child alone is almost negligible as compared with that used by the entire household, the advertiser here again recognizes the influence which habits formed in childhood will have upon a woman. Colgate & Company have gone still further by continuously advertising to children of the primary school grades.

For advertising purposes, generations are not to be classified by age exclusively, but also according to future buying potentiality. For example, the junior members of an organization might be regarded as a distinct advertising generation. Then there are the college students who will, before long, take their places in the ranks. Groups of individuals who will be in a position to affect sales tomorrow represent a distinct generation for the advertiser. Advertising to a younger generation is particularly feasible when the product or service is used by a person over an extended and continuous period of years, or where new prospects are constantly coming into the field. Such a policy enables the advertiser to address an additional market of possible buyers when they are at an impressionistic age—at a time when their esteem may be secured with less effort than will be possible when others compete for their attention. This policy furthermore secures customers who will buy over a longer period of years than will those of the advanced buying generation.

**To dispel "mal-impressions."**—Often the success of a product is hindered by a single objection which may exist in the minds of the people, even though it is not justified by the quality of the product itself. The impression may seem too ludicrous to countenance, or be too apparently the work of gossip-mongers to recognize. Unless some statement is made to counteract it, however, the public may remain under a false apprehension and avoid buying the product. Many women regarded a soap as "impure" because of its brown color and naphtha odor, whereas a white soap seemed "cleaner" to them —an impression which hindered the popularity of the former type of soap and consequently its sale. Advertising was accordingly designed to disclose the falsity of this impression, by showing how groundless it was. Another instance of advertising, designed to dispel an erroneous impression, was that of the bonding company, to remove the stigma of being a bonded employee. The purpose of the advertising was to show that bonding was not a reflection upon an employee's integrity, but a mark of character. New labor-saving devices invariably have to overcome the fear that they will replace the very workers whose services are often required for the satisfactory operation of these devices, especially during the period of approval. This is no simple situation, for it is necessary to show how these workers will be more productive with the machines than without them.

Where the unpopularity of an article is based on a valid

fact, the product or else condition should be corrected before further advertising is contemplated. Where the impression is unwarranted, the advertising can be planned to dispel the impression, but it must not do so in a manner which would suggest the objection to those who had not thought of it before. If possible, the advertising should interpret the bothersome features in terms of distinctive advantages; this was done for Fels-Naphtha soap, whose "clean naphtha odor" was made a real virtue.

To meet price-cutting and substitution.—The most insidious form of "mal-impression" is caused by those imitators who mislead the public to believe that the infringing brand of goods is the genuine one. As soon as an article successfully enters a new field, others immediately seek to follow. This course of events is to be expected. Some firms with droves of small imitators following in the wake of their advertising prefer to ignore them. The leading house may feel that as long as it obtains all the business it can accommodate, others are welcome to the rest. Often it is healthy to have "competitors" in an industry for the sake of strengthening the entire field. Instances are many where a single far-seeing advertiser in an industry deliberately helped others in the field to avoid its pitfalls. The action of other firms in a trade may, however, warrant drastic action when they degrade the standing of a product in the public esteem and when they misrepresent an inferior article as the one advertised.

A trade-mark may offer some protection, but to depend on it alone would require constant resort to the courts. Firms may spring up for the sole purpose of manufacturing the substitute article; they may lack any financial standing and disappear as quickly as they are discovered. In forestalling such competition and in meeting it when it does arise, advertising is often effective.

The best policy to follow in presenting a new idea is to establish it firmly before anyone has a chance to follow. Many firms have used this strategy and as a result, their sales have continued in satisfactory volume. It has often happened, however, that a firm has not been quick enough to establish its product with the public, and, worse still, makes little effort to

Smaller, but Delicious

# Oranges

were never better than
right now

Here are smaller oranges as juicy, sweet and luscious as any larger fruit you ever ate.

Nature has made these smaller oranges especially fine this year. Of course they cost less, so they are twice a bargain.

Buy two dozen therefore where you've bought one before. Or buy them by the box.

Get them for your table, for your salads and desserts and for the children's school lunches.

Rich in essential vitamines—just what every growing child requires.

Phone your dealer now. Let the entire family enjoy them. Ask for—

*California* **Sunkist** *Oranges*
Uniformly Good

ADVANTAGES FROM DISADVANTAGES

This advertisement turns a predicament into an opportunity. Note (1) how simply it mentions the size of the oranges; (2) shows why that circumstance is really a boon; and then (3) emerges from the defensive position and recommends quantity purchase.

*Examining Your Investments*

*Number Two*

### Effect of a Change in a Company's Relative Position in Its Industry

The dominant position and correspondingly high credit which certain companies at one time enjoyed in their field have in some instances been impaired by growing and aggressive competition. As a result their securities have declined to the point of adjustment to the changed conditions.

*A careful analysis by us of your holdings will acquaint you with such a condition and enable you to make timely and appropriate changes.*

## Clark, Dodge & Co.
ESTABLISHED 1847
### 51 Wall St., New York
790 Broad St., Newark
Members New York Stock Exchange

THE FINANCIAL ASPECT OF LEADERSHIP IN AN INDUSTRY

do so until its position is jeopardized. This delay is invariably due to its assumption that a lasting success has been attained, as the initial rush for a new product often gives a deceptive assurance of further sales.

People will not, as a rule, buy an article of a certain make in preference to that of another brand just because of the justice involved. They will buy it, however, if they can appreciate that one product is more reliable than another, or offers more advantages than are afforded by others. It will be recognized that an article confronted with this problem is in a highly competitive stage and requires all its resources to protect itself.

To meet the competition of substitute articles and of price-cutting on similar products, the distinctiveness of a product should be stressed. Its special features of merit should be emphasized. At least one point of distinction in the article itself should be found—the more essential the point the better —and attention should be directed to it.

**To be recognized as a leader in the field.**—Until now we have considered advertising a tool to be applied to some peculiar and immediate problem facing a product. We have not introduced advertising in the capacity which represents one of the most far-reaching purposes to which it can be dedicated— that of having its product recognized as the foremost of its kind. To strive to be regarded as a leader in a certain line is not a form of vanity; it is one of the most effective methods for having a given brand specified whenever a person is in the market for that product. The leader is one who stands above those around him; so with merchandise, the very fact that a product is a leader gives it an individuality which causes the name to be immediately associated with that product.

Jewelry, Tiffany; Fountain pens, Waterman's; Collars, Arrow; Underwear, B. V. D.; Rubber Heels, O'Sullivan's; Soda Crackers, Uneeda Biscuits—what a paying triumph it was for those advertisers to have their names regarded almost as synonyms for their respective products! [2] Especially in a highly competitive field, where the chief reason for buying one brand instead of another is the confidence which the manufacturer inspires in the quality of his product, it is a wise policy to make a bid for leadership. A fallacious belief exists that leadership in an industry is always bestowed upon that concern which is longest established in that field. The fallacy lies in the incorrect use of the word "establish" which means to fix firmly, place on a permanent footing, settle securely. How is a business established? By erecting buildings? No, that establishes only the house of the business. By printing letterheads, calling a meeting of the board of directors and declaring that "on this day the business is established"? Again no; these actions merely indicate the intention of beginning

---

[2] The possible danger to which this situation may give rise is discussed in a later chapter, on Trade-Marks.

operations. Upon what, then, can a business be established? Upon the esteem with which the public regards it. Upon that all businesses are built. A man may be in business by himself, but no man is in business for himself; he is in business for his customers. They are the ones whom he has to serve. The degree to which they know the product, and their satisfaction in using it, measure the firmness with which the business is established. The reputation of being the foremost in the field usually goes to the *first* firm in that industry to make a uniformly good product and *to advertise it.* Age offers to a concern a longer period of years in which to become known. But if that concern fails to employ those years in establishing the knowledge of its existence among the possible customers, it drops in the procession behind the concern which, better appreciating the part played by public opinion, advertises for that esteem. A good product, the advanced age of a house, and plenty of capital are factors contributing to prestige, but they do not constitute it. Advertising is necessary to mould these elements into an entity which may assume leadership. Leadership requires character; to earn it the product must be of exceptionally good value. Leadership demands initiative; to attain it advertising must be quick in turning situations into opportunities. Leadership requires force; to achieve it, advertising must be dominant. Finally, leadership demands consistency; to deserve it, a product must maintain the high standards expected of it, and above all, the advertising for it must be continuous.

In a highly competitive field where there are a legion of advertisers, such as that of gas ranges in one market, where 93.2 per cent of the households own one, and 82 different makes are offered, it may be unduly costly for a new advertiser to forge sufficiently far ahead of the others merely to be regarded as the leader. In many industries there has been so little consistent effort on the part of any one member that a most favorable opportunity exists for some alert advertiser to raise his name to leadership in that field.

**To increase strength of entire industry.**—All the members of an industry may be losing business as a consequence of conditions outside the industry itself. Two piano dealers may regard each other as "competitors" in a mediæval sense of the word. They are not, however, to any extent. Before parents buy a piano for their family they probably consider a number of alternatives—shall they buy the piano or perhaps a new rug—or shall they save the money toward the purchase of a new automobile, or put it in the bank and start a "college" account for the youngster? Again, they might hold the money for a few years and then take a trip with the family (anyway the child is studying too hard now). From another point of view, perhaps it were better not to spend the money at all now—conditions may change . . . and besides . . . So the alternatives conflict. Whether to go to dealer Smith or dealer Brown is a very incidental question. But whether to buy any piano at all—that is the real issue.

The real competition for a product consists of all the factors which tend to keep business from it. Furniture and jewelry might well be regarded more competitive than one form of furniture is to another form; likewise flowers and candy, automobiles and player-pianos or automobiles and homes (depending on the price of the car), bonds and insurance, books and motion pictures, fireless cookers and radios, these are combinations of alternatives the importance of which should be recognized in judging the competition of a product.

Frequently a general condition may offer a common competition to all engaged in a pursuit, as a business depression does. Perhaps it is the change of a preference such as the one which confronted the manufacturer of phonographs when people took to radios, or the change may be one of style such as the one which prompted men to discard suspenders for belts, starched collars for the semi-soft ones, or which affected the hairpin business when the bobbed hair came into vogue.

In the planning of advertising, it is necessary to survey all the spheres of the prospective buyers' interests and habits to determine the importance to them of the product as compared with that of other commodities. Advertising can then serve in directing preference to an entire industry, just as it does to any one concern.

One of the inspiring activities in advertising has been the united work of entire industries in spreading the popularity of their products through associated efforts. Flowers, linen, fruit, tea, milk, coffee, and walnuts have been advertised by their respective associations, as have lumber, cement, coal and gas, wall paper and paints, bicycles, toys, and savings banks. The increased favor of the public towards these products in general is naturally reflected in the sales of the respective members, who, by organized co-operation, accomplish what no individual advertiser could afford to accomplish by himself.

Advertising of services.—Frequent references have been made to the advertising of products. The same forces of group education (which is the nature of all advertising) may be applied as well to aiding in the dispensation of services rendered by bankers, accountants, and members of the medical and legal professions. They have come to recognize the apparent ignorance which exists among the laity as to the true nature of the services they perform. The popular conception of a banker is that of an unapproachable person who should be seen only as a last resort; an accountant is a necessary expense which can be avoided by working the bookkeeper overtime—in fact, he who renders a personal service is all too often thought of only when a visit to him is unavoidable. Services rendered by professional men will always be in demand in some measure, but there is much to be done in informing the public of the constructive and preventive work which they can perform.

The feeling exists among some engaged in the professions that a man should be known by his work—not by what he says about his ability. The correct form of group education for the appreciation of professional services bears out that policy. It tells about the various phases of work that are performed by the men in a profession. It makes more people appreciate the services which may be obtained, thus bringing more clients into the entire field. To whom will they go? Most naturally, to the advertiser who brought the facts to their attention. In this way, the individual in the profession is benefited without resorting to competitive claims of his ability. Such a plan does not compete for the present clients of the profession, but educates more people to use the knowledge offered. The true distinction between "ethical" and "unethical" advertising of professions rests between the helpful and constructive information it gives as contrasted with the making of competitive claims only.

Group education has also been used by municipalities to tell of their advantages to prospective residents and to desirable industries, and by foreign countries to describe the opportunities they afford to commerce; it is useful also to governments in presenting their ideals, their problems, and resources to their own people, and to the people of other lands.

**Advertising of beliefs and ideals.**—In the realms of spiritual, economic, and social improvement, advertising has its great uses. Churches have successfully advertised, not the individual advantages of one sect over another, but the need for religion in the lives of the people. If religion is recognized as an idea in the pioneering stage, surely beliefs not as long established can do equally as well by going back to first principles and doing pioneering work.

**In conclusion.**—For commodities, the essential task of advertising is to secure sales. For services, facilities, and beliefs, advertising has the definite objective of securing acceptance. In addition to situations here outlined, an undertaking may be confronted with unusual conditions which directly affect the purpose of the advertising. What the possible contingencies may be there is no need to discuss. The skill lies in recognizing the exact nature of the circumstances affecting the sale of a product, in deciding how the sale could be helped in view of that situation, and finally, in defining clearly what the purpose of the advertising shall be.

# PART II

# THE PREPARATION OF ADVERTISEMENTS

## CHAPTER III

## THE COPY APPROACH

EVER since the early days of printing, the compositor, upon receiving the manuscript to be set into type, has been given instructions to copy it; many years ago the manuscript itself became known as "copy", and today the text of an advertisement is referred to by the same name, whether that text consists of only one word or of many pages of reading matter. Just as an advertisement is a tool used to accomplish some definite purpose, so the copy is an instrument of expression enabling the advertisement to do its work. What the work is, depends upon the intention of the advertisement, but regardless of what the purpose may be, the only usefulness of copy is to prompt each of its many readers to heed the advertiser's wishes in that respect.

**The point of view.**—The curbstones of a city boulevard were lined with people out to greet a noted official. They crowded in rows five deep along the sidewalks and buildings. They stood on crates and boxes. Those in the buildings had clambered out upon the bunting-decorated window-ledges where they too could await the great personage who was expected momentarily to leave the hotel where he had attended a formal luncheon. At the hotel entrance the official appeared. The crowd shouted as one its deafening greeting; window watchers shouted their welcome, and the official started on his ride up the avenue, standing in his car with head uncovered. What an occasion for a grandiloquent bow! How dramatic and appropriate would a beautiful flourish of his hat have been! But no. This man seemed to pick out one group along the curbstone, smile, and raise his hat unmistakably *to them*. Then his eye lighted on a party nearby. He greeted *them*. All along the route he could be seen to pick out a definite face or a definite group of faces when he bowed a return to the greetings. Did the people feel, after he had passed, that here was a superficial hero acting as though he descended from loftier heights? Certainly not, for he had left the impression of having addressed them personally, man to man. He was remembered.

An advertisement rides in a carriage before people. **Crowds are not standing in expectancy for it. Flags are not waving.** Its arrival is not anticipated by many people, nor noticed by most of them, yet it must rise and speak to a large number— perhaps several million—in one appearance. The grandiloquent advertisement speaks *at* multitudes of people, and leaves them unmoved. The individualized advertisement seems to speak *to each one* of those millions, or thousands, or hundreds, but it leaves no doubt of the fact that it is speaking directly *to* the reader himself.

The great temptation which confronts a writer of copy is that of preaching at multitudes and expecting that in some way, through some power, the individual reader will divine the fact that the advertisement applies to him, and be awestruck into heeding its message. The difference between the individualized advertisement and the mob preachment may be seen in the following instances:

| *Mob Preachments* | *Individualized Advertisements* |
|---|---|
| 'You keen-headed business men, men upon whose shoulders rests the responsibility of keeping the wheels of the world's commerce running smoothly, you know the value of an efficiently conducted business. Use this dictating machine service in your offices and help the nation's tide of progress. | You can save the time of every member of your organization who dictates, and save the time of the stenographers as well. The dictating machine enables each correspondent to do his work without wasting the time of another. It does your present work at just half the cost. |
| All you who are looking for an automobile whose performance meets the world's expectation for workmanship and beauty —— | Ride with us in a Roadster. You will sense the smooth, silent, power, the easy throttling down, the instant pick-up of the supple motor —— · |

Housekeepers, you know that it is necessary to spend your household money thoughtfully, intelligently. Yet what do you look for when you buy a gas mantle? Do you buy it for price alone? Is that the way you get best value in your other purchases?

You would not measure the value of your children's eyesight by price. Surely, then, you will not judge your gas mantle by its cost—rather by its ability to give soft steady illumination.

The good advertisement, like the good host, has its thoughts centered strictly on the person addressed, when speaking to him. The reader of an advertisement is of course aware that others may read it also, yet he does not like to be considered as a negligible part of a vast audience. When he is addressed in that spirit, he becomes the bored listener in a crowd who quickly edges to the outside and away.

The man who is reputed to be a most highly paid editorial writer has his articles widely reprinted and nationally read. Yet the quality which has earned for him his high rank is not his ability to shout sermons loud enough to be heard by millions of people, but the power to address himself to just one man—who is representative of the many. So well does he picture his reader that each reader considers himself the one man. The same point of view in copy enables the entire advertisement to speak to many readers at one time, but intimately to each.

**The spirit of copy.**—People, as a rule, are quicker in judging the character of other people than in judging the value of products. They form their opinions largely from the amount of confidence other people inspire in them. "I don't know everything about this," says a prospect to himself. "The advertiser surely knows more about it than I do. If he really thinks it is good (and I think he is sincere) it must be all right." This is the reasoning which often precipitates the decision to buy. There has been no new form of sincerity created for advertising; the sincerity of an advertisement does not vary from its writer's genuine belief in the merits of his product. In no other part of the advertisement will this characteristic—or the lack of it—be more evident than in the copy. As Roy Durstine has said in his refreshing book "Making Advertisements and Making Them Pay," the one trait most essential to a good advertisement is none other than the age-old quality of sincerity. This observation is borne out repeatedly in the day's work.

**The purpose of copy.**—Though the absence of sincerity is quickly sensed in an advertisement, its presence alone is not sufficient to make the advertisement effective. Many a man who was bursting with a realization of the worthiness of his ideals or his product has found himself at a loss to make others appreciate them, has found himself floundering for words and groping for the thoughts which would convey his belief to them. That is why many owners of business institutions are often obliged to call upon another man with the ability of conveying thoughts to people through print. To believe in a fact is the beginning of persuasion; to express a statement of the fact may likewise be insufficient. The fact must be impressed upon them in such manner that they will act in accordance with the suggestion it offers. Through the ages, if legend records correctly, gallant young suitors have found themselves inarticulate in proposing to the ladies of their choice. Here we have the personal experience of a man who knows what he wants to say, who, in most cases, possesses sincerity of the noblest stamp—yet who has difficulty in making someone else appreciate his thoughts. Happily, on such occasions, man can speak in languages other than that of the tongue—he may even enlist the aid of a Cyrano de Bergerac in expressing his thoughts (or thoughts meant to be his). But until he does so, his trail is a lone one. An advertiser may likewise know his subject thoroughly and have the fullest confidence in its worthiness, but he must be able to convey the reasons for his belief to others before he can expect them to share his views and act in accordance with them.

**The opening wedge.**—The question which next arises is that of actually getting the advertisement started. How should the copy go about presenting its thoughts? Would it not always be sufficient simply to state that such-and-such products are being offered for sale? Well, perhaps it would. Let us see. What is the first thing a man looks for when he examines a banquet photograph? How often will he buy such a picture unless he recognizes one of the upturned faces in the foreground—preferably his own? The same human self-concern measures a man's interest in an advertisement. Man is interested in himself. If he can perceive at the outset that in some way the advertisement refers to him, to his satisfaction, or to the happiness of those around him—he will go further into the matter. Otherwise, the "advertisement" is but a verbal self-portrait of the man who paid for the space. The good advertisement, therefore, always presents a thought of interest to the reader before logically leading to the idea whose adoption would be to the interest of the advertiser. These are the two steps of every effective advertisement, regardless of its size, as the following examples illustrate:

> *"Do you want to make more money?*
> Write for this booklet."

> *"Cool off* with a G-E Fan."

> *"Keep your hold on youth and health.* Brush your teeth with Forhan's."

> *"Guard your children from city contagions* by washing your hands with Lifebuoy Soap."

> *"Tired out at night?* Tell your shoemaker that you want O'Sullivan's."

In each of the foregoing instances, two elements will be recognized. The first, the idea of interest to the reader, set in italics, serves as the entering wedge for the second idea, whose acceptance would be to the advertiser's interest.[1]

**Creating the idea of interest to the reader.**—What type of idea constitutes one "of interest to the reader"? It is the same which gains success for the salesman—giving to the prospect some helpful information, some constructive sugges-

---

[1] An illustration can also be used to picture the idea which will form the entering wedge. If an advertisement showed a summer scene in which a man was enjoying the breezes of a fan, with copy reading, "get a G-E Fan," the two steps would be taken.

tion, touching upon a topic which is giving that person considerable concern.

The real salesman informs; he shows ways of doing something better; he imparts news, knowledge of which will be to the prospect's advantage; he advises in a becoming manner. Johns-Manville have advertised the fact that their salesmen of asbestos are practical counsellors in matters of heat insulation. The salesmen get into overalls, go through the prospect's plant, study the particular requirements—and then recommend the proper treatment, if any is necessary. Helpfulness is the kindling power of salesmanship. Sally Smith, back of the counter showing her customers how to knit sweaters (thereby selling more yarn), is following the same principle. And when a yarn company such as Fleisher undertakes the instructional work on a gigantic scale, their advertising is built in identically the same spirit—that of *giving* the reader a useful and interesting idea. Both campaign and advertisement must embody some idea of value to the reader. This thought serves as an entering wedge to the rest of the advertiser's message.

When an advertisement embodies no entering wedge, it is not an advertisement but a droll announcement, tossed to the reader with a "take-it-or-leave-it" attitude—and generally the reader decides to leave it. Compare the ideas in the left hand column with those in the right:

We announce the sale of Beaver Board, made of the quality for which this house is renowned.

Change your attic into a playroom—with Beaver Board.

Le Page's Glue is for sale at your stationer's. You should buy a tube.

Save the cost of replacing things around the house. Buy a tube of Le Page's Glue.

While the first examples would fail to prompt a further thought, the second, starting with an idea of interest to the reader, cause him to go further into the advertisements.

**The copy approach.**—The idea serving as the opening wedge of an advertisement may be expressed in a number of different ways. It may be presented in a cut-and-dried manner. This would be comparable to the kind of a hit you would make if you placed your fist against an object and then pushed. Such a hit lacks power, it lacks momentum, it lacks swing. An instance of a correspondingly weak idea would be:

"Save your energy by washing your clothes with Rinso."

Were you to stand before the object at a distance and then deliver the blow, there would be an increase in power which could be compared to an advertising approach which is said to have some punch, as:

"Your clothes will wash quickly with Rinso."

An idea, in addition to being approached from a distance, may be approached from many angles. Sometimes this fact is referred to as the "Copy Slant" or the "Copy Angle." It is more than an angle, however. It is the unusual perspective in which the idea is seen; it is the swiftness of approach—the cleverness and aptness of vividly expressing an idea. It is truly the *copy approach,* the presence of which in the following excerpts imparts that quality which, for lack of a more exact expression, has been described as "originality";

"Don't rub your youth away;
Rinso soaks clothes clean."

It is the degree and success of such wholesome originality in the copy approach which makes one advertisement stand and leaves another obscure; it is the *approach* which shapes the copy for the whole advertisement. The original presentation of a thought may be injected by applying any of these three "I's":

1. The Imaginative approach.
2. The Interpretive approach.
3. The Initiative approach.

**The imaginative approach.**—A. S. M. Hutchinson, in **"If Winter Comes,"** introduces Mabel Sabre, a very human character indeed—"Whatever she saw, or heard, or read," it was said of her, "she saw or heard or read exactly as the thing presented itself. If she saw a door, she saw merely a piece of wood with a handle and a keyhole. It may be argued that a door is merely a piece of wood with a handle and a keyhole and that is what Mabel would have argued. But a door is in fact the most intriguing mystery in the world because of what may be on the other side of anything. She saw and heard nothing behind it. . . ."

Advertising speaks to a legion of people who have no more imagination than had Mabel Sabre. To them a door is a door, a room a room, a lamp just a lamp. And if you tried to tell them about lamps, let us say, they would pass by the advertisement as one dealing with an article of no concern to them. "For isn't a lamp a lamp—with a polychromed base, and a shade attached by a wire frame?" You can almost hear the Mabel Sabres exclaiming, "Oh—a lamp—why certainly, anybody would know what it is—just a lamp! What else could it be?—and I'm not in the least interested in lamps," they would conclude, turning away from the advertisement.

To some, however, a lamp is more than a lamp. It is the light of the home which adds, by its beams, to the happiness of the family. It is the companion of childhood under which the girl grows to womanhood, the boy to manhood. Its soft light makes the room a home and makes the home an influence. Its presence makes the house a place in which one is prouder to receive guests and makes the visit of a friend more pleasant. No, a lamp is not just a lamp. But it takes imagination to see that, and advertising must fill the void for those who are not possessed with that gift.

The good advertisement is developed from an idea within the realms of the reader's personal interest. It may not be the physical product advertised. But an entering wedge may be found in the satisfaction which the article may render to him, in the "idea behind" which can be found only "on the other side of the door." Where the reader does not appreciate what the product may mean to him, the advertising seeks to awaken his own imagination which, according to Deland, is the ability to construct around an object its probable or

# The Personality of the Doorway

No part of a home expresses individuality as does its doorway. It sounds the architectural keynote of the entire house. It offers a cheery welcome to the visitor. It is the gateway to the delightful hospitality to be found within the home.

The massive door swings open, noiselessly and smoothly—and when the visitor steps within, like a shadow it glides back into place.

This smooth motion, this silence is not accidental. It is the result of forethought and care in the designing of the door and in the selection of those vitally important details which make all doors possible—the hinges.

For more than half a century McKinney Hinges and Butts have met the exacting requirements of the most careful architects and builders. The care and precision with which McKinney Hinges and Butts are made give the home-owner long years of service and make possible throughout his house doors which open and close with ease and in silence.

McKinney Butts are made in a wide variety of finishes to harmonize with every style of woodwork.

*Garage-door Hardware Sets.* This is one of the latest McKinney developments for the convenience of architects, builders and home owners. Everything necessary for the hanging of garage doors packed complete in a box. Let us send you a booklet which fully illustrates just what kinds of attractive doors these sets make possible. Designs cover all sizes and styles of doors.

McKINNEY MANUFACTURING COMPANY, Pittsburgh
Western Office, Wrigley Building, Chicago.          Export Representation

# McKINNEY
## Hinges and Butts

### THE IMAGINATIVE APPROACH
" . . . *a door is more than a door* . . . "
This approach bestows an imaginative significance to a commonplace idea.

possible environment, to realize what produced it and what it will produce. Thus there is created the imaginative approach, such, for instance, as that used for a fixture which is only a part of the lamp itself—the Mazda bulb. The same imaginative approach has been employed in creating advertisements for articles as prosaic as the following:

| Product | The Imaginative Approach |
|---|---|
| Beds | "Enjoy a peaceful night's sleep." |
| Billiard Tables | "Keep your family together in the evenings." |
| Cosmetics | "Are you having the pleasant times other girls are having?" |
| Automobiles (in cities) | "The green fields await you." |
| Automobiles (in the country) | "Why be isolated from your friends?" |
| Furnaces | "You can't be happy in a cold house." |

To find an opening by means of this imaginative approach, those satisfactions which the product may render to the reader should be analyzed, then that one which will be closest to him should be chosen.

The interpretive approach.—Many are the ways of saying the same thing, and advertising must ever be resourceful in saying an old thing in a new way. The interpretive approach is the one which presents a known fact about a product in a new light to the reader; it converts a matter-of-fact statement graphically into one which inspires greater respect for that fact. Colgate and Company wished to say "Your teeth are working for you incessantly." The idea is good, but this statement of it is very inane. They interpreted the idea by saying, "*You* may have been on a vacation but your teeth worked all the time," and the improvement in the copy is an appreciable one.

Take another instance in an allied line. The opening wedge for the Ivory Soap advertisement was the idea that the pores of the skin had to be kept clean in order that they might function properly. To express that idea by saying, "Your skin must be allowed to function properly" would be literally correct, but would lack in poignancy. Accordingly, the idea was expressed in a less matter-of-fact way. "Your skin has

# Why men crack . . .

An authority of international standing recently wrote:
"You have overeaten and plugged your organs with moderate
stimulants, the worst of which are not only alcohol and tobacco,
but caffein and sugar." . . . He was talking to men who crack
physically in the race for success.

YOU know them. Strong men, vigorous men, robust men—men who have never had a sick day in their lives. They drive. They drive themselves to the limit. They lash themselves over the limit with stimulants. They crack. Often, they crash.

You have seen them afterward. Pitiful shells. The zest gone, the fire gone. Burnt-out furnaces of energy.

"He was such a healthy-looking man—"

He was. His health was his undoing. His constitution absorbed punishment. Otherwise he might have been warned in time.

For every ounce of energy gained by stimulation, by whipping the nerves to action, an ounce of reserve strength is drained. If the reserve is great, its loss may not be felt immediately. But repeated withdrawals exhaust any reserve. Physical bankruptcy. Then the crash.

The last ten years have been overwrought. People have disregarded much that they know about hygiene—about health. "Keeping up with the times." It is time to check up. It is time to remember some of the simple lessons of health everyone learned in school.

Avoid stimulants. You remember the rule. It was not meant for children only.

*Borrowed Energy Must be Repaid!*

Two million American families avoid caffein by drinking Postum. And two million American families are better off for it. They have deprived themselves of nothing.

The need they feel for a good, hot drink is amply satisfied by Postum. They like its taste. They like its wholesomeness. They prefer the energy—*real energy*—of body-building grain in place of artificial energy *borrowed from their own reserve* by drug stimulation.

Postum is made of whole wheat and bran, roasted. A little sweetening. Nothing more.

It is not an imitation of coffee or anything else. It is an excellent drink in its own right.

It has a full, rich flavor, inherited directly from nourishing wheat and system-tuning bran. Instead of retarding or upsetting digestion, it is an actual help, making the whole meal more appetizing and warming the stomach without counteracting these good effects by drugging.

There isn't a wakeful hour, a taut nerve, or a headache in it. Your family can drink it every meal of the day, relish it, crave it, knowing it is a help, not a hindrance, to health and efficiency.

So we speak to you—the wife, the mother—because the well-being of your household is largely in your hands. Your finger is close to your family's pulse. You know how the men in your family look rather helplessly to you for a certain amount of "mothering"—you know how you can usually detect significant variations in their welfare before they are aware of them themselves.

*An Experiment in "Mothering"*

Those who depend on you have a good many years yet to live, we hope. A good many years to do with as they please. In the interest of their health, efficiency, and happiness during these remaining years, we are going to ask you to see that they try Postum for thirty days.

We will give you the first week's supply of Postum. Enough for a cup with every meal for a week. All we ask is that the trial be carried on from there for thirty days. The accumulated effect of a habit of years cannot be shaken off in two or three days, or even a week.

There is a woman in Battle Creek, Mich., famous for her Postum. She has traveled all over the country, preparing it. She has personally served it to over half a million people, at expositions, food fairs, and at Postum headquarters in Battle Creek, where she has 25,000 visitors yearly.

Her name is Carrie Blanchard. People who have tasted Carrie Blanchard's Postum have the habit of remembering its goodness.

We have asked her to tell you about Postum made in the Carrie Blanchard way. She wants to start you on the thirty-day test with her own directions—in addition to the week's supply.

As the guardian of a man who has not cracked—it might be well for you to accept Carrie Blanchard's offer.

*Carrie Blanchard's Offer*

"Men have always been partial to my Postum. Any woman can please her men folks with it, made my way—but there are a few simple things to remember.

"I have written these things down, and will be mighty glad to send my directions to anyone who will write. I also want to send enough Instant Postum, or Postum Cereal (the kind you boil), to get you well started on your thirty-day test.

"If you will send in your name and address, I'll see that you get the kind you want, right away."

- TEAR THIS OUT—MAIL IT NOW

POSTUM CEREAL CO., Inc., Battle Creek, Mich.
I want to make a thirty-day test of Postum. Please
send me, without cost or obligation, one week's supply of

Instant Postum . . . . ☐ Check
Postum Cereal . . . . ☐ which you
. . . . ☐ prefer

Name_____

Street_____

City_____State_____

If you live in Canada, address
POSTUM CEREAL CO., 45 Front St., East, Toronto, Ont. L.M.J. 4-34

*Healthy children love Postum made this way!*—You know how much youngsters like to have the same drink as the grown-ups! You know, too, that many of them do not get the milk they need, because they do not like its flavor. Make Instant Postum for them with hot (not boiled) milk, instead of water. It has the wholesomeness of a warm drink, all the nourishment of milk and Postum, and the real goodness of Postum flavor. . . . For hot summer days, both children and grown-ups find iced Postum delicious, made with either milk or water.

YOUR GROCER SELLS POSTUM IN TWO FORMS. Instant Postum, made in the cup by adding boiling water, is the easiest drink in the world to prepare. Postum Cereal (the kind you boil) is also easy to make, but should be boiled 20 minutes. Either form costs less than most other hot drinks.

## THE INTERPRETIVE APPROACH

This approach confines itself to the statement of a fact, but presents that fact from an interesting aspect.

five miles of pores. Are they open or closed?" asked one advertisement. "Is your skin like a clear stream or a muddy swamp?" another asked. "Your millions of pores are rivers of health," explained a third advertisement, while a fourth showed how a lily would die if its skin were varnished, indicating that objectionable soap oils are likely to have the same effect on the skin. And in this manner the same idea was interpreted in many different ways, each driving home the significance of that idea in a different manner. Were the imaginative approach used, it would have spoken of the joy of health made possible by the use of the soap. The initiative approach, however, confined itself to the physical fact but presented that fact in a more graphic manner.

The General Electric Company wished to convey the idea: "You ought to have many convenient electric outlet switches in your home." They so worded this idea that it would speak to the reader in the language of his own interests. "Can you light your house from the front door?" asked one advertisement. "You could, if you had a convenient outlet switch," it went on to say. "Must you stop ironing when lights are needed?" asked another advertisement, while a third spoke of the convenience of controlling the cellar lights from the head of the stairs. A fourth advertisement approached the idea by showing that enough switches in the living room enabled a person to read anywhere in the room without the inconvenience of moving his chair up to a lamp.

In a corresponding manner, every interpretive approach translates a dry statement of a fact into one that means something alive to the reader in his own sphere of thought. Thus the first wedge is formed.

The interpretive device is by no means a tool used exclusively in advertising. Speakers use it when they base their talk upon one point and seek to impress that point in as many different ways as possible; editorial writers avail themselves of its effectiveness by continually harping on one idea, but always approaching that idea from a fresh viewpoint, as the writer of advertisements will do well to observe. It is excellent practice to see in how many synonymous ways a given fact may be presented; the results of this experiment will show that no thought is so old or so commonplace that it cannot be expressed in a new manner.

The initiative approach.—Just as the witness, who was asked by the opposition's barrister whether he was still beating his wife, would have incriminated himself by saying either yes or no, so the third or initiative approach places the reader in position where he must fall in line with the advertiser's suggestion regardless of whether he wishes to or not. The two best known instances of this approach are provided by those advertisers who ask the reader to choose one of the several alternatives offered ("Which do you prefer—a shaving soap, tube, or powder?"), or confront him with a problem which it will interest him to solve (typified by the "What-would-*you*-do-in-this-case" type of advertisement). Salesmen know that the man who sits before them with a noncommittal face is one of the most difficult types to meet. Merely to engage such a prospect in a discussion is an important victory in the case of a man of this sort. For similar reasons advertisements try to break down the barriers by putting the reader in a position where he must enter into a discussion with the advertiser.

Narrative story-form copy employs this device very skillfully by having the reader overhear a conversation or a discussion. At first he thinks he is not an interested party, but he soon finds himself in the center of the stage engaging in the argument very directly. The success of this approach lies in its ability to have the reader assume the initiative of going further into the matter.

Still other tactics of the initiative approach consists in presenting a thought which serves as a notice that responsibility for failing to heed it will rest on the reader. It will really throw the initiative and responsibility of action entirely upon him, and practically tell him so, too. "If you should have a fire to-night," asks the Safe-Cabinet Company, "would your records be destroyed?" This is not a very comforting question to ask, nor is it intended to lull the reader into further comfortable indifference to his security from loss. It deliberately seeks to jolt him into a realization of his danger; the

# Where was your office towel last week?

*Don't confuse ScotTissue Towels with harsh, non-absorbent paper towels. Remember, it isn't Thirsty-Fibre unless it bears the name ScotTissue.*

**Thirsty Fibre Really DRIES**

*Every ScotTissue Towel contains millions of soft Thirsty Fibres, which absorb four times their weight in water. They make ScotTissue the quickest-drying, most satisfactory towels made.*

You never question a ScotTissue Towel. You never wonder who used it last—or how long it has been on the rack or what else it was washed with—or whether it is damp or dry.

You *know* that every ScotTissue Towel you reach for is fresh, clean, individual—that it is dry, thirsty, soft—that you are the only one to use it—that you can wash your hands or face as often as you wish, and *always* have a fresh towel.

Especially in warm weather, will you enjoy the refreshing, cooling, comforting feel of these quick-drying Thirsty Fibres—found only in ScotTissue Towels.

Whether you buy towels for your personal use or whether you buy them in larger quantities for the use of others, you will find ScotTissue prices as attractive as you find the towels comfortable and pleasant to use.

Send us your order or write us for price per carton of 150 towels or per case of 25 cartons (3750 towels). Less in larger quantities of 5, 10 and 25 case shipments. If you need fixtures we have them moderately priced to meet all requirements.

**Scott Paper Company, Chester, Pa.**
New York      Philadelphia      Chicago      San Francisco

## Scot Tissue Towels
### for "Clean Hands in Business"

### THE INITIATIVE APPROACH
The opening idea here engages the reader in a discussion and places him on the defensive.

more the reader thinks of the idea, the more keenly he feels prompted to go on with the advertisement.

A study of the initiative approach shows that it is the highest development of the interpretive approach, going farther than merely translating an idea interestingly; it plunges the reader immediately into an idea.

The importance of the copy approach.—The imaginative approach, it will be remembered, takes a product as it is and shows it to be something more than the physical article itself. The interpretive approach takes any given statement of fact and presents it, still as a statement of fact, in a new light. The initiative approach puts the reader in such a position that no matter what he says, or what he does, he will be heeding the advertiser's invitation to go further into the matter.

If a large number of advertisements were to be taken— effective advertisements, weak advertisements, and those in the twilight zone—and if the last quarter of each were cut off and compared, an unusual similarity in their copy text would be apparent. The observing reader will notice that the nearer he gets to the end of an advertisement, the more closely will its copy resemble the respective piece of copy in other advertisements and the more obscure will become the distinction between the good advertisements and the bad. This is due to the fact that advertisers have similar objectives in their work. The closing paragraphs are naturally directed toward similar goals. It is in the opening of the advertisement that the greatest difference exists; it is here that an advertisement is made or "broken," and it is at this point that the copy approach is of chief value. The three methods, the imaginative approach, the interpretive approach, and the initiative approach, are approaches in presenting a story, to be regarded strictly as such, and not as types of advertisements. For if the approaching idea is well conceived, the succeeding ideas will follow step by step, until the closing is reached. A copy-writer, in actual practice, will devote his greatest effort to conceiving the idea upon which he will write the advertisement. He knows that once he determines the approach, the rest of the copy will suggest itself easily enough.

The novice encounters an insurmountable difficulty unless he regards advertisements in terms or ideas rather than style. These ideas depend upon the purpose of the advertisement, upon the approaching idea, and upon the method of developing the approach, as next discussed. However, a writer should not think of advertisements in terms of patterns, one of which he shall seek to follow.

**Headlines.**—A mere statement of the approaching idea may also serve as the headline and provide the keynote for an illustration. In creating the idea, however, it may be difficult to phrase it immediately for headline purposes. At first the writer should devote his efforts to the conception of the approaching thought, then to epitomizing it into headline form. The headline may serve in several capacities:

1.   It may summarize the text of the advertisement.

2.   It may arouse the reader to inspect the advertisement further.

3.   It may seek the attention of a certain group of readers only.

4.   It may assist an illustration in performing one of the above functions, or it may combine several of them.

**Summary headlines.**—A summary headline, also known as a news headline, is one which tells the entire story at one glance. It finds its greatest usefulness in newspapers since they are read hurriedly and tell their message quickly. The effectiveness of this form of headline depends upon the importance to the reader of the statement it makes at the outset. Assuming the responsibility for the entire advertisement, it must be particularly succinct and replete with information. Instances would be:

"Hot Water *Instantly*—Any Time You Want It."

"You Get More Battery—You Pay Less Money."

"This Blade Saves One-half Your Shaving Time."

The copy which follows a summary headline merely has to amplify it. As in a newspaper story, the gist of the news is at the top; that which follows simply elaborates upon it.

**Headlines arousing curiosity.**—Another form of headline is one which seeks to invite further reading, rather than endeavors to digest the copy for the reader. It merely serves as an entering wedge in drawing his attention to the ideas which follow. It is employed for advertisements in which a mere statement of an idea in one sentence is not sufficient to convince the reader of its importance to him. Among the many good instances of such "teaser" headlines are the following:

"Even His Wife Wouldn't Tell Him."

"When Your Feet Go To Your Head."

"The Luncheon She Never Gave."

The entire purpose of a teaser headline is to make the reader interested in that which follows. These curiosity-inspiring headlines should not be too far-fetched. If they trick the reader through a misleading or irrelevant statement, they may cause a natural resentment which will militate against the entire advertisement. Even when the irrelevant headline does not provoke antagonism, it starts the reader thinking in a direction which fails to serve as a wedge for the ideas which follow in the advertisement.

**Headlines which select their audience.**—Where it is desired to reach a definite type of person from among a varied group of readers, the headline can address itself to the people it wants to reach and automatically select them from among the readers. Of course it would be possible to say:

"To Newly Wedded Wives Who Are in Doubt About Their Cooking."

"To Bankers and Business Men Interested in Having Healthy Feet."

"Attention of Those Who Are Experiencing Static Trouble with Their Radio."

or

"Dealers who are interested in delivery problems."

But while the foregoing may serve a good purpose, they lack any personal touch. The following instances show a better development of selective headlines in that they say something which has little interest to those outside the desired group, but immediate significance to all those within it.

"After You Serve This Dish,
He'll Forget His Mother's Cooking."

"Are Your Feet Good 'Collateral'?"

"Don't Kid Yourself About Static."

"Do You Want to Deliver Cheaper?"

The second grouping automatically chooses its readers by implication of interest, in the first three instances, or by direct selection, as in the fourth illustration.

**Further suggestions in headlines.** —Among the characteristics of a good headline are brevity, aptness, distinctiveness, and interesting approach. The success of a headline depends upon the impression it can make quickly. The length regarded best for most headlines is five words or less. Where there are more words, the headline should be examined to see if the thought can be transposed, thus:

"We Always Carry in Stock for Our Customers
A Complete Line of Couplings."

Revised, the heading would read:

"Couplings Always in Stock."

The following is of course too lengthy:

"This Will Serve to Announce
That the Housecraft Decoration Book
Is Now Ready for Distribution."

A more effective headline would be:

"The Housecraft Decoration
Book Now Ready."

Where it is necessary to break up a headline into two lines, it is well to break at phrase pauses, in order to preserve the thoughts. "Breaking by sense," as that master typographer the late Benjamin Sherbow described this method, avoids giving emphasis to secondary words, as is done in the following instance which is broken abruptly:

> "The Housecraft Decoration
> Book Now Ready."

This headline is also broken abruptly:

> "The Housecraft Decoration Book Now
> Ready."

However, the advertisement is not speaking of "Housecraft Decoration" or "Book Now" but "The Housecraft Decoration Book."

> "The Housecraft Decoration Book
> Now Ready."

**Distinctiveness.**—"Something is said in this advertisement which you won't find elsewhere" should be the message of every headline. The caption should apply as specifically as possible to the product advertised. Generalities and platitudes are the great foes of specific headlines. Here, for example, are three headlines, each of which is so general in conception that an endless list of products to which it might be applied could be prepared:

> "Every woman likes to have the *Best*.
> Why not give her the *Best* for a Christmas gift?"
> > *To advertise sewing machines!*

> "It deserves the Preference."
> > *From an underwear advertisement.*

> "Worthy of their increasing success."
> > *This happened to refer to ties.*

Here is another headline whose weakness lies not so much in its vagueness as in its platitudinous spirit:

"All Parents Want Their Children to Be Healthy."

True enough, they do; what of it? The headline fails to show that the advertisement will help the parents keep the children healthy, as would:

"A Healthful Food for Children."

This idea, in turn, is even more specific in the following form:

"Makes Kids Husky."

The reader is not particularly impressed by:

"Enormous Shirt Sale."

He finds the following more definite:

"Sale of 2143 Shirts."

And as between the two headlines which appear below, he gets far more information from the second than from the first:

"Simplifying Your Lawn Appearance Problem."

"Cuts Your Grass 5 Times Quicker."

Headlines can be made specific by saying something concrete and individual about the product.

Aptness.—Pithiness and appropriateness are particularly desirable, as the following headlines show:
Precise but unwieldy:

"Did You Ever Have a Breakdown on the Highway
When Out in Your Automobile?"

This one is more apt:

"Why Be a Roadside Tinker?"

And here is another example of lack of aptness, and aptness:

"It Is Possible for You to Secure Two-fold the
Amount of Light You Have in Your Basement."

"Double Daylight for Your Basement."

Other examples of apt headlines are:

"Two Minutes from Griddle to Grin."

"A Trickle of Power or a Torrent."

"Teeth Glisten Now."

A headline will be apt if its thought is an appropriate one and if the word-choice is picturesque.

**Original approach.**—The headline itself can use an interesting approach to advantage. It is the originality of approach that gives the following headlines their interest. The imaginative approach here enables the reader to see more than the product itself:

"When She's 18, Mother."
*Brunswick Phonograph.*

"Make It a Holiday Week-End for the Kiddies."
*Mayfair Toy Shop.*

Drive Those Cares Away."
*Overland Car.*

An interpretive approach offers a fact in a more significant manner:

"Move with a Screw-driver and Not with an Axe."
*Improved Office Partition Co.*

"The Deep-Chested Bumper."
*Weed Spring-Bar Bumper.*

"Keep That Schoolgirl Complexion."
*Palmolive Soap.*

The initiative approach, on the other hand, inveigles the reader to continue reading the advertisement. Note the following:

"Women Resented This Man's Statement."
*Odorono.*

"I Would Have Gone to College, But——"
*New York University Endowment Campaign.*

"Which of These 12 Are You?"
*Equitable Trust Company.*

Terse, direct questions add the piquancy of interest to a headline. Questions which lead directly to the point are invariably best for the purpose. It may not be possible for a headline to embody all the desirable qualities. If the thought itself is a good entering wedge, a very direct statement of that thought will suffice. Yet it stands to reason that the better the presentation, the more effective will the headline be. With a good idea, well expressed, as the keynote to the advertisement, the method of developing the copy follows with surprising ease.

CHAPTER IV

DEVELOPING THE COPY

**The Copy Wedge-Ladder.**—The steps of an advertisement after the entering wedge, will follow closely those of a salesman who, let us say, is offering a new type of article for the first time to an interested prospect. He will approach his prospect with some information or an idea of interest to that prospect; that is his opening wedge. Step by step he will then show why it would be to the prospect's advantage to order the product, which is of course the principal object of the salesman. Specifically, the salesman at the outset will briefly explain the general usefulness of the product. Once the prospect has evidenced an interest, he will go into a detailed description of the product, and prove his points; subsequently he will explain matters of price, terms, and delivery; then he will make a general suggestion to order, finally producing the order form and definitely requesting the prospect's signature. The more expensive the article, the more thought a prospective buyer will naturally give to it, and the more calls the salesman will accordingly be required to make. On the occasion of each call after the first, he may seek to further his presentation by impressing just one additional feature, not attempting to discuss the matter of ordering until he feels the time is ripe.

The salesman does not delve into a description of the different models he offers until he is sure that the prospect understands the general usefulness of the product, nor does he go into details of shipping before the prospect is satisfied with all details of the product. Furthermore, he does not explain what may be accomplished by a product if that is already well known to the prospect; instead, he will get right into details. The experienced salesman arranges his presentation in a series of steps, each making it possible for him to go to the next, and finally culminating in the order. He determines for himself at just what point he shall begin his sales presentation.

The structure of every advertisement is likewise a series of wedges, one thought leading to the next. As a guiding principle, advertising should interest a person first in his general need for a product, and then in his need for the particular brand. Having done this, the advertisement may go into a description of details and finally present a definite proposition for an order.[1]

Where the first step is sufficient to prompt the reader to carry out the advertiser's wishes, the advertisement would be completed in two wedges, thus:

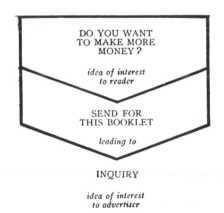

A similar situation prevails when the reader is already on the verge of buying—which accounts for the brevity of description in retail store advertising, and the brevity of copy in retentive advertising as well. But in pioneering advertising, as in most of that in the competitive stage, considerable explanatory work is necessary to secure acceptance of the advertiser's recommendation; consequently, more steps are necessary between the opening and the closing of the adver-

---

[1] Pioneering advertising will be recognized as a huge wedge making way for competitive advertising—which would be of little value without the preceding explanatory work.

# *!* fear

*Are you self-conscious about the impression you make on people?*

FEAR is probably the greatest handicap anyone can have in life. It keeps you from being your own real self—from doing your downright best and from getting on in life as you should.

Personal appearance has a lot to do with the way you feel. Clothes count, of course. But still there is one thing so many people overlook—something that at once brands them as either fastidious or careless—*the teeth.*

Notice today how you, yourself, watch another person's teeth when he or she is talking. If the teeth are not well kept they at once become a liability.

Only the right dentifrice —consistently used—will protect you against such criticism. Listerine Tooth Paste cleans teeth a new way. The first tube you buy will prove this to you.

You will notice the improvement even in the first few days. And, moreover, just as Listerine is the safe antiseptic, so Listerine Tooth Paste is the safe dentifrice. It cleans yet it cannot injure the enamel.

What are your teeth saying about you today?

*LAMBERT PHARMACAL CO.*
*St. Louis, U. S. A.*

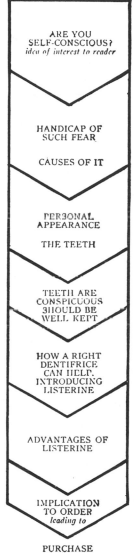

ARE YOU SELF-CONSCIOUS?
*idea of interest to reader*

HANDICAP OF SUCH FEAR

CAUSES OF IT

PERSONAL APPEARANCE

THE TEETH

TEETH ARE CONSPICUOUS SHOULD BE WELL KEPT

HOW A RIGHT DENTIFRICE CAN HELP. INTRODUCING LISTERINE

ADVANTAGES OF LISTERINE

IMPLICATION TO ORDER
*leading to*

PURCHASE

*the idea of interest to advertiser*

A COPY WEDGE-LADDER

tisement. Here, too, the sequence of the steps follows closely the presentation of the personal salesman—one wedge leading to the next.

Graphically, the wedges may be represented by means of a wedge-ladder. The number of wedges which shall be contained in any one advertisement depends upon the number of thoughts which will have to be introduced between the opening wedge, the idea of interest to the reader, and the closing wedge, the idea of interest to the advertiser. The size or depth of these wedges varies with the amount of explanation necessary to establish one thought before it leads to the next.

An idea can be developed in a particular advertisement by making one fact lead directly to the next, until the final suggestion is reached. Once the wedges are conceived, no statement should divert their sequence. The wedge-ladder drawn on paper offers a test of coherence after the ideas have been woven into a piece of copy. It is at best a mechanical division of the thoughts which are spun together in one advertisement. The practical copy-writer is able to secure continuity in his copy with grace and smoothness, for he conceives the wedges before he writes. Facile expression becomes second nature with him just as it does with the well-trained public speaker. Until such fluency in writing is acquired, however, it is best to outline the ideas of a proposed piece of copy by means of a wedge-ladder, inspecting all parts until they dovetail logically one with the other, and with the closing idea.

Unity.—The effective advertisement uses all its force to impress one idea before passing on to the next. Some advertisers seek to deliver only one message at all times. For many years the Hupmobile has been featured as a "Comfort Car," and Educator Shoe advertisements have consistently been advocating, "Let the Bones Grow Straight."

The underlying idea of course may be changed from season to season, from campaign to campaign,[2] or from advertisement to advertisement, depending upon the changes in the purpose of the advertising. It is a matter of judgment to

---

[2] "Campaign" is here used in the sense of an organized plan involving two or more advertisements.

# What is getting into your boy's mind?

Back of that matter-of-fact exterior, which your boy shows to you and the world, is a brain bubbling with impressions. Out of his confused observation of human emotions, his mind, plastic as wet clay, is forming opinions about life, honor, truth and principle. Alone, he weighs, measures and makes judgment. He is fashioning his future.

The years between ten and twenty are the formative period of a boy's life. Then he is a bundle of contradictions. He instinctively loves fair play. He hates preaching and moralizing. But, bless his heart, how nobly he responds to right suggestion and example, when they are invitingly put.

This is the secret of the success and popularity of

"The Biggest, Brightest, Best Magazine for Boys in All the World"

Its stories are about boys like you boy, human, lovable fellows, who in a real world, meet conditions, temptations and trials of character just as your boy is meeting them and will have to meet them.

Hungrily reading these stories boys learn facts, facts of business, facts of science, facts of history, facts of nature, the motives back of life, the problems of industry and commerce, the advantages of education and training—all woven into tales that fire the imagination, quicken ambition and leave healthy ideas of sincerity, simplicity and faithfulness to the highest ideals.

Its authoritative articles instruct boys in mechanics, games and sports. They teach them the principles of health and physical well being.

THE AMERICAN BOY is helping a half-million young Americans to become real men, real citizens. Every boy should have it. Your boy will profit by it. Give him and that other fellow you would like to see get ahead, a year's subscription to THE AMERICAN BOY.

*$2.00 a year by mail. 20 cents a copy at news-stands. Subscribe for a year or leave a standing order at your news-dealer's.*

A COPY WEDGE-LADDER

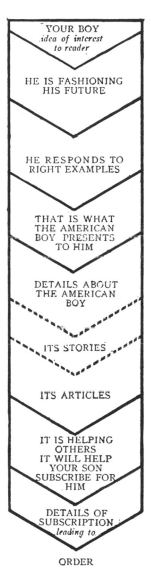

YOUR BOY
*idea of interest to reader*

HE IS FASHIONING HIS FUTURE

HE RESPONDS TO RIGHT EXAMPLES

THAT IS WHAT THE AMERICAN BOY PRESENTS TO HIM

DETAILS ABOUT THE AMERICAN BOY

ITS STORIES

ITS ARTICLES

IT IS HELPING OTHERS
IT WILL HELP YOUR SON
SUBSCRIBE FOR HIM

DETAILS OF SUBSCRIPTION
*leading to*

ORDER

*idea of interest to advertiser*

determine the attention which shall be accorded one idea before broaching the next one. In a single advertisement, however, only *one* outstanding idea should be expressed, stressed, and unmistakably impressed. When it is appreciated that advertisers consider years of effort none too long in which to drive home one thought, surely a single advertisement should not seek to offer a variety of them.

If, for example, the campaign idea, "The Carr Check-Writer Gives *Protection*," were adopted, all the advertisements in that series should bear out that thought. They should not feature this protector as one which matches the woodwork in color, or as being light in weight and simple to operate. Only those ideas which show that the device gives *protection* would be eligible for use in the advertising. And if the machine were regarded as being in the competitive stage, those ideas would be desirable which show how this device affords *better protection* than do other machines. Each advertisement would then show in a different way how the machine protects its users. Unity would furthermore be secured within the advertisements themselves by including in each only those statements which would corroborate the idea to be conveyed. There is always the temptation of trying to introduce too many different ideas at one time and not substantially presenting any one of them. It is far better to present a single thought, and support it with enough facts to impress the message.

A test for unity in a series of advertisements is to see whether they can be summarized in a single sentence; in the case of a paragraph, try for a single phrase.

**Emphasis.**—Emphasis in copy means giving prominence to ideas in order of their importance. Emphasis may be obtained through:

1. Amount of space devoted to an idea.
2. Position.
3. Construction.

**Emphasis through amount of space.**—It is an accepted practice for department stores to charge the respective departments for the space allotted to them in their newspaper advertising. Every inch of space used is thereby given the responsibility of securing definite results. It naturally follows that an article of most consistent profit will be allotted most space.

Talking points in an advertisement may be similarly regarded. Space should be allotted to them in proportion to their relative importance in conveying the idea. The great weakness to avoid in copy is that of obscuring the most significant idea, as far as the reader is concerned, with unessential talking points.

**Emphasis through position.**—People, events, and advertisements are judged largely by the first impression they make—and the one they finally leave. The beginning and the ending of a piece of copy are crucial positions. They are more likely to be read than any other part; what they say will be remembered longer. Through its position alone, a statement made here always gains emphasis. The same principle holds true of sentences within paragraphs, or even words within sentences, as exemplified by comparing

"That pity which does not open the purse is not of help,"

with this sentence, the emphasis of which is well placed:

"Pity is no help that does not open the purse."

**Emphasis through structure.**—A dependable method of making copy read with force is through the use of short sentences, that is, sentences having less than fifteen words. The writing of sentences in this staccato length leads the writer to express his thoughts more succinctly, and helps the reader to grasp the idea more readily. The danger of monotonous cadence can be avoided by varying the structure of the sentences themselves.

Short paragraphs also aid emphasis, for paragraphs are capable of making the copy look like "hard reading" or "easy reading" as the case may be, before readers even learn their substance. Very short paragraphs, containing only one or two lines, are the simplest to read and to follow. They are effective in getting attention and holding it at a high pitch. Especially in the opening of an advertisement they are useful. If continuously used to any extent, however, very short paragraphs become tiresome.

Short paragraphs, of from three to seven lines, are very pleasant for the average person to read. Most magazine stories and advertisements are written in paragraphs of this length. Other things being equal, long paragraphs, consisting of from eight to twenty lines, give an effect of calmness and deliberation, as contrasted with the abruptness of the very short staccato paragraphs. Many advertisements combine the advantages of the different paragraph lengths by using very short ones at the opening, then increasing the length of the subsequent paragraphs to the size they wish to follow.

Emphasis may be secured through so many mechanical devices of illustrations and typography that its value in the copy is liable to be overlooked, yet it is a method which, if skillfully used in copy, can give a statement all the force that is desired.

**Developing the copy.** —Advertising copy makes liberal use of the descriptive and narrative methods of developing a theme. These two methods serve as a basis upon which the writer may build to suit his individual taste, in keeping with the particular assignment.

**Description.**—Description as used in copy may be either:

1. Direct.
2. By effect.
3. By detail.
4. By analogy.
5. By suggestion.
6. By logic.

**Direct description.** —This form of copy literally pictures the article in words. It endeavors to describe an idea in such a way that the reader can see it as vividly as though he beheld it with his own eyes. Direct description is valuable where the possession of the physical article is the strongest appeal, the satisfaction which it may give being thoroughly appreciated as in the case of competitive advertisements. Its effectiveness lies in its ability to portray the product realistically, as though the writer had it in his own hands.

**Description by effect.**—A second form of description portrays the effect of using the product, or tells what the product will be, as in the following instances:

> "Pebeco—leaves the mouth cool and fresh."

> "When Hyclorite is applied to sunburned skin, the burning sensation soon disappears. Not only is the pain alleviated, but the skin loses its sullen redness and is restored to its normal color."

> "Cyclone Lawn Fence keeps children at home—off the street; out of doors, yet out of danger.
> "Cyclone Fence establishes privacy; bars unwelcome outsiders; permits you to select your children's playmates."

In the foregoing instances, the copy does not picture the product itself, yet it does leave a distinct impression of the article. Where that which the article will do for the reader is more important than possession of the tangible goods, description by effect can be employed to advantage. Description by effect also permits the use of the imaginative approach which makes it vivid. Its disadvantage lies in the fact that it does not actually identify the product; for this reason direct description may be introduced in a secondary capacity.

**Description by detail.**—Still another method of description is that of stressing a few details of the product itself, as was done in the following instance:

> "On the Remington Portable you will find the single shift, back-spacer key, two-color ribbon mechanism, and valuable line spacer."

A description of all the product's details may be appropriate in offering a set of specifications, but may be uncalled for in an advertisement which seeks to emphasize one point rather than elaborate upon a score of them. By stressing a few details or instances, however, the advertisement may suggest by inference that all remaining details of the product are of equally good character; the copy may then invite further inquiry into the other features.

Description by detail is useful in the advertisements of products in the competitive stage because it permits emphasis to be directed to a distinct, useful feature of the product. In describing by detail, points of difference between the advertised product and similar ones should be chosen. Where no difference to speak of exists, any detail which has not previously been emphasized may serve the purpose. A well-known clothing shop became famous by emphasizing the advantage of hand-tailored clothes for men, and heralded the fact that all its clothes were of this type. The idea was quite effective, for many people had never thought of the distinction before, though many other stores were also selling hand-tailored clothing. Because this department store was the first generally to stress this detail, it was credited by the public as being "the one with the tailor-made clothes"—merely because the advertising was the first to emphasize the fact.

Description by detail is of special help in selling to the layman products of a technical or mechanical nature; though he may have little patience with technical details, his interest may be aroused by showing him a few of the essential features. In addressing an audience of technically trained men, this form of description is even more effective.

Description by analogy.—Analogy draws a parallel between the idea to be conveyed and one that is already established, as in these instances:

"On the foot of Cæsar was laced the ancestor of the modern boot. Laced! Science hasn't yet invented any better method for doing that important work. Since its invention, more than one third of a century ago, the Mimeograph method has remained unchanged."

"Acid Mouth is the Gimlet that Bores into Healthy Teeth."

Another metaphorical effect may be secured through personification. Thus Ovington's, the gift shop, is referred to as "A Friendly Little Shop"; the Big Ben Clock is presented as "The Pal Whose Smiling Face Helps Begin the Day Right," and the Emeralite Jr. Lamp is "The Lamp That's Like His Daddy" (a young father must have written that advertisement).

A well-chosen analogy, metaphor, or personification has great descriptive power. The first precaution to observe in using this device is that of basing the analogy on an idea which is well known. If "As easy as tuning in" were used in 1921, many readers would have politely inquired, "What in the world does that mean?" Equally meaningless at all times is any analogy which is not founded on an idea already familiar to the reader.

The second weakness that may be encountered in using analogy is that of being far-fetched. A test for aptness in the use of a comparison is to measure the space required to introduce the analogy and to show its application to the present idea. If the analogy is well chosen, the point made will be quite obvious; hence the explanation will be very brief.

**Description by suggestion.**—Suggestion starts a thought and lets the reader's imagination finish it. It plays upon his emotions, his recollections, and his imagination, instead of using logical argument which calls upon his reasoning faculties. People have many experiences before they come upon a given advertisement. To revive the memories of those experiences and impressions, the advertisement need say very little to suggest a great deal. The advantage of suggestion lies in its ability to express a world of meaning in a limited time and space, as did the White Rock advertisement which said, in the most Volsteadian manner, "Makes It Last Longer."

**Epigrammatic description.**—Epigrammatic copy is a higher form of description by suggestion, implying its entire meaning in very few words. Of all the forms of suggestion it is the most subtle. "The Office Safe Isn't," says the advertisement of The Mercantile Safe Deposit Company. "It's A Wise Hammer That Never Loses Its Head" reads the copy of Billings and Spencer, the toolmakers. "If I Couldn't Get Good Tires, I'd Hire a Chauffeur" says the venerable gentleman in a Hood Tire advertisement, to indicate how little trouble he had with these tires.

Epigrammatic copy is terse and succinct. It doesn't depend upon logic for support, but relies upon the smack of its aptness. It lacks conviction but is rich in suggestions. It condenses ideas and reduces the number of words used to express them. It does not try to start any arguments, but merely to move the imagination. Because epigrammatic copy is subtle, its point may be too vague for its readers to grasp. Because of its suggestiveness, it may convey more meaning than a dissertation. It offers a distinctive style of presentation for articles in the competitive stage which have little physical superiority over similar products. It is inadequate for most pioneering work.

In writing epigrammatic copy, it is necessary to find the one thought which will thoroughly convey the idea. If a number of thoughts are necessary, it is not wise to eliminate all but one, but to create one that will be as strong as all of them. Words should be picked which will not need qualification. Epigrammatic copy uses mostly nouns and verbs. A balanced or parallel structure helps to simplify the copy, if it has any length. That manner of expression which will best present the character of the product should be used, but it is worth remembering that a piece of copy is better when understood than when merely admired.

**Description by logic.**—Opinion and assertion of a controversial point can always be questioned, but proof based on fact is irrefutable. Claim alone raises doubt of the authenticity of a statement; evidence of a fact tells its own story. And since an advertiser is naturally biased in favor of his own product, his assertions alone may be totally unconvincing. Those articles, such as cosmetics, bought because of a whim or a fancy, may be advertised in a vein to please whims and fancies. But where the reader ponders over the whys and wherefores in buying (as is often the case in articles of pure utility), the advertising should prove why, and give evidence of wherefore, what, and how. On the strength of proof alone, the advertisement should ask consideration of the product. Not upon what the advertiser says, but upon what the facts show; not upon what he thinks, but upon what evidence and reasoning prove should such an advertisement be built up.

The proof itself may be founded upon public or private demonstration, or impartial tests; it may be established through satisfaction of customers expressed in testimonials and indorsements, through samples, trial offers and guarantees; or it may be demonstrated through logical argument based upon other facts specially compiled, or upon self-evident facts.

Though it may not be practicable to submit all the proof of a statement within a magazine or newspaper advertisement because of space limitation, the advertisement itself should be based upon fact, and be specific and thorough in the statements it does make. By presenting concrete facts instead of glib assertions, the advertisements can show convincing reasons for the conclusion reached, and invite further investigation.

**Narrative copy.**—Reading the "short-story," or narrative form of copy is the nearest approach to actually hearing a person speak. Because it seems to come from the mouth of some definite character, it carries its point directly and vividly. Narrative copy can assume the form of monologue, of dialogue, or be in the third person. Usually no more than three people enter upon the scene, seldom do more than two speak, preferably only one.

**The elements of narrative copy.**—Narrative copy, other than that in the monologue form of an "open letter," usually consists of:

1. The plunge into the story.
2. The story which reveals a moral.
3. The transition from the character to the reader.
4. The direct suggestion to the reader.

**The plunge.**—The story in narrative copy should get under immediate headway, for the entire effect depends upon getting the reader absorbed in its action. Action may be obtained by opening in the middle of a conversation or in the middle of an incident. The prelude may be disposed of either by omission, if it appears self-evident, by headline, by illustration, by explanatory note, or by doubling back after the start of the copy (like a motion picture which has a scene "cut in" showing what happened prior to the opening of the story).

At first, it may be found advisable to write out the entire story in chronological order. Then it can be inspected for the point where explanations seem to be finished and where the action begins. In whatever way the introduction is treated, the copy should get going at the outset.

**The story itself.**—The story should illustrate a definite point, for this is the part of the copy which does most of the selling. It should, therefore, be complete in the moral it seeks to prove or to suggest. Narrative copy differs from a stenographic report of a conversation in that it presents the entire substance of an idea, whereas an extract of equal length from the stenographic report might merely be a detached excerpt. The conversation of narrative copy should be natural to the speakers. The best narrative copy is that in which the speakers actually seem to be giving their experiences and opinions rather than paraphrasing the advertiser's claims.

**The transition.**—Once the story has told enough to establish its point, the scene shifts to the reader. At first he was an impersonal hearer of the narrative, but now is suddenly drawn into the place of the man who had been addressed or discussed; or else the transition takes place as though the speaker turned around in his swivel chair and addressed the reader. The transition draws the moral of the story and shows that it might apply to the reader as well.

A good transition is a delicate piece of copy craftsmanship, which draws the reader into the advertisement quite naturally while his interest in the story is at its height. Immediately following the transition amplifying details may be supplied the reader in case it was impracticable to have this information embodied as a part of the story itself.

**The direct suggestion to the reader.**—The last step which the narrative copy takes is to tell the reader what he should do. Its purpose is to arouse the reader to a realization of the benefits portrayed in the conclusion. Since the success of the advertisement will be measured only in the response secured, and not by the mere excellence of its narrative, special attention must be given to the ending itself.

**THE PLUNGE**

**THE STORY**

**THE TRANSITION**

# "I put it off—just put it off"

Merely changing the names to protect his pride, let us tell his story in his own words.

He had written to the Institute asking for information about the Modern Business Course and Service; and our representative found him in his "office"—a box-like structure eight feet square attached to a ramshackle building which was the "works."

ALEXANDER Han.'lton Institute!" he exclaimed with a pathetic smile, "Will it be any use I wonder, now that the funeral is over?"

He paused a moment and then went on—

"Six years ago I clipped a coupon to send to the Institute, but—I didn't send it. I put it off . . . . . just put it off. I was thirty-nine then, with a flourishing business—and considerable property besides. Now I am forty-five and all I own is the tools out there in the shop . . . . . Last week I sent in a coupon—six years late . . . . .

"You know where the Emerson Store *was*, don't you?" he asked. "Well, I'm it. I'm the bankrupt."

"Lack of experience?" the Institute man ventured.

"On the contrary I've had a pretty broad experience. I've made money as a retailer, as a salesman and a jobber. And I know the heating and sheet-metal business as well as any man in this country—

### *"But I didn't know enough*

"The National Homes Company built a hundred homes here during the war. I got the contract for the heating and roofing work. It was my big opportunity. But I'd never been thorely grounded in the fundamentals of business; I didn't understand all the underlying currents that can carry a man forward or hurl him on the rocks.

"Rising material and labor costs got me . . . . The business and $18,000 is gone . . . . And so you see me here today . . . . with one man, and my tools— all that is left after twenty years' work. At home it's pretty tough."

He stopped and lighted his pipe, then his slightly stooped shoulders straightened.

"But it's not too late to begin again," he declared. "And this time I'm going to start right. That's why I sent in the coupon and asked you to call . . . . But what a world of difference it would have made to me," he concluded, "if I had acted on my impulse six years ago, instead of putting it off!" . . . .

### *Opportunity can either make or destroy*

Some day, you say to yourself, your opportunity will come. And it will. It comes sooner or later to almost every man, giving him the chance to do bigger things and make larger profits than ever before.

Some men are ready. They seize their chances and establish themselves for life. Countless other men also seize their chances—men who know enough to handle smaller things but lack absolute knowledge of one or more vital departments of business. So the opportunities that should lift them overwhelm and destroy them instead.

### *We save years of men's lives*

The Alexander Hamilton Institute was established to teach business as a profession, as law schools teach law or medical schools teach medicine.

With the help of leaders in the various departments of business—sales, accounting, factory and office management, costs, merchandising, advertising, transportation, corporation finance—its Course was prepared.

On its Advisory Council are leaders in education and business—Frank A. Vanderlip, the financier; General Coleman duPont, the well-known business executive; John Hays Hammond, the eminent engineer; Jeremiah W. Jenks, the statistician and economist, and Joseph French Johnson, Dean of New York University School of Commerce.

With such a Course under such counsel, the Institute has had the privilege of helping thousands of men to reach a higher place at a younger age, to save the years that must men lost in dull routine, or in energy misapplied.

### *You may put it off but—*

The Institute urges no man to accept its training; it wants no man who needs to be urged to consult his own best interests . It seeks only the opportunity to lay the full facts of its Modern Business Course and Service before you, leaving you to decide. The facts are contained in a 116-page book entitled "Forging Ahead in Business." It was this book that the man whose story is told above *meant* to send for six years ago. Considering what this training has meant to so many other successful men, isn't it worth while for you to send for it now? It will be sent without obligation.

### ALEXANDER HAMILTON INSTITUTE
512 ASTOR PLACE     NEW YORK CITY
Canadian Address:     C. P. R. Building, Toronto

Send me "Forging Ahead in Business" which I may keep without obligation.

Name _____ Business Position _____

Address _____

**AMPLIFYING DETAILS**

**SUGGESTION TO ACT**

THE ELEMENTS OF NARRATIVE COPY

Closing the advertisement.—The sentence which begins an advertisement may also be considered to begin its closing. It is a well-established wedge-ladder principle of all selling, however, that a person is not interested in the details of a product if he is not interested in the product itself; he is not interested in terms of purchase for a stove if he has no intention of buying one; the instructions for filling out a return card are of no consequence to him if he has no thought of mailing the card, and to be told where to ask for a product is not of concern to him if he has no desire to possess such a product. As a corollary, however, it is evident that a man will go to serious effort to get a thing if he wants it strongly enough, either because of whim or through need. Because of the mental process whereby man can be prompted to act largely through his own desires, the advertiser's suggestion is usually reserved for the closing of the advertisement—after the reader has been shown why he should heed its advice.

A few methods.—The closing suggestions may endeavor to make a single impression upon the reader, who is asked to do nothing else but appreciate one point. This represents an early wedge in a campaign. It may ask the reader to send for literature or else for a sample, this inquiry to be followed by a recommendation to buy. The closing may lead the reader to go to his dealer for the advertised article (where distribution has been provided for) or else it may make a direct bid for an immediate cash order. The strongest advertisement has only one objective. Where two are included, as, "Go to Your Dealer," or "Write Us," one is usually presented as subordinate to the other.

Good advertising strategy makes the copy conform to the advertising plan. All necessary provisions should be made so that the reader will not be put to useless trouble. Not infrequently the reader is told to ask for a product "at your dealer's" when the goods may not be stocked in his store. Instructions should be precise and complete. All questions which might possibly arise should be anticipated. "Get the summer catalogue. Out soon," leaves the reader wondering when it will be out, where he can get it, whether he can write for it, and whether he will have to pay for it. "Go to a Jones Dealer.

There's one in most towns," is less effective than "Go to the Dealer that shows this sign," or, "For Sale at Richard Mayer, 334 Park Street" (where the local address can be given). It has even happened that such important elements as firm names and addresses have been overlooked in advertisements which required their presence. Costly details are they, worth careful watching.

**Forms of closing.**—The ending itself can be in the tone of:
1. Implied suggestion.
2. "Soft" suggestion.
3. Command.

**Closing with an implied suggestion.**—

"Kebo, a Very Popular Arrow Collar With Young Men."

The foregoing is the entire copy of an advertisement. Its implication is "Get one at your dealer's"—yet it does not use those words. An implied suggestion such as the foregoing can be used where the advertiser wishes merely to leave an impression in the reader's mind, or where the reader obviously knows what to do in case he likes the idea presented.

**Closing with a soft suggestion.**—"We shall be glad to discuss it with your architect" is an instance of the soft suggestion. "Why not look over your furniture now, with this 'neglected inch' in your mind?" is another instance of this ending referring to casters. The soft suggestion is a refined type of closing, stronger than the implied suggestion, possessing a courteous, gracious charm which is effective with some people, necessary in advertising many products, and appropriate in forming an early wedge.

**Closing with a command.**—Surely charm, poise, and restraint are delightful on all occasions. Yet an advertisement may have more serious work at hand than conforming to an etiquette which frowns upon over-anxiety for business. It may have to produce orders countable at the end of the month in dollars and cents. For obtaining such tangible results, advertising has a manner more brusque and more direct in its method; it tells the reader what he should do in terms which he can't mistake, as in these instances:

"Speak to Your Own Engineer About It."

"Ask Your Barber for a Stacomb Rub."

"Place Your Order with Your Newsdealer at Once."

A statement can often be commanding in tone without being considered a personal affront. This is true because of a person's inbred training in taking orders. From the time a child is told to say "Pa-pa" until the day he is given the enjoinder, "Do take care of yourself, grandfather!" he is quite amenable to orders. A command, however, can be effective even when quietly said. Some people have a ring of authority in their voice which makes a command of their soft-spoken word. An advertisement likewise would do well to possess such a grace.

**Getting immediate response.**—It is a common trait to put off any duty until attention to it becomes quite imperative. The closing thought of the advertisement has to overcome the tendency to procrastinate. The reader may be quite sincere in believing that he "will do it next time." As soon as the advertisement passes from his sight, however, he starts forgetting it. The only way to make sure that he *does* take care of the matter, is to get him to do so right then and there. Though many devices exist for inviting action or for assuring early attention by means of "urge" lines, the concluding message in advertisements still offers abundant opportunity for further improvement. The urge line may tell how restricted the offer is:

"Only 280 pairs in stock."

"The edition of this booklet is limited."

"We can insure copies only to those who write at once."

It can stress the value of that which is being offered:

"This report was prepared at great expense. It is not for general distribution but a copy will be sent upon your letter-head request."

The urge line can reiterate the convenience of acting and the subsequent satisfaction:

"Get a jar at your druggist's and have this beauty treatment tonight."

CHAPTER V

## FINER POINTS IN COPY

A VETERAN advertising man once declared that he could tell how long an advertiser had been in the field by the simplicity of the language used in his copy. Experience teaches an advertiser that simple, direct and understandable language is the most effective. The new advertiser unthinkingly tries to prove himself a mighty factor in the industry; consequently he often uses pretentious, sonorous phrases instead of the simple, straightforward language which would be vastly more impressive.

**Gauging the language.**— The choice of language in copy may be gauged by any of three factors:

1. The readers.
2. The character which the product is to reflect.
3. The medium in which the advertisement is to appear.

**Language as affected by readers.**—Advertising copy should be written so that it will sound natural to most of the audience for which it is intended. It would be addressed to school children in one manner; to treasurers of public utility corporations in another manner. Copy would describe valves to a layman in a language different from that in which it would describe them to an engineer. To use technical language to the former would be meaningless; to use elemental descriptions to an engineer might be equally unsuited, for an engineer is capable of comprehending scientific description. The advertisements of even a single product do not endeavor to establish a definite level of diction, but to adapt themselves to their immediate reader.

**Language as affected by character product is to reflect.**—An object acquires personality from the character of its surroundings. Language is an effective device for helping define the grade of a product. The language in cigar advertising is

97

often facetious, while the language of investment brochures is at times very reserved indeed. Yet both extremes have been successful for they are in keeping with the respective characters of their products.

Occasion may arise for elevating a product above the class which its price might indicate. The copy in these circumstances has to appeal to a social stratum higher than that of the people who have been buying the product. An importer of cosmetics faced the stigma of having his line considered cheap just because of its low price. He introduced a high-class Parisian spirit into his advertisements and deliberately used French phrases which were above the comprehension of most of his readers. These tactics secured a fair acceptance by some people of the higher level addressed, and rapid acceptance by those who refused to trail behind in their appointments. The advertiser purposely aimed high, knowing that in the matters of appearance and of luxury women follow those on a social rung above their own. Men are likewise susceptible to the selfsame flattery, as the advertisements of cigarettes with their atmosphere of "big business" show.

**Language as affected by medium.**—A third guide-post in determining the choice of language is the medium in which the advertisement is to appear—such as a newspaper, a magazine, a letter and so forth. The very nature of the medium may reveal the interests of the reader and give a clue to his language. An advertisement could speak of loaded drafts in an export magazine, of indicator charts in an engineering paper, push binders in a farm publication, or articulation in a dental folder, with the assurance of being understood better than if entire sentences were used to describe the thought.

It may be known that a reader is interested in golfing, in social work, in automobiling, or in other activities. Every additional interest gives its followers a distinct category of experiences and a new vocabulary. Once again the copy receives an additional fund of specific language. In the matter of better adapting copy to particular occasions, advertising has an opportunity not yet thoroughly appreciated.

**The tone of copy.**—Tone is the quality of copy which gives inflection to its statement, corresponding to the tone of the

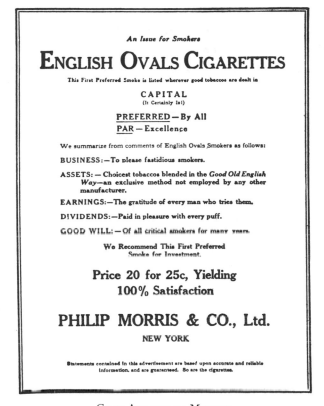

An Issue for Smokers

# ENGLISH OVALS CIGARETTES

This First Preferred Smoke is listed wherever good tobaccos are dealt in

**CAPITAL**
(It Certainly Is!)

PREFERRED — By All

PAR — Excellence

We summarize from comments of English Ovals Smokers as follows:

BUSINESS:—To please fastidious smokers.

ASSETS: — Choicest tobaccos blended in the *Good Old English Way*—an exclusive method not employed by any other manufacturer.

EARNINGS:—The gratitude of every man who tries them.

DIVIDENDS:—Paid in pleasure with every puff.

GOOD WILL:—Of all critical smokers for many years.

We Recommend This First Preferred
Smoke for Investment.

### Price 20 for 25c, Yielding 100% Satisfaction

## PHILIP MORRIS & CO., Ltd.

### NEW YORK

Statements contained in this advertisement are based upon accurate and reliable information, and are guaranteed. So are the cigarettes.

COPY ADAPTED TO MEDIUM
This advertisement appeared on the financial page of a newspaper.

voice in speaking. Because copy is printed and cannot be varied to meet the change of expression on the reader's face, as a conversation can, the tone must be tempered so that there is no possibility of its being misconstrued. A man accepts a slap on the back smilingly from a friend. Yet let a stranger slap him with equal grace and even the calmest man will hardly express pleasure. He may go so far as to cast an unpleasant look at the stranger, and if the look fails to obtain an "I'm sorry—made a mistake" expression, bystanders may be forced to separate the two. Yet, the occasion was the same, and likewise the act. Only custom and the attitude of the people concerned fix the fine line of distinction determining appro-

priateness or good taste. Copy, too, has its amenities of conduct as may be seen in the following examples:

*Addressed to sporting men:*

"Get aboard the Speedy Six. Go over the bumps with her.
She doesn't care how hard the bounces are, and you won't
either."

*Addressed to women:*

"You are invited to enjoy a drive in the Speedy Six, noting
particularly its quiet smoothness."

*Lack of copy courtesy in a beverage advertisement:*

"YOUR WIFE AT HOME—Whether your other half is
young or old, blonde or brunette, you should remember that
she gets as thirsty as you do."

**Making words work.**—Copy is at all times a device for
conveying a thought. It should do that adequately. Frequently the question has arisen, "How many words will a
person read in an advertisement?" Various estimates have
been given but as quickly discarded, for a man will read as
long as the copy says something that is of interest to him. He
would read a 500-word will, or one of 13,500 words, if he
thought his name were mentioned somewhere in it. He would
read an advertisement equally as long if he thought it might
be of advantage for him to do so; otherwise he would not read
even a 50-word advertisement.

Length, judged in number of words, may vary, but every
word must count. Every sentence in a piece of copy must
justify its presence, for length is a matter of impression;
not merely of inches, time, or words. Everyone knows that
some days are "longer" than others; some pages of reading
"shorter" than others. And because the advertisement asked
the reader for his attention, the copy ought to express its
message in a way which will not call for undue effort on the
reader's part. This quality may be secured in an advertisement by using no unnecessary words, and by making sure that
those which are used convey the writer's meaning in the best
possible manner. It is understood that the sense of the copy
is of more importance than its structure; that meaning and
clearness are not to be sacrificed for effect.

**Making copy specific.**—Copy thrives on specific facts. Generalities fail to bring out distinctive features; they are superficial. The true significance of their message is obscured by their vagueness. Advertisements can be made specific if the writer is thoroughly familiar with his subject, thinks clearly, and expresses himself precisely.

We have here, as a case in point, a piece of copy typical of the bubbles of generality which may be seen floating around:

> "We start with the finest material that money can buy, and place it in the hands of the most skillful craftsman that money can hire. Then we inspect each tire individually to make sure that it is 100% before it leaves us. For pride is a part of every tire we make, pride in the 76 years of quality manufacturing which this house stands for."

Here are further illustrations of copy which does, and copy which does not, make use of all available facts:

*Specific Facts Lacking.*

The world's masterpieces of mechanical skill are rivalled in sturdy and reliable construction by our Tractor. A distinctly serviceable product, known and appreciated by the best farmers for many years. When you behold our Tractor you see a superb piece of craftsmanship, created by master makers to perform your work at the minimum of expenditure and resulting in the maximum of service. With its mighty engine, it does all that you want it to do, and more.

*Vague.*

This serviceable trunk is well-built throughout, and finished in a manner unsurpassed. Designed just right for travelling. Has room for anything you might want to take along with you.

*Real Information Given.*

The Richards Tractor starts making the seed-bed as soon as it finishes plowing. It gets right back into the field with the discs and other fitting tools, riding the fresh-turned earth as easily as a wheelbarrow on a plank. The two broad tracks get positive traction on the uneven ground. There is no power lost through slipping —no dragging or wallowing. The Richards Tractor always delivers the full rated draw-bar pull of its heavy duty motor.

*More Specific.*

Open-top trunk model sturdily constructed of three-ply veneer basswood, covered with vulcanized fibre and finished with brass plated trimmings and locking bar. Fine roomy compartments for hats, shoes and laundry bags.

| *General.* | *More Exact.* |
|---|---|
| Textile mills require all kinds of pipe for every purpose. These mills use pipes in practically every room and every department. | Textile mills use water pipes for fire protection and for processing in dyeing departments; air pipes for cleaning and humidifying systems; steam pipes for heating and processing in finishing machines. |

A good suggestion for a copy-writer to follow in making his copy concrete is to request the technical specifications from someone who knows their details.

Superlative claims to excellence are well-known offenders against exactness in copy. There is something pitiably futile about extravagant language. Even where such language is warranted, a better impression is made by singing an article's praise in some other way.

Words should be chosen to express an idea and not to serve as a substitute for one, as is the case in these bromidic expressions:

"Efficiency is the watchword."

"Stop! Look! Listen to this announcement!"

"The early bird catches the worm. Come to the sale early."

Such lines are hollow, trite, and lazy. They do not help sell the product, a fact which in itself is the chief objection to their use. The copy would be more descriptive if the writer had asked himself, "Just what do I want to say?" and had used his own answer as the text for the advertisement.

**Making copy concise.**—In advertising copy it is especially necessary to say what has to be said in as few words as possible. A good test for the usefulness of a word is to see whether the meaning of the sentence is altered by its omission, or whether the sentence could be simplified by transposition, as in the following instances:

| *Verbose.* | *More concise.* |
|---|---|
| It is a fact that with a Stevens Reversible Toaster, all you have to do when one side of the bread which you are toasting is browned and it is your wish to have the other side browned also, is simply to turn the knob on the side. | On a Stevens Reversible Toaster, just turn the knob to turn the bread. |
| *(48 words)* | *(13 words)* |

*Verbose.*

The systematic organization of data and papers is one of the major problems confronting any man engaged in business. However, the fact may not be fully appreciated that one of the elementary principles of order is applied in the Elvira Guaranteed Letter File. This principle will be recognized as being identical in every respect with that of the dictionary and telephone book, well-known in every business house and office. In both of these compendiums you find your word or number, as the case may be, without delay. Through the application of the identical principle the Elvira Letter File similarly enables you to find your letters equally as expeditiously.

*(108 words)*

The following corporations which have used the Stenophone, when asked how they were satisfied with it, have expressed their fine approval by forwarding to us their orders, after a short trial of ten days' use of the Stenophone in their own offices.

*(42 words)*

*More concise.*

You want a word in the dictionary or a name in the telephone book; you find each quickly—naturally. No delay. No excuses. You want a letter from a file equipped with an Elvira Index. You find it immediately. No waiting. No mental calculations.

*(44 words)*

These corporations have expressed their satisfaction with the Stenophone by ordering it after ten days' trial.

*(16 words)*

In endeavoring to secure conciseness, however, it is necessary to avoid the effect of curtness or incompleteness. Conciseness is not obtained by eliminating words that would help the reader get the idea clearly, but rather by using effectively every word which the writer has selected.

**What is the word?**—An object may be "set," "placed," "planted," "stationed," or "located"; "fixed," "established," "settled," "appointed," "arranged," "disposed," "regulated," or "adjusted." All these words approximate each other in meaning. But they would not all be equally exact when used to describe a single idea. Every word has to be weighed for its suitability to the particular thought it is desired to express. The word has to be examined, first for its literal meaning, or *denotation*. Is it used precisely? Second, it must be judged for its implied, or associated meaning, its *connotation*. Often words assume a character which is quite different from the one they originally played. "Propaganda," for example, is defined in the dictionary as "a society of cardinals for the education of missionary priests." But is that the meaning the word conveys today? Its connoted meaning, not its denoted meaning, is now dominant. There is a third quality in copy, obtainable by the discriminating use of words—that of vividness, as illustrated in the following paragraphs:

> "Change your attic from a dusty mysterious catch-all into a snug winter playroom."
>
> *(Beaver Board)*

> "Hothouse Strawberries are piled high on a tiled table. A white-garbed chef slips a tiny wooden paddle under a berry, whisks it into a shining copper kettle of fondant, turns it over once, and flips it out again."
>
> *(Stix, Baer & Fuller)*

> "The thrill of the strike—as a mighty bronze-back grabs your plug; the sing of your line and the whirr of your reel— as down he goes through the cool, shady depth; the splash!— as up he darts to the surface and, in a frenzy of fight throws his shining, quivering mass before you; then—tense moments of play, a futile dash or two, and finally—the catch. That's bait-casting for game fish!"
>
> *(South Bend Bait)*

Finally, the sound of a word can help to make it harmonize with the thought. In the fishing excerpt just given, notice the harshness and force of the italicized consonants in *"mighty bronze-back grabs* your *plug;* the music of the *ng* and *n* in "the si*ng* of the li*n*e"; the rolling of the *r*'s in "the whi*r* of your *r*eel"; and the sputter of "the spla*sh* a*s* up he da*r*t*s* to the surface." The selection of words with such nicety was the work of a master.

# Where Use Approaches Abuse

A big butt log is coming in merrily at the end of the logging line. Suddenly it swerves and brings up, bang! against a stump or tree.

Something has got to give.

If the wire rope doesn't stretch, it will break. If it stretches and stays stretched, chances are it will break next time. If it stretches and returns to its original shape, it will still be good for many another racking strain.

Yellow Strand Wire Rope, by its very nature, is supreme in withstanding unusual stresses. The steel wire is especially drawn to our own specifications. Powerful machines, designed and built by us, make this superior wire into superior rope.

One strand is painted yellow to distinguish it in appearance, as it distinguishes itself in performance, from all ordinary wire ropes.

For economy and real wire rope satisfaction, you will do well to specify "Yellow Strand."

This company also makes all standard grades of wire rope for all purposes.

**BRODERICK & BASCOM ROPE CO., ST. LOUIS**
Branches: New York and Seattle  Factories: St. Louis and Seattle

Basline Autowline and Powersteel Autowlock, two indispensable automobile accessories made of Yellow Strand Wire Rope, have strongly entrenched themselves in the hearts of motorists the nation over.

## YELLOW STRAND WIRE ROPE

No Words Wasted Here

**Making copy move.** —"What size, sir?" greets you as you step into a store of one of our large retail hatters. The clerk does not ask, "Do you wish a hat?" when you enter, or "What can I do for you?" but directly "What size, sir?" These sales tactics are not recommended for general use, but they can often be fittingly applied in advertising. Copy can often omit unnecessary introductions and obvious preliminaries. The space and time thus saved can be used to better advantage.

The first sentence of an advertisement should start the reader thinking in final direction of the idea to be presented. Every sentence should carry the action forward. In this way, the reader continues in his own mind with the idea where the copy leaves off—sure evidence that the impression has been made. Action may be aided by:

1. *Omission of top-heavy introduction.*—It is not necessary to say, "In this advertisement we are going to bring to your attention the fact that—." The copy can start right in with "the fact that."

2. *Good word choice.*—Verbs do the most work. They should be pungent. Nouns should be used which are exact; adjectives and adverbs which are vivid.

3. *Use of short, simple sentences.*

4. *Avoidance of obvious statements.*—The essential facts should be given, but the reader's imagination should be drawn on for part of the copy. It is not hard to picture the bagging of game as the sportsman described it: "Bang!—Missed! Bang!—Dead!"; and the Chinaman's impression of a toboggan slide: "Z-Z-Z—walk back a mile."

**Humor in advertising.**—A sense of humor is always acceptable at the proper time, but in advertisements its only function lies in helping to convey some definite idea. Humor can be applied either by taking a humorous view of some person's predicament or else by presenting a thought in a good-natured spirit.

A predicament which might be humorously viewed would be that of the bridegroom who had forgotten the ring, or that of the autoist who has had a blow-out. To the person involved, such situations are far from humorous. The man who slips on a banana peel can seldom see why everyone around him laughs, yet when he sees another man slip, he laughs too.

Of course, it is less dignified to laugh on such an occasion than it is to slip. A person of breeding checks his laughter, and his chuckle escapes in the form of a gasp; he generally smiles in spite of himself. Using this same foible of human nature, an advertisement may picture another's predicament merely to appeal to the reader's humor.

The second use of humor is to develop a thought good-naturedly, as this advertisement from *Life* does:

"IMPROVE YOUR FORGETTERY.

"This isn't a memory advertisement. Everyone knows the value of a good memory. Not everyone knows the importance of a good forgettery. If you have one, you'll live longer and live happier. You'll have more friends and will be popular. Forget your woes, your worries, your cares, your annoyances, and your hates. You can improve your forgettery if you read *Life* every week. Buy it or make sure of getting it regularly by heeding the annexed coupon."

Humor does not have to come as an outburst to be of use in advertising. A light touch of it often enables an advertisement to handle a subject which otherwise would be difficult of treatment. Insect powder would come in the class of goods about which little could be mentioned in polite society, to say nothing of exhorting the public in behalf of its use. Yet note how the following copy presents its argument untrammeled by the false restraint which a serious treatment would have demanded:

"WHY ASK A BUG TO FIND AND EAT A POISON?

"—— this way he simply breathes—and dies: Even the little bug with the high forehead might be a grandfather before he found your morsel of poisonous powders or liquids. Why wait? Why have the mess and danger, when all he needs to do is—breathe and turn ghost! Equipped as he is with a score of breathing pores—tiny doors—he takes one whiff of El Vampiro and dies!

"A few puffs of El Vampiro into the air, and all the flies in the room will kiss the world good-bye. A puff or two around beds and into the wall crevices, and the rest of the beggars will declare an endless holiday. And remember, the whiff that knocks out papa bug this minute, will be strong enough an hour from now to handle his posterity."

In handling humor a word of caution is necessary. There is a great temptation to be funny and to forget what the advertisement started out to do. The novice would do best to avoid using humor until selling qualities are consistently present in his work. Then he can afford to smile at these restrictions.

**Actually preparing the copy.**—The construction of an advertisement usually follows one of three plans. The copy may have to be fitted to the illustration or layout. This is a poor method which, at best, invariably reveals its artificial structure. Good practice at this, however, as well as good sport, can be had by taking illustrations of advertisements and writing new headlines to them.

An alternative to the foregoing plan is that of illustrating the copy. In this case, the artist has to get the copy-writer's idea. This too is no easy matter, but is a far better method than the first. In many offices a copy-writer and an artist team up in their work because of their quick appreciation in grasping each other's ideas. Such an arrangement is almost ideal.

The third method combines the copy-writer and the visualizer in one person. He may not be an accomplished artist, but he embodies the ability to conceive an idea, to visualize it graphically, and to express the copy thought. To develop this skill, so valuable in advertising, it is well to suggest the picturized idea and the layout when preparing the copy.

It is very interesting to note the methods which men follow in the actual writing: The two plans in most common use are writing out the copy in longhand and then having it transcribed, or writing directly upon the typewriter; other methods are dictating, and making first drafts in shorthand. The only rule laid down by good sense and by practice is to use the method which you personally prefer. Typing direct is the most expedient way of getting an advertisement written. Men trained in newspaper work, and in department-store writing in which copy has to be rushed through to catch an edition, invariably employ the typewriter. Those to whom the typewriter is a mechanical distraction, write their copy in longhand; then have it typed. Here again the choice is optional. The concluding suggestion is to find the way which suits you best and cultivate it, for then you will be able to write your most effective copy.

## CHAPTER VI

## SLOGANS

THE word "slogan" comes from the old Gaelic "sluagh-gairm," "sluagh" meaning army, and "gairm" a call or cry, together meaning an army cry. Today a slogan does not mean a soldier's war whoop, but rather the whoop of an advertiser, if the metaphor may be permitted. In fact, it is for lack of a more exact understanding of slogans that their correct value in a serious advertising undertaking has been generally overrated, their true usefulness little understood.

**What is a slogan?**—A slogan may be described as any phrase containing an idea whose acceptance by readers would be to the advertiser's interest. Often a slogan is spoken of as a "catch-line." Catch what? Attention? To catch attention is no virtue in advertising unless the attention is directed to some idea which will make the reader act in accordance with the advertiser's wishes. Even the "line" part of the "catch-line" definition is misleading, for the slogan is primarily an idea; secondarily a phrase. *An idea* is the first quality which a slogan must embody—an idea which represents good selling thought measured in the same terms as copy itself.

Frequently the slogan is regarded as an entity which can set at naught all precepts of sound advertising. This misconception has given rise to popular but false formula of advertising, which declares that "if you want to advertise, all you need is a snappy slogan, then splurge." This conception is palpably incorrect; in successful work the slogan does not enter upon the scene until all the preliminary work of advertising has been done. Then it takes its cue from the purpose of the advertising and is supported at the outset by an accompaniment of copy or illustrations. As the performance progresses, the slogan plays a more and more conspicuous part. But not until the entire selection is so well-known that the phrased idea requires no amplifying support to impress its significance is the slogan called upon to play an advertising solo.

**Usefulness of slogans.**—When, then, is it advisable to have a slogan? Mainly when the advertiser is planning a consistent and continuous campaign designed to convey *one* outstanding idea. Upon such an occasion the slogan may serve as the motif running through all the advertising, acting also as a pithy summary of the message. Because of its influence in the copy as well as its own conspicuity, the slogan often merits serious consideration. Many advertisers using a slogan do not dedicate their entire efforts to its glorification, but regard the phrase essentially as the central copy idea for their advertisements. "The air is so full of things you shouldn't miss," "Save the surface and you save all," and "It beats—as it sweeps—as it cleans" were more than isolated phrases in the respective campaigns; they were themes around which their advertisements were written. The true keynote of copy as epitomized in a good slogan may so thoroughly permeate the advertisement that it may not be necessary to feature the slogan at all, yet the slogan may be doing its work all the time. Think of a slogan as a copy idea and you discover the source of its power; if it gains significance with use, it has the elements of a good slogan.

**Forms of slogans.**—According to their meaning slogans may be divided into the following groupings:

*What the product is.*—

"Only Refill Shaving Stick"...........................(*Colgate Shaving Stick*)
"Watch Dog Of Your Battery"
                    (*Western Electrical Instrument Company*)
"Evinrude Is Rowboat Motoring".........................(*Evinrude Motors*)
"The Magazine of a Remade World"............(*Red Book Magazine*)
"The Watchman Of Your Coal Pile"...................(*Hoffman Valves*)

*What the product does.*—

"Chases Dirt"..................................................(*Old Dutch Cleanser*)
"Makes Night As Safe As Day"................................(*Benzer Lens*)
"The Cletrac Way Makes Farming Pay"............(*Cletrac Tractors*)
"It Beats—As It Sweeps—As It Cleans"....(*Hoover Suction Sweeper*)
"They Keep You Looking Your Best"
                    (*David Adler & Sons Clothing*)

*Description by comparison.—*

"As Easy As Pointing Your Finger"...........*(Colt Patent Firearms)*
"Built Like A Sky-Scraper"......*(Shaw-Walker Steel Filing Cabinets)*
"Like A Clean China Dish"...............*(Grand Rapids Refrigerators)*
"As Strong As The Rock of Gibraltar"
*(Prudential Insurance Company of America)*
"Clear As A Bell"...............................................*(Sonora Phonograph)*

*Description by recommendation and reputation.—*

"Ask Dad—He Knows"..............*(Sweet Caporal Cigarettes)*
"Covers The Earth".....................*(Sherwin-Williams Paints)*
"The Saw Most Carpenters Use"................................*(Diston Saws)*
"The Mark That Is 50 Years Deep"
*(Billings & Spencer Drop Forgings)*
"No Rolls-Royce Has Ever Worn Out"....*(Rolls-Royce Automobiles)*

*Description by effect.—*

"Happiness in Every Box"..................*(United Retail Candy Stores)*
"A Skin You Love to Touch"................*(Woodbury's Facial Soap)*
"They Satisfy"............................ ...............*(Chesterfield Cigarettes)*
"The Recollection of Quality Remains Long After the
Price Is Forgotten"..............................*(Simonds Hardware)*
"The More You Eat, The More You Want"..*(Cracker Jack Candy)*

*Explanation of operation, construction, or merit.—*

"Made In The Cup at the Table"
*(George Washington Prepared Coffee)*
"Ink That Absorbs Moisture from the Air".............*(Stafford's Ink)*
"Always Sharp—Never Sharpened".......... .........*(Eversharp Pencil)*
"It's Toasted"..............................................*(Lucky Strike Cigarette)*
"From Contented Cows"...................................*(Carnation Milk)*

*Direct suggestion to use product.—*

"Say It With Flowers".......................*(Society of American Florists)*
"When You Think of Writing—Think of Whiting"
*(Whiting Correspondence Paper)*
"Let the Gold-Dust Twins Do Your Work"....*(Gold Dust Powder)*
"Drink Coca-Cola"........................................... *(Coca-Cola)*
"Never Say 'Dye'—Say 'Rit' ".....................................*(Rit Dye Soap)*

*Indirect suggestion to use product.—*

"A Clean Tooth Never Decays"..............*(Prophylactic Tooth Brush)*
"Save The Surface And You Save All"
*(Paint and Varnish Association)*

"Never Neglect A Break In The Skin".............................*(New Skin)*
"The Air Is Full of Things You Shouldn't Miss"
*(Eveready Radio Batteries)*
"Look at Your Shoes!".............................*(Shinola-Bixby-Dalley)*

*Aid to identification.—*
"The Candy Mint with the Hole".............................*(Life-Savers)*
"Know Them By The Jet Black Tread"..........*(Pennsylvania Tires)*
"If It Isn't An Eastman It Isn't A Kodak"..........*(Eastman-Kodak)*
"The Yellow Package With The Gable Top"....*(C. N. Disinfectant)*
"The Wilson Label Protects Your Table"
*(Wilson Company Products)*

An interesting peculiarity that may be observed in slogans is their tendency to feature points of individuality of articles in the competitive stage.

**Construction of slogans.**—The slogan should be simple to understand, easy to remember, and pleasant to repeat. Since the success of a slogan depends largely upon its repetition, the qualities of brevity, aptness, and original approach are imperative. Seven short words would seem the maximum to use in a slogan, six just few enough to be within the margin of safety, and less than that even more desirable.

Aptness may further be aided by alliteration, by rhyming ("The Cletrac Way Makes Farming Pay," "An Apple a Day Keeps the Doctor Away," "When You Think of Writing—Think of Whiting"), or by parallel structure ("A Little Thing to Look For, a Big Thing to Find," "The More You Eat the More You Want"). Euphony and a swinging cadence are helpful. ("Never Neglect a Break in the Skin," "You See What You Write as You Write It.")

Originality in copy approach serves to make the slogan interesting and vivid, as shown by "Happiness In Every Box," which uses the imaginative approach to suggest a satisfaction; "Save the Surface and You Save All" says a commonplace thing in a new way, with an interpretive approach and "Never Say Dye—Say 'Rit' " adroitly puts responsibility for further action upon the reader, true to the initiative approach.

**Precautions in creating slogans.**—Epigrammatic structure is but the shell of a slogan which must be strong, to be sure, but which must not be confused with the idea of the slogan itself.

A headline may be "newsy," of transient interest, valuable mainly at the time it is used. But the slogan should say something about an essential feature of the product which will be as true and interesting tomorrow as today. It should also be kept in mind that the purpose of the slogan is to convey a message. When occasion for a new message in the copy arises, there should be little hesitancy in changing the slogan to suit. There is always danger of losing sight of this fact and using the advertising to perpetuate a slogan when, in fact, the slogan should be helping the advertising say something vital about the product.

Following are some of the other serious weaknesses which should be guarded against in creating slogans:

1. *Idea reflects little reason why a person would buy the product.—*

Compare

"Making the World Sweeter" (Candy)

with

"Happiness in Every Box."

Compare

"Shoe That's Standardized"

with

"Shoe That Fits the Foot."

Compare also the value of the appeal in

"Put Your Sweeping Reliance on a Bissell"

with

"Gets the Dirt, not the Carpet."

2. *Slogan not based upon inherent quality of a product.—*

"I'se in Town, Honey"

Called more attention to Aunt Jemima than to her pancakes, and at that, said nothing which would make a person think of the pancakes when they thought of her.

3. *Idea not distinctive.*—

Superlative self-praise is the keynote of these:

"America's Smartest Car."

"The Most Beautiful Car in America."

"Say It with Flowers" was distinctive but to say "Say It with" anything else would only add bouquets to the florist's advertising.

4. *Idea Ambiguous.*—

"Have You A Little Fairy In Your Home?"

(Proving what feature about the product thus advertised?)

"Where Accuracy Counts—We Win."

(How many would guess that this advertised a boring machine? Which one?)

"Roll Your Own."

(Tennis courts or tobacco? Which brand?)

"Bear For Wear."

(Furs? No. Tires! Which make?)

A good slogan is one which refers specifically and exclusively to the product advertised. In this manner it prevents confusing the public, and simultaneously, will prevent appropriation by an infringing advertiser.

A slogan for a product may have become so well known that it acquires a value despite shortcomings in meaning. Under these circumstances some advertisers have not suddenly eliminated their slogan but have gradually subordinated it to a newer one, until it has entirely faded out and been replaced. These experiences, expensive as they have been, have conclusively shown that it is an idea within a phrase which makes a slogan, not quotation marks around it.[1]

---

[1] No provision is made by the government for the recording and protection of slogans, with a few legal exceptions not applicable in most instances. *Printer's Ink* has established a "clearing house" where a record of slogans is kept for the convenience of advertisers.

The secondary slogan.—Often the slogan calls upon the support of a descriptive line which becomes a secondary slogan, as:

Runkel's "The Cocoa With That Chocolaty Taste, *For Drinking, Baking, Cooking.*"

"Beauty Begins Where The Light Comes In
BRENLIN—*the long wearing window shade material*"

The secondary slogan may be changed more freely than the slogan proper. Together they may form apt copy for car-card and poster display, but the importance of the transient phrase should not be confused with the slogan itself, nor should it be dragged into the advertisement as a matter of form only.

A suggestion on slogans.—The simplest slogans are the hardest to create. Rarely indeed is the slogan finally used in an extended campaign, spontaneously created the moment a need for it arises. The slogan is often the result of painstaking effort. A good way to create one is to define the idea for the copy in as many words as necessary. Then proceed with the writing of the copy, in the course of which the idea may be crystallized into a pithy phrase. Even if the slogan so evolved is not flawless at first writing, it may provide an idea which can be improved until it does become—the perfect slogan.

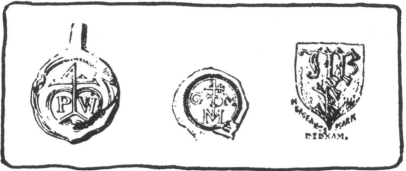

*Leaden Package Seals.*

## Chapter VII

## THE "A B C" OF TRADE-MARKS

IN the year 1266, just about 500 years before the industrial revolution started the ball of advertising rolling, a law of far-reaching effect in modern advertising was enacted by the English Parliament. "Every baker shall have a mark (*signum*) of his own for each sort of bread," it was decreed, so that the public might know what kind of loaf it was purchasing.[1] One hundred years later it was enacted that—"no goldsmith or silversmith in the city of London shall sell wrought silver of less than sterling fineness, the mark of every goldsmith to be known to the wardens of the craft." [2] How significant that ordinance was! It standardized the quality of the product, and made identification possible.

Early uses of trade-marks.—Identification marks on goods and wares are not a matter of law, but of public convenience. Unearthed Roman pottery dating back to Byzantine times has revealed the use of makers' marks centuries ago. In the medieval ages, before the masses knew how to read and write, signs and symbols were used to aid identification. Shopkeepers adopted signs for their stores. Very often they copied the

---

[1] Report of the British Archaeological Association, Volume 50, page 47.
[2] "Marks of Gold and Silver Smiths," by F. W. Fairholt.

116

armorial signs of the lords and nobles of that day. Subsequently these merchants' marks were reproduced on rings which would be impressed on the leaden package seals. Then came the custom of engraving these marks upon the wares themselves. At first the nature of the designs was purely arbitrary, but in 1300 the English Parliament found it necessary to establish a standardized code for the two commodities which were the center of trading interest at that time—gold and silver. On articles made of these precious metals there first had to appear a "lion passant"—the heraldic guardian lion, indicating that the wares came from England. Scotland was represented by a thistle, and Ireland by a crowned harp. Then there had to appear the mark of the city. (London had a leopard's head crowned, Edinburgh the castle, Birmingham an anchor, Sheffield a crown.) In addition, a duty mark and a date mark had to appear, and finally the surname or initials of the individual silversmith. The survival of this practice may be found in the stamping of silverware today.

**Modern influence of trade-marks.**—The outstanding event which gave to trade-marks their present importance was the advent of the steam engine and machinery in the eighteenth century. Factories then began to spring up. The men who

SILVERWARE MARKS OF FOUR
CENTURIES
These trade-marks come in sets.
Top set—1528
Second set—1698
Third set—1765
Bottom set, used by the Gorham Mfg. Co., in the present day.

MERCHANTS' MARKS

made the goods were further and further removed from those who finally bought the merchandise.

During the nineteenth century, an entirely new industrial system arose, based upon quantity production and country-wide distribution aided by advertising. At the foundation of the entire structure is the identification of wares by means of trade-marks. To the manufacturer the trade-mark says, "I am your representative, telling everybody that the object upon which I appear is made by you to the best of your ability." To the public it says, "Know all men that the product which bears my impress comes from one who has a reputation of quality to maintain." He does not endeavor to hide inferior wares under the cloak of anonymity. And to the advertising man the trade-mark says, "You who will broadcast the merits of my product, see that the product is worthy of the public trust. And please, sir, see that I appear attractive to the public eye."

**What is a trade-mark?**—What was at first a simple custom of mute identification has evolved into a technical system occupying the attention of the bar and of the advertising profession alike. In its broad sense a trade-mark is any device which tells who made the product or who sold it. In other words, it indicates the product's origin. More specifically, it is any symbol or device attached to goods offered for sale in the market, which distinguishes them from similar goods, or identifies them as the wares of a particular trader.[3] A trade-mark may consist of any distinctive picture, symbol, word, or device which satisfies these three conditions.[4]

1. It must be *physically* affixed to a commercial article or to its container.

2. It must point *distinctively* to the origin of the article.

3. It must be of such a nature that it can be lawfully appropriated to the use of one person, *to the exclusion of others.*

In the United States the two very important facts which must be clearly understood at the outset are that a trade-mark applies only to the specific article of merchandise to which it

---

[3] 38 Cyclopedia of Law, 678.
[4] Based on A. C. Paul, "The Law of Trade-Marks," Section 22.

must be affixed,[5] and that a word or any other design usually understood when the term "mark" is mentioned may be a trade-mark as well as a picture.

What "registering a trade-mark" means.—The purpose of a trade-mark is to protect the owner from unfair competition and the public from being deceived. The judicial attitude toward it is based on the principle that a man is not to sell his own goods under the pretense that they are the goods of another man. He cannot be permitted to use names, marks, letters, or other indicia by which he may induce purchasers to believe that the goods which he is selling are the manufacture of another person.[6]

In the United States the first actually to use a trade-mark is considered its owner *for that class of commodity*. Common law, founded on custom and usage, has been established to prevent unfair methods of competition. The Federal Trade-mark Act, passed in 1905, with amendments in later years, was designed to give uniform statutory protection to the rightful users of trade-marks. In order to come under the shelter of this law, an identifying mark which meets certain legal requirements may be entered or recorded at the Patent Office in Washington. This procedure is called "registering a trade-mark."

Registration gives a trade-mark these advantages if a question of infringement should arise:

1. It helps to prove the exact nature of the trade-mark in case a question should arise as to whether a second mark infringes on the first.

2. It puts the burden of proof in a litigation upon the other party, if they did not likewise register their mark.

3. The date of registration is accepted as evidence of the trade-mark's use.

(An unregistered trade-mark has to show prior use by means of old containers, records, and witnesses, often difficult to produce.)

4. It gives Federal courts jurisdiction in action against infringements. (An injunction issued by this court is enforce-

---

[5] This provision makes it difficult to trade-mark services rendered, such as those of a bank or accountant.

[6] L. B. Sebastian, "The Law of Trade-Marks," page 1.

able anywhere in the United States; that of a State court, in one State only.)

5. Domestic registration is necessary in many foreign countries. (Many countries require that the trade-mark be registered in the United States first, before accepting registration under their own laws.)

The act of registration alone, however, does not make a trade-mark any more than obtaining a patent makes an invention. Neither does this procedure automatically protect it from litigation. Once the trade-mark has been registered, the Patent Office, which has charge of this work, will seek to prevent infringing ideas from being registered, but the owner himself has to defend it or bring suit, if he believes another has unlawfully appropriated his trade-mark. Registration, furthermore, does not prevent another from proving the mark to be his, even though he did not record it, for a trade-mark rightfully belongs to the first person who has used it for a class of products; registration merely affords greater convenience in proving prior usage.

A large number of trade-marks were already in existence in 1905 when the present trade-mark law went into effect. To protect these, there was introduced a "ten-year clause" which provided that any trade-mark in active use for ten years prior to the passage of the Act be accorded the protection of the law, even though that trade-mark might have been disqualified under the more stern requirements of the new law. These old trade-marks form many of the present exceptions to the current law. In creating a new trade-mark, the actual intention of the law should serve as the basis of understanding, not the confusing precedents of the trade-marks which existed when the law went into effect.

What is a trade name?—Legally a trade-mark applies only to the vendible article of merchandise to which it is affixed, whereas a trade name is one under which a business is carried on.[7] It applies to a business as a whole, although that business may be engaged in the sale of many articles. Thus words like Mazda, Palmolive, Charms, Pebeco, Old Dutch Cleanser, and Kodak are trade-marks, but Westinghouse, Colgate, Huyler's,

---

[7] A. C. Paul, "The Law of Trade-Marks," Section 140.

Gulden's, Vacuum Oil Company, Cudahy Packing Company, Marshall Field, Wanamaker, and Tiffany are trade names.

When a business is opened under a name which does not completely reveal the true ownership of the company, the name must be entered at the office of the county clerk (in some States, at the office of the county register or the town recorder). The filing of this name is a very simple and inexpensive procedure. Once this has been done, a competitor would not be allowed to appropriate the name for his store or business; if he should attempt to do so, he could be haled to a court of equity *on the grounds of unfair competition and prevented from continuing the practice.* However, a name for a specific article of merchandise registered at Washington as a trade-mark would be protected *under the trade-mark law.* To prove "unfair competition" in a court of equity is no simple procedure, and to secure the protection of the trade-mark statutes is a far easier matter.[8]

If a man sells merchandise under his personal name, he may experience great difficulty in protecting that name if an infringer with the same name appears on the scene. Even in cases of the most flagrant misuse of a family name, the courts have refused to keep a person from using his own name, as they would absolutely enjoin the use of a trade-mark under similar circumstances. The second party does not necessarily have to stop using that name, as the courts may compel him only to "nullify his wrong" by using in connection with his name a distinguishing mark. This distinguishing mark may consist merely of a line of copy to point out the difference as:

WILLIAM H. BAKER
(Distinct from the old chocolate manufactory of
Walter Baker Co., Ltd.)
or
ROGERS MANUFACTURING Co.
(Not connected with the original Rogers)

---

[8] Instead of going to the Court of Equity to prove unfair competition in interstate commerce, an advertiser may go to the Federal Trade Commission. This body has accomplished much in eliminating unfair methods of competition; its action on a case, however, is slow. It awards no damages but merely restrains unfair practices. It is not interested in statutory infringement of trade-marks, devoting itself primarily to the question of goodwill.

It is evident that the best the courts do to protect a trade name seldom overcomes the objection which a trade name may offer. In the foregoing instances the name is "distinguished" according to law, but is thoroughly confusing as far as its advertising value is concerned. The average purchaser sees only the word "Baker" without bothering to figure out which Baker is meant. Or to be considered on the safe side, they may avoid buying even the genuine Baker's Cocoa. In either case the original firm often loses because it has used a trade name and not a trade-mark. Unquestionably it is better as a matter of expediency to protect a commodity with a trade-mark rather than to rely upon a trade name. This fact has been demonstrated again and again when occasion arises for seeking legal protection. As Nims points out in his excellent book on the subject, the difference between the two methods is not one of principle but of degree and method of proof.

In view of these facts it is most important to distinguish between a trade-mark and a trade name. In advertising parlance, words used for trade-mark purposes are often spoken of as trade names. Though this practice is a common one, it is incorrect and extremely confusing. Such terms are really trade-mark words clearly coming under the category of trade-marks; not of trade names.

**Meeting the requirements—affixing the trade-mark to the product.**—The first requirement of a legal trade-mark is that it be affixed to the product itself or to its container. The mere use of a device in the advertising, on the stationery, or even in the architectural design of the factory does not qualify it as a trade-mark. The mark must appear on the product itself or on the package.[9]

In the case of shoes, soap, tires, or typewriters, it would appear simple enough to affix the trade-mark. The nature of the product, however, often makes fulfillment of the requirement a difficult mechanical task when the article is one such

---

[9] This clause makes it necessary actually to produce or manufacture the article to be trade-marked before such protection is obtainable. An interstate sale of the article must also be made, for Federal registration. The individual States have trade-mark laws obtaining within their respective borders only; for practical purposes these laws have been superseded by Federal registration.

# Mulsified

## Vaseline

# Keds

### CATERPILLAR

# THERMOS
# Nujol

# Radiola

as cheese or raisins. Manufacturers of cheese have overcome the difficulty by having the trade-mark stamped around the rim of the cheese so that every half-pound slice would bear an impression of its complete name. Raisins, on the other hand, have been put into packages upon which their trade-mark was duly affixed.

From the standpoint of advertising, it is not enough to get the trade-mark on the product. *The trade-mark must adhere to it until it reaches the consumer.* Wrappers bearing the trade-mark for oranges were often lost before the fruit reached the housewife. A better method was found in the use of small labels which were pasted on the fruit, and a subsequent improvement resulted in a machine which actually stamped the trade-mark on each individual orange. *The trade-mark must be inexpensive to apply.* The expense of trade-marking may involve the device itself, the machines necessary to affix it, and, of most importance, the slowing up of production. Finally, *the trade-mark must not be injurious to the product.* Over $30,000 was spent in perfecting the machine which could stamp oranges of different size without mashing the fruit itself. It is quite evident that the advertising office is not the only department whose wishes are to be considered in creating the trade-mark.

**Meeting the requirements — distinctiveness.**—Since the trade-mark is merely an identifying device, it has no original value. Only after it has been used on a product does it begin to have any worth, based on the reputation which the article has created for itself or which advertising has created in its behalf, plus the degree to which people associate the product with the trade-mark. At the very outset, the trade-mark seeks to be distinctive that it may overcome confusion with competing articles, help the reader recollect the advertised brand when he thinks of buying the product, and assist him to recall previous advertisements whenever he sees the trade-mark.

The law does not say what a trade-mark must look like. It simply states that the trade-mark is "to point to origin of product," and suggests that this could be done by a "symbol, sign, word, or device." Mulhall divided trade-marks into the groupings which follow. He then conducted a series of tests to determine their respective effectiveness, with this result:[10]

Pictures .......................Highest Score
Geometric forms ..................Next best
Words ..........................Next best
Syllables, or disconnected letters .......Next best

The inference that may be drawn is that pictures, being best, should be used whenever possible in trade-marks. In order that the trade-mark may be described in conversation, the use of a word is most advisable. Syllables and disconnected letters alone should be avoided, for they contribute little connotative sense. A single trade-mark can embody several of these classifications, as is done when a picture and a word are combined, or a symbol and a syllable. A design containing a word, or a distinctive style of lettering a word, may be registered as a trade-mark though the word itself is not eligible for registration. When the phrase "Trade-mark Registered" appears under a device in an advertisement, it does not necessarily follow that the entire device has been appropriated as a trade-mark, for only one element within it may be so regarded. This element may be a word but not the ornamental border in which it appears, and vice versa, or a word without the descriptive term accompanying it; or else it may be a style of lettering but not the word alone. When a device such as this is offered for registration, a "disclaimer" listing the parts to be excluded must accompany the application. This is not necessary, however, when the entire mark is distinctive.[11]

**Suggestions on distinctiveness.**—The trade-mark should be simple. It should require no explanation. If a design is used, it should have one distinguishing feature easy to remember and put into words.

If a picture is adopted, it should be of a permanent character. Which trade-mark, as an example, appears more out of date: the Rock of Gibraltar as used by the Prudential Insurance Company of America, or the Smith Brothers on their

---

[10] Tipper Hotchkiss, Hollingworth and Parsons, "Advertising, Its Principles and Practices," page 127.

[11] There are, of course, forms of trade-marks other than those here considered—such as the colored strand in rope, the band of color around an electric motor, or the strip of color on the edge of a shovel. Mulhall's groups include the devices used in about 95 per cent of all trade-marks.

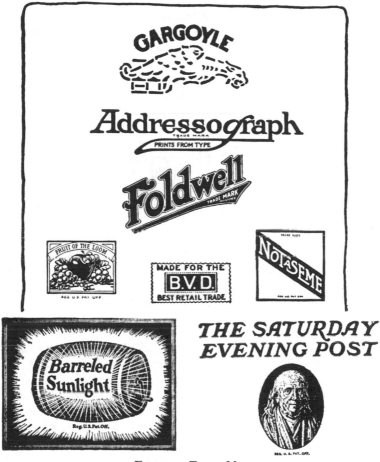

FIND THE TRADE-MARK

*Gargoyle* (as applied to oils, greases and waxes).—The registered trade-mark consists of the picture of the gargoyle when associated with the word "Gargoyle," also of the word "Gargoyle" alone, regardless of the illustration or of the style of lettering (*No.* 43,284, *Reg.* 1904).

*Addressograph* (as applied to printing machines).—The word alone is the registered trade-mark, regardless of the lettering, and not the phrase "Prints from Type" (*Nos.* 34,056, *Reg.* 1900).

*Foldwell* (as applied to paper).—The lettering only and not the word unless lettered in that style, constitutes the registered trademark (*Nos.* 130,050, *Reg.* 1923).

*Fruit of the Loom* (as applied to textile fabrics).—The illustration, word, and lettering are each an element of the registered trade-mark (*Nos.* 174,998, *Reg.* 1923).

*B.V.D.* (as applied to suspenders, belts, shirts and drawers).—The registered trademark embraces the initials only, regardless of lettering and not the accompanying phrase (*Nos.* 23,183, *Reg.* 1893).

*Notas\-eme* (as applied to hosiery).—The word and the style of lettering are each elements of the registered trade-mark (*Nos.* 141,794, *Reg.* 1921).

*Barreled Sunlight* (as applied to mixed paints).—The phrase alone, regardless of the lettering, not the illustration, constitutes the registered trade-mark (*Nos.* 146,385, *Reg.* 1921).

*Saturday Evening Post* (as applied to a weekly magazine).—The registered trademark consists of the medallion of Benjamin Franklin (*Nos.* 44,432, *Reg.* 1905); also the phrase, regardless of the lettering (*Nos.* 44,443, *Reg.* 1905).

box of cough-drops? The Rock of Gibraltar will be an up-to-date trade-mark for many years to come but the Smith Brothers would have to be given the most expensive shave in history in order to modernize their trade-mark. No element which the normal progress of time and custom may make obsolete should be introduced in a new trade-mark.

In designing a trade-mark, cognizance must also be taken of the method whereby it is to be reproduced. Automobiles usually carry their trade-marks on their radiators and on the hubs of their wheels. Simple, open-faced designs are here particularly necessary. For jewelry, a trade-mark even more simple is required to permit of reduction in size. For most package goods, a trade-mark with its width three-fifths its height will be found adaptable to the container and to adver-tisements alike.

**Meeting the requirements—legal stipulations.**—The law makes several stipulations which a trade-mark must meet be-fore it can be registered by one firm to the exclusion of others. Some of these are quite clear, whereas others are matters over which judicial opinion itself is finely divided. Adver-tising in this instance enjoys greater latitude than the bar, for while the court seeks to apply the meaning of the law to trade-marks which have already been used, the primary inter-est of advertising is in the creation of new trade-marks. To the advertising man, the legal restrictions should indicate danger which it is his place to avoid at the outset. The ques-tion is not how close the trade-mark can come to the limits of the law and still win the decision of the court, but how the trade-mark can comply with the principles of good adver-tising and win the decision of the buyer when it comes to secur-ing the sale.

**What the law says.**—The trade-mark is granted for use on a definite product. The registration of a trade-mark for one product does not automatically enjoin its use for an article of a different "descriptive quality." The legal test of whether goods are or are not "of the same descriptive properties" rests on the answers to two questions: 1. Would there be ac-tual confusion in the goods themselves; would people use one product for another unknowingly? 2. Would there be con-fusion of origin (tea and coffee were held to possess the same descriptive properties for this latter reason, though anyone enjoying a cup of tea would know it was tea, and not coffee he was drinking) ? It is often a delicate matter for courts to decide whether two products are or are not "of the same class," or "of the same descriptive properties." It has been held, for instance, that shovels and pick-axes, after-dinner mints and chocolate candies were of the same respective classes, while ice-cream and ice-cream cones, fire extinguishers and automobiles were not of the same class, and, hence, ineligible to secure the protection of the same trade-mark, though in each instance both were made by the same house. The advertiser would have to register the trade-mark separately for each product. In that case, priority of trade-mark use for one product would be of no avail if another firm had already employed the identical trade-mark for the second product. As an illustration, we have the "Packard" Automobile and the "Packard" Piano, each made by a different firm, as well as the "Cadillac" Car and the "Cadillac" Vacuum Cleaner; and "Beech-Nut" is registered as a trade-mark for bacon by the Beech-Nut Packing Company, and for cigarettes by the P. Lorillard Company. To forestall any unwelcome borrowing, a trade-mark may be registered separately for each product. The objectionable feature of this legal provision which confines trade-mark right to a single class of goods may be entirely avoided by choosing a distinctive group of names for a family of products, as Pep-O-Mint, Wint-O-Green, or else by prefixing a trade name lettered in a style distinctive to the product.

Some firms, finding themselves with various trade-marks on their hands, have pushed one product and made that the leader. Other concerns have sought to standardize gradually the varieties of the trade-marks on products issued by their houses.

**What a trade-mark must not do.**—A trade-mark must not include the flag, or any insignia of the United States, or of any State or municipality, or of any foreign country. It must not be the insignia of the Red Cross or of any organization which has adopted and publicly used this emblem.

A trade-mark is not registrable if it is used for deceptive purposes. If it indicates a quality which does not exist, the mark is regarded as being equally misleading. (Syrup of Figs and Fruit Vinegar were excluded from registration on these grounds.)

**Must identify only.**—The sole function of the trade-mark is to identify the maker or the seller of goods. It must not be a quality of the article or a description of it. Furthermore, the trade-mark must not affect the utility of the product or be an ornamental feature, for if it does, it is no longer an identifying device but the article itself. The idea thus loses its status as a trade-mark in that it becomes a simple manufacturing feature which others may have the right to adopt. "A red edge on a shovel can be appropriated exclusively by a manufacturer because it adds nothing whatever to the utility of the goods, but a red tread on an automobile cannot be appropriated. Rubber which is colored red by the use of antimony is a common product in the trade and has qualities which make it superior for certain purposes and under certain conditions. Any manufacturer has the right to make use of such common practices which belong to the art and it would be against public policy to grant to any one concern an exclusive right to manufacture tires with red treads." [12] Another instance is that of a roofing paper which had a unique design over its entire surface; this device was likewise held ineligible for registration as a trade-mark, because it was not a mere identifying design but a decorative feature which added value to the product itself.

The name of any living person can be used only if it is drawn in a distinctive way or used in conjunction with his picture. In such a case the distinctive style of lettering or the picture, and not the mere name, really forms the trade-mark.

The name of a historically famous person may be used, if it is not of a descriptive or geographical character. In fact, descriptive and geographical terms cannot be registered as trade-marks. It is within these classifications that most of the adapted and coined words in advertising fall—and in which most of the troublesome trade-mark questions arise.

---

[12] Roy W. Johnson, "Trade-marking 'Difficult' Merchandise," *Printer's Ink Monthly*, June, 1921, page 13.

**When is a trade-mark descriptive?**—A term may be regarded as descriptive if the public has a need for the word in describing that particular article. Comparative terms such as "superb," "best," "grade A," and "high-class," are clearly parts of the accepted language as applying to almost anything of which we speak. Hence to grant their exclusive use by one manufacturer would be giving him an unfair right to appropriate a term which may properly be used by the public as applying to his competitor's product as well. As a rule, therefore, comparative terms are totally unsuited for use as trade-marks.

Though the law says that adjectives of the English language are the common property of all who speak it or write it, an adjective may be acceptable if it is not ordinarily applied to the particular type of article under consideration, though it is a familiar term when used in a different sense. "Ivory" was regarded as only a suggestive use of the word when applied to soap, but descriptive when applied to manicure and toilet sets. Likewise, on the same principle, "Elastic" was accepted as a trade-mark for bookcases because the public would not ordinarily refer to bookcases by that term, but "Elastic Seam" for hosiery was regarded as descriptive, because, in that case, the word pictured a quality frequently demanded by purchasers of those goods.

Terms such as these have been considered descriptive by the courts:

| | |
|---|---|
| Autoguard | *(Bumper for autos)* |
| Vacuum Cup | *(For tires)* |
| Mahogany | *(For shoe polish)* |
| Infallible | *(Smokeless powder)* |

whereas these terms were held non-descriptive:

| | |
|---|---|
| Vogue | *(Magazine)* |
| Teller | *(Recording safe)* |
| Trucker | *(Plows)* |
| Woolknap | *(Blankets)* |

A study of acceptable words reveals that the courts themselves have laid down no set rules on the question of descriptiveness. When the validity of a trade-mark depends upon an interpretation of what is and what is not descriptive, and

when claims of its legal eligibility are based upon the precedent
of trade-marks which are even more descriptive, all experiences would indicate that it is advisable to leave trouble alone
and create a new idea. Richard H. Paynter, the psychologist,
selected a list of names against which infringements had been
charged in court.[13] He then held a series of practical tests
of the names by questioning the public about them in a manner
similar to that in which an advertising research is conducted.
The results revealed one outstanding fact—that the fairest
efforts of the court to decide upon a trade-mark do not necessarily insure its meeting the requirements of advertising. It
can not be too strongly emphasized that the value of the
trade-mark is determined in the mind of the public. It is
toward the public that the advertising man should direct his
efforts. There his ideas will prove more fruitful than in the
province of the lawyer where he might hope to gain his point
on the strength of a debatable precedent.[14]

When may a geographical name be used?—"No mark which
consists merely of a geographical name or term shall be registered under this act," says the law. The acceptability of a
geographical name depends upon the meaning conveyed by
its use. The name of a city may imply much more than a
spot on the map. With an insight into the principle involved
in the use of geographical names (or "community names" as
Rogers more appropriately calls them), advertising may here
find greater opportunities than are generally recognized. A
geographical name may indicate:

1. Origin only, without implying a definite quality.
2. A certain process or quality of manufacture.
3. An arbitrary choice.

Name indicating origin only.—A term is said to indicate
origin only when it is construed to mean that its article is "a
product coming from that place." Thus California oranges
are taken to mean oranges from California; Blue Lick Water,
water from the Blue Lick Springs; Georgia peaches, peaches

---

[13] Richard H. Paynter, Jr., "A Psychological Study of Trade-mark Infringements."

[14] It may not be amiss to call the attention of the court to the practicability
of testing disputed words upon the public, thus determining fairly the degree
of confusion which actually exists.

from that State only. The term does not, however, indicate any exact grade or quality, since two Georgia peaches may be quite unlike each other in size and in lusciousness.

A product whose name is obviously chosen to indicate origin must come from the designated source. Peaches grown in New York could not be called "Georgia peaches," nor could a mineral water taken from a Maine spring be called "Blue Lick Water," if for any reason that were contemplated. This necessity for truthfulness accounted for the fact that steps had to be taken to prevent clothing manufacturers from marketing their garments as "Rochester Clothing" unless they were actually located in that city. No one producer of an article coming from a territory whose name implies origin only may appropriate the name for his own exclusive use. Hence such terms are unsuited for trade-mark purposes. But a local association may well raise the standards of the goods emanating from its district, and then use advertising to secure wide public recognition of their excellence (as has been done so well by the fruit growers' associations).

**Name indicating process or quality of manufacture.**—Very often a name comes to mean more than a place from which a product comes. It expresses a definite process of manufacture or quality of product for which the place has become renowned. Lubricating oils can be divided into two general classes: those refined from an asphaltum base petroleum, and those refined from a paraffine base petroleum. The paraffine base oil deposits are chiefly in Pennsylvania, Southeastern Ohio, West Virginia, and New York. Buyers of pure paraffine base oil speak of it and ask for it as "Pennsylvania" oil, even though the oil may have come from one of the other states in the paraffine base oil belt. One oil producer in Pennsylvania consequently was restrained from calling his oil "Pennsylvania" oil because it had a mixed base, and not the pure paraffine base that buyers expect of oil under that name. "Pennsylvania" thus lost its identity as a geographical term when applied to oil, and became the label for a specific quality of oil.

The name may go even further than indicating a process or quality of a product, and indicate the product of a single house, which may or may not be made in the city whose name it bears, as Elgin Watches or Kalamazoo Stoves. "Where a geographical name is first adopted to denote a place of manufacture and afterwards becomes known as a synonym for superior excellence, persons elsewhere in town will not be permitted to use it on similar goods." [15]

Name arbitrarily chosen.—The greatest source of registrable trade-marks, among geographical names, is that of arbitrary choice. The legal requirement for an arbitrarily selected name is that it shall not mislead. Thus Paris Garters hardly give the inference that the supporters are made in the capital of France, any more than the name Vienna Rolls tends to lead the housewife into believing that the rolls have been baked this morning in Vienna.

Furthermore, the law must be satisfied that an arbitrary name does not seek to benefit by the reputation created in its behalf by another. Philadelphia Cream Cheese was an arbitrary name chosen many years ago by a New York dairy. At that time Philadelphia Cream Cheese meant nothing at all to the trade. It might just as well have been called Kansas City Cream Cheese or Kokomo Cream Cheese. Since then, however, the name Philadelphia Cream Cheese has gained the reputation of being the product of a certain dairy only. Another company, subsequently offering a "Philadelphia Cream Cheese," was restrained in court from using that name, as it was no longer an arbitrary use of the name, but one calculated to benefit by the prestige of the original user, which was another matter entirely.

The advertising requirement for an arbitrary name is that it connotes a pleasant idea in a distinctive manner. "Bermuda Hot Water Heaters" is a good example, suggesting water that has tropical warmth on a bleak January day. Palm Beach Cloth and Old Dutch Cleanser likewise possess an excellent connotative significance. Nicknames such as Keystone, Granite State, Empire State, and Hoosier often acquire the same meaning as the official names and should be regarded in the same light.

Appearance of goods no trade-mark.—The color of a product does not by itself form a valid trade-mark. Nor is the

---

[15] A. C. Paul, "The Law of Trade-marks," Section 241.

shape of the article or the style of its packing registrable as a trade-mark. One concern always wrapped its parcels in a light orange-colored paper tied with a red string. That distinctive wrapping alone could not meet the legal requirements of a registrable trade-mark. A match company was likewise unable to obtain trade-mark registration of the color of its match-heads; a soap manufacturer could not register the color of his soap; nor could a perfume manufacturer enter merely an unusual-shaped bottle as his trade-mark.

However, where a distinctive shape, color, or mode of packing has been extensively used for a product *in connection with an affixed label,* the entire combination can be protected from infringement on the grounds of unfair competition, even though the individual elements cannot be separately protected. The use of identical color and shape together may be considered an element in the imitation of another's trade-mark or dress of goods, and in such case be enjoined. In other words, the laws against unfair competition give no rest to the infringer who takes advantage of the fact that another cannot register an idea as a trade-mark; still the man who cannot register an identifying idea should get a trade-mark which can be protected as such.

A special feature in package construction should be patented if possible. This keeps others from copying it for 17 years, during which time the product has ample opportunity to enjoy its exclusive feature and to establish itself as "The Article With The Blank Construction Package." The time to advertise the patented feature of a product is when the patent is issued, and not the season before it expires, as unfortunately is so often done.

**Trade-marks on patented articles.**—When a new article is patented and is given a trade-marked name, a curious situation may arise. After the patent expires, the name becomes a generic term. It is then common property and may not be retained exclusively by its originator as a trade-mark. When the patents on the Singer Sewing Machine expired, other people obtained the right to manufacture this machine. Since the machine was known only as Singer Sewing Machine, that term went into the dictionary and out of the category of

## Comparison Chart
### Legal Protection of Ideas in the United States

| IDEA | METHOD OF PROTECTION | REQUIREMENTS FOR THIS PROTECTION | DURATION | COMMENTS |
|---|---|---|---|---|
| **A TRADE-MARK** Any device which identifies the origin of a product, telling who made it or who sold it. | Registration with the Patent Office, Washington, D. C. | A. Must be physically affixed to a product or its container. B. Must point distinctively to origin or product. C. Must be eligible for appropriation by one person to the exclusion of others. | 20 years, renewable for similar periods upon expiration. | I. A word may be a trade-mark. II. The first to begin continuous use of a trade-mark is its owner for that class of goods, whether or not he registered the trade-mark. Registration serves to establish priority of usage. III. A trade-marked article can be made by another unless that article is patented. The trade-mark itself, however, must not be used by another for that type of product. |
| **A TRADE NAME** A name which applies to the *business as a whole*, not to an individual product. | Infringer can be restrained in court on grounds of unfair competition. In major cases, infringer can be haled before Federal Trade Commission. | A. Owner of name must show in court that another is leading people to believe that they are purchasing from the original user of that name, when in fact they are buying from the infringer. | Perpetual. | I. The term "Trade Name" is used in a confused sense. A TRADE-MARK WORD IS NOT A TRADE NAME. There is an important difference between the two, both in their application and in the ease of defending their use against infringers. |
| **A SLOGAN** | A slogan as such cannot be copyrighted or registered. | | | |
| **AN ADVERTISE-MENT**, a piece of copy, an illustration. | Copyrighting with Copyright Office, Library of Congress, Washington, D. C. | A. Must represent an original intellectual effort. B. Must bear copyright notice when published, then submitted with application for copyright. | 28 years, renewable once. | I. Copyright fee only $1. Procedure very simple. II. Must not be attached to product. If it is, it comes under the classification of labels. |
| **THE TITLE** of a newspaper, house organ or magazine. | Same as Trade-Mark. Registration with the Patent Office, Washington, D. C. | A. Must be physically affixed to the newspaper, house organ or magazine. B. Must point distinctively to origin of product. C. Must be eligible for appropriation by one person to the exclusion of others. | 20 years, renewable for similar periods upon expiration. | I. The title is really the trade-mark of the publication. II. Does not include the title of a book (such as a novel or a text book). III. The phrase "Registered," U. S. Pat. Office" or "Trade-Mark Registered," or a similar phrase must always appear in conjunction with a trade-mark so registered. |

| IDEA | METHOD OF PROTECTION | REQUIREMENTS FOR THIS PROTECTION | DURATION | COMMENTS |
|---|---|---|---|---|
| A LABEL | Copyrighting with the Patent Office, Washington, D. C. | A. Must be attached to product. B. Must be descriptive of contents. C. Must tell who made the goods or who sold them. | 28 years, renewable once. | I. Notice this is not copyrighted with the copyright office but with the patent office. II. A label differs from a trade-mark in that it is descriptive and in that the label includes the entire print while a trade-mark applies to the device regardless of the printed matter with which it appears on a package. |
| DESIGN OF FABRIC. | By securing letters of design patent, from the Patent Office, Washington, D. C. | A. Must be a new, original and definite form into which a physical substance is moulded or shaped, which gives it a distinguishing appearance (such as ornamental design or pattern of texture, or furniture decoration). | 3½ years, 7 years, 14 years (optional). | I. This applies essentially to textile designs. II. The fee is nominal; varies with duration of patent. |
| AN INNOVATION IN PACKAGE CONSTRUCTION. | Patenting with the Patent Office, Washington, D. C. | A. Must be a new discovery or invention of an art, machine, manufacture, composition of matter, or else a new and useful improvement on one. | 17 years, not renewable. | I. A new feature in the product itself, or in the construction of its package is especially desirable when the product is in the advanced competitive stage, since it provides to the product a basic point of individuality. |
| AN INNOVATION IN PACKAGE DESIGN | Infringer may be restrained in court on grounds of unfair competition. | An advertiser cannot register a color, as such, as his trade-mark, but he may succeed in registering an arbitrary combination of colors used in conjunction with his label, as his trade-mark. An advertiser may restrain another from imitating the color scheme, package dressing or label arrangement, so as to be mistaken for his, on the grounds of unfair competition. | | |
| AN INNOVATION IN THE PRODUCT ITSELF. | Same as innovation in package construction. Patenting with the Patent Office, Washington, D. C. | | | |

trade-marks.[16] Goodyear Rubber now likewise means rubber made by the Goodyear process, regardless of who makes it. Aluminum, linoleum, and aspirin are other words in popular usage today, which were originally trade-marks for patented articles.

While the patent on a product continues, however, its trade-marked name remains the exclusive property of the advertiser, legally speaking. In every-day affairs, however, such a name may suffer the penalty of success. People may apply it to all products of that type instead of to the article of one concern only. For example, a Thermos Bottle does not mean *any* vacuum bottle but only that made by the Thermos Bottle Company. The only firm which makes Victrolas is the Victor Talking Machine Company, yet people inquire of a dealer, "What brand of Victrolas have you?" "Vaseline" is the trade-marked property of the Chesebrough Manufacturing Company and may not be used by another manufacturer. "Celluloid" is likewise a trade-mark. By the irony of fate some advertisers struggle first to popularize a name and then have to begin another struggle to "privatize" the name. We find one advertiser imploring, "Don't Say Underwear, Say Munsingwear," while another is warning, "If It Isn't An Eastman It Isn't a Kodak." To judge from past experience, we may some day see the Munsingwear advertising reach the enviable plight of Eastman-Kodak advertising, and declare, "Not All Underwear is Munsingwear."

The question therefore arises whether an advertiser is better off if his name is not so well-known that it becomes a part and parcel of every man's language, or whether he is in a better position if he is obliged to defend his exclusive right to a name. It is a very interesting question indeed—and as such we shall leave it here.

**Copy demands of a trade-marked word.**—The suitability of a word for use as a trade-mark can well be decided by good copy sense. The word should be as adaptable as some of the patented reading lamps, which can be hung, clamped, or stuck anywhere and still give forth their light.

---

[16] The Singer Sewing Machine Company did not lose its right to the peculiar style of lettering whereby it had presented its name. The lettering design remains to this day the trade-mark.

# HOUDAILLES
### (Say Hoo-dye)

**Clicquot**
Pronounced Klee-ko

# Unguentine
### UN-GWEN-TEEN

FIRST AID TO PRONUNCIATION

The following qualifications help a trade-mark in its work. A single trade-mark may not embody all of the virtues enumerated, but it may at least strive to achieve them.[17]  Words chosen for trade-mark purposes should be:

1. Simple and crisp.

Such words are typified by Kem, Lux, Zonite, Mazda, Fab.

2. Easy to say.

What is the average reader to do with names such as Houdailles, Hyomei, Telekathoras, Glycothymoline, Sempre Giovine?

Advertisers of such names may find it necessary to run an explanatory line spelling the name phonetically. This is one of the two ways out of the difficulty. The other is to change the name before it is advertised.

3. Pronounceable in one way only.

Is Olivilo to be pronounced Ah-leev-eye-lo or Olive-eelo; Pall Mall, Pawl Mawl or Pell Mell; Michelin, Mish-elin or Mike-elin?

The public's pronunciation may be corrected by a simple

---

[17] In judging trade-mark words, care must be taken to distinguish between the popularity of a word because of its aptness, and popularity because of its previous advertising. We speak of "Kodak" as an excellent name—and it is, but are we not influenced by its advertising as much as by its own merit as an "advertisable" word? We should be fair in comparing a new name with one that is well-known, and not expect the recent creation to make the impression which a well-established trade-mark makes.

expedient such as was used by the Standard Oil Company. Their name, Socony, was mispronounced "Sock-ohnee" and "Soak-ohnee." The desired pronunciation was So-co'-nee, which they impressed by printing their name SoCOny and So*cony*.

4. Distinctive.

The trade-mark should possess individuality both in its construction and in its application to a product. One issue of Hendricks' Commercial Register listed 95 "Nationals," 122 "Champions," 134 "Stars," 142 "Ideals," 149 "Universals," and 184 "Standards." What individuality would a new name possess if it consisted of, or included, one of these terms?

5. Suggestive of product.

The trade-mark must not literally describe the product, but it can suggest the nature of the article, as does *Tarvia* Road Mixture, *Sheetrock* Wall-board, *Palmolive* Soap, *Dromedary* Dates, *Gainaday* Electric Washer, *Sealdsweet* Fruits. The word choice itself is important as revealed by comparing the effect of Orange *Squash* with that of Orange *Crush*, of Soap *Chips* with that of Soap *Flakes*.

**Registering the trade-mark.**—A new trade-mark may be registered for a term of 20 years with privilege of renewal for the same term, on an application made not more than six months before its expiration. Trade-marks granted before April 1, 1905, remain in force for the original term and may' then be renewed as in the case of an original. The fee for the registration alone is $10 but with lawyer's fee included may amount to $75 or more, depending upon the searching necessary.

Every article whose trade-mark is registered must bear the notice: "Registered in U. S. Patent Office," or "Reg. U. S. Pat. Off.," or a similar phrase. When the article itself cannot bear the impression, the notice may be placed on its container.

Should the trade-mark infringe upon one that is not even registered (it is estimated that there are over 160,000 trade-marks without registration), the lack of knowledge of that unregistered trade-mark or the lack of intention to mislead will not prevent the court from ordering the advertiser to change his mark, or pay damages if such damages can be

# Some Trade-mark "Don'ts."

1. Don't try to imitate another trade-mark. The money spent will only advertise the original user. And if the imitating mark does make a success, it will have difficulty in being protected from infringers.
2. Don't depend upon a doubtful legal precedent. The value of a trade-mark is not measured by the money spent for its protection but by the extent to which people associate it with an advertised product of merit.
3. Don't depend upon any idea whose absence will not be as conspicuous as its presence.
4. Don't depend on a mere circle, square or other commonplace idea. The simplicity of such a device is excellent, but its commonness fails to recommend its use.
5. Don't use an idea that is not adaptable to a package, to other articles of a line, or to advertisements of different sizes.
6. Don't include a contemporary style or fashion of dress. It will quickly antiquate the trade-mark. Better go back into history, if you wish a costumed effect.
7. Don't depend upon color where you can avoid it. The trade-mark may have to be reproduced in black-and-white.
8. Don't depend upon an explanation of the trade-mark to clarify its meaning. The success of the trade-mark depends on its own aptness.
9. Don't fail to register the trade-mark both at home and abroad.
10. Don't overlook the importance of having a good trade-mark at the outset.

proved. It is therefore advisable to have an attorney handle all details of filing the papers and searching.

The Commissioner of Patents, Washington, D. C., is in charge of trade-mark registration. His office will forward, upon request, a helpful booklet, entitled "United States Statutes Concerning the Registration of Trade-marks (with Rules of Patent Office)."

**Copyrighting.**—A copyright grants its owner the exclusive right of printing, publishing, or reproducing a work of art or literature for a period of 28 years and is renewable once. Trade-mark registration protects an identifying device from imitation. Copyrighting protects an "intellectual work" itself from being copied by another. In trade-mark cases, the infringer simply copies the trade-mark idea and offers it on his own product. In the case of copyrighting, the infringer reprints or otherwise duplicates the product itself.

The copyright applies to 13 classes of "intellectual efforts" of which the following are of special interest to advertisers:

(a) Books, directories, and other compilations.
(b) Periodicals, newspapers.
(f) Maps.
(g) Works of art, models, or designs for works of art.
(h) Reproductions of a work of art.
(i) Drawings or plastic works of a scientific or technical character.
(j) Photographs.
(k) Prints and pictorial illustrations.

**How to secure a copyright.**—A copyright may be secured by the advertiser himself. The simplicity of the procedure, in fact, is one of the most pleasant things encountered in an advertising man's work. It is merely necessary to secure a copyright application card from the Register of Copyrights, Copyright Office, Library of Congress, Washington, D. C. No charge is made for this card, but the class of work to be copyrighted should be stated in writing (as a, b, j, k, and so forth, according to the list given).

. When the work to be copyrighted is published, it should bear the imprint, "Copyright 19— by ——," for articles in classes (a) and (b) in the preceding list. In the case of articles in the other classes, it is merely necessary to print "©" accompanied by name, initials or else by a symbol, providing the full name is evident somewhere on the copies.

After the work has been printed, two copies of it are to be sent to the Register of Copyrights, with the application blank and with a fee of $1. Postmasters are authorized to mail these packages without postage charge and to issue a receipt as well.

In case of an illustration or photograph, a blue-print or photostat [18] should be forwarded bearing the title of the drawing on its back. If it is desired to copyright a drawing before its completion to protect the artist pending its finish, the same procedure may be followed; "©," "Copr.," or "Copyright" should be used (not "copyrighted").

It is well to note that a name to be used as a trade-mark cannot be copyrighted, nor can a slogan be so protected. The copyrighting of advertisements is done chiefly for its moral effect. The title of any publication issued periodically (as a magazine or a house organ) comes under the trade-mark provision.

**Protecting labels.**—A label is protected under the law of unfair competition; it is treated in a manner different from that in which a regular trade-mark or copyright subject is handled. The label to be acceptable must be attached to the article, and be descriptive of it. The label must give the maker's or seller's name; it must be an "artistic production." When the label is printed, it should bear a line "Reg. U. S. Patent Office." Ten copies of the label should be sent to the Commissioner of Patents (not to the Library of Congress, as in other copyrighted works) with the formal application blank, procurable upon request. The Patent Office fee is $10. If for any reason the copyright is not granted, no harm will come from the use which has been made of the registration line on the label; it will merely be necessary for the advertiser to refrain from using that clause on his subsequent labels. The facts bear repeating that registration or copyrighting does not of itself enjoin others from using the idea; the act merely im-

---

[18] A photographic print, described in the chapter on engraving

proves the chance an advertiser has to win his legal action against any infringer.

**Canadian trade-marks.**—The Canadian Trade-mark and Design Act, passed in 1919, divides trade-marks into two classes, "general" and "specific." Under general trade-marks come the names of firms and institutions corresponding to what in the United States would be trade names. The specific trade-mark, on the other hand, is one which applies to a particular article only, as does the trade-mark in the United States.

The chief requirement for registration is the qualification of distinguishing the goods of the owner. The term of registration of specific trade-marks is 25 years, and is renewable. General trade-marks, once registered, continue to enjoy this legal privilege as long as they are used.

The government application fee for a specific trade-mark is $25; for a general trade-mark, $30. These figures, of course, are exclusive of charges for any legal services which an applicant would undoubtedly wish to employ.

Upon request, the Commissioner of Patents (Trade-mark and Copyright Branch), Ottawa, will forward the informative statement of the Canadian trade-mark laws and rules of practice, entitled "Circular of the Patent and Copyright Office Containing 'The Trade-mark and Design Act' and 'The Timber Marking Act.' "

**Trade-marks in the United Kingdom.**—Under the Trade-marks Act of 1905 and 1919, a trade-mark to be eligible for registration in the United Kingdom must contain or consist of at least one of the following features:

1. The name of a company, individual, or firm, represented in a special manner.

2. The signature of the applicant for registration, or some predecessor in his business.

(The above two groupings correspond to trade names which would not be registered in the United States, and to general trade-marks registrable in the Dominion of Canada.)

3. An invented word or words (*aptly* called *word-marks*).

4. A word or words having no direct reference to the character or quality of the goods and not being, according to its ordinary significance, a geographical name or a surname (an

<br /><br />

Courtesy American
European Patent
Co.

LOST, STRAYED, OR STOLEN

Each of these well-known American trade-marks has been registered abroad,
or submitted for registration abroad, by some one other than the original owner
who thereby lost his rights to the trade-mark in that country. The above are
taken from the *Official Lista General de las Marcas,* and from the *Boletin
Oficial,* Argentine Republic.

explicit way of saying that "descriptive" and "geographical" terms are excluded).

5. Any other distinctive mark.

In addition, any mark which has enjoyed bona fide use as a trade-mark in the British Isles for not less than two years, if it distinguishes the goods, is eligible for registration.

Excluded from registration as trade-marks are those devices which fail to distinguish or which are deceptive. The law also excludes those marks which represent British, royal or imperial arms, crests, crowns, flags, Admiralty seals, and similar official devices; the words "Royal," "Imperial," and "Crown," indicating royal patronage, are deemed unsuited for registration, as are also armorial signs, unless the applicant can show justification for the use of the latter.

Consent must be obtained from the owner of a name for its use, if the owner is living. If he is recently deceased, approval must be obtained from his estate.

A valuable provision in the British Act is that of "registration at the customs," whereby the customs authority will notify the owner of a registered trade-mark when goods wrongfully bearing that mark are being imported.

Among the other differences between the registration requirements in the United States and those in the United Kingdom is to be noted the fact that the former requires actual use of the trade-mark on a product which has been put into sale; whereas the latter will register a trade-mark if there is merely a bona-fide intention of using it within a reasonable length of time.

The period of registration is 14 years and is renewable. Application for registration costs £1. Here again, this amount does not include the cost of searching and legal counsel. Owing to the proportions reached by industrial activity in the British Isles and the length of time many of the businesses have been established, searching and legal counsel are extremely important.

The official government brochure on the subject, "Instructions to Persons Who Wish to Register Trade-marks," may be obtained from The Registrar, The Patent Office, 25, Southampton Buildings, London, W. C. 2. It should be remembered that registration in the United Kingdom does not apply to the Colonies.

**Trade-marks in other countries.**—Under the laws of the United States and England, the entire trade-mark concept is based on the principle that the owner of goods, who first uses a mark to identify his wares, is the rightful owner of that mark. But in many other countries, ownership of the mark goes to the first person to register it, regardless of his actual or intended use of that mark to distinguish his merchandise. This policy has the virtue of encouraging owners of trade-marks to register them and thus enable others to ascertain that the mark is in use. But the same principle offers an ideal opportunity for plunder to those pirates who specialize in registering all the trade-marks they can clip from American and British magazines, thus becoming the rightful owners of the trade-marks of those two countries. Their game depends upon the laxity of the true owners of those trade-marks in registering them abroad. The profit lies in selling back the marks to the manufacturers who wish to enter the country with their trade-marked wares. The only way these indignities may be avoided is to register a trade-mark in all countries abroad before much money is spent in advertising it even in the domestic field.

Most foreign countries require that a trade-mark first be registered in its domestic land before they will permit registration in their provinces.

**Conclusion on trade-marks.**—To summarize, the most important thing to remember about trade-marks is this: that the real value of a trade-mark lies in the reputation which a product earns for itself, both through inherent worth and through good advertising of that quality. In choosing a trade-mark word, sheer cleverness should not be the sole criterion; the most desirable qualities are ability to wear well in continuous use and power distinctively to identify merchandise of merit.

## CHAPTER VIII

## VISUALIZING THE IDEA

WHAT is Eternity?
How long is it?
How would you go about describing Eternity, if you were called upon to do so? Quite an assignment, no doubt, but just see how Hendrick Van Loon in his entrancing "Story of Mankind" handles the task: "High up in the North," he says, "in the land called Svithjod there stands a rock. It is one hundred miles high and one hundred miles wide. Once every thousand years a little bird comes to this rock to sharpen its beak. When this rock has been worn away, then a single day of eternity will have gone by." And there you have Eternity, endless thought that it is, clearly visualized! Surely if a conception as indefinable as Eternity can be picturized, there should be no difficulty in translating into graphic form the ideas of advertisements.

The genesis of every advertisement is a thought. A simple statement of the idea in the mind of the advertiser may serve the purpose of the advertisement, in which case no picture would be necessary. The copy may be so graphic, so vibrant in its descriptive power, that an accompanying illustration becomes superfluous. Often, however, a thought is better expressed by illustration than by words. More frequently, illustration can be used to reinforce written copy, both methods of presentation being used to advantage in conveying a single idea.

**Visualizing defined.**—To visualize an idea is to crystallize an abstract thought and present it in its physical form, or else, to evolve a vivid manner of picturing a concrete statement. The methods of visualizing are many. Take "Boys Playing Ball" as an instance. Were two artists asked to draw their conception of this theme, one might show a happy ragamuffin with a bat in his hand standing before another who is catching.

148

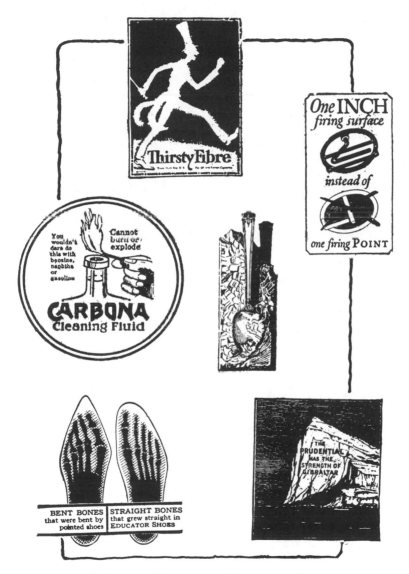

A GROUP OF NOTEWORTHY VISUALIZING IDEAS

A second artist might show a well-laid-out diamond with uniformed players covering the bases. And a dozen artists would probably offer a dozen different interpretations. It is evident, therefore, that the variety of ideas whereby a thought can be pictured is limited only by the imagination of man.

**Visualizing vs. Layout.**—Closely allied with visualization, but not to be confused with it, is the making of layouts. Layout concerns itself with the arrangement of the units within the advertisement, whereas visualization interests itself in the conception of these elements. When "The Greatest Mother in the World" was created, it represented a visualizing idea. When it was decided whereabouts in an advertisement this picture was to appear, the question was one of layout. When the famous "Thirsty Fibre" was born, he was the offspring of a visualizing idea. But all decisions upon the exact place he will occupy in the advertisement, or upon his size, come within the province of layout. Visualizing creates; layout arranges. Visualizing takes a thought and gives it definition in the shape of a drawing; layout takes the drawing, together with the copy, and fits the two together into an advertisement.

In large offices the work of visualizing is done by a person who devotes his time exclusively to interpreting ideas in black and white. Generally, visualization is regarded as the first step in preparing the layout of the advertisement. In fact, when an advertising man "draws up a layout," he may in truth be evolving the visualizing idea as well. The performance of the two tasks may be almost simultaneous, but the nature of each should be clearly appreciated. The ability to draw well is a decided advantage, but is secondary in this phase of advertising to the power of creating the idea to be illustrated. With this ability it is a comparatively simple matter to convey the idea to an illustrator who prepares the finished drawing. If one is fortunately gifted with the ability to draw, he need only learn how to conceive of ideas which are essential in advertising. It is the idea in an illustration, not the illustration alone, which is so highly valued in advertising.

**The purpose of visualizing.**—The purpose of any illustration is to convey an *idea*. The only ideas eligible for use in an advertisement are those which help express the message underlying the advertisement. If it is the purpose of the advertisement to show the simplicity of operation of a check protector, the illustration must in some way show how simply that check protector operates; it would not do merely to illustrate that advertisement with a view of "big business"—a panorama of tall office buildings—though those buildings be excellently drawn. Conversely, if the purpose of the advertisement is to drive home the fact that "the largest offices use check protectors," the panorama of tall buildings would be quite appropriate. A mere barren close-up of the machine itself would leave the advertisement quite void of any visualizing power.

*Everything which enters into an advertisement is a part of that advertisement and must help that advertisement in its work.* Recognizing that the work of an advertisement is to deliver a message, illustrations admittedly are to be used only in conveying that thought. If the idea is "This is a beautiful product," the illustration will have to portray the beauty of the product. If the idea is "See how this little pinion works," the illustration must show how the pinion works. If the idea is "Be sure you buy this brand of breakfast food in this package and not any 'similar brands,'" the illustration must feature the package as emphatically as possible. In the message of the advertisement lies the visualizing idea. Learn to recognize the message and to translate it into illustration, and you have learned to visualize.

**Functions of visualizing.**—Since the purposes of advertisements vary, the underlying ideas of illustrations will differ; since no two men would express a thought in exactly the same way, the methods used in visualizing these thoughts will likewise differ. According to their functions, however, visualizing ideas may be likened to nouns, verbs, and adjectives. Illustrations in the first group are created to say, "This is the product," "Here is the product," "Notice that this is the product." They turn the spotlight on the *noun* of the advertisement. Illustrations of the *verb* type say, "Here is what the product does," "See how this feature works," "This is how the product operates," or "This is what the Service will do for you."

The illustrations of the *verb* family are in large measure explanatory. The third or *adjective* type of visualizing idea devotes itself to glorifying the beauty, distinctiveness, elegance, or exclusiveness of the product, not merely by adjectives (for these would be too blatant), but by beautiful pictures which say as much, and more. Hart, Schaffner & Marx Clothes advertisements sell men's clothes, not by picturing the internal construction of the suits but by bringing out their distinctiveness. McCallum Hosiery advertisements have not endeavored to show the weave of the hosiery, nor its reinforced heel. They seek rather to convey the spirit of refinement and elegance which surround the people who purchase McCallum Hosiery. Over the advertisements of Arrow Collars there is cast a halo of elegance by the fine drawings and borders. The illustrations are the adjectives of these advertisements.

**Methods of visualizing.**—Once the true scope of visualizing is appreciated, it becomes an easier task to go about actually creating the pictorial theme of an advertisement. Following are some of the effective methods employed in visualizing ideas:

1. Illustration of product alone.
2. Illustration of product in setting.
3. Illustration of product in use.
4. Illustration of result of product's use.
5. Dramatization of a headline.
6. Dramatization of a situation.
7. Comparison.
8. Contrast.
9. Emphasis on detail.
10. Diagram.
11. Phantom effects.
12. Symbolic illustrations.
13. Legendary signs.
14. Decoration and ornament alone.
15. Odd and grotesque figures.

**Illustration of product alone.**—To familiarize the reader with the actual article so that he will recognize it when he sees it, the simplest form of illustration is used. It simply

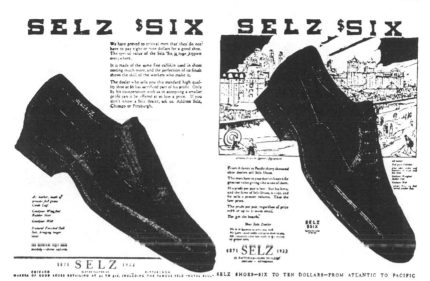

PRODUCT ALONE      PRODUCT IN SETTING

Here we have two shoes, one presented alone, the other in a setting. If the design, appearance, or style of a product is in itself the chief point of interest, the product can well be shown by itself. If the distinctiveness of a product is to be enhanced, a setting is useful. Competitive products which have little physical distinctiveness over similar products are the chief users of settings, and, in fact, often become known by those backgrounds.

shows a picture of the product. Such an advertisement tells the readers that this is the article they are reading about. The illustration of the actual product may be advisable when the product is ordered direct from the advertisement; when it is purchased mainly because of its pleasing or appetizing appearance, as in the case of clothing and food; when it is in an intensely competitive market (in order to establish individual brands and prevent substitution); and when it is desired merely to keep the name or package of the product before the public.

Where the product comes in a package, it is invariably good to show the article itself as well as the container. The advantages of this method over that of showing a conventionalized, staid package are manifold: it gives proper emphasis to both contents and package, lends more interest to the picture, and gives more life to the advertisement.

A. The Product Alone            B. The Product in a Setting

E. The Product in Use            F. Dramatizing Headline
                                 *"A Lamp for Every Room"*

*Specially drawn for* ADVERTISING PROCEDURE *by George L. Hollrock.*

EIGHT METHODS OF

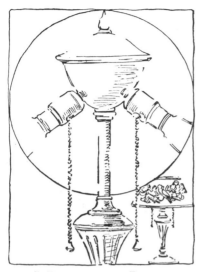

C. Detail of the Product

D. Contrast

G. Ornamental

H. Symbolic

Visualizing an Idea

**Illustration of product in setting.**—The surroundings of a product may suggest certain qualities with better effect than would a lengthy exhortation. Lamps, standing on finely designed table runners; silverware photographed against a background of old lace; a bottle of ink shown alongside an engineer's set of drawing instruments—all these let the background do the talking. The product itself modestly stands by content to let the reader draw his own inference.

The art of showing a product in setting—and it is an art—lies in keeping the background as simple and as unobtrusive as possible, yet in having it unmistakably define the article as possessing the desired qualities and as belonging in the environments pictured. All details must be correct. If a chair designed in the style of the Sheraton period were to be shown in a home, all surrounding objects would need to be of the same period. It would never do to introduce a mission footstool or a Louis Quinze table. No detail is too trivial to overlook in having the setting of a product consistent with its style.

Then, too, it is important to avoid presenting an article out of its class, with surroundings either too ordinary or too aristocratic. A certain brand of coffee was constantly pictured as being served by butlers in elegantly furnished homes and clubs. The impression created was not in keeping with the reasonable price of the coffee, leading the public to conclude that here was an "exclusive" coffee—far too expensive for the home of the person of ordinary means. Subsequently the advertisements pictured scenes in more modest homes where the enjoyment of the coffee was just as great. The purpose of a luxury-setting campaign may be designed to lift the product above the mediocre class. It is essential to know when the impression has been conveyed and when the time is ripe for a reversal to the simpler idea.

**Illustration of product in use.**—To show a monkey-wrench alone may appear most uninteresting, especially if this wrench looks like any other wrench. To show it in a kit of tools lends interest, but to show a person actually using the wrench on an automobile wheel places the tool in another category en-

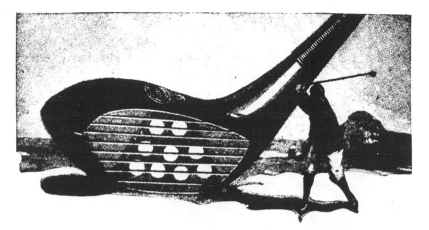

THE PRODUCT IN USE AND IN A SETTING

If a product would be lost if shown actual size in its setting, the device here used is effective—magnifying the product in comparison with its surroundings. Regardless of the size of an advertisement, an object within it can be made to appear big by introducing a smaller reproduction of an object actually known to be larger.

tirely. It now becomes a decidedly interesting article to any automobilist. He is brought into the picture. It is no longer a wrench that he beholds, but a tool which would serve him to good purpose—a tool which he ought to have.

Show a package of pancake flour. It is a package. Open the box and let some of the contents be seen. Still nothing startling. But take the flour into the advertising kitchen and come back bearing a platter of pancakes covered with molasses, a light cloud of steam rising, and the butter on them melting—the flour now looks like breakfast.

Very effective indeed is a picture showing the product in use. In arranging a picture of this character, it is essential to choose an apt setting and eliminate as much distracting detail as possible. The skill lies in making the product the center of interest and in preventing the article from becoming hopelessly involved with the scenery and actors. All parts of the illustration should direct the eyes, naturally and casually, to the product which is to be emphasized.

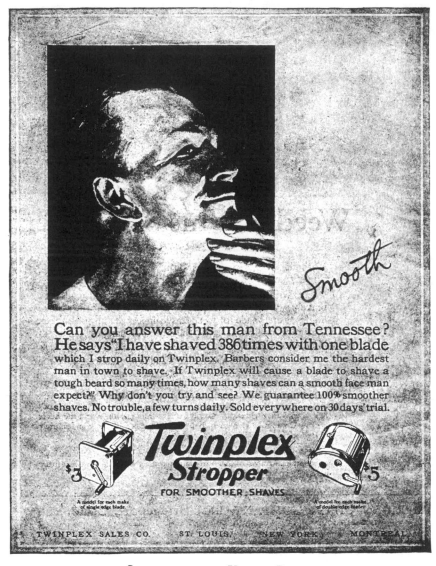

SATISFACTION FROM USING A PRODUCT

The man is smiling. Why does he smile? Because he has just had a smooth
shave. How did he get a smooth shave? He used a Twinplex Stropper. That
is the story of this illustration, showing the result of using a product.

**Illustration of result of product's use.**—It would seem that a picture of the article advertised would be effective in any advertisement. But to the reader the article itself may not be as important as that which it will do for him. Suited to the purpose, there is a form of illustration which shows the *effect* the article has had upon some person or object. A man with sound teeth as the result of using a certain tooth-paste, a housewife in a spic-and-span kitchen cleaned by the advertiser's soap, an unearthed farm fence still unrotted because it had been treated with the advertiser's wood protector— these are typical instances of this form of visualizing. Where it seems that nothing new or different can be said about a product, interest can invariably be aroused by picturing the result and effect of the use of the product. An alternative idea is offered in showing the need for the product. The advertisement for O'Sullivan's Heels asks: "Are you all tired out at 6 o'clock?" and pictures a pair of tired feet to indicate the need for rubber heels.

**Dramatization of the headline.**—Dramatizing the headline translates the thought of the caption into an illustration. An elementary though crude instance within this category is the picture of the pair of scissors cutting a dollar sign in two, with the caption reading, "Prices Cut In Half." In their own language, these illustrations say what the copy expresses in words.

The latitude offered to the visualizer in dramatizing the headline is very wide indeed. Often one pauses to inquire whether the headline or picture came first, so closely united they appear to be.—The answer invariably is that both came in the same mental breath—*the visualizer was simply using a fresh copy approach* and in doing so suggested the pictorial idea as well. It is worth close study to see how a simple idea can be originally presented through a new copy approach and how such an approach invariably suggests its own illustration. An examination of the illustrations contained in advertisements excelling in copy approach will demonstrate this fact. In dramatizing a headline there is a temptation to make a forced pun of that headline, or else to wade into some remote generality. When aptly applied, however, this form of illustration is strikingly vivid.

Ginger Ale
Sarsaparilla
Birch Beer
Root Beer

## "Well," said the little Eskimo, "I'll tell you all about it

"LONG, long ago there was a King whose boast it was that he had the best feasts that men could devise or cooks could cook.

"He had a beautiful daughter, as all Kings of olden time had. When she was old enough, the King announced that he would give his daughter's hand to him who would bring a new beverage that would be as beautiful as golden sunlight, would be icy-cold and hot at the same time, would sparkle and live through a whole feast, and which, while it quenched the thirst of the moment, would awaken desire for it in young and old, rich and poor, male and female.

"And in due time it came to pass that a handsome young Prince, aided by an old wizard, brought some roots from one island, some canes from another, and some fruits from a third. From below the ground he drew the living waters of a magic spring. Then the old wizard blended the essences of the roots and the fruits, sweetened them to a nicety, and infused the whole with the bubbles that gave it life. And at the next feast the Prince won the King's daughter with the wonderful new beverage, which fulfilled all the King's conditions.

"'And what is the name of this beautiful golden liquid?' asked the King when the feast was over.

"But the Prince had walked into the garden with the King's daughter, and there was no answer.

"So, my dears, we must assume that then and there was discovered the universal beverage, Ginger Ale— the one of which we say '*They all like it*'."

Under the ground at Millis, Massachusetts, are bed-rock springs of pure, cold water. The ginger used in Clicquot Club Ginger Ale comes from Jamaica. The sugar is from the cane. Lemon and lime juice are combined in the Ginger Ale that is cold and hot, is alive and golden, and which pleases everybody.
For your feasts, for meals and between meals, drink Clicquot Club Ginger Ale.

THE CLICQUOT CLUB COMPANY, Millis, Mass., U. S. A.

**Clicquot Club** GINGER ALE

Pronounced Klee-ko

### DRAMATIZING A SITUATION

An enchanting legendary visualization based on the narrative element with the copy.

Ouch!

When insects bite and sting
Unguentine—*quick!*

If your house is an Ice-Box,
*See the man who applies Improved Asbestocel*

# VIBRATION—DESTRUCTION!

EVERY tremor you feel is a punishment for your car. Protected by
springy upholstery and agile springs, you
do not realize the terrific pounding that

any given strength—stronger for any given
weight—Mo-*lyb*-den-um Steel possesses
greater resistant properties to wear, shock-
strain and fatigue than any steel hitherto

### Dramatizing the Headline

We now come to a group of superb illustrations. Each truly dramatizes its
headline. How simple and complete is the visualization of "Ouch!" The
ice-box illustration also makes its conception self-evident. The riders in the
back seat of the automobile could hardly feel more jarred than does the
reader who looks at the lower illustration. That is the best evidence of its
success in visualizing "Vibration."

**Dramatization of a situation.**—Not alone in the headline but in the copy itself may a visualizing idea be found. A scene depicted in the body of the copy may lend itself well to dramatization in a picture, as though the advertisement were enacted in life and a photograph of one incident were snapped. Any illustration which secures its ideas from the narrative element of the copy may here provide the visualizing idea.

The difficulty in dramatizing a situation is not, as a rule, that of finding an incident to picture, for a piece of such copy may be rich in settings. Rather the difficulty lies in picking just one scene from the many possible ones. When an artist is called upon to illustrate a magazine story, he does not endeavor to draw a picture for each paragraph. He chooses just one or two incidents from the entire story. Therein lies his art. In the foyer of a motion picture theatre, "stills" are shown of the entire picture. It will be noticed that these "stills" are not random photographs clipped from the motion picture film, but show only the more tense moments of the photoplay. The visualizer's task in advertising is to snap the "stills" of the copy. The idea most suitable for illustration may be the climax of the story, the dénouement scene, or even the final setting which reveals the substance of the entire advertisement in picture form.

The characteristic which makes a situation most desirable to illustrate is the completeness of the story it embodies. It should suggest a mass of action without feverishness of motion, and without excitement. The craftsman in dramatizing a situation does not show an incident when it is at its height of activity, but rather suggests, in a subtle way, the action which has already taken place, or is about to take place.

**Comparison.**—One of the simplest devices for explaining a new thought is that of showing its resemblance to one that is already established. In copy, logic proceeds from the known to the unknown; pictures may likewise compare a recognized idea with the one to be portrayed. The simplicity of refilling a shaving stick was compared with the ease of screwing in a flash-light battery; the tread of rubber heels was compared with that of a cat.

# *Is there any* Real Difference?

Even today in some countries women yoked with oxen share the cruel drudgery of plowing the fields

# Drudgery *tears down—destroys—kills*

A WOMAN yoked with an ox—wearily dragging a heavy plow. A woman yoked to a washboard—rubbing, scrubbing—straining her back. Is there any real difference?

Hard tasks both. Monotonous—spirit breaking—dreary. Both are drudgery. Against the soul-crushing bonds of just such kinds of drudgery, womankind has struggled since the beginning of history.

Bit by bit she has gained ground—at last she's coming into her own.

Above all, the American woman. For the American woman doesn't follow hidebound custom merely because it *is* custom. She wants to know *why*.

And she asks why so long and so hard that finally the world sits up and takes notice—and helps her to find the answer.

Today, even in civilized countries of the old world, women still take their family wash to the streams—get down on their hands and knees, and scrub as women did four thousand years ago—to get them clean.

IN America, our great-grandmothers, too, rubbed and scrubbed—but in their own homes and on rough washboards. They used crude, harsh, home-made soaps, lye soaps that ate holes into clothes like

wildfire. Then came bar soap—good soap —excellent soap—but it, too, had to be rubbed in to get results, and backs still ached over the washboards. Monday was still blue Monday.

But the American woman was questioning—questioning more and more this terrible weekly drudgery. Why should she be submitted week after week to this torture? Why could not a soap be made that would get the clothes clean without all this rubbing? That would simply do the work that *she* had to do?

And the more she complained and questioned the harder science worked for an answer.

TODAY there is a new soap—Rinso— that is freeing millions—yes *literally* millions—of women the world over from the deadly, nerve-racking drudgery of scrubbing and rubbing their lives away on the big family wash. Though it has only recently been introduced, seventy million packages of this new soap were used last year!

Turn to page 162 and read all about Rinso, the wonderful new kind of soap that will relieve you of the hardest work of washday.

Lever Bros. Co., Cambridge, Mass.

## COMPARISON

The task of many pioneering advertisements is to awaken people from their apathy towards present methods. The comparison here made is properly a bold one. One great fault of pictures in pioneering advertisements is that they are not daring enough to convey the idea.

163

Comparison is an exceedingly effective device for expressing an idea. Care must be taken, however, that it does not become too far-fetched, that the factor with which an object is being compared is familiar to the readers, and that the comparison carries the point favorably. (The cat analogy for rubber heels found disfavor among people to whom the picture suggested a stealthy tread.) An advertiser wishing to show the small size of his motor had it photographed in the palm of a studio model's hand. In the photograph, however, the motor appeared one-half as large again, because the man's hand was that of a well-groomed artist's model. The motor was re-photographed in a mechanic's large, work-grained hand, and this time the comparison told the story effectively.

Contrast.—Contrast is used to emphasize the difference in detail or principle between two products or two ideas. The object or idea may be contrasted with another object or idea. Showing a store which has a cash register beside a store using the counter cash-drawer system; picturing a mechanic packing a valve with an advertised tool, in contrast with a workman without one; comparing the man who reads good literature with his brother who fails to do so—these are instances of visualizing which use contrast.

An object may also be contrasted with itself at a different time, as in a "before and after" picture—the first scene presenting a product or situation before the advertised article was applied, the second scene showing the result of its use.

The chief precaution to observe in using contrast is to keep all conditions equal in both instances with the exception of the one stressed, and to show clearly the distinction without obvious exaggeration. It would be misleading to contrast two stores using different cash systems, if one were a general cross-roads store and the other an exclusive large-city specialty shop. In each of these stores, different conditions prevail. It is further advisable in a "before and after" photograph to keep the point of view of the camera the same, as well as its focus.

THE ANGLE OF RELAXATION

Some newspapers are read with indifference—folks run through them in a half-interested, nonchalant manner. Often indeed this is the fate, especially of evening newspapers at the hands of tired, busy men and women. And, naturally, advertising in these papers gets only a passing interest.

VS.

THE ANGLE OF INTEREST

Watch the way folks read OTHER papers—such as the Morning Courant in Hartford. They rush to the doorstep mornings to get it—or quarrel with the newsstand boy if the supply's sold out. They read every line BECAUSE EVERY LINE IS WRITTEN FOR THEM TO READ. And they even study the advertising with real avidity.

CONTRAST

You do not need a double-page advertisement to visualize an idea, as is shown by this simple use of contrasts.

**Emphasis on detail.**—Just think of the opportunities a salesman has, when he is showing his product, to bring out all its merits. "See that little point in there?" he can ask his prospect. "Notice how it works. That detail is an exclusive feature with this machine." Or else, "This hair comb may look like any other comb to you. But examine closely the teeth." Thus the salesman can discuss the superiority of the details of the product, one by one. Perhaps there is only a single point of difference between his article and competing ones, or there may be many. In any event, he can emphasize the advantage when occasion to do so arises.

An advertisement, however, cannot invite the reader to pick up the picture and scrutinize it the way he would a product. The picture as a rule appears in reduced size, and the detail appears still smaller, oftener than not being totally ob-

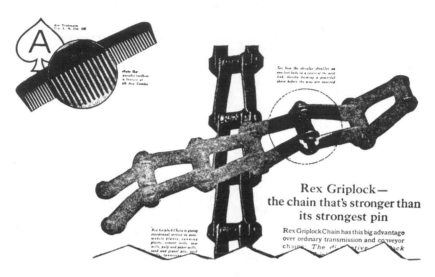

Rex Griplock—
the chain that's stronger than
its strongest pin

Rex Griplock Chain has this big advantage
over ordinary transmission and conveyor
chain.

EMPHASIZING DETAILS

The upper illustration shows a simple method for focusing attention on a single
feature of a product. The lower illustration goes two steps further by exposing
a cross section of the detail and lightening the color of the rest of the product.

scured. The visualizer may here use his talents to good purpose by discovering a method for emphasizing the article's
features. The detail may be removed bodily from the product itself and pictured alone; it may, by means of a special
device, such as an arrow or a circle, have attention focused
upon it. Or it may be enlarged as though it were seen through
a magnifying glass. Changing the perspective of the object,
or presenting it from an unusual angle, constitute other ways
in which emphasis may be given to important details. The
relationship between the part emphasized and the rest of
the product should, if possible, be shown. The function or
the advantage of this distinct feature should also be made
apparent.

Where a product is in a highly competitive field, in which
its physical details rather than its general qualities give it individuality, the illustration can be advantageously employed
to impress its features upon the public.

ILLUSTRATED BUT NOT VISUALIZED

What has the illustration t

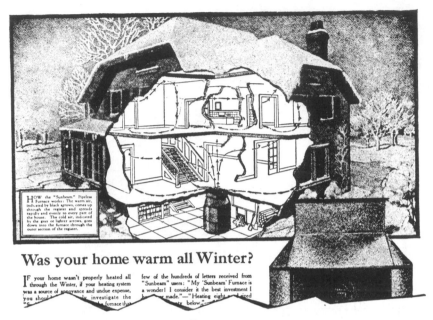

HOW the "Sunbeam" Pipeless Furnace works: The warm air, indicated by black arrows, comes up through the register and spreads rapidly and evenly to every part of the house. The cold air, indicated by the grey or lighter arrows, goes down into the furnace through the outer section of the register.

## Was your home warm all Winter?

IF your home wasn't properly heated all through the Winter, if your heating system was a source of annoyance and undue expense, you should _____ investigate the "S_____ furnace tha_____

few of the hundreds of letters received from "Sunbeam" users: "My 'Sunbeam' Furnace is a wonder! I consider it the best investment I h_____ ever made."—"Heating eight _____ sized _____ below._____

DIAGRAM

From the engineering draughtsman the advertising man learned how to cut away sections of products, large and small, to show the inside construction. A simple graph is also embodied to trace the current of warm air through the house.

**Charts and diagrams.**—Charts and diagrams date back to man's first writings. They were the forerunners of present draughtsmanship. Little wonder, then, that advertising finds in graphic presentation a very convenient method of clarifying and impressing its ideas. Charts and graphs permit the reader to summarize lengthy copy at a glance. They vividly reveal the gist of a set of facts, as was done in a kitchen cabinet advertisement which showed by a simple diagram the steps saved the housewife who owned such cabinet.

Charts and graphs are employed extensively in the engineering professions. They are recognized as indispensable tools in all technical fields. For the layman, however, they ordinarily appear "dry" and mathematically cold. Consequently, other illustrations are frequently combined with them to lend the warmth of human feeling to the austerity of facts.

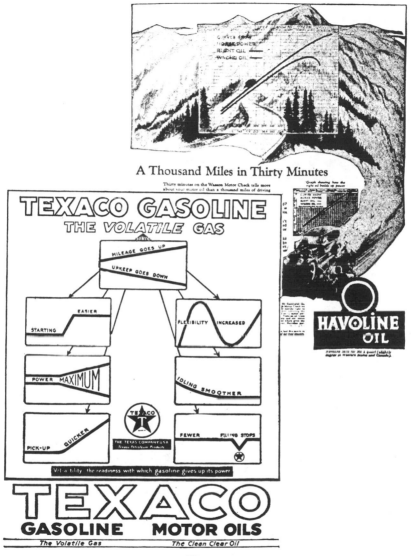

A Thousand Miles in Thirty Minutes

CHARTS

Charts and graphs come in handy whenever a technical explanation must be presented. The Havoline advertisement aptly places the chart in a setting. Each chart in the Texaco advertisement has the virtue of simplicity. For advertising purposes, the qualities desired in charts are interest, clarity, and impressiveness.

**The phantom or ghost diagram.**—Very often it is desired to present an internal view of an article, especially in picturing mechanical parts. In such a case, the visualizer learns from the draughtsman how to expose the hidden section. The outer shell of the part is broken away, permitting a view of the internal workings, or else an "X-ray" picture is taken of the hidden part, the result being a phantom view.

The phantom method offers excellent possibilities where an explanation of concealed mechanism or internal functioning is necessary. The possible disadvantages of this method are the secondary importance which such a picture may reflect upon the part advertised, its complexity, and the increased expense of drawing and engraving a "ghost" effect.

**Symbolic illustrations.**—When the ancient Greeks were confronted with an idea so vast and so vague that they could not comprehend its true nature, they promptly created anthropomorphous gods to represent their conceptions. Every quality in man had its god. Atlas was the strong man and Mercury the quick one, while learning had Athena as its goddess. Each god represented a conception of some abstract quality or omnipotent power.

When modern advertisers first began their work, they too found themselves quite inarticulate in proclaiming the virtues of their products. They, too, climbed Mount Olympus, returning with their arms full of characters to portray their ideas. Happiness, a robust, sheet-clad woman, would be shown offering the reader a package of the advertised product. Strength, a muscular giant, would be leaning against a building to show the strength and character of the house which was advertised. Before long, the entire retinue of gods was paraded before the public—Health, Love, Knowledge, Prosperity, Joy, Speed, and Endurance, as well as others.

For advertising purposes, such characters are both trite and introspective. They indulge in self-praise of a product and do not illustrate how the reader is going to be benefited. They are effective only when they seek to interpret ideas whose vastness and abstractness make the other methods of visualizing difficult.

SYMBOLIC

The noble, the menacing, the fleeting, each represented in a magnificent symbol.
Symbols may be used appropriately to visualize abstract ideas. They should
be used with discretion in picturing the physical qualities of products.

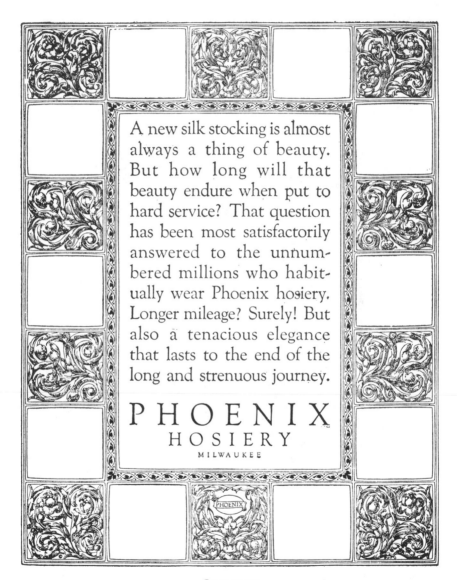

A new silk stocking is almost always a thing of beauty. But how long will that beauty endure when put to hard service? That question has been most satisfactorily answered to the unnumbered millions who habitually wear Phoenix hosiery. Longer mileage? Surely! But also a tenacious elegance that lasts to the end of the long and strenuous journey.

PHOENIX
HOSIERY
MILWAUKEE

ORNAMENT

A STUDY IN VISUALIZING
Dramatizing a headline, emphasizing a detail, and symbolism.

**Legendary signs.**—A horse-shoe is supposed to be an emblem of good luck; a laurel wreath, achievement. For advertising purposes, these legendary signs may be effective in conveying simple ideas, since they speak in a blunt, elemental language, easily comprehended by readers of all ranks of intelligence. Their chief handicap is lack of personal application to the reader, and lack of novelty.

Sometimes a new design may be employed, such as the Egyptian motif of the sun's far-reaching rays, used by an advertiser to represent the immensity of his organization. Where a symbol such as this one requires its own interpretation, however, it may be better to devote the illustration to the idea itself, rather than to a picture requiring explanation.

**Decoration and ornament.**—An advertisement may require no pictorial illustration, yet seek to make a more attractive appearance than is obtainable through the use of type alone. Decoration is then introduced to accomplish this purpose. Decoration and ornament may manifest themselves in the form of borders, backgrounds, fancy letters, and similar devices. Their use in an advertisement is entirely a matter of appropriateness and helpfulness. The only measure of their merit is an inspection of the complete advertisement. They should help the impression to be conveyed (if it is an impression rather than a clear-cut message which is to be presented) and make the message more inviting to read. Interesting though decoration and ornament may be, their use is commended to the trained visualizer only. The novice will do well to avoid them; and in following this caution, he will discover how effective his simple advertisements can be.

**The odd and grotesque.**—Comedy may be introduced into illustration as into copy but it should not be so interesting as to compete with the point of the advertisement. The caricature, the freakish, the unconventional, are potent devices for attracting attention. They should be employed only where they illustrate some definite idea, or else where they immediately pass the attention they command to a more important part of the advertisement.

NOVEL

An unconventional treatment like this one conveys the idea of something refreshing and novel. Despite the liberties which the illustration takes, the reader sees a hat in a window—the chief subject of the advertisement.

**Further suggestions on visualizing.**—Each method of visualizing an idea has its peculiar advantages. In one advertisement, several illustrative devices may be employed, each serving its own purpose. Thus a picture dramatizing a situation may serve as the top-piece to the advertisement, accompanied by another illustration enlarging some detail of the article. Or a package may be thrust boldly over a before-and-after scene.

And Now —
The Barrett
Specification Roof!

The Floor is The *Producing* Part

WELL VISUALIZED

From the floor to the roof, the advertiser meets a similar problem—that of showing the product in its natural setting in a manner other than those in common use. A bit of imagination, a hand, and a pencil make the Barrett advertisement stand apart. A dextrous treatment makes the Kreolite Floors illustration graphic.

The combinations are as endless as the ideas themselves.[1] It is well, however, to bear in mind a few general rules. One apt illustration is better than a poor one supported by others of a mediocre nature. The varieties of visualization methods should be limited within an advertisement. Continuity in a series of advertisements can be secured without monotony by steadily employing the same methods of visualization and letting the individuality of the ideas provide distinctiveness. Some advertisers adopt a style of visualization which they continually employ on a campaign, during the course of a season or over a number of years.

There is an unmistakable similarity between the methods of visualizing and the methods of developing a piece of copy. Direct description in copy corresponds to picturing the product alone; description by effect, to showing the result of the use of the product; description by suggestion, to picturing a product in a background. This similarity would indicate that both copy and pictures can be used to convey the same thought. Most people are copy-minded in expressing themselves, since copy corresponds to our every-day language. Illustrators are, of course, the exception, for they naturally think in terms of pictures rather than in the language of copy. A good suggestion, therefore, is to determine what type of mind you have, and perfect your ability to express yourself in that manner, learning at the same time to express yourself in the other way as well. When you think of copy, try to inject the graphic spirit; when you think of illustration, consider it not as a personal exhibition of skill, but as a vehicle of an idea.

Just as it is the test of any idea to see whether it helps the advertisement fulfill the purpose for which it was created, so it is the test of visualization to see whether it conveys the idea which underlies the advertisement.

---

[1] In studying the illustrations in contemporary advertisements the various visualizing elements should be separately considered, if several are combined within one advertisement.

## CHAPTER IX

# LAYOUTS

THE finished advertisement is put together from a working drawing known as a "layout." The layout is designed to help the man creating the idea to present his thoughts to the advertiser, in order that the appearance of the idea in its final form may be pictured. The layout gives the copy man a basis for estimating the amount of copy required; it tells the artist the proportion to which drawings must be made; it enables the mechanical department to specify the size of the photo-engraving; finally it provides the printer with the shop instructions necessary for putting the copy into type.

The amount of effort necessary in the preparation of the layout depends largely upon the purpose for which the layout is being prepared and upon the understanding of the person for whom it is intended. If the layout is designed for a printer, a box showing the area in which the type is to be set, plus a few marginal notations, may serve all purposes. But for a person who is not familiar with the display of an advertisement during its metamorphosis, the layout may have to be a carefully hand-drawn model, showing in every detail just how the advertisement will look when completed. The only guide to follow in this work is to determine the experience of the person who is to use the layout, then draw the layout so clear that he cannot mistake its plans.

The layout is important for still another and most important reason. Upon the conception of the layout depends the attractiveness of the advertisement when seen as a whole. The arranging of the layout involves creative work of a highly skillful nature. Copy and illustration have to be assigned to their positions in such a manner that the reader will feel tempted to go through the advertisement, as it passes before him in the procession of other advertisements. The layout

179

must further make it easy for the reader to get the message contained in the advertisement.

**The general plan.**—When a surveyor draws a map, he first fixes the boundaries of the grounds. Within that area he marks the most conspicuous landmarks, then makes note of the lesser features. Finally he adds the minor details. The layout, as the map of the advertisement, is similarly built. First its exact size and shape are determined, then the chief elements are given their place, after which the other units are considered in the order of their importance. The first step, accordingly, is to determine the exact size of the advertisement, knowing which, most layout men proceed by drawing on a sheet of paper large enough to leave ample margins, a rectangle of those dimensions.

All the elements which are to be included in the advertisement are then gathered together and scrutinized. Among these features may be the following:

*Illustrations:*
　　Main visualizing idea.
　　Other illustrations (such as package).
　　Border.
*Copy:*
　　Headline.
　　Sub-headlines.
　　Paragraphs of regular copy.
　　Paragraphs of copy to be specially emphasized.
　　Price, if that is to be emphasized.
　　Slogan, if important.
*Standing detail:*
　　Name-plate and address.
　　Trade-mark.
　　Dealer's address.
　　Coupon.
　　Other instructional lines.

All of the foregoing seldom go into one advertisement. But it is into these respective units that the advertisement is divided for the sake of drawing the layout. There is now before the layout man a sheet of paper bearing nothing but a penciled frame. Alongside, he will have the copy manuscript

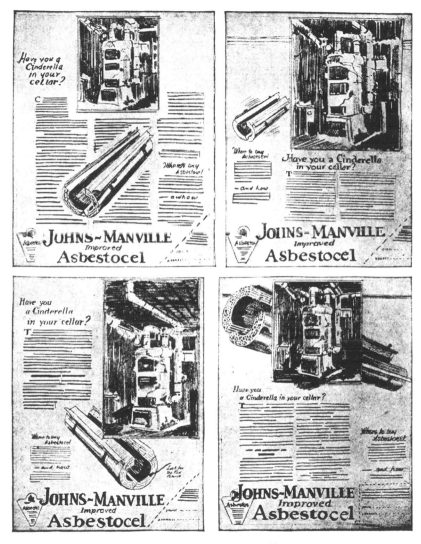

*Specially prepared by the Art Department, Newell-Emmet Co.*

A STUDY IN LAYOUTS

These layouts show the same advertisement arranged in four different ways. The lower right-hand layout was finally chosen. (*See frontispiece.*)

and the visualizing idea, or he may have these in his mind. He is now ready to determine just how the material should be assembled, in accordance with two factors: first, their meaning; second, their structural requirements.

Arrangement according to meaning.—The layout consists of parts. The layout man thinks in terms of these parts. How much space should be allotted to each? This is the first question to answer. The measure of all things is the proportion of qualities within them. In layouts, all the units which we have just mentioned are evaluated in accordance with their *importance.* The most important idea of the advertisement deserves the most prominent display, the least important gets the least display; by this standard of value, the comparative space to be allotted to each item is determined.

If the headline or copy is very important and the name of the advertiser secondary, that fact determines the prominence which the headline or copy gets. The headline could be very bold, and the copy could occupy most of the space, the nameplate being presented in small unobtrusive type. If the purpose of the advertisement is to tell people that the product bearing that name is still being sold, the name could be elevated and emblazoned as large as the advertisement will consistently permit. If the advertisement is to feature price, as is often the case in retail clothing copy, the type will accordingly be set in an imposing size; if question of the price barely enters into the discussion, it can be run in with the text of the advertisement in a size of type no larger than that of the rest of the copy. If an illustration conveys the whole story of the advertisement, and a paragraph of copy is purely supplementary, the illustration deserves the greater part of the page, and the copy the smaller. If the conditions were reversed, the dominance accorded to the illustration and to the picture would also be reversed. "How important is it?" is the question which must be asked of every part which will appear in the layout. Then the outstanding element is given its place; everything else is worked around it.

Let us take, for example, the accompanying eight layouts for a kitchen cleanser. The first layout gives the headline prominence. The copy is important and hence it is given most of the space. The name of the advertiser is not very important; neither is a picture of the can. Hence these are both subordinated. The trade-mark, represented by a triangle with a hanging cross-bar, likewise is relegated to comparative obscurity. In each case, however, the prominence accorded the various elements is in keeping with the respective importance of that feature.

We now move on to the second layout. This uses visualization of the idea to form the opening wedge, rather than a headline. Accordingly there is less copy, and it is given less space than copy in the first layout. The picture of the product gets more publicity than previously.

In the third and fourth layouts we meet a change. The copy is shorter than before, the picture of the product demands more attention than before. The name and trade-mark are likewise considered of growing importance and therefore appear larger than before.

See how the product has grown in importance, in layout number five; the trade-mark is brought to the foreground close to the can and the name—to which increased attention is being invited.

In the sixth layout the product is the thing; likewise the trade-mark. The name is given a more conspicuous position than ever. The headline has disappeared altogether and there is need for but little copy—hence it receives an unassuming amount of space.

In layout number seven, the name, the can, and the trade-mark are the whole show, for a very good reason. For the purpose of this advertisement they are regarded as everything. The paragraph of copy is purely supplementary. What it says is not nearly as important as the message conveyed by the package and name.

In layout number eight we revert to the visualizing idea and add a headline to the copy to tell our story. For this advertisement the name, trade-mark, and picture of the product are of incidental importance. That explains why they have been dropped from the dominating position they possessed before.

It is interesting to trace the themes running through this

LAYOUT 1

LAYOUT 2

LAYOUT 5

LAYOUT 6

LAYOUT 3

LAYOUT 4

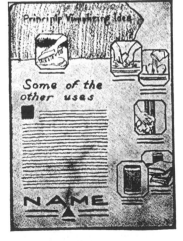

LAYOUT 7

LAYOUT 8

symphony of layouts; to note how the name begins in small type and is gradually enlarged as its importance is increased; likewise how the trade-mark and the can grow in importance. The headline and the copy, on the other hand, begin in a full burst of glory, and are gradually retired from the scene, until the final layout, which really represents a revival. It may have occurred to the reader that this series of layouts is parallel with the change which takes place in a series of advertisements as the product passes through the pioneering, the competitive, the retentive, and the new pioneering stages. At the outset there is a large amount of explanatory work to do, which gradually gives way to the competitive tactics of featuring the package, the trade-mark, and the name, and finally entirely new uses are introduced. The parallelism is true enough, though it is not the chief lesson of the layouts. The series simply illustrates how the various elements of an advertisement can be given varying degrees of prominence through size and position, the measure of consideration accorded to each being its relative importance in the telling of the story. The series does not imply that a single set of layouts need repeat all the antics which are played here with the different features. In fact, an advertiser may find that, as in the first layout, he needs all the room he can obtain for copy, and that emphasizing his trade-mark is the least thing he has to worry about. In this case, all his layouts would be proportioned as is layout number one. Similarly, he may use any of the other seven, depending upon his requirements.

Upon first thought, it would appear that preparing layouts is purely the work of an illustrator. But the illustrator has to be an idea-editor. He has to be one whose wits are sharpened to pick the wheat of news from the chaff of material handed to him—chaff not being used in any deprecatory sense, but merely as a relative term to indicate that in all advertisements some ideas are more vital than others. Before a stroke of work is done on the layout itself, too much time can hardly be spent in studying the content of a proposed advertisement and picking out the most important element.

**Arrangement according to structure.**—The first part of the job is done. The elements of the layout have been graded according to the importance they are finally to receive. The second part of the work is to assemble the different pieces of the advertisement in such a manner that they will give to the whole advertisement an interesting appearance. Until now the layout man was concerned with the meaning of the advertisement; now he is dealing with its structure. Meaning can be said to appeal to the intellect; structure does not go that far. It seeks to arrest the attention of the reader, invite reading of this particular advertisement, and make it easy for the eye to go through the entire advertisement. Meaning is the appeal to the mind; structure is the appeal to the eye. Meaning implies what things say; structure, how they look. And just as a good choice of clothes depends upon having everything, from hat to shoes, picked with a regard to their effect when worn together, so the composition of the objects within the layout is planned chiefly with a view to their final appearance.

Balance.—One characteristic of all great illustrations is their appearance of stability in structure. They are comfortable to behold. They appear soundly built and self-sufficient. A layout must likewise be soundly built and possess that quality known as balance. Balance in layouts means that one-half the advertisement possesses the same characteristic of power as does the other half. Optically, the advertisement is not divided into horizontal halves, at a point equidistant from top and bottom, but at a point about five-eighths of the way up the page, known as the optical center. It is this point which the eye invariably chooses as being the center of a printed surface—an illusion which can be tested easily by taking a sheet of white paper and pointing quickly to the center of the page, afterwards determining the actual center with a ruler.

A line crossing the optical center will be found to divide the layout into two comfortable parts which just seem to balance each other. This same optical center represents the position of greatest attention within the advertisement.

A mathematical way of securing balance is to place similar objects on opposite sides of the center in corresponding positions, the center lines being either the optical center, the vertical center, or a diagonal line. This form of balance, known as bi-symmetric balance, is the easiest to secure, because it can be judged precisely. As skill in obtaining bi-symmetric balance increases, the effect of stability may be obtained in a more elastic and subtle form—through "occult" balance.

The parts of the advertisement are here considered like two persons at the ends of a see-saw. The board on which they are swinging rests at the point where the optical center crosses the vertical center. Two units of equal weight at equal distance from the center balance each other. A lighter one could easily balance a heavier element by being further away from the center. The "weight" of a part of an advertisement may be gauged by its size, by its degree of blackness, or by its oddity of shape. Because of the difficulty in comparing these elements, their arrangement requires more careful thought than does a mere attainment of bi-symmetric balance, but possibilities for interesting effects are more numerous.

Gaze-motion.—Another characteristic of good advertisements is that of well-employed "gaze-motion," the quality whereby everything in an advertisement leads the eye naturally from part to part, or else, focuses all attention on the leading element. Where an advertisement consists of reading matter only, the sequence of the copy guides the reader right through the advertisement. No special devices are required here. But where illustration and copy are combined within one advertisement, it is necessary to insure the unity of the entire ensemble, by having one element point, lead, or look towards the next one, or seem definitely related to it. The effect is obtained crudely but with a degree of success by means of arrows and lines. To show faces looking in a certain direction or people walking that way causes the reader to follow suit and look there, too. In a more adroit manner, the eye can be guided through the parts of the advertisement by offering it a line of direction to follow, or by providing convenient "stepping stones" in the form of initial letters, captions, or illustrations.

An advertisement which shows a face deliberately looking at an adjoining advertisement rather than toward its own copy or towards the reader, a shoe pointing directly at a neighboring display rather than calling attention to its own advertisement, represents some of the grosser violations in good composition. Even more to be guarded against than these obvious faults is the inclusion of aimless units which do not seem to belong anywhere or to contribute to the effectiveness of the advertisement as a whole.

**Distinctiveness.**—Besides possessing fundamentally good structure, the effective layout must make a quiet advertisement stand apart from the rest. It must encourage the reader to put aside for a moment the distracting thoughts passing through his mind and heed the particular message before him. The day will be dark indeed, when all advertisements will look exactly alike, and darker still people's lives, when that happens. For the very fact that individuals are unlike each other, and often unlike themselves, requires that advertisements be equally as varied. The style of advertisements is but a mirror of the mental style of the people to whom the advertisements are addressed. With many advertisements striving for the attention of one person, it follows logically that each of the many will endeavor to obtain preference through some distinctive device. Layouts are not apart from the struggle.

The close observer of advertising will discover that the general style of advertisements changes from season to season and from year to year. Like all evolutions, this one is gradual, steady, and incessant. The leaders strike a new note in their advertisements, and for several years the followers reflect that influence. Even before these effects have passed all the way down the line, the leaders have evolved another idea. Instead of using a picture of the products as a background, printing their copy upon it, they will use a picture at the top of the advertisement only; instead of showing one large illustration, they will scatter several small ones through the copy. Instead of using a second color for the initials of every word in a headline, they will confine the use of the second color to pictures; and then, instead of using the color generously, they will use just a spot of it, after which the pendulum swings back to the use of color in solid, massed effects for backgrounds. So the style in advertising goes, impelled by the same force that influences style anywhere—the desire to be a little bit different from another—only in this case, it is a matter of accomplishing a definite purpose, and not of satisfying a vanity. The method generally followed, therefore, in planning layouts, is that of studying the style of competing advertisements competing both as to products and as to media, and conceiving a general style quite unlike those already presented. Good taste at all times, but distinctiveness as well, must be the rule.

Distinction through odd shapes.—One of the best-known methods employed to obtain distinctiveness is that of using odd illustrative devices, such as a uniquely drawn border or fanciful picture, the very novelty of which serves to attract the attention. To create a freak effect would seem easy enough, but to make that drawing occupy as little of the precious advertising space as possible, to make the attention device represent a visualizing idea as well, and to create an odd design which is more pleasing than jarring, require no mean skill.

Advertisements with very brief copy can afford to apply their energy to securing attention, in which circumstance, surroundings permitting, they can well use the most novel design, border, or picture it is possible to obtain. The only criterion in such case is that the effect be in good taste—and distinctive. Advertisements with very limited space also do well to use odd-shaped illustrations which dominate the entire space. Through their concentrated uniqueness alone, these layouts may then be able to compete with their larger neighbors. By far the greater proportion of advertisements are those which have at least fair-sized copy messages to convey, and which use publication space larger, say, than one newspaper column wide and six inches deep. To these advertisements, the layout man has to apply care in gaining distinctiveness without sacrificing too much copy and visualizing space. One of the very popular devices employed is that of using the product itself as a border, or drawing an arbitrary bold border to focus attention on the product, name, or copy; or the product itself may be shown in such a way as to provide a border or "binding" for the entire advertisement. Instead of borders, hand-lettering in its various manifestations can be used to introduce an element of distinctiveness.

DISTINCTIVE SMALL ADVERTISEMENTS

The initial letter makes the Marshall Field advertisement stand apart. A good spot of color and clear typography characterize the Thayer A B C advertisement. An appropriate border distinguishes the Brooks advertisement. An interesting copy approach, simply visualized, gives charm to the Himebaugh & Browne advertisement. Pears' advertisement makes good use of color composition. Note the contrast in tone between foreground and background, producing that effect—depth—seldom used well in layouts.

This is the third announcement published by this house for the purpose of informing the public that our prices on jewelry and kindred wares are based on the present cost of replacement.

Nordlinger prices were lowered to meet the new price levels when those levels. were reached—in accordance with our half-century-old policy of giving our patrons right values.

Los Angeles' oldest jewelry house has enjoyed the confidence of the entire public for over 51 years—a tribute to a sincere endeavor to maintain high merchandizing ideals.

DISTINCTIVENESS THROUGH HAND LETTERING

**Distinction through white space.**—The next general method employed to make layouts distinctive is the judicious use of white space. Among the earliest users of modern advertising space, were the patent-medicine venders who crowded their advertisements with copy. Their style should not be underestimated; it is still used extensively with variations and with good results in mail-order advertising. Those copy-jammed advertisements had a decided influence for many years on all advertising. There was a time when it was considered extravagant to leave exposed a bit of space in an advertisement. Paragraphs of copy were slapped into crevices of space like mud between the logs of a hut. Then came the reaction. Advertisers deliberately left a wide margin of space around their copy and illustrations so that they would stand out from the surrounding advertisements. This plan has proved far more fruitful to advertisers and decidedly more pleasing to readers. The desire for still more effective use of white space has led to the development of a third type of white-space advertisement—a very ingenious one—that in which the white space of the advertisement is blended into the white of the pictures used in the advertisement.

**Distinction through action.**—Simple pictures of people or things in action seem to hold fascination for readers. A man standing still is a man standing still, but that man running after a train becomes a very interesting person indeed. Why is he so anxious to catch that train? Will he make it? What if he doesn't? Is some one waiting at the other end for him? Or for the papers in his black bag? Why? More quickly than it takes to read these queries, they run through the mind of the person viewing the picture, and direct his attention to the advertisement itself.

**Distinction through technique.**—Automobile manufacturers have been particularly ingenious in discovering new methods of illustrating their cars. Their success in doing this shows that there are many ways of drawing the same object. They used photographs of the family riding in the machine, then they took out the family and left the machine standing alone on the road; finally, even the roadway was taken out of the picture and only a side view of the car appeared. The scene shifted and automobiles were pictured in front of famous homes and institutions; expensively dressed people were shown entering the tonneau. That effect gave way to the picture in which only head-on views were shown; subsequently backgrounds, ranging from white-capped mountains to tapestry, were called into the picture. Photographs gave way to wash drawings, these to pen-and-ink drawings, and pen-and-ink drawings to oil paintings. The search for fresh styles, new techniques, new effects, and a new note in advertising has been relentless and untiring.

**Distinction through additional color.**—Though technically not a color, black is regarded as one in advertising. Most advertisements are printed in black ink on white paper. Contrast is obtainable in such instances by the use of additional colors, when this plan is practicable. The hue, intensity, and value of the extra colors is guided by the purpose for which these colors are to be employed and the impression they are to convey. The number of colors is restricted by fitness and by mechanical limitations.

Color may be used to reproduce in their natural tones products such as fabrics, foods, and other commodities, in the sale of which appearance represents an important factor. The illustration for such purposes has to be specially drawn to accommodate the color. The most common difficulty experienced in this connection is the mechanical task of matching up inks to the actual tone of the product. An advertiser who issued a shoe catalogue to retailers received numerous inquiries for a sample of "that new-colored leather"—the shoes in reality were the well-known light tan.

Color may also be used merely to emphasize a detail of the products, a bright spot serving to focus attention on some feature which is to receive special mention. Though the color for such purposes is used sparingly, it may serve to make the entire advertisement stand out among its black-and-white, or massively colored neighbors.

A third use to which color is put is that of supplementing the advertisement itself. It either clamors for attention by the very intensity with which it is applied, or invites consideration by the restraint of its appearance. In either case, the color is dedicated to securing attention only—for which task it is a very handy tool.

Whether or not color shall be used is a matter of alternatives. Is the additional expenditure involved worth while? Would it be better to devote the funds to buying more advertising space, or to procuring more illustrations? Then there is the matter of practicability. If an advertisement were to appear on the outside back cover of most magazines, it would be obliged to use color; in a newspaper (with the exception of the colored supplements) it would be restricted to black-and-white; while for street-car signs and outdoor advertisements, the use of color is particularly opportune.

**Suggestions on planning layouts.**—An advertisement should be self-assertive. There should be something about it which commands attention—whether that something is a device within the layout, or the decidedly pleasing effect of the entire display.

If the advertisement is to appear in clamorous surroundings, provide it with an air-cushion of white space so that it cannot be rammed into obscurity. If the layout requires a bold treatment, be bold and let there be no mistake about it; if reserved treatment is necessary, let it be gracefully reserved and not affectedly restrained.

The advertisement should be so self-contained that no part of it may be construed as belonging to an adjoining advertisement. The layout should be so planned that no matter in what company of layouts it may find itself in a publication, it still maintains its individuality.

Just as in writing copy, so in planning layouts, there is an ever-tempting goblin urging fanciful arrangements and complicated devices. An examination of the advertisements prepared by the highest-priced layout men discloses exquisite simplicity of arrangement even when an abundance of material is included. The chances are that the reader of these advertisements never pauses to observe their layout, so natural do they seem. In that very naturalness lies their strength. True cleverness in layouts consists not in devising freak exhibitions of arrangement, but in making the layout so simple that a person is pleased by the appearance of the advertisement without knowing why he likes it.

When it is considered that a small, distinctive advertisement can do far more than a large unimpressive one, when it is realized how much money can be saved even in a single campaign by the use of less space if such distinction in layout is attained—to say nothing of the greater effectiveness of the large advertisement when its layout is distinctively drawn—then the opportunities in this phase of advertising work will begin to be appreciated.

**Suggestions on drawing the layout.**—The final layout is seldom identical with the first suggestion—it is the result of arrangement and rearrangement of the various parts until they are satisfactorily combined.

Instead of making the layout in full size, experiments can first be made with thumb-nail sketches, in which illustration, headline and copy are indicated in different positions.

Instead of sketching in the illustrations of a layout by hand, a proof of a unit from a former advertisement can often be pasted into place. This is especially applicable where the same name-plate, package, trade-mark, or perhaps border are always inserted. Where no proofs are available, photostatic [2] prints of the desired parts can be made for pasting up. These are inexpensive, light gray photographs and provide an economical way of reproducing the parts which are uniform in all drawings.

Another aid in making a simple layout, when a line plate [2] is already made but when no proofs of it are at hand, is the rubber-stamp inking pad. The plate is pressed against the pad and then imprinted on the layout sheet in the proper place. When a layout is designed for the printer, it is a good plan to place the engraving on the sheet, draw a line around it, and then write in the rectangle thus formed, "Plate 'A' here," at the same time identifying the engraving with a corresponding mark on its block.

When a large number of layouts of a specified size are to be drawn, it may be helpful to cut a sheet of tin, or heavy cardboard to that size, using that sheet as a pattern for drawing the outline on the layout paper. Specially ruled "layout sheets" are often printed for an advertising office, to help the layout man and the printer.

## Buying the Art Work.

That part of the advertisement which has to be drawn by an illustrator is referred to as the art work, a term applied alike to a painting of colorful splendor or to a small drawing. Art work describes only the nature of certain elements in many advertisements, not their character.

---

[2] These engraving terms are more fully described in a chapter which follows.

This subject brings us to a very interesting practice in advertising. Whereas men who write copy are, as a rule, members of the staff in the advertising office, illustrators generally work independently in their own studios; assignments are commissioned to them by the various advertisers as occasion arises. Large department stores and mail-order houses constantly requiring illustrations may have on their staffs a limited number of artists who take care of their recurrent needs. With this possible exception, however, the practice is to engage the services of outside, or "free-lance" artists, whenever occasion arises.

**Facts to consider.**—Upon what factors does the choice of an artist depend—since there are many to whom the advertiser may turn? Artists differ in the matter of ability and this fact must be borne in mind. The difference may be either in:

1. The general style.
2. The medium[3] or tool used in drawing.
3. The nature of the subject to be drawn.
4. The price.

**Technique.**—Art is the expression of an idea seen through the eyes of man. Two men viewing the same thing will see it each in a different light. In the method of seeing things lies the first distinguishing trait of artists. When one man views a factory, he sees it with the camera-like eyes of an engineer. Another beholds it in an impressionistic sense, viewing it as a bundle of tall girders with a gaunt cloud of smoke belching from above and swarms of workers emerging from the doorways. Or suppose two artists look upon the face of a child. One sees it as a smiling cherub; another sees it as a mass of straight lines and deep shadows. By the very interpretations which artists place upon the objects of the world they live in, is their fitness for an assignment determined.

**Medium used.**—The tools which an artist uses are spoken of as the medium. This may be pencil, crayon, or pen and ink; the illustrator may use a brush with wash colors, with water colors or else oil colors. His work may be black-and-

---

[3] Medium as used in this sense should be distinguished from a medium in the sense of a publication.

*Specially drawn for* ADVERTISING PROCEDURE *by George L. Hollrock.*

## PEN AND INK

Here and on the following pages are four doorways, identical in design but each drawn with a different tool ("in a different medium"). This one is drawn with pen and ink. Note the fineness of the strokes and the delicacy of the entire effect! The doorway seems to sparkle with sunshine. This must be the home of a young couple.

For future reference, we may note that this is printed from a line plate and is suited to reproduction even on the roughest stock (as news, or antique book).

198

*Specially drawn for* ADVERTISING PROCEDURE *by George L. Hollrock.*

PENCIL

How soft and gray are the lines in this picture! The shadows seems to blend into each other. This must be a finely preserved old home, with a well-filled family album on the parlor table. The artist obtained this effect through the use of his medium in drawing.

Printed from a high-light (drop-out) halftone, 120-screen. Will reproduce **well on a highly finished stock.**

*Specially drawn for* ADVERTISING PROCEDURE *by George L. Hollrock.*

### CRAYON

Here's a rugged doorway, rather masculine in its effect. Probably the entrance to a club. Note the lack of detail and gradations in the beadwork at the top, also in the bushes at the side. The tones are simple and definite.

Drawn on a rough-surfaced ross-board (to aid the mottled effect in the shadows). Reproduced from a line plate. Will print on any rough-surfaced stock—especially an antique cover.

200

*Specially drawn for* ADVERTISING PROCEDURE *by George L. Hollrock.*

WASH

This doorway was drawn by brush in "wash," giving the effect of photography.
Note the broad flat strokes. The doorway looks rather formal and quite
stately, and yet shows the warmth of a real personality—probably the home
of a foreign service official.
Reproduced from a 120-screen silhouette halftone, with whites liberally tooled
out and blacks carefully burnished. Suitable for reproduction on **machine-**
finish paper or better, as discussed in a later chapter.

white, two-color, three-color, or full—the latter meaning the
three primaries, yellow, red, and blue, plus black. The camera
itself provides a useful medium, with its pictures taken in a
soft or "fuzzy" focus to lend atmosphere, or else in sharp
focus to stress details. The choice of medium is determined
largely by the method to be used in converting the drawing
into a plate, since some effects do not lend themselves to the
making of certain photo-engravings, as discussed at greater
length in the chapter dealing with that subject.

Subject.—Artists differ also in their ability to draw certain things. Some are better able to illustrate men's clothing
than ladies' millinery; others are more at home when drawing
engine parts than when illustrating cozy homes; while a third
group can produce a suite of furniture to precision, yet feel
utterly uncomfortable in endeavoring to draw a symbolic character, or to do justice to a landscape view. A study of the
advertisements for any period of time will reveal the work of
various artists for different advertisers, each artist being identified, however, with a certain type of subject.

It is sometimes necessary to commission several artists to
execute for a single illustration, each artist handling that part
of the work to which he is best suited. Thus, one illustrator
may draw a woman in a kitchen, working over a bowl. Another will later draw the egg-beater in her hand, while the
wording to appear across the illustration may be added by
a third artist, a specialist in lettering. It need hardly be added
that an advertiser's choice is necessarily restricted by the number of artists available in his own city.

Price.—The fourth consideration, price, requires that the
expenditure be consistent with the assignment. The money
appropriated for art work should be in keeping with the total
cost of the advertisement. Every artist, on the other hand,
has placed a standard of value on his or her work. Some
there are whose canvas would cost several thousand dollars;
the work of others may be commanded at a cost as low as five
or ten dollars. The amount charged by the artist depends
upon his reputation, experience, and finally, upon the skill and
time required in performing the task itself.

If an artist is to supply the idea for an illustration, its cost

ART CONTRACT *and* BILL

*in account with* DATE_____

NAME_____

ADDRESS_____

DESCRIPTION OF WORK:

ROUGH SKETCH ☐   FINISHED DRAWING ☐

OK *for Payment*

ART DEPT.   PROD. MGR.

DETAILED INSTRUCTIONS_____

_____

_____

_____

_____

_____

_____

MEDIUM—Line, Wash, Color, Crayon, Photo

SIZE JOB MUST SCALE TO_____

DUE DATE (Preliminary Showing)_____(Complete)_____

PRICE_____

This order, when completed, will constitute bill for the work, and is the only bill necessary or receivable. This bill will not be recognized for payment, however, unless signed by the person or firm from whom work is ordered, in space under terms of contract on reverse side.

CLIENT_____PRODUCT_____

JOB No._____REQ'N No._____AD. No._____

PUBLICATION_____ISSUE_____

An Order for Art Work

is invariably higher than when he merely applies his time to executing a definite assignment. It is best to agree on a price in advance. Some illustrators prefer to fix the price after they see how much work is required. This method may be satisfactory where an advertiser has worked with the individual before and knows his methods, but it is always best to set a limit. An artist's work may be worth all he asks for it, yet the illustration may not be worth that amount to the advertiser. The only safe rule is to set a fixed price in advance, and issue a written order confirming it.

**Working with the artist.**—Any office, especially if it is located in a large city which is known to create or issue advertising, is invariably visited by the artists with their portfolios. It is an established principle in many offices to see every visiting artist, whether he be a "free lance" working by himself, or the representative of a studio. A large number of artists have thus been "discovered" by advertising men who were amply repaid for the courtesy and time necessary to inspect the samples of their work. A card file system is maintained in most offices, the cards bearing a note of the type of work in which the artist specializes. Large agencies go even further and keep a file of proofs submitted by the various illustrators. Then, whenever a job comes up, the files can be consulted.

When an artist is commissioned to do some work, he should be instructed as to the.effect wanted, the purpose of the illustration, and the proportions. He should be supplied with as much information as possible, especially that which will help him get the spirit of the advertisement. All technical data should be furnished, and whenever possible, a copy, model, or photograph of the subject itself. If there are any special details which are to be emphasized but which may possibly be overlooked by the artist, it is well to point them out to him definitely. For instance, if a garment needs to be pictured with a certain seam prominent, or a machine with the handle turned up, it is, of course, essential that the artist know these things before he starts to work.

Shortly after the artist has undertaken the commission, he will generally submit a pencil sketch of the drawing, known as a "rough." This is inspected primarily for its technical accuracy and its general scheme of composition. If any revisions are to be made, they should be made at this stage.

The original layout may sometimes serve as the "rough" for the final drawing. It is an occasional practice to make the finished illustration right over this rough, to insure carrying out the idea submitted, incidentally saving the cost of entirely redrawing the illustration. The most common practice followed is that of having the artist make the drawing on a canvas or board in a size about twice that in which the illustration is to appear. The separate drawing gives the artist an opportunity to work up his detail, besides permitting the typographical department to start its work from the original layout. Another plan is to take a "silver print" of the rough sketch. On this light-gray print the final drawing is inked in, thus making it possible to preserve the delicate effects so hard to re-sketch.

A "reducing-glass"—the opposite of a magnifying glass—

is used to inspect an original drawing to see what it will look like when reduced to the size necessary for the advertisement.

Artists desire engraver's proofs of their work, for their portfolios. These proofs are the clearest reproductions of an illustration. Only organization policy and courtesy can establish rules for their issuance. It is also a matter of courtesy to inform the artist where his illustration will finally appear.

In buying art work it is always necessary to judge how the drawing will reproduce in the printed advertisement. Closely allied with layouts, therefore, are the mechanical processes through which the advertisement will pass before it appears in the final state, the discussion of which brings us to the doorstep of the next chapter—printing.

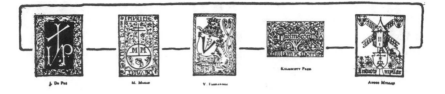

## CHAPTER X

## THE ADVERTISEMENT IN PRINT

IT is quite easy to imagine, in this age of machinery, a huge contraption into which the layout sheet, the artist's canvas, and the copy manuscript could be poured at one end and emerge at the other as a completed advertisement. What a wonderful machine that would be! Though this particular device has not yet been developed, the fact remains that pictures and words are transmuted into finished advertisements, and these advertisements are reproduced a million-fold. How is all this done? Through what steps does the advertisement pass from the time it is an embryonic idea on paper until the time it appears in print?

These questions are of interest to the advertising man, for it is the finished advertisement which concerns him most; unless he knows how that advertisement is developed, unless he recognizes the limitation of certain mechanical processes and appreciates the opportunity afforded by others, unless he knows how to give the proper instructions and have the necessary material prepared, he cannot hope to have his ideas carried out with any degree of effectiveness or economy.

The mechanics of advertising divides itself into two major divisions: first, the work of the printer, who puts the copy into type and prints the advertisements; second, the work of the photo-engraver, who makes plates of the pictures which are to be used with the copy. This chapter is devoted to the printing of advertisements.

**Principles of printing.**—It is first necessary to understand the principles whereby the work is performed. There are

206

three different ways of imprinting words and pictures on paper:

1. Letter-press printing.
2. Lithographic printing (which includes offset).
3. Intaglio printing (which includes rotogravure).

**Letter-press printing.**—A clerk who receipts a bill by means of a rubber stamp and inking pad applies the principle of letter-press printing. The message on the stamp is raised above the surface. When the stamp is pressed against the inked pad, the raised portions (or the design) are covered with ink, and when it is tapped against the paper, the raised portion transfers the ink to the sheet, reproducing the very design which appears on the rubber stamp. For the sake of printing in quantity and with speed, metal type is used instead of rubber type. But any printing from a raised design, standing in relief like that on a rubber stamp, operates on the "letter-press" principle.

**Lithographic printing.**—In 1796, a young Bavarian artist by the name of Senefelder was disconsolately wondering how he could reproduce his pictures in a manner less costly than the prevailing one—in which the illustrations were carved out of wood, just as letters were, and reproduced on the letter-press plan. Quite by accident he discovered a method which opened an entirely new avenue to printing—now known as lithography.

Lithographic printing in principle is quite unlike letter-press printing. Strange to say, the printing surface bears no raised characters, but is a perfectly flat surface—either stone, or sheets of metal plates. The stone is a special kind—a very fine quality of limestone—which is quite porous. The design to be printed is drawn, or transferred, to the surface of the stone, or metal plate, with a greaselike ink. The entire surface of the stone or metal plate is then dampened with water, which naturally affects all parts except those to which the greaselike ink has been applied.

When the inked rollers are passed over the entire surface of the stone, or metal plate, the ink, being an oily substance, will not adhere to the dampened parts, but will stick only to the part which bears the illustrations and type drawn, or transferred, by the artist—the design to be printed. When paper is applied under pressure to the surface it immediately accepts the impression of the inked design on the stone or metal plate. The reproduction is printed! Of course, the actual lithographic process is not as crude as this explanation makes it appear. But with all its perfections and refinements, it operates on the principle here described.

Offset printing is a form of lithography whereby the design is transferred not to the paper directly, but to a rubber-sheeted cylinder which, in turn, is brought into contact with the sheet of paper.

**Intaglio printing.**—An example of the third printing method, intaglio (pronounced intalyo) printing, is the little "engraved" visiting card. By passing the finger lightly over this card, it will be noticed that the letters are raised. This is because the card is printed from a small sheet of copper, or perhaps steel, on which a skilful artisan etches out by hand the name which is to appear. When the ink roller is applied to the plate, it fills these etched grooves with ink. When the surplus ink is wiped off the face of the plate, the ink in the etching remains, and, when the plate is pressed against the printing surface, adheres to that paper in its mountain-like ridges of minute height. This form of printing, incidentally, is known as copper-plate or steel-plate engraving, distinguishing it from "photo-engraving," the method used in making plates of illustrations, soon to be described.

Rotogravure, the process made famous by the Sunday newspaper supplements, is a form of intaglio printing in which the etching is not done by hand but by means of a photo-chemical process. The etching is not as deep as it is when done by hand.

**Comparison of principles.**—The letter-press method is the simplest and most extensively used. Lithography and its child, offset printing, require much preliminary work. Both are costly for small quantity work, but prove superior for color work in large quantities, such as labels; also for color work covering large areas, like outdoor posters. Intaglio is little used except as it appears in the rotogravure form. Most daily newspapers are printed by the letter-press method (the

exceptions are the rotogravure sections). Magazines, likewise, are generally printed by the letter-press method. The
large outdoor posters are practically all done by the lithographic method. Letter-press printing is the one used most
in advertising and to this method the remaining section of
this chapter is devoted.[1]

**Methods of setting type.**—Not all letter-press printing is
done in the same manner, for there are several different ways
whereby type may be assembled or set.

A study of these takes us back to the earliest days of printing. It was during the reign of Ming Tsong I, second em-
peror of the Tartarian dynasty in China, that printing is believed to have been invented (about 926 A. D.). A page
of type was made by taking a wooden block and carving as
much of the message on that block as it would accommodate.
The reason for carving entire pages of type at a time (known
as the xylographic method) was undoubtedly due to the fact
that the Chinese alphabet was a very large and complex one.
It was easier to recut an entire new page than to endeavor to
assort and assemble words out of separate letters. Indeed,
it may never even have occurred to the Chinese of that day
to make their characters separable. To them, a page was the
unit of type.

**Origin of type-letters.**—The art of printing came from the
Orient to Europe in the thirteenth century, through Venetian
merchants who traveled great distances in their trading ven-
tures. Whereas the Chinese alphabet was an involved one,
the European alphabet consisted of only 22 letters, which
could be arranged into any combination to form the respective words. It is therefore not surprising to find that shortly
after printing made its appearance in Europe, the xylograph
method was discarded in favor of the practice of composing
a page from individually carved letters. To make the word
"ever," for example, the printer would take the letter "e,"
then "v," an "e," and finally an "r," put them all together,
and thus form the word. He could do the same for each

---

[1] Further reference to lithography and rotogravure will be found at the
end of Chapter XI.

word in the sentence, and, letter by letter, set up or "compose" the page.

This change was a decided improvement and simplified matters somewhat, but still the printer was confronted with the necessity of carving by hand the original letters.

What a task! Each page of the Gutenberg Bible, the first one printed[2] (1438) contained between 2,300 to 3,000 letters to a page, every one of which had to be originally carved by hand. Peter Schoeffer, formerly a workman in Gutenberg's shop, developed a method for moulding letters and opened the first type foundry in 1455, thereby making it possible to cast letters in quantity. The printer could now obtain enough type to print several pages at a time. To this day, the method of setting type by hand, letter for letter and word for word, is used for certain work. But two revolutionizing improvements have opened new opportunities in printing—machines which set type, a line at a time, and machines which set type, a single letter at a time. All three methods of setting type play important parts in advertising.

Hand-set method.—By the hand-set method a person known as a "compositor" picks the letters of type from their nest of boxes or compartments (called "cases"), "sets" them into words, and unites the words of type into sentences and paragraphs, just as in the old days. After the printing is completed, the letters are "distributed" or returned by hand into their proper boxes where they remain until needed for another job. They are then again picked by hand, and the process is repeated. In this way, the same piece of metal type is used over and over again, always being picked by hand and returned in the same manner.

The hand-set method is an arduous one, particularly where a large body of type, such as newspaper text, is to be set. Despite its limitations, however, the hand-setting method does offer certain advantages. It permits a flexibility in arrangement and nicety of appearance not easily obtainable by the

---

[2] Whenever this statement is made, claims invariably arise that a Dutch printer named Coster (or Koster) of Haarlem. preceded Gutenberg. The evidence offered in support of both sides is profuse, with the supporters of Gutenberg in the lead.

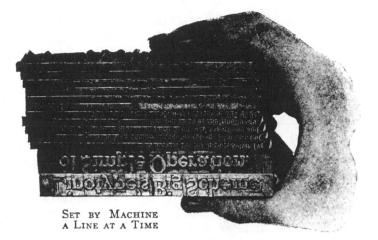

SET BY MACHINE
A LINE AT A TIME

speedier devices soon to be described. For composition which requires large-sized type or type of different sizes, for setting up advertisements where there is not much copy, where the type arrangement is very important and a distinctive effect is desired—in fact, for most of the display advertisements which appear in publications, hand-setting is extensively used.

**Machine-set: line-at-a-time.**—Not until a machine known as the Linotype was invented, was it possible to set type quickly. When it is realized that the news columns of practically all of our newspapers and magazines and much of our advertising booklet work is set up by the line-casting machines, the value of this principle will be appreciated. To look at one of these machines, one would hardly imagine it capable of producing such wonderful work. The layman is first impressed by the keyboard, resembling in general appearance that of the typewriter. Before this keyboard sits an operator clicking away as dexterously as ever did a typist at her machine. But every time he touches a key, he sets into motion a mechanism far more complex than that of the typewriter. A bystander will hear a lot of clicking, will observe some wheels move and some levers pass back and forward, and then will behold a metal slug emerge, bearing a line of copy completely moulded into type! Just what happened is a story in itself. Suffice it to say that the linotype casts letters already formed into words as they are written in the copy.

The saving in time is manifold; first, because of the speed whereby the operation is performed; second, because the compositor can handle lines of type easier than individual letters, some of whose metal bodies are no wider than a match-stick; and third, because the letters (or matrices) within the machines from which the lines of type were moulded return automatically to their compartments, ready to help another line to be moulded. These matrices do not leave the machine, and the line of type which is formed does not have to be returned to the machine. After the slugs are used, they are melted up, and the lead can be cast over again.

There is one particular characteristic in linotype composition, however; if it is desired to change one letter, or one punctuation mark, it is necessary to recast the entire line in which that letter or mark is contained. Of course, where no changes will have to be made, this objection does not exist, but there is certain work which may involve considerable revising, and for this kind of work, the method described below is best.

Machine-set: letter-at-a-time.—The Monotype offers some of the speed of the Linotype and the flexibility of arrangement possible with hand-set type. The monotype really consists of two machines whereby, when the process is complete, the type is set in line widths but each letter in that line is separate and detached from the next letter. A change is readily made by removing the wrong letter and replacing it with the correct one. The fact that the letters in a line are not moulded together also permits the printer better to arrange the fine spacing between them. Monotype is extensively used for fine book work, for tabular work, and for composition in irregular widths, such as is necessary in setting around cuts. As in the linotype process, the metal type is remelted after the printing is completed.

As far as advertising is concerned, hand-setting is generally preferable for short copy consisting of large-sized type, linotype for long pieces of copy to be set in uniform type and in regular column widths, and monotype for long pieces of copy in which many revisions may be made, or else in which the type has to be accommodated to irregular column widths.

SET BY MACHINE—EACH LETTER IS SEPARATE

**The presses.**—Passing from the composing room where the type is set, to the room where the printing is actually done, the visitor is greeted with the whir and clatter of the presses. Upon examination, he will discover two kinds of presses— those known as "job presses" and those called "cylinder presses." A job press is the small but industrious member of the press family. It takes up even less floor space than does an office desk, and it can handle sheets up to 14 inches by 22 inches in size. Job presses have a capacity of from 1,000 to 3,000 impressions an hour, and are well suited for work such as that required on letter-heads, envelopes, leaflets, and folders, in moderate quantities.

For work which is larger, either in page size or in quantity, the cylinder (or flat-bed) press is used. This can accommo date sheets up to 54 inches by 72 inches or even larger; each one of these sheets may bear any number of printed pages which are subsequently cut or folded into the desired size. In this manner 64 identical copies of a single advertisement can be run off at the same time, or a group of different advertisements printed in one impression.

There is still a third style of press known as a rotary press —the speediest and largest of them all. It is used in printing newspapers, and only for that advertising work which is to be produced in large quantities. Rotary presses may be seen in action at the plant of any large newspaper, while cylinder presses will be found in print-shops of moderately large size. Job presses are used in large shops also, but usually comprise the entire press equipment of the small print-shops. Though most newspapers are printed on rotary presses, the advertising man, through his printer, will have most of his work done on job or cylinder presses.

## Type Faces.

To the uninitiated, the styles of type used in advertisements are innumerable, and he finds the multitude of type designs quite confusing. And when he tries to memorize the characteristics of the various type faces he is confronted by an uncanny similarity among many of the designs, and a roster of strange names whereby these types are known.

The first step necessary, therefore, in studying type faces is to erase for the time being the miscellany of impressions which have been gathered on the subject. If the reader has time to memorize the features of different type faces, he should hold that information in reserve for awhile, and first discover the why and wherefore of the whole subject. He will then find it a far simpler matter to make type the servant of advertisements and not have the fate of advertisements depend upon the pranks of type.

History of type faces.—Anyone with the price of a newspaper can today purchase a splendid example of printed work; with a few cents more, he can buy a magazine. A book or even an entire library of books is hardly considered a luxury. Before the Venetian merchants had brought the idea of printing from the East, however, there was no such thing in Europe as a newspaper, nor was there printing in any form. The few books which existed were written entirely by the hands of the patient monks during the dark ages preceding the thirteenth century. Reading and writing was an art which they cultivated. So precious were the manuscripts that these works were bought only by the wealthy and, along with the jewels and other precious family heirlooms, were handed down from father to son.

When printing was first introduced in Europe, it was not hailed as a boon to civilization. Those who knew of it guarded their secret closely for it was viewed as a device for "forging" original manuscripts by printing the pages which were supposed to be hand-written. The influence of printing since that

time speaks for itself. The only significance of the early
attitude towards printing is that the first type faces were designed to imitate the style of the letters used by the monks.

Those plodding souls employed wide-pointed reed pens,
making broad, heavy strokes, with many fancy curves. The
letters were especially well adapted for use in the psalm books
and psalters which were read in the dim light of the churches.

## 𝔄𝔇𝔙𝔈ℜ𝔗𝔌𝔖𝔌𝔑𝔊 𝔓ℜ𝔒𝔠𝔈𝔇𝔘ℜ𝔈

This black-letter type originated in the Germanic states.
In its modified form, it was brought to England by William
Caxton when he opened the first print-shop in 1474. Here it
received its present-day name of "Old English." [3]

Just before the time that type was receiving attention in
northern Europe, Italy was passing through its Renaissance.
Learning was making great advances. The Italian monument
cutters had copied and developed a simple style of lettering
taken from their Roman monuments. This was quite unlike
the black-face letter of their northern neighbors.

## ADVERTISING PROCEDURE

Legend has it that the recognized designers disparaged the
Italian, or Roman, style. "Why, that is going back to old
fashioned lettering," they declared. "That type is antique;
it is old style." And to this day the names "Antique" and
"Old Style" cling to type with the characteristics of the first
Roman lettering. Chief among these characteristics are the
fine strokes of almost equal shade. There is only a slight
contrast between the strokes of a letter in Old Style type.

But designers all over Europe continued to experiment for
new effects. In 1790 a certain Didot of Paris, and Bodoni
of Parma, introduced the roman letter here shown. This is
now known as Bodoni. It looks like Old Style, but has a
greater contrast in the weight of its strokes.

## ADVERTISING PROCEDURE

---

[3] Also known as "Tudor," "Text," and Black Face.

Instead of all being about even, one part of the letter is a fine
and the next heavy line.

"If you call the other type 'Old Style,'" said the admirers of the new type, "then this is modern." And "Modern" to this day is the general term applied to any Roman
type having sharp contrasts in the shading of its strokes.

The little bars at the top and bottom of Roman letters are
known as "serifs." They were introduced by the monument
cutters who marked the tops and bottoms of their letters with
a stroke of the chisel. A characteristic of Old Style lettering
is that its serifs are oblique; in modern lettering the serifs
are horizontal.

The early Roman letters were always constructed in the
perpendicular until a Venetian designer by the picturesque
name of Aldus Manutius created a slanting face in imitation
of the Italian script writing. And there was born of his work
the type named in honor of his land, Italics (1496).

During the fifteenth century, small letters were also introduced (small letters being the ones we use in writing). Capital letters are more technically known as "upper case" (U. C.
or "Caps"); small letters as "lower case" (l. c.)—the terms
being derived from the parts of the printer's type case in which
the respective types are kept.

THIS LINE IS SET IN CAPITALS (OR CAPS).

this line is set in lower case letters.

This Line Is Set in Caps and Lower Case.

THIS LINE IS SET IN CAPS AND SMALL CAPS.

We have now traced to their lair these four styles of type:
From the Gothic school of monks—

### 𝔒𝔩𝔡 𝔈𝔫𝔤𝔩𝔦𝔰𝔥

From the Roman school of Italian monument cutters and
scribes—

### Old Style

### **Modern**

### *Italics*

BLACK FACE
(Old English)

Taken from a title page
designed by Bergomensis
(1492).

OLD STYLE: taken from a Roman monument.

A B C D
E F G H
I L M N

MODERN

Taken from Bodoni's
Type Specimen Book
(1808). Note resemblance
to Old Style, the chief
difference being extra
shading in the strokes.

MARC: TULLIUS
CICERO
PHILOSOPHUS

FORERUNNERS OF PRESENT-DAY TYPE STYLES

It is very important to remember that, historically speaking, "Roman" indicates the pedigree of an Old Style or Modern type. In advertising parlance it has come to mean an Old Style or Modern type which is not in Italics. Instead of saying, "Do not set this in Italics," the printer's instructions will simply read, "Set Roman." This distinction between the origin of a name and its current use should be kept clear. Old Style likewise often means that light-face member of a family of type. The same caution is necessary in referring to "Gothic" type, which at the present time refers to a Roman style of letter with no serifs whatsoever, and with all its strokes of uniform width LIKE THESE LETTERS.

Black-face or Old English type is no longer common, and in advertising its use is quite limited. From the two Roman faces, however, endless variations have been evolved. Countless designers have endeavored to make departures in their lettering. Little wonder, then, that a modern type-foundry specimen book includes a formidable array of type faces which are little known and less used. Many are antiquated, many duplicated, few individual. It will serve most practical purposes to know just these six faces, learning the characteristics of one at a time by studying the general effect of a paragraph set in each, also shading, the formation of the letters, the curves, the angles, and the serifs of the letters themselves:[4]

| Caslon | Scotch Roman |
|---|---|
| Bookman | Bodoni |
| Cheltenham | Goudy (or else Cloister) |

From one face of type, a series of other faces may be designed, with the same general characteristics, differing only in one feature; these are known as a "family." For example, there is a Caslon Old Style (mostly used for text matter), and Caslon Bold (generally used for display work); then there

---

[4] Types are usually named after the men who designed them, or men for whom they were designed. Caslon is named after its designer, William Caslon, 1720. Bookman appears to be an arbitrary name, with year of introduction uncertain. Cheltenham was designed by two men, Goodhue and Kimball, for the Cheltenham Press, England. Bodoni is named after Giambattista Bodoni, 1790; Goudy, after Fred Goudy who is actively engaged in typography as this book is written.

# A Headline Set in Cheltenham Bold
# A Headline Set in Caslon Bold
# A Headline Set in Scotch Roman
# A Headline Set in Cloister Bold
# A Headline Set in Bookman
# A Headline Set in Bodoni

A SHARE of stock represents a most conspicuous example of multiple inheritance taxation. It is possible that the same share of stock upon the death of its owner may be subject to taxation first by the Federal Government; then by the state where its owner was domiciled; then by some other state which may also claim him as a citizen;

*8 POINT CASLON OLD FACE*

A SHARE of stock represents a most conspicuous example of multiple inheritance taxation. It is possible that the same share of stock upon the death of its owner may be subject to taxation first by the Federal Government; then by the state where its owner was domiciled; then by some other state which may also claim him as a citizen;

*8 POINT CHELTENHAM OLD STYLE*

A SHARE of stock represents a most conspicuous example of multiple inheritance taxation. It is possible that the same share of stock upon the death of its owner may be subject to taxation first by the Federal Government; then by the state where its owner was domiciled;

*8 POINT BOOKMAN (also called Antique)*

A SHARE of stock represents a most conspicuous example of multiple inheritance taxation. It is possible that the same share of stock upon the death of its owner may be subject to taxation first by the Federal Government; then by the state where its owner was domiciled; then by some

*8 POINT SCOTCH*

A SHARE of stock represents a most conspicuous example of multiple inheritance taxation. It is possible that the same share of stock upon the death of its owner may be subject to taxation first by the Federal Government; then by the state where its owner was domiciled; then by some other state which

*8 POINT BODONI*

A SHARE of stock represents a most conspicuous example of multiple inheritance taxation. It is possible that the same share of stock upon the death of its owner may be subject to taxation first by the Federal Government; then by the state where its owner was domiciled; then

*8 POINT BODONI (2 Point Leaded)*

---

SOME GOOD COMBINATIONS FOR HEADLINE AND TEXT

Chelt. Bold with Chelt. Old Style     Scotch Roman throughout
Chelt. Bold with Caslon Old Style (or Old Face)   Bookman throughout
Caslon Bold with Caslon Old Style (or Old Face)   Bodoni with Scotch Roman

You are always safe in specifying a bold-face member of a type family for headline, and the light face for text.

219

are Old Style Italics and Caslon Bold Italics, Caslon Bold Condensed, Caslon Bold Condensed Italics, and a Caslon Recut (between an old style and modern). Type faces are designed in the family manner to permit having varied types in a piece of printed matter and still retain a harmony throughout.

Type measurement.—Type faces vary in size as well as in style. That dimension of the printed letter running from north to south, as it were, or the vertical measure of the letter, is referred to as its depth. The width of type varies with the shape of the individual letter. Ordinarily type size is specified by giving its depth only, which is measured in "points."

The point.—When Benjamin Franklin opened his printshop in Philadelphia he ordered his type from Fournier, a Frenchman, credited with being the founder of the "point" system of measuring type. In accordance with this method, in use at the present time, the inch is divided into 72 parts, called "points." Thus 8-point (abbreviated 8-pt.) type is 8/72 of an inch in depth. Nine lines of this size of type, without spacing, would take up an inch on paper. 12-pt. type is 12/72 of an inch deep, 36-pt., 36/72 of an inch, etc.

If a 36-pt. letter were to be measured with an ordinary ruler, it would be found that the letter is not quite ½ inch deep; neither is an 18-pt. letter quite ¼ inch deep, and so on, right through the sizes. The reason for this apparent discrepancy lies in the fact that a so-called 36-pt. letter is mounted on a piece of metal whose depth is exactly ½ inch. Between the edge of the metal and the top of the letter which appears in print there may be a little "shoulder"; likewise, on the lower part of the type there is another shoulder. The space required by both of these makes the actual type face a trifle smaller than the equivalent of its point size in inches.

The smallest type for most practical purposes is a 6-pt. Then it advances in point sizes as follows (the most popular sizes are here shown in italics):

6, 8, *10* points.
*12, 14, 18, 24, 30, 36, 42, 48* points.
*60, 72,* 84, 96 points.

From 12-point to 48-point the size advances in multiples of 6 (except 14-point) ; from 48-point to 96-point in multiples of 12. Not every type face is made in all these sizes, while, for odd effects, some foundries cast intermediate sizes.

Type up to and including 14-pt in size is, in many quarters, referred to as "body" type; that above 14-point, "display" type. The terms are merely descriptive, and do not preclude setting the body or text of an advertisement in "display" or headline type, and vice versa.

The pica-em.—Though the width of a letter need not be specified when its depth is given, it is necessary to give the width of the line in which the type is to be set. Strange as it may seem, width in printing is not measured by points, but by another unit known as a "pica-em" or "pica," of which there are six to the inch.

Originally pica was the name applied to all 12-point type. The letter "M" it was observed, was the nearest approach to a square letter in the entire alphabet. The width of that "M" in pica-sized type was therefore taken as the unit of width and called the "pica-em." There can be 10-point "ems," and 24-point "ems," or an "em" in any sized type, but the pica-em which is the standard unit of measuring printing areas is always 1/6 of an inch wide. A line or advertisement 2 inches wide is 12 picas wide; 3 inches, 18 picas wide; 3½ inches, 21 picas; 6 inches, 36 picas, and so forth.

The agate line.—We now have seen how type is measured in depth by points. The width of its individual letters, for most purposes, need not be specified, but the width of the lines in which it is to be set must be stated and this is measured in pica-ems.

There is still another unit of measurement to be considered, namely, the depth of the space in which the type is to be set. In advertising, space is a very precious thing. It must be paid for dearly. Hence the inch with its cumbersome divisions of quarters, eighths, and sixteenths, is put to one side. Not even the pica-em is used. A unit known as an *agate line,* of which there are fourteen to the inch, is employed. A space 1 inch deep has 14 agate lines; 2 inches, 28 lines; 4 inches, 56 lines; 5 inches, 70 lines, and so forth.

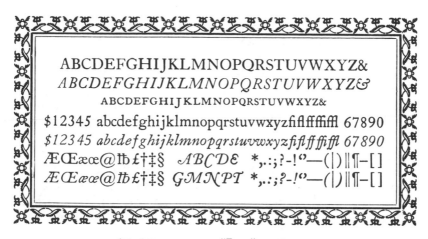

AN ASSORTMENT OR "FONT" OF CASLON

Caslon designed this type in England during an age of elegance. The Caslon letters reflect a lightness and charm of spirit, as is especially evident in the swash letters (center of lower two lines). Caslon type combines both classicism of form and freedom of line, and is a readable letter. You are always safe in specifying it.

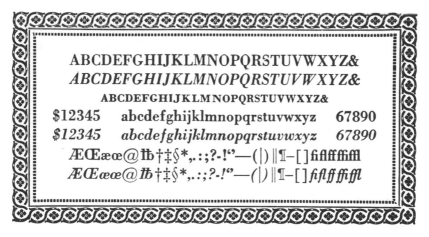

AN ASSORTMENT OR "FONT" OF BODONI

Giambattista Bodoni shared the desire of other Italian designers of his time to restore Italy's preeminence in typography. He set out to design a new Roman letter, unlike the even-stroked "old-style" Caslon letter, which had become the model of the northern countries. The result was a shaded or "modern" letter, now named after him. Bodoni type has a sharp, incisive character, with long ascenders, descenders and flat serifs. It makes a legible, distinctive page. Suitably designed decorative material accompanies the various fonts of type.

The agate line is extensively used in ordering publication space, where it always means 1/14 of an inch deep, and one column wide.[5]

There are 14 agate lines in every inch of space, measured from the top of the page to the bottom, *regardless of the printed lines actually set up within that space.* The printer should be told the width of the advertisement (in picas) and the depth of the advertisement in agate lines.

A special ruler known as a "type gauge" is used for measuring type sizes and printing areas. Instead of being divided into inches or centimeters, this ruler has a *point* scale for measuring depth of type, a *pica* scale for measuring width of advertisement spaces, and an *agate line* scale for measuring the depth of advertisement spaces. To repeat, 72 points to the inch, 6 pica-ems to the inch, 14 agate lines to the inch.

**Specifying type.**—To specify type it is necessary to state:

1. Size of type.
2. Type face, including particular member of type family.
3. Line width, where there are several lines of copy.

For example:

"Set 12-point Caslon Bold Caps and lower case, 21 picas wide" (abbreviated, "Set 12-pt. Cas. Bold, C & l. c. 21 picas wide).

"Set 24-pt. Goudy Bold Caps."
"Set 12-pt. Goudy O. S. l. c., 25 picas wide."
"Set 48-pt. Chelt. Bold Italics, C. & l. c."
"Set 8-pt. Bookman C. & l. c., 13 picas wide."

Type instructions are marked right on the copy manuscript on the layout sheet opposite the corresponding paragraphs of copy.

It requires both training and experience to estimate and specify exactly the size of type which will best fit into a given space. A number of valuable tables have been worked out for this purpose. The man untrained in this field work will do well to study type sizes carefully. In actual work he had best draw on his layout the grouping of type and the comparative blackness of different lines and paragraphs of copy, specify his choice of type faces, as "Goudy Bold and Goudy O. S.," "Chelt. Bold and Cas. O. S.," as the preference may be, and then request the printer to follow the general layout idea, setting the copy in a size "to fill the space indicated."

## Typography.

After the foregoing introduction to printing, we leave the print-shop with a better appreciation of its work and its tools and return to the advertising desk where the copy and layout have patiently been awaiting us. Quite distinctly, we remember how much work was required to prepare the copy, and how much thought was given to its purpose, its approach, and its development. What is the best way for setting up that copy? Which type-faces should be used? These are the questions which now arise. The answer is close at hand.

The purpose of type is to convey the message of its words. It is not an instrument for filling up space, but a vehicle for thought. The choice of type-face is therefore dependent entirely upon its ability to express *the idea* of the advertisement. Artistry in typography lies in conveying the idea without calling attention to the devices used in delivering that message. The typographer is very much like the public speaker. He will decide whether he wishes to present his major story first, followed by the supporting details and interesting sidelights, or whether he wishes to go right through his text, giving each fact equal significance. Next, knowing his audience and the nature of the occasion, he will decide upon the tone to use. Will he begin calmly and maintain this even tenor throughout, will he dramatize his introductory remarks and then settle down to a lower pitch, or will he start off dramatically and resort to frequent emphasis throughout his presentation?

Similarly, in selecting a type style, the first step is to read the copy. What does it mean? Is it all one continuous thought or does it possess one outstanding idea with incidental amplifying features? If the former is the case, the type will be set in uniform size and style throughout; if the latter, some of the sentences will be accorded prominence, with the less important thoughts subordinated. Does the headline of the copy make a calm statement with the rest of the copy equally subdued, or is there an exclamative thought in the headline followed by a series of statements, each of sharp significance? In the former case, the headline and the rest of the copy would be set in continuous, even sequence; in the latter case, the copy would be broken up into paragraphs between which the subcaptions would appear in bold face.

The illustrative matter, as well as the copy, may also give a cue as to the proper type-face to use. A drawing with a blazing poster treatment would require a type sufficiently black to accompany it. A delicate pen-and-ink border would, on the other hand, call for a lighter face of type.

By its very design, lettering can be made to the capacity of pictorially describing an idea, causing the word which it forms to be only an incident. Considerable attention has been accorded this possibility of type and has resulted in some very ingenious effects. But this aspect of type has serious limitations, both mechanically and pictorially. It can be seen how machinery can appropriately be depicted by a heavy, solid type like Cheltenham Bold, and lingerie by an effeminate type like Goudy Old Style, but if type is viewed solely in this light, what can be regarded as the typographical equivalent of oranges, window shades, oil cans, lawn-grass seeds, cigars, automobiles, or any of the other innumerable objects which are advertised? Products, even more than people, lack an individuality whereby they can be described. Consequently, the endeavor to choose type solely as a reflection of a product's characteristics has serious limitations, and the advertising man is invariably made to realize that type generally best serves in one all-important capacity—that of making the copy inviting to read, and letting the copy carry the burden of the message.

Orderliness.—That advertisement whose message (not appearance alone) is best remembered, invariably possesses Spartan simplicity in arrangement. The type matter is so laid out that a person will see instantly where the message begins.

Once started, the typographical arrangement offers no difficulty to the reader as he follows the sequence of the copy;
in fact, it encourages the reader to go further. Where an advertisement lacks a logical arrangement, the copy seems to
run all over the page, with neither beginning nor ending. The
reader finds its appearance uninteresting, regardless of the
excellence of its copy. On the other hand, it is not uncommon
for readers to go through full-page advertisements set in
small type, presented in a sensible, orderly arrangement.

**Uniformity.**—More often than not, a single type family provides all the variety necessary for an advertisement. For a headline, Caslon Bold may be used; for a sub-
head, the same face in smaller size, upper and lower case, or
italics. For the text matter, Caslon Old Style again. Thus,
a single type family can provide an advertisement with all
the facts necessary to make it sparkle. A combination of two
families may sometimes be deemed advisable, but as a rule this
practice should be avoided.

**Emphasis.**—Typographic emphasis is used to direct attention to an element of importance in the advertisement. It is
also used to relieve the monotony of a set-up, and to call attention to the advertisement as a whole. It may consist of a
caption in heavier type, of a paragraph in contrasting size, of
a word in italics, of underscoring, of boxing, of an initial letter, or of extra white space surrounding the part to be emphasized.

Emphasis by any of these devices secures its effect through
contrast with surrounding type. But when a piece of copy
overindulges in typographic emphasis, especially that of the
same kind, the very attention which it seeks is lost. It must
always be remembered that printed matter will more surely
be read if it does not rely entirely upon artificial emphasis
for holding the reader's attention. An advertisement which
used all of its typographical energy to secure the eye of the
reader is like the speaker who says, "I want only five minutes
of your time," and then spends four minutes of them in enlarging on this fact. It is far better to make people want to
read the advertisement than it is to devote the advertisement
to saying that you want them to read it.

To make the advertisement easy to read, the lines should not be set too wide for a given size of type.[6] It is far better to set the material in a double column. Neither should the lines be set too close together (too "solid"). There should always be a fair amount of space between the lines, regardless of the size in which the type is set. Space between the lines is obtained by inserting leads—thin strips of metal of varying thicknesses. It is important to note that a certain relationship exists between type size and lead between the lines. The advantage of a fair-sized type face may be entirely destroyed by failing to lead. A page of 10-point set solid, for instance, is far more difficult to read than a page of 8-point type set on a 10-point body, that is, with 2-point leading between each line. By giving close study to the proper amount of space between the lines, experienced advertisers succeed in making their advertisements pleasant to read, even though the space carries a profusion of copy.

Among the other effective devices for making an advertisement inviting to read is that of breaking up long pieces of copy into logical units, these units being presented in short paragraphs. Plenty of white space, convenient sub-captions, tabulations, and indentations are other useful devices for relieving the dullness of a printed page.

The skill of the master lies in utilizing at any one time only a few of the typographical tricks at his command. The wisdom of the novice lies in avoiding stunts and adhering to the simplest arrangements.

**The initial letter.**—The initial letter is a larger-sized letter than the body type at the beginning of which it is used. It originated long before the advent of printing, in the old illuminated manuscripts where it served as a colorful ornament on the page. The present use of the initial letter is to suggest the starting point of the reading matter, to indicate a new group of thoughts within the advertisement, and to relieve the severity of the set-up. Initial letters are known as 2-line, 3-line, or 4-line initial letters, depending upon the number of lines of adjoining type they span. Some initials

---

[6] See Appendix for tables of type measurement.

may extend above the copy, others drop into the copy. A test of the effectiveness of initials is to note whether they call attention to the advertisement and cause a person to begin reading the copy, rather than attract attention to their own charms or oddity.

**Hand-lettering.** —An advertisement may have a style of lettering specially created for itself. This is known as "hand-lettering." An artist writes or prints the desired copy on a sheet of drawing paper. This copy is photographed and made into a photo-engraving plate which, in turn, is given to the printer.[7]

Hand-lettering offers individuality. Hence it is used chiefly for headlines, name-plates, and for short pieces of copy. But few artists are given the time or are endowed with the talent to create lettering as good as that of the standard type designers for general text matter. Consequently, a hand-lettered advertisement is often unique to behold but trying to read. Of course the extra additional expense of hand-lettering would be warranted if it insured more effective advertising than standard type faces, but as a rule there is little to be gained.

## Paper Stock.

Paper mills sell either through their own mill agents, or through paper jobbers who handle other brands as well. These in turn deliver the paper to the printer. In most instances, the printer provides the stock as a part of the complete printing job. Where the advertiser is qualified to judge paper stock, and is familiar with the prevailing prices, he may find it advisable on large quantity work to order direct from the paper house, thereby securing the trade discount. Unless he is thoroughly conversant with paper stocks, however, he would do better to depend upon the printer, whose knowledge of the technical requirements of the work and whose familiarity with the paper market make his counsel invaluable.

**Kinds of stock.**—The base of all paper is cellulose fibre, the best being that found in linen and cotton. However, hemp, jute, wood pulp, and waste paper are also used extensively.

---

[7] As described in the chapter on Engraving.

Paper varies according to the texture of its body, depending upon the kind and quality of fibre selected, and upon the finish of its surface. The stocks most used in advertising come within one of three groupings, known as:

1. Writing.
2. Book.
3. Cover.

The classifications within each of these divisions, a description of the qualities of each classification and a note regarding its suitability to different photo-engravings, is given in the accompanying Comparison Chart of Paper Stocks.

**Other stocks.**—Among cardboards, there are those known as coated, and bristols, the former of which is the stock most commonly known. It comes in white and in colors, the color appearing on the surface only. Bristols belong to the stock which, in its better quality, is used for wedding announcements. They come in many weights, both white and colored, the entire body of the sheet and not merely the surface being pigmented. Cardboards may be ordered by weight, by specifying heavyweight, medium, or lightweight, as the paper-maker may have classified them, or by specifying plies, the ply being the number of sheets pasted together to constitute the thickness. The number of plies is purely a relative term, and two cardboards of the same number of plies may yet differ in their thickness.

For use in direct lithography and offset lithographs, special paper is used, known respectively as lithographic and offset stock.

**Measuring paper.**—The customary unit in buying paper is the ream of 500 sheets.[8] The size of paper is measured in linear inches; its weight by its weight per ream. In specifying paper, the size is given first and the weight afterward. Thus, 17x22—20 (read seventeen, twenty-two, twenty) means that a ream of paper, each sheet of which is 17"x22" in size, weighs 20 pounds. 25x38—80 describes a sheet of paper cut to the size of 25"x38", of which one ream weighs 80 pounds. Likewise, 22x26—20, 32x44—80, 26x40—150, each mean that a

---

[8] The count of 1000 sheets to the ream is being introduced.

ream of paper in the specified size is of the given weight.

At first it would appear that the variety of sizes and weights is unlimited, and as a matter of fact, until recent years, they were. Subsequently, several sizes and weights were taken as a standard or basic size. These are:

```
For writing paper ......................17x22
For book paper ........................25x38
For cover paper .......................20x26
For cardboard .........................22x28
```

Regardless of the size in which a sheet of paper may be furnished by the mill, it can be quoted by its basic weight, i. e., its weight per ream if cut to the basic size for that paper. One very often hears references made to a "20-pound bond" or a "24-pound bond," meaning that 500 sheets of that paper, if cut to the size of 17x22, weighs 20 lbs. or 24 lbs., irrespective of the fact that the paper in question may be 19x24, or 17x28, or some other size. Similarly, a 70-pound book paper means paper a ream of which 25x38 in size weighs 70 pounds.

When possible, jobs are printed on large sheets to save presswork. After being printed, these sheets are cut up into the number of advertisements which it was possible to get on a wide sheet. The most economical sheet-size, then, is one which leaves no waste margin to be trimmed off after the sheets have been cut into the allotted number of advertisements. In planning folders, the sheet-size is chosen which will best accommodate the desired page-size, and vice versa. It is most important to consult the printer and determine whether or not a contemplated job will cut well out of the basic sized sheets. If it will not, find out which of the other standard sizes kept in stock by most paper houses could best be used.

## Working with the Printer.

Printers differ in facilities and ability. One plant may be especially equipped to handle book work, another fine color work, and a third, "job" work, such as letterheads and smaller printed matter.

Choosing the printer.—The plan which has proved most satisfactory is to give trial orders to a number of printers whose work appears satisfactory and whose prices are rea-

# Comparison Chart of Paper Stocks
### including only the better known
### WRITING — BOOK — COVER

| Paper | Specification | Description | Photo-Engraving Recommended | Comments |
|---|---|---|---|---|
| WRITING<br>Basic Size:<br>17 x 22<br>Other Standard<br>Sizes:<br>17 x 28<br>19 x 24<br>22 x 34<br>28 x 34<br>24 x 38 | Flat Writing. | This is the paper used in the making of inexpensive school writing tablets and note books. Better grades of it are used in correspondence stationery. | A. Line plates. | I. Not used extensively for advertising purposes.<br>II. As the quality of a Flat Writing stock becomes better, it moves into the class of Bonds. |
| | Bonds. | Most letters received in the business office are on this stock. Its grades vary from that in which wood pulp and sulphite are used, to the better qualities made of linen rags. The weight in most common use is 20 lbs. (17 x 22-20). | A. Line plates.<br>B. 110-screen halftones.<br>C. Highlight halftone. | I. Bonds provide a large variety of tints.<br>II. Some come in finishes such as "crash," simulating the cloth; also glazed. Most bonds come in a plain unglazed finish.<br>III. Engraving plates for use on bonds should be etched deep. |
| | Ledger. | A very high class sheet of writing paper, used mostly for documents and accounting work. Has a tough, sturdy body, and a surface finish which has been plated (compressed between sheets of metal). Is heavier, as a class than bonds; also more expensive. In its lighter weights it is also used for executive stationery. | A. Line plates.<br>B. 120-screen halftones. | I. Comes mostly in white and buff. |
| BOOK<br>Basic Size:<br>25 x 38<br>Other Standard<br>Sizes:<br>30½ x 41 | Newsstock. | Received its name from its use for newspapers. The least expensive of book papers and sometimes considered as a class by itself. Has a thin, porous body and a rough surface. | A. Line plates.<br>B. 65-screen halftone, tooled well.<br>C. Quartertones. | I. Comes mostly in white (which varies in its tones).<br>II. Qualities vary. Finish does not have to be specified. |

| PAPER | SPECIFICATION | DESCRIPTION | PHOTO-ENGRAVING RECOMMENDED | COMMENTS |
|---|---|---|---|---|
| 32 x 44<br>38 x 50<br>41 x 61<br>44 x 46 | Antique. | A book paper whose body is of higher quality and heavier weight than that of news, but which likewise has a rough, uneven surface. | A. Line plates only. | I. Limited range of colors.<br>II. Has a number of different finishes, as *egg-shell, antique wove, antique laid.* |
| | Machine finish (M. F.) | The least expensive of the book papers which can take half tones dependably well.<br><br>Represents an additional process through which antique paper goes. The stock is "sized" or submersed in chemicals, which fill up the pores, making the paper less absorbent. It is then "calendered," or ironed, giving the surface the smooth finish which permits the use of half-tone. Sometimes known as "S. & C."—Sized and Calendered. | A. 120-screen half-tones. | I. Moderate range of colors.<br>II. A very utilitarian paper. **Permits** reproduction of wash drawings and photographs. Creases well. Especially good for booklets and catalogues to be issued in quantity. |
| | English-finish. | A grade smoother than machine-finish, but not as high as the one next described. For most purposes in which a half-tone is to be used this offers a serviceable, attractive stock. | A. 133-screen half-tones. | I. Moderate range of colors.<br>II. Folds well. Can withstand fingering and usage. Good for leaflets and booklets, house-organs, and moderately high-class catalogues. |
| | Sized and Super Calendered ("S. & S. C." Super). | This is a machine-finished paper which has been "sized," like Machine Finish and English Finish, but which has been given an additional ironing. The surface is consequently glossy. | A. 133-screen half-tones. | I. Moderate range of colors.<br>II. Folds well. Suited for uses similar to those of English-finish, when a more attractive effect is sought. |

(Cont.)

# Comparison Chart of Paper Stocks
### including only the better known
### WRITING — BOOK — COVER

| Paper | Specification | Description | Photo-Engraving Recommended | Comments |
|---|---|---|---|---|
| BOOK (*Cont.*) | Enamel Coated ("Coated"). | The smoothest of book papers. This is a machine finish paper which has been given a coating of clay and glue, then passed through the calender rolls at high speed. The result is a hard surface, dull, or glossy. Is brittle. Does not fold well. Otherwise shows reproductions to very best advantage. | A. 133, 150, 175-screen halftones. Can take vignette finish. | I. Most expensive of the book papers. Looks good. Good for extra fine work. Cannot stand much fingering and usage. |
| COVER Basic Size: 20 x26 Other Standard Sizes: 23 x 33 26 x 40 33 x 46 | Antique. | Refers to the rough-surfaced finish. Antique cover is usually rougher than antique book. | I. Line plates. | I. Broad range of finishes, including *ripple*, *linen*, *crash* and many fancy patterns. II. Good for folders, and for booklet covers. |
| | Plated. | The surface has been pressed, as in ledgers. | I. 120-screen halftones. | I. Folds well. Good for booklet covers. |
| | Enamel Coated ("Coated"). | A cover stock which has been given a treatment similar to book cover stock. | I. 133, 150, 175-screen halftones. | I. The acme of cover stocks in appearance. Does not fold well. |

Note I. Book papers come in a greater variety of weights than do bonds, bonds in greater variety than covers. Cover stocks have a greater variety of colors and of finishes than have books; books a greater variety than bonds.
II. Antique stocks cannot take halftones; only line plates.
III. If a job is wanted in a hurry, an antique stock is preferable, since the ink on it dries more quickly than in the case of a smooth-finish paper.
IV. The above sizes are based on a ream of 500 sheets.

sonable. With this experience as a basis, work is given out to the printer or printers with whom the advertiser has had the most satisfactory business dealings, without competitive bids. Of course, on large jobs, competitive bids should be called for. Issuing competitive work at random on a price basis alone, however, is seldom satisfactory. A printer to whom an opportunity on an account has been given before will often figure very closely on the first job in order to get new business. When once he secures the work, he may either effect false economies at the expense of quality or else endeavors to make up on the next job for sacrificed profit on the first.

The advantages to the advertiser of fixed and continuous relations with the printer are many. In the first place, his ideas are better understood by a printer who has done work for him before, and this fact constitutes the most important advantage which is gained by dealing with one print-shop. Furthermore, the advertiser is able to secure the benefit of any economies which the printer may be able to effect, since the latter does not have to work on a speculative basis in the case of a steady account. A printer can always find ways of saving money for the advertiser—either in the 'selection of stock, in the employment of odd stock, in the press work, in binding, and in numerous other ways not apparent to one unskilled in the work.

Finally, a faithful printer can be depended upon when an occasion arises for doing exceptionally quick or exceptionally difficult work, and such occasions arise all too often in advertising. For the sake of speed, one advertiser will often have a number of accredited shops working on different jobs, allocating the work according to class or quality.

Handling the job.—For each job the printer will, upon request, furnish an estimate, which is the best known way of avoiding misunderstandings. When arrangements have been completed, all copy, plates, and layouts should be turned over at one time. The copy should be typewritten on 8½x11 inch sheets, on one side of the paper only. If there are several pages of copy, each should be numbered. On the layout, proofs of the plates supplied by the engraver may be pasted to indicate the exact position of the respective illustrations.

The printer will send for approval proofs of an advertisement at different stages of the work. Thus there are proofs known as:

*Galley Proofs.*—If type for a booklet is being set up by machine, it will be set up one line after the other and placed in a long tray, known as a galley. Two sets of proofs will then be pulled. One set is read for typographical errors; the other is cut up and dummied into pages.

*Page Proofs.*—With the advertiser's dummy as a guide, the printer breaks up the galleys into pages and submits page proofs showing more nearly how the type and engravings look in the finished advertisement.

*Stone Proofs.*—A "stone" is the work-table on which the composer locks up the pages for press. After he has the type assembled here, he can make or "pull" a proof. This will give the general typographic arrangement, but will not show halftone engraving plates clearly.

*Foundry Proofs.*—Foundry proofs resemble page proofs and show how the plates and type look just before they are moulded into electrotypes. After this, all desired alterations will have to be made in the electrotype itself—a pretty costly proposition.

*Press Proofs.*—Press proofs are exact reproductions of the job when the forms are on the press and ready to be printed. This is the last call for changes and only those which are absolutely necessary should be made.

Not all jobs require each of the proofs described above, one proof alone sufficing in many instances. Frequently, however, several revisions on galley proof or foundry proof will be found necessary. When a proof is received, it is compared for accuracy with the original copy which the printer returns at that time. If satisfactory, the proof is marked "O. K." with the date and name of the person "O. K.'ing" the work. Otherwise, the necessary revisions are indicated, and the copy is marked "O. K. with C." (O. K. with corrections), provided no further proofs are necessary. If it is believed advisable to see another proof containing the corrections, the printer is instructed to "Send Revise." In all cases, the orig-

| | |
|---|---|
| ℒ | Dele, or delete: take it out. |
| ℊ | Letter reversed—turn. |
| # | Put in space. |
| ◌ | Close up—no space. |
| V/\ | Bad spacing: space more evenly. |
| wf | Wrong font: character of wrong size or style. |
| tr | Transpose. |
| ¶ | Make a new paragraph. |
| □ | Indent; or, put in an em-quad space. |
| ⊏ | ⊏ Carry to the left. |
| ⊐ | Carry to the right. |
| ⊓ | Elevate. |
| ⊔ | Depress. |
| × | Imperfect type—correct. |
| ↓ | Space shows between words—push down. |
| ⫽ | Straighten crooked line. |
| ‖ ＝ | ‖Straighten alignment. |
| stet | Restore or retain words crossed out. |
| ⌒ | Print (æ, fi, etc.) as a ligature. |
| out see copy | Words are omitted from, or in, copy. |
| ⑦ | Query to author: Is this correct? |
| caps | Put in capitals. |
| sc | Put in SMALL CAPITALS. |
| lc | Put in LOWER CASE. |
| rom | Put in roman type. |
| ital | Put in italic type. |
| bf | Put in bold face type, |

inal manuscript, or else proof checked against, should be returned with the corrected proof. The printer will send a duplicate set of proofs for the advertiser's file. The further a job advances, the more expensive it becomes to make any alterations. It therefore follows logically that the best place to make changes is on the original manuscript before it reaches the printer.

Proofreaders' marks are a set of symbols which tell the printer in the language of the shop just what is to be done. These marks are very useful to know. If there is any question, however, as to the mark to use for a certain correction or change, it is always best to explain exactly what is wanted in plain Anglo-Saxon language.

Suggestions in printing.—Folding, or binding, represents the final step in the work of the printer. Since the sheets are printed flat, arrangements must be made to fold them by hand or by machine into the respective sizes. When the pages are to be bound together, "wire" or "saddle" stitching is in most cases the most practical.

If a reprint of the job is contemplated and electrotypes have not been made, the printer should be instructed to hold the type.

The factor which takes the most time in printing is not always the actual set-up or press run, but the waiting for complete instructions, for plates, for proofs to be read and O. K.'d, or for one side or one color to dry before proceeding with the job. Those delays are unavoidable and must be taken into consideration in making up a schedule for any job; but no time should be lost through lack of dispatch in handling the work.

Paper companies issue cabinets or folders containing samples of their stock. These can be obtained without cost, either direct from the paper dealer or through the printer. Paper companies are also generous in distributing samples of printing produced on their different stocks. These mailings range from small cards to elaborate monographs, rich in their content. A user of printing can have his name placed on their mailing list upon request. Publications dealing with advertising usually contain advertisements of paper companies offering to send their latest literature.

Advertisers may often find it advisable to have their own printers set up an advertisement which is to appear in several publications. From this one set-up, a number of plates can be made of the entire advertisement, each of which may then be sent to the respective periodicals. Because of this practice, it is possible to see the identical advertisement appear in different publications without the slightest variation in style. Advertising composition, as this phase of printing is known, is assuming large proportions.

**Summary of steps.**—The work of putting through an actual job entails certain routine steps. Their sequence may vary with the individual advertisement, but from the time the copy and layout are ready for the printer, the procedure will follow these lines:

1. Copy is prepared.
2. Printer's layout is made with type instructions.
3. Printer is chosen.
4. Estimate is O. K.'d and orders for job are issued.
5. Paper is ordered.
6. Galley proofs are O. K.'d.
7. Page proofs are O. K.'d.
8. Material is printed.
9. Material is sent to bindery, if necessary, for stitching of sheets together, or for folding.
10. Material is delivered.

When the copy and layout for a job are given to the printer, the plates for the illustrations will also have to be turned over to him, and to get these plates we shall pay a visit to the photo-engraving shop.

*A group of rare imprints used by early printers to identify their books.*

## Chapter XI

## ENGRAVING FOR THE ADVERTISING MAN

ONE of the causes of surprise and wonder in any advertising office is the plate from which pictures are reproduced in advertisements—surprise to those who have not seen these plates before, wonder even to those who are familiar with the reproduction of illustrations, but who are not quite sure how the plates are made, and consequently are not certain of what they may expect. It is even more puzzling to see how a man critically views an illustration on his desk, matches it with a ruler against a layout, and then marks several notations along the margin. Off it is sent to a "photo-engraver" and when it comes back it is accompanied by a reproduction of the illustration in reduced size, along with the plate from which that reproduction was printed, and from which many more imprints can be made. What did that man consider when he determined upon the instructions to give? How was the picture transferred to a hard metal surface from which it could be reprinted a million-fold? There lies a story!

**The photo-engraving method.**—In the old days, illustrations were carved by hand from wood, just as were the original type letters. For special purposes this method is still used to a very limited extent, but by far the greater proportion of illustrations, such as we see in publication advertising, is made by the speedy method which combines photography and metallic engraving, called photo-engraving. The process resembles that of regular photography in principle and makes possible actually to reproduce pictures in advertisements.

The camera in snap-shot photography uses a negative film, on which all white parts turn out black and all black parts white. The film is placed over a sensitized paper—the positive—and both are exposed to light which can pass through only the white parts of the negative in varying degrees, the dark areas shutting it off. When the paper is placed in the developer, all portions darken to the intensity in which the light registered, reproducing the original scene. This print is spoken of as the photograph.

In photo-engraving, the negative undergoes a process similar in many respects. The illustration to be reproduced is photographed by means of a glass-plate camera, like the one used in photographic studios where pictures are taken on plates rather than on roll films. This plate is then developed, the negative which finally appears on it looking almost as though it were painted on the glass itself. It is necessary, however, to separate the negative from the glass. For this purpose a transparent substance which looks like "Newskin" is poured over the plate and is permitted to dry. When this coating is gently lifted off the glass, it carries along the impression of the picture. This very sensitive tissue is known as the *engraving negative.*

In regular photography, the negative is printed directly on a piece of paper, while in photo-engraving it is desired to print the negative on a sheet of metal. To do this, the negative film is placed upon another sheet of glass—a very thick one. Against this, a sensitized sheet of zinc or copper is applied and exposed to light. The action on the metal is identical with that on paper. Where the light shines through, the plate is darkened to that extent, and before long, the picture appears printed on the flat metal surface.

· We now have a thin plate of metal bearing a fac-simile of the original illustration. But this plate is still unsuited to letter-press printing because it has no elevations or depressions like those on a rubber stamp. To get a relief effect from this flat sheet of metal, it is coated with an acid-resisting chemical which adheres only to the parts representing the objects photographed and which ultimately are intended to be printed. The entire plate is subsequently immersed in a tank of acid which eats into the metal, biting into the crevices of the unprotected areas (the parts which are not to be printed according to the original picture). The original illustration finally appears, standing out in relief like fine ridges on metal. To facilitate handling, the engraving is mounted upon a block

A PHOTO-ENGRAVING PLATE

From plates like this the pictures in advertisements are printed. The plate of metal is tacked down to a block of wood. The above plate was used to reproduce Illustration E, the 120-screen square halftone, shown on a following page. The plate itself appears larger than its reproduction because of the bevel edge all around, but the printing surface is identical in size with the print itself (1½-inches wide).

of wood. A plate from which illustrations can be printed has now been created. The finished product looks as though some master artisan of infinite patience had chiseled a reproduction on the metal, copying every gossamer line and every elusive shadow.

**Steps in making engravings.**—Stripped of their technical detail and verbiage, the essential steps in making a photo-engraving are these:

1. The illustration or object to be reproduced is photographed.

2. A negative tissue is developed.

3. The print is made from the negative tissue on metal.

4. The metal plate is treated, then placed in a chemical bath which etches into the metal.

5. The result is a reproduction of the original subject on a sheet of metal (the engraving).

6. Workman finishes plate, tooling and otherwise perfecting the engraving by hand.

7. The plate is mounted, if desired, after which it is ready for printing.

Between these steps the plate may be manipulated and improved by the workman, upon whose skill the finished engraving is entirely dependent. That bichromated glue or gamboge is used in the engraving process may be of little interest to the advertising man, but it is essential for his success and economy in ordering plates that he understand at least the principles of photo-engraving.

**Line plates.**—The two major classes of photo-engraving are known as (1) line plates and (2) halftones. The simplest form of engraving plate is made from a drawing which is of one tone of blackness only, that is, consisting of solid blacks or pure whites. Such a drawing can be reproduced into the least expensive form of original engraving, the line plate. The single tone of blackness referred to may appear in the drawing as lines of various weights—or even dots of various sizes. But each one is a distinct tone of blackness which the eye can separate into distinct lines or masses.

Zinc is the metal generally used in the making of line plates, or zinc etchings, as they are sometimes called, but where the details of the illustration are of extreme delicacy, copper is preferable. Copper line plates are more costly than zinc, but they hold the very fine lines better than do zinc line plates.

**Halftones.**—Unlike the drawing of line plate technic, in which the lines appear distinctly apart, a photograph has tones which blend. Black merges into white with such fine gradations that the different shades cannot be sharply distinguished by the eye. For illustrations of this character, whether photograph, wash drawing, or oil painting, an engraving known as a halftone has to be made.

The halftone method breaks an area of blending tones into dots varying in size and in their distance from each other. In the final reproduction, the dots may appear so close together that the untrained eye will mistake the illustration for an actual photographic print. But the camera gets each dot separately and transfers the picture to the metal plate—dot

A.—Line Plate.    B.—Line Plate with Ben Day Shading.

by dot. The effect is particularly noticeable in photographic reproductions which appear in newspapers.

Breaking the picture into dots is accomplished by placing a screen just in front of the plate in the camera. From the back of the camera the illustration resembles a view seen through a screened window. No common garden variety of screening is used in the camera, however, but one of glass on which hair lines are very finely cross-ruled. The number of these lines varies with the different screens. Halftones are described as 60-screen, 85-screen, 100-screen, 110-screen, etc., according to the number of cross lines per inch.

The negative film is put through a developing process similar in principle to that of the line plate, but the resultant print has a mass of dots in relief. Some of them are larger than others, in keeping with the value of the corresponding part of the original illustration. When the plate is inked, the dots with a larger surface retain more of the ink and print heavily, making solid tones, while the smaller dots print very fine indeed, giving the light gray effects on a halftone. The difference in the area, the arrangement, and the proximity of dots gives the varying tones of light and dark shades appearing in the original illustration.

Screens are made in the following lines (per inch). Those most frequently used are shown in italics:

55-*60-65-85-100-110-120-133*-150-175

Higher (meaning finer) screens than 175 are obtainable but are not in general use. *The fineness of the screen affects the*

C.—Square Halftone. 65-Screen.

D.—Square Halftone. 85-Screen

E.—Square Halftone. 120-Screen.

F.—Square Halftone. 133-Screen

G.—133-Screen Halftone, square at bottom (without line) vignette sides and top.

H.—Silhouette (outside) Halftone. 133-Screen.

COMPARISON OF PHOTO-ENGRAVINGS
*Specially designed for* ADVERTISING PROCEDURE
*Illustrations by George L. Hollrock.*
*Plates by Powers Reproduction Corp.*

*fidelity (or legibility)* of the detail in the engraving. The more dots per square inch in the screen, the finer is the detail, and the more perfect the subsequent reproduction.

The screen to be used for a halftone is dependent mainly upon the finish of the surface of the paper upon which the plate is to be printed. A coarse-finished paper takes a "coarse" screen (low number of lines, like 65 or 85 screen); a more highly polished (or coated) paper would require a 120 or 133 screen halftone. The amount of detail to be reproduced in the picture also helps determine the screen; the more the detail, the higher the screen needed to reproduce those details with clear definition. For most purposes it is safe to specify 120-screen when the picture is to be reproduced on a machine-finish paper, and 133-screen when super-calendered or coated paper is to be used. Trade publications are generally printed on a machine-finish paper, while the higher class of "consumer" periodicals appear on a super-calendered or on a coated stock.

For unusual effects, special screens are sometimes used, as the one-way screen, in which cross lines are not used; and mezzographs, in which wavy lines replace straight vertical and horizontal rulings. These unusual effects should never be attempted, however, without the special advice of an experienced engraver.

It is always desirable to make a halftone from an original illustration itself and not from another halftone picture. When a halftone is made from a halftone print, the two sets of screens break into each other, producing a mottled, cross-hatched effect.

With the exception of the very low-screened half-tones, the metal used for this form of engraving is copper. Halftones are more costly than line plates.

**Halftone finishes.**—In the case of a line cut, the camera reproduces the illustration exactly as it appears. If the illustration is only a circle, the reproduction will be only a circle. In making a halftone, however, the screen covers the entire picture. If the camera is set to take a picture 8″x8″, the screen will appear over that entire area. A circle, if it were photographed, would appear with a light-gray screen inside of it, and another outside, the whole being eight inches square. The screen does not confine itself to the subject—it covers the entire plate. There are times when the camera includes portions of an illustration which are not wanted, but of course the engraver can eliminate these before the plate is finished. Where everything but the subject is cut away, leaving a pure white background, we have a *silhouette*. (See Illustration H.) This is a very practical finish which gives the subject character, and economizes on the space it uses in the advertisement. For a silhouette plate, the background should be painted out on the original illustration. The silhouette is also known as an *outline halftone*.

A less expensive finish is obtained by letting the screen surrounding an object stand, at the same time giving the whole a definite shape, usually rectangular. This is known as a square finish. (See Illustration C.) A square finish may be had in any size or shape; even oval, an oval background being called by the paradoxical name of a squared oval finish. A squared oval finish is more expensive than a plain rectangular one.

On square finishes a line border can readily be added by the engraver, and is obtainable by specifying "square finish with line." Where no border appears, the effect is said to be a "square finish, raw edge." A line border serves as a frame for the picture and also gives more strength to the plate itself, especially when that plate is to be printed on a coarse stock.

The sharp edges of a square silhouette halftone can be softened by giving its background a cloudy, fade-away effect, known as a *vignette,* as in Illustration G. This effect is a difficult one to use successfully. Without good paper and presswork, it smudges instead of fading, and is practicable only on high-class work. A vignette finish is one of the most costly of the halftone finishes.

**Ben Day.**—The Ben Day process, named after the man who perfected the method, is one whereby the engraver can create shading and cross hatching effects in line plates by a purely mechanical device. It makes possible in the line plate some of the sparkle appearance and gradation of color found in halftones. The principle of the Ben Day process is somewhat similar to that of the rubber stamp. Instead of printing words, however, it reproduces pattern effects upon the

EFFECTIVE USE OF BEN DAY
How many different patterns (shadings) do you see here?

engraving. In Ben Day work, a number of frames is used, each having a strong, transparent, gelatin-like film stretched across it, like the sheepskin on the side of a drum. These are known as the Ben Day screens.

The Ben Day is "laid on" before the plate is chemically etched. All parts upon the plate which are not to receive the Ben Day impression are covered with a protective film. The Ben Day Sheet is then inked with an acid resistant, pressed against the exposed areas which have the design stamped upon them. After the protective film is removed, the plate continues through its etching process. The final plate bears the stippled, shaded, or Ben Day effect.

It is often cheaper to use the Ben Day method than to have the design drawn by hand and furthermore, the mechanical stippling gives a more uniform appearance to the reproduction. The Ben Day pattern can be reproduced in an illustration of any given size, or in an area of any shape. Frequently several Ben Day patterns are introduced into different parts of a single illustration. A skilled workman can produce many odd combinations and dainty effects with this process.

**Combination plates and surprints.**—Often it is desired, for the sake of embodying the delicacy of a halftone with the boldness of a line cut, or for some other reason, to combine a line plate and halftone in a single engraving. This is quite practicable.

It must be borne in mind that finished engraving plates are made from negatives. At a certain stage these negatives are nothing but thin, transparent, rubber-like tissues. If one negative is laid over another and printed with it, the final plate will bear their combined pictures. If the negatives are suitably arranged, the resultant plate will show the respective pictures combined.

In a *surprint* (or *double print*), a line plate illustration is made to appear *upon* the halftone picture (or vice versa). Surprints are commonly used to make lettering appear across a photograph or to place any object of emphasis upon the face of a halftone illustration.

In a *combination plate* the line plate and halftone negatives intermingle or *adjoin* each other, giving a composite effect. Combination plates are extensively used where a standardized border effect is employed throughout a campaign and different photographs are to be shown within it—the border being in line, the photograph in halftone. A skilled engraver can strip both negatives together so well that the eye will detect no joints on the final print. Money may be saved, however, by first making a distinct line plate and a distinct halftone engraving, and then tacking both plates together on a single block. Of course, this is possible only when the appearance of such a joint or gap on a combination plate does not affect the design of the reproduction.

**Re-etching, burnishing, and tooling.**—A halftone illustration can be improved at three different stages in its career. The first opportunity comes when the advertiser turns the copy for the illustration over to the engraver to be photographed. It is hardly necessary to say that an illustration should be in its best possible shape before an engraving is made of it. Yet many advertisers hope to get a good plate from a poor illustration, trusting to the engraver and to luck. The engraver may be depended upon to do his best, but if the advertiser is lucky with his plate, he cannot expect to be equally lucky with the bill, for it costs money to atone for the shortcomings of the original drawing or photograph.

The second opportunity for re-touching a picture is offered when the negative is being developed. The engraver may then "tone down" or else accentuate the detail of the illustration by chemical washing.

The final occasion for improving the engraving is offered when the metal plate itself is completed. Parts to appear perfectly white can be chiseled away or "tooled out." The engraver can make dark parts on a halftone appear darker, by rubbing a tool over the desired area, thereby spreading the surface of the dots. This finishing process is known as "burnishing." Or he can soften [1] or lighten other parts by means of chemical retouching.

Mortising.—After the metal plate is made, an area within it may be entirely cut out by machine to permit the insertion of type or of a smaller engraving. Cutting a hole through the metal and the block upon which it is mounted is called "mortising." Tooling of surplus metal on the plate so that it will not show on the reproduction when printed is called "routing out."

It is frequently optional with the advertiser to decide whether a printer is to set the type, pull a proof, and then have an engraver use it with the original illustration in making a surprint or combination plate, or else have the plate of the illustration mortised and let the printer set up the type within it. The former is better on a high-class assignment; the latter may be entirely suitable for the ordinary job, and is usually less costly. In ordering combination or surprint plates, it is always necessary to decide whether the type is to be reproduced in the same proportion as the illustration.

High-light halftones, or drop-out halftones.—Owing to the presence of the screen in a halftone, the purest white will appear a light gray. To remove the screen, it is necessary to etch or tool the plate by hand. Where a halftone requires a great amount of such tooling, a "high-light" or "drop-out" halftone can be made. The original illustration for a high-

---

[1] When an engraving is said to be "softened," the term is understood to mean that the dark areas of the pictures are to be made less harsh and less severe—the blacks are made grayer. The metal plate itself is not made plastic.

light halftone is drawn as it is to appear in the final, all lines representing their correct color value.[2] The high-lights are then chemically etched by the engraver, whose skill must be that of an expert to prepare such plates. The cost of high-light halftones is about four times that of the basic price of an ordinary halftone.

**Quartertones for double-process halftones.**—Bold effects in halftones, so often desired for newspaper advertising, are obtainable through quartertones. By this method, a halftone is made of the original subject half its final size and double the final screen value desired. The proof of this plate is then retouched, fading grays being painted out and the blacks exaggerated. From this proof, a line plate double its size is made, the screen pores thus being enlarged until they reach line plate boldness. The cost of a quartertone is that of a halftone plus a line-cut, plus extra time for retouching.[3]

**Plates for colored illustrations.**—When a plate is printed in only one color of ink, it is referred to as black-and-white plate, though the ink be orange, blue, brown, or any other single color. When two or more colors are to appear in illustration, extra sets of plates have to be made accordingly.

**Color line-engravings.**—Color line plates are made from an illustration which is actually drawn in black upon white background. The illustration itself is not colored, but the colors in which the engraving is to appear are indicated upon a flap of tracing paper which is folded over this drawing, or else are specified on a separate drawing which shows the color scheme. This drawing, however, does not have to be as detailed as the black-and-white drawing which is the one photographed.

From the black-and-white drawing the engraver makes, by the usual line plate method, two, three, or four identical metal prints, as required by the number of colors. With the color scheme before him, he treats the different plates so that all

---

[2] In a regular halftone the engraver can lighten or darken parts of the illustration.

[3] This method of making quartertones is being improved upon to effect greater economy.

parts other than those in their respective colors will be eliminated.

Each plate then prints only the part where its color is to appear. When the resultant set of plates is used for printing, "A" plate—showing all areas in which the first color appears —is run off with that colored ink; "B" plate, showing a second color, is printed over it with that ink, and so forth. The final effect is a single reproduction in the various colors. This is the simplest and least expensive photo-engraving method of reproducing colored effects. It is to be observed that the colors are separated by the engraver and also that the plates themselves bear no colors until placed upon the press.

The engraver making colored plates prints or "pulls" a separate proof of each plate, in its respective color, then shows the combination of two colors, three colors, and finally a proof showing all the colors printed in correct sequence ("progressive proofs").

When color plates overlap each other exactly when reproduced, they are said to "register." When they do not coincide exactly, they are "off" (or "out of") register.

**Color halftones.**—*Original halftone illustrations to be reproduced in colors are sent to the engraver in their natural colors,* not in black and white, as may be done in the case of an illustration for color line plates. The picture may be an oil painting of food, or a portrait study in water colors, in fact, any illustration in colors may be reproduced by this method, which is known as "process work." The camera, not the engraver, in this instance, separates the colors.

The subject to be reproduced is photographed through color filters. Each filter shuts off all colors other than its designated tone, every trace of whose character is recognized by the filter. For three-color halftone, the colors are analyzed for their primary tones, three photographs being made, each with a different filter. Three halftones are then produced, one bearing all the yellows, the other all the blues, the third all the reds, each in its varying hues, intensities, and values. When the plates are printed over each other in the proper sequence of their colors, the original color effect is produced.

When a fourth plate is used, as is generally the case for

black, which serves as a "key plate," the method is then referred to as the "four-color process." Four-color process plates are capable of faithfully reproducing a subject even though it be remarkably variegated. The perfection of color engraving suitable for high-speed presses has been one of the landmarks in the development of advertising.

Often it is possible to combine color plates at a saving. Thus a black-and-white halftone plate may be used as the key plate which will contain all the detailed features of the illustration. Accompanying this there will be a line or Ben Day plate serving to give emphasis to desired areas. Another effect which may be secured economically is obtainable by using a second color for background only. Here a line plate, or a Ben Day "tint-block," may be made by the engraver—the tint-block printing a solid area of color which is printed first, with the illustration over it. These various methods do not produce the same fineness of detail but do permit of economies when their effect serves the purpose at hand.

Other forms of plates, such as wood-cuts, duotypes, chalk plates, wax engravings, and linoleum blocks, which will interest the person seeking detailed information on this subject. They are commended for further attention.

**Duplicate plates.**—The plates which have so far been considered are original plates in the sense that they are the initial conversion of an illustration into metallic form. Once such an original is made, however, many duplicate copies can be produced at a fraction of the cost of that original.[4] Duplicates may be desired in order to run an illustration or advertisement in several different periodicals simultaneously, or to economize the printing cost by running a number of imprints off at one impression. Also they may be needed to save the originals for future use, since the wear and tear of long "runs" on the press is hard on plates and type.

---

[4] At the time an engraver makes an original plate, he can make several extra plates from the same negative. The engraver refers to these as "duplicate plates" but they are generally regarded as the original plates themselves. Their cost is slightly less than the original engraving, but is considerably higher than the duplicate plate, here described, which is made by the electrotyping or stereotyping process.

The forms of duplicate plates are as follows:

1. Electrotypes.
   Made from
   Wax Mould of original plate.
   Lead Mould of original plate.
   Special Mould of original plate.
2. Matrices.
   Made from the original plate and from which can be made
3. Stereotypes.

**Electrotypes—wax mould.**—The wax mould electrotype is the one in most common use. By this method the original plate is pressed into a sheet of wax, and then placed into an electrolytic "bath" which plates the wax with a coating of copper. When the wax is removed, a thin shell of copper deposit remains, a perfect fac-simile of the original plate. This is given a backing of about one-quarter of an inch of metal to strengthen it for handling. An electrotype can be made from another electrotype but each succeeding plate will be less true in sharpness of details than the original.

**Electrotypes—lead mould.**—Lead mould electrotypes are used for color reproduction, and for advertisements in which greater precision is required than can be obtained with wax mould electrotypes.

The process is quite an interesting one to watch. The original plate is stamped into a sheet of lead under great hydraulic pressure (5,658 pounds per square inch). This bed then becomes the mould for the subsequent electrotypes. Greater accuracy is secured because of the enormous pressure of the original impression and because of the firmness of the mould itself. Furthermore, fine halftone dots may be reproduced without the impediment of graphite dust which is necessary in wax moulds. Lead mould electrotypes, however, cost more than do the wax mould variety.

Nickeltypes, steeltypes, and other special plates will prove of interest for further investigation. The new developments of those shops which are constantly seeking to improve the forms of electrotypes are well worth watching.

**Matrices and stereotypes.**—A less expensive form of duplicate plate than the electrotype is that known as the matrix. The original plate is pressed into a damp piece of papier-maché pulp. When the latter is dried, it looks like a piece of baked cardboard with the illustration or type stamped in it. This is a matrix, spoken of as a "mat," over which metal is poured. The metal cools, hardens, and forms a plate known as a stereotype. The stereotype is then used for printing. If the mat is not needed for another stereotype, it is destroyed.

The matrix can be curved and a corresponding stereotype made to fit on the cylinders of a rotary press. As many newspapers, especially those in large cities, print on such presses, their shops are generally equipped to make stereos from mats. An advertiser using a large number of publications may consequently save money in making plates—and on postage also —by merely forwarding a matrix of the advertisement and letting the newspaper in which the advertisement is to appear make a stereotype for its own use. It is to be noted that a mat cannot be printed from directly, since it is only a mould to be used in making a stereotype.

**The size of the illustration.**—It is desirable, but not absolutely necessary, to have the illustration drawn in a size one and one-half to twice that in which it is finally to appear. In this way, the crudity of detail is lessened when the size of the drawing is decreased. It must be remembered, however, that all parts of a picture will reduce in similar proportion when the picture is reduced. If a flag-pole standing before a building appears two stories high, and the illustration is reduced one-half, the pole will still appear two stories high on the smaller reproduction. This reduction of an illustration to the final size of the plate is known as "scaling down." The size of an illustration must be so proportioned that the final plate will reproduce to the desired dimension. If the engraving is to be 2″x3″, or as 2 is to 3, the drawing must be as 2 is to 3, that is, 4″x6″, 8″x12″, or 10″x15″. Conversely, an 18″x42″ illustration reduced to two-thirds in height (to 12″) will automatically be reduced to two-thirds in width (to 28″).

In ordering the illustration from which an engraving is to be made, the *proportion of its dimensions* must be given to the artist; in ordering the engraving from the engraver, only one dimension need be given.

Sometimes it is desired to change the proportion of a plate after the drawing has been made. This change may be effected by the engraver, who can cut off or "crop" a part of the foreground, background, or sides on the negative. The engraver can also change the proportions of some plates by making an additional negative of the illustration and inserting a part of it in the original negative which he cuts in two. He really grafts a part of one negative into the other, thereby increasing the size of the final plate as desired. "Stripping in," as this operation is called, is possible only where the subject will not be destroyed by such patching. Thus a symmetrical border may have a half-inch of its own design added to its height by the engraver. If he did the same to an automobile, however, the result would appear as an engineering abortion.

Another thought to bear in mind is that an illustration which is to be reduced must have its details so drawn that they will not close up the space between them when reduced. They must not "blur" or "fill in."

**Ordering the plate.**—When the engraver receives a drawing, he wishes to know:

1. The kind of plate wanted—whether halftone or line plate.

If halftone, the screen number and the finish.

2. The exact size of the plate.

If several are to be made, the number and size of each. The size of the engraving should be indicated either in height or in width and this information should be marked in blue pencil on the margin of the drawing. The measurement ought to indicate just how much of the illustration is to be included, dimensions being given in exact inches, not in terms of column width

3. Whether the plate is to be mounted or unmounted.

This depends upon the kind of press on which the plates will be printed. (Plates are mounted unless otherwise specified.)

4. Special features of the job.

These may include the Ben Day process, mortising, cropping, hand-tooling, stripping-in of the negatives, or other details.

5. Time wanted.

6. Where plate is to be shipped.

It is necessary to state whether the plate is to be sent to the advertiser's office, to printer, direct to publication, or to electrotyper.

Where a plate is sent to be electrotyped, the electrotyper wishes to know:

1. What kind of plate to make.

Whether electrotype, matrix, or stereotype. If electrotype, kind of mould. If none is specified, wax mould is understood.

2. The number of plates.

3. Whether plates are to be mounted or unmounted.

The same consideration as with the engraver.

4. Time wanted.

5. Shipping instructions.

Whether plates are to be mailed, and to whom, or what disposition advertiser wishes made of them.

**How the advertisement is put together.**—The electrotype plant may be a separate one from the engraving or printing shop but the work of all three is closely allied. The advertiser will send the original illustration to the engraver who makes the original plate, which, in turn, he sends to the printer. The latter will set up the type for the advertisement, and insert the plate in its proper place, following the layout. The advertisement is now ready to print. For a small number of impressions the printer may place the entire form on the press and "run it off," as printing a job is called. Otherwise one or more electrotypes of the entire advertisement may be made. These plates may take a number of courses:

1. They may be returned to the printer who sets them on his press and prints the advertisement, thus printing several productions at the same time, instead of only one.

2. One of the plates may serve as a master plate from which other electrotypes may be made when needed. These are sent to the printer, to publications, or to dealers for their local advertising.

3. The electrotype may be used for making matrices which

are sent out to the publications or to dealers. As a rule printers will not permit mats to be made *directly* from type.

4. From these matrices, stereotypes can be made. Stereotypes may be sent to the newspapers in which the advertisement is to appear, or to dealers for use in their local advertising.

The electrotyper disposes of all plates at the advertiser's instructions, returning the type directly to the printer who holds the original engravings for the advertiser.

**Keeping a record of engravings.**—A record of plates can be made by a system involving three steps:

1. The engraving is numbered, usually on the edge of the mounting.

2. A proof of the plate bearing a corresponding number is pasted in a scrap-book, or better, on a filing folder, for convenient reference. It is easier to refer to proofs than to plates themselves.

3. A shipping record, telling where the engraving is at any particular time, is entered, either in a book, on a card, or on the filing folder itself.

Engravings are usually filed in shallow drawers. They may be further grouped in shallow boxes, to prevent scattering.

Used engravings may be disposed of either by salvaging parts which can be used again or by unmounting the plates and selling them for old metal.

**Further suggestions—the illustration.**—Red photographs as black. Blue will not show in line engravings. Hence all notations may be made in blue.

The face of the illustration should be carefully protected by a drop-sheet pasted along the top edge.

Drawings should be carried flat. Rolling them may cause the heavier ink on them to chip off and furthermore the curling of the illustration is bothersome.

The illustration ought to be substantial enough to withstand handling. Where this is not the case, it should be mounted with rubber cement (an excellent adhesive) on a sheet of heavy, non-curling cardboard.

A black-and-white illustration may be reversed by the engraver either in color or in position. Reversing color means that black appears as white and white appears black. White lettering on a black background may be obtained by giving the engraver the lettering in black on white, with instructions to reverse the colors. In reversing position, left and right are transposed. For example, a man walking from the left to the right of an illustration can be made to appear walking in the opposite direction. In reversing position, however, the sense of the illustration must not be altered. A car with a right-hand drive would appear as having a left-hand drive if the plate were reversed in position. If lettering appears anywhere in a picture, the picture cannot be reversed, for it will look as though it were printed "backwards."

Money can be saved in plates by reversing the position of those borders and illustrative effects which are to face each other, as on the opposite pages of a catalogue. Even this expedient is not necessary when the opposite elements are identical, in which case an electrotype of one will serve the purpose. When an order for a reverse plate is given, it is always necessary to specify whether color or position is to be reversed.

The area over which the Ben Day is to be laid on the plate should be left blank on the illustration. Boundary or "guide" lines need merely be drawn to indicate the parts within which the Ben Day is to be used, blue pencil "x" marks serving to indicate the parts on which the pattern is to appear, or else the spaces may be painted in with light-blue wash. The pattern number should be specified in the margin. (The engraver can furnish a Ben Day book giving these pattern numbers.)

Instructions can be placed on a tissue overlay as well. In case of doubt about the style to use, it is best to tell the engraver what effect is desired, showing him a sample if one is available. He will then specify the appropriate design.

It is often possible to break up a black area by means of a Ben Day pattern which is reversed in color. When this is desired, the engraver may be instructed to "gray down by means of a Ben Day"—instructions which are less confusing than "lay a Ben Day."

If one-half of an illustration is identical with the other (as in borders) the illustrator need draw only one such part of the drawing. The engraver can duplicate the negative of that part, reverse the position of one, strip both together, and make a complete plate.

**Further suggestions—the plate itself.**—The quality of a plate depends largely upon the clearness with which its lines stand out. A plate is said to be "shallow" when its chemical bath was too weak or too brief to etch deeply into the metal. It is "undermined" when the chemical was permitted to gnaw into the lines themselves, weakening their ability to withstand printing. Undermining is usually the result of hasty workmanship. Deep etching is especially desirable for all plates to be electrotyped, stereotyped, or printed on a very hard-surfaced paper (as bond paper).

The face of an engraving, particularly a halftone, is very delicate and should be carefully protected in handling. Every scratch appears as a blemish in the final advertisement. Even the chemical effect of a rubber-band stretched across a halftone engraving will sometimes cause a streak to appear in the final reproduction.

The size of the plates used in one advertisement may not be right for an advertisement which will appear in another publication. It is therefore desirable to make a layout elastic, thus permitting its adaptation for any size or shape. Where the advertisement is one engraving unit, it may still be adapted for a second advertisement by cropping off a part of the background, by eliminating side scenery, or by increasing the spacing between the different elements within the layout. For the smaller advertisements in a campaign, it may be well to use only a part of an illustration, rather than try to reduce the entire drawing to the small size.

Very often a plate formerly used in a publication can be reproduced with a solid colored "tint-block" (a line plate evenly covering an area) in a piece of direct advertising. Similarly, trade-marks and other engravings can be prepared to appear in either one or two colors.

**Further suggestions—duplicate plates.**—A number of small plates may be placed alongside each other on the same mould to reduce the cost of electrotyping. Similarly, in making matrices, several engravings can be stamped into the same sheet, which can subsequently be cut with scissors.

In rush electrotyping jobs, the original plate can be returned after the mould is made, several hours before the new plate is completed. However, electrotypers generally prefer to keep the original until the others are produced. Then, should the new electrotype be spoiled in the process, as it is occasionally, no time is lost in making another. Some plants therefore renounce responsibility for perfect electrotypes when the original plate is returned in advance of the duplicate plates.

An engraving used continuously in newspapers may, after a time, become warped and worn. Vertical sides of a border are apt to become concave from the printer's handling in "locking-up," and when this happens, new plates should be supplied to avoid the unbecoming appearance.

It is advisable to have made at the outset, in necessary sizes, a number of electrotypes of name-plates, trade-marks, or other standing pictorial detail. A little foresight in securing electrotypes has saved many a situation from becoming a predicament.

The expense of a master-plate for making a few matrices from type may be saved by using linotype or monotype composition. The printer may not permit matrix-making direct from his hand-set type because the pressure distorts the type faces; he generally requires instead that the advertiser make an electrotype of the type from type and then make the mats from this electro. Machine-set type is remelted after use, however, and consequently can be used for a limited number of matrices.

Converting illustrations for campaign use.—There are many occasions in the course of the day's work when the ingenuity of the man ordering the engravings is taxed. Here is a wash drawing, for instance. It has been reproduced in magazines from a set of halftone plates. What can be done to convert it into a line-cut for newspaper use? How can a black-and-white reproduction be made from an oil painting which appeared in colors? A printer is ready to set up an advertisement—he must have the engraving or a proof of it at once so that he can proceed with the type composition. The illustration is just leaving for the engraver and it will be eight hours before the halftone is finished. What instructions shall be given? Questions such as these test the skill of an advertising man and determine the economy of his production. It is good to know, therefore, of these special prints which can effect a saving in time and in effort.

**Orthochromatic prints (Orthochromes).** —Orthochromatic prints are extensively used to convert a colored illustration into a black-and-white subject. The ordinary plate makes a black and white photograph, whether the original be in red, orange, yellow, green, or in any other color. It does not retain their distinguishing tones, however, and if used in photographing a colored subject, loses much of the tone. Red, for example, comes out black, while blues fade into whites. An orthochromatic negative interprets colors into their proper black and white values from which a one-color halftone can be made. To give the colors better definition, the photographer may also use a special color filter and further retouch the final print.

**Panchromatic prints (Panchromes).**—Panchromatic prints are even better than orthochromes when red appears in the original picture.

**Silverprints (or Bleached Prints).**—Silverprints are used to convert a halftone subject, such as a photograph or wash drawing, into one suited for line-plate use. Their principle is quite a simple one. If a sheet of tissue paper were placed over a photograph and its features copied in sharp pencil line, an illustration fit for line-plate purposes would be obtained. The silverprint is made on a similar principle. A print of the original halftone is made on a special paper. An artist goes over it with a pen, drawing only those features which allow for line-plate reproduction. The print is then washed chemically. The halftone effects which were not redrawn are bleached out but lines are left which were specially included. The illustration is now converted into such form that a line-plate can be made from it.

Where a silverprint drawing would appear too mechanical, the artist of the original drawing should be commissioned to make a new drawing specially designed for line-plate use. Often a second artist skillful with pen-and-ink has to be called, as the first specializes in wash and oils only. The silverprint method, however, is obviously more economical than that of completely redrawing an illustration.

**Blue-prints.**—A blue-print may be made from the same negative as the engraving itself, and can be delivered sooner than can the actual plate. Its position and color are the reverse of the original but otherwise it indicates very closely just how the final engraving will look. Blue-prints are ordered for use in layouts when the plate itself is not needed as much as is a proof of it.[5]

**Photostats.**—A photostat is a very inexpensive print on which the lettering appears white on a gray background. A photostat can be made from a photostat to have the black appear on white, as in the original. The photostat shows the illustrations in reversed colors and is used extensively for making individual reproductions of manuscript, of advertising layouts, and of advertisements themselves.

It may be precarious to experiment with an original and costly layout for coloring or arrangement and for such experimental purposes a photostat may often be used to advantage. If a number of people are to receive dummies or layouts and it is not practicable to pass one around to all, it may be cheaper to give them photostats than it would be to redraw the original for each. Artists, also, use photostats as roughs for their final illustration, working right over the print, thus insuring correctness of proportion, anatomy, and other technical detail.

**Ordering for lithography.**—Illustrations to be lithographed should be presented as they are to appear, or in the case of simple flat color designs, an outline drawing accompanied by the color scheme may be provided. Separate drawings can be supplied for different units of the reproduction, to be combined in the final. If type matter is to appear, a printer must

---

[5] Blue-prints ought not be used as original illustrations for an engraving, as blue does not photograph on a regular camera. An orthochrome print has to be made first. The blue-prints referred to above are made from the original illustrations by the engraver.

set up the text and supply a proof of it, as the lithographer cannot use the metal type itself.

**Ordering rotogravure.**—Rotogravure is an intaglio process. The rotogravure method differs essentially from photo-engraving in that the lines to appear are eaten out of the plate of the copper cylinder, whereas in photo-engraving the areas *not to appear* are eaten away. The depth of the etchings on rotogravure is very fine—so fine that even a person with a sensitive touch can barely feel them when he runs his finger across the metal. Revisions cannot be made on the final plate and there are no proofs before it is run off. It is furthermore impossible to make electrotypes of gravure cylinders. Duplicates are made by etching from "positives." Special inks, generally sepia-colored, or dark green, are usually employed for rotogravure.

Illustrations for rotogravure should be of mass technique, rather than in delicate pen and ink style. Frilly hair lines are lost through rotogravure, but pictures with high lights and deep shadows, such as photographs or drawings in wash, black and white oils, and charcoals, can be superbly reproduced. Halftone proofs should not be used.

All the members of a rotogravure advertisement must be assembled and pasted up exactly as they are to appear in the final; there is no manipulation in size and position of negatives, as in photo-engravings.

The proportion of the advertisement's size must scale exactly to that of the space ordered. The units may be pasted up, with type proof of the copy inserted wherever the reading matter is to appear. No rotogravure proofs can be sent in advance of publication date, but blue-prints of the advertisement as it is to appear can be obtained.

# PART III

# THE SCHEDULING OF ADVERTISEMENTS

## CHAPTER XII

# NEWSPAPERS

THE object which carries an advertisement is spoken of as the advertising medium. It acts as the intermediary in bringing the advertisement to its readers. According to their chief characteristics, media may be grouped as follows:

1. Newspapers.
2. Magazines.[1]
    a. General magazines.
    b. General magazines of specialized interests.
    c. Women's magazines.
    d. Farm papers.
    e. Technical papers.
    f. Trade papers.
3. Outdoor advertising.
4. Car cards.
5. Direct-mail advertising.
6. Dealer displays.

If an unlimited advertising appropriation were made without a corresponding obligation to accomplish a given purpose, the sum could be spent readily enough by making a list of all the known media and scheduling advertising space in them with joyous abandon. But the size of an expenditure alone is no assurance of successful results, for a fraction of the amount, well directed, might prove far more productive.

**The skill in choosing media.**—In the play, "It Pays to Advertise," Rodney Martin starts a company to sell "13 Soap, Unlucky for Dirt," in competition with the business of his father, who is an extreme conservative. Martin Junior seeks

---

[1] A magazine may be regarded as being in any of the several advertising groupings given here. When the individual character of a medium is so well known that its distinctive qualities are recognized, the need for grouping it with others is automatically obviated.

to impress the elder Martin with the power of advertising. He plans, therefore, an overwhelming campaign of advertising for "13 Soap, Unlucky for Dirt," just for the sake of convincing father.

When Martin Senior arises the next morning, he beholds the advertisements of 13 Soap. In his breakfast newspaper he sees "13 Soap, Unlucky for Dirt," on his way to the office, "13 Soap, Unlucky for Dirt," and even when he takes an out-of-town business trip, he sees nothing but "13 Soap, Unlucky for Dirt." And, as the story goes, he finally capitulates, impressed by the prestige of the new firm largely because he has seen the soap advertised "everywhere."

The reason was that the son knew his father. He knew through which streets his father passed on his way to the office, what views faced his windows, where he went to lunch, which barber-shop he frequented, in which train he traveled. And there the advertising was placed. Because there was a definite plan, Rodney's small appropriation proved ample for his purpose.

Though the play was written to entertain rather than to teach, it illustrates two principles in the selection of media: first, it is important to know the habits and customs of your prospects; second, to reach the prospective buyer economically, it is necessary to have a definite plan. The world in which a person moves is the only one which exists, as far as *he* is concerned. It is his "everywhere." The people he meets in it are the "everybody" to whom he so often defers in his private decisions. All the advertising placed where the reader's path never crosses may just as well not be placed at all, but the advertising man who knows where his prospects may be reached can put advertising dollars to work most profitably.

**Plans for using media.**—Here we see why media are selected not only for their intrinsic value but for their appropriateness in the advertising plan. The field tactics employed in advertising may be described as zone campaigns, cream campaigns, and national campaigns. In the first, the advertiser selects a definite and restricted geographical territory, puts forth his entire effort in securing all the business available in that district, and then passes on to another zone, and repeats the performance there. In a cream campaign, the advertiser seeks to secure the best business first, no matter how scattered the prospects may be. Having done this, he reaches for the next best business, and so on down the line (taking the cream off first). A national campaign is a zone and cream plan combined on a mammoth blanketing scale; the advertiser endeavors to get as much of the business in his industry as is possible, wherever it is.

The zone plan.—The zone plan permits the advertiser to secure an early cash return on a given appropriation. He can, by following such a plan, conduct a campaign with limited funds, making the advertising pay for itself quickly, and reinvesting the income if he wishes, in more extensive advertising. Zone campaigns are used to meet attacks of competition, sudden changes in conditions, or unusual trade emergencies. The zone may consist of a town, city, county, State, or group of States.

If there are any weaknesses in the product or in the selling method, they may be discovered in a zone campaign and corrected before damage has been done, either to the reputation of the house or the bank account.

The zone plan is used extensively for staple articles in generally accepted use, such as food products, soap, hosiery, shoes, cigarettes, and other commodities for which one person is as likely a prospect as his neighbor. Provided it does so thoroughly, any medium may be used which reaches people in a given zone only, such as local newspapers, outdoor signs, car cards, direct-mail advertising, and dealer-display advertising.

The cream plan.—Unlike the zone campaign, which seeks to "cover" geographical territories thoroughly, the cream campaign approaches the question by going after the most profitable business first, wherever it may be—after which it looks around for the next best business. Applying the cream plan to the sale of a new office device, the advertising would first be directed to the largest offices in which such device could be used; the advertising of gaskets for valve connections and pipe joints would be directed first to the largest power plants; the advertising of expensive vases and lamps would first be directed to the wealthier homes. Thus the cream plan divides prospects into strata of potentiality—then endeavors to reach only the most promising class. This plan also divides a prospective market into its respective industries and goes after the most likely one first. The manufacturers of adding machines, to cite an instance, first approached banks, then business offices, then retail stores. After tractors were offered to the farmer, the largest apparent market, they were sold to the lumber manufacturers, to contractors, and to municipalities.

The cream plan is extensively used for higher-priced articles of limited use—articles for which the presence of one prospect is not an assurance that another as good is in the office or home alongside of him. In the cream plan, media are desired which reach prospects of the desired class, regardless of their location, rank, or station. Magazines of specialized interest are here used extensively. Direct-mail advertising also affords an ideal means of reaching these hand-picked prospects

Both the zone plan and the cream plan are suitable for use by new advertisers. In fact, it is advisable that the advertiser confine himself at the outset to either of these plans; otherwise, his appropriation melts away before the advertising has had a chance to serve its purpose. It is possible to combine the two plans by picking the zone which is the cream of all zones, then picking from within it only the cream prospects. But in the case of every new undertaking, it is advisable to limit the audience—then reach it thoroughly.

**The national plan.**—A national campaign is a zone undertaking on a large scale. The plan is usually put into effect either after a firm has been in business long enough to have distribution of its merchandise wherever the advertising is to appear, or is the culmination of a series of zone campaigns which can be helped by a single campaign covering the gaps between the zones. The national plan requires an abundance of two things—capital and experience—the first to provide for the facilities of production, personnel of selling, and cost of advertising; the latter to recognize the feasibility of the plan and to guide its course. The media most frequently used in national campaigns are general magazines, newspapers, and billboards.

In all instances, the selection of one form of medium rather than another is entirely a matter of the advertiser's discretion, for each form offers its distinct advantages. As a guide, however, this principle may be of help: A product seeking sales in a clearly defined field will require a medium whose circulation can be clearly directed to the desired prospects. As the campaign broadens in scope, these will be supplanted by media with more indiscriminate circulation, as that quality proves desirable, in fact, and the cost of reaching the people is reduced per person. The new advertiser is strongly cautioned against following preferences instead of a plan, and against scattering a modest appropriation among too many media. The largest national advertisers of today started by using a single medium consistently.

**Newspapers—general influence.**—In the United States there are about 425 morning newspapers, 1,600 evening newspapers, and 550 Sunday papers;[2] in Canada, 26 morning and 86 evening English language newspapers—a fact which is less significant to the advertising man than the fact that there is hardly a hamlet in the country not served by its local paper. Many sections of the country are served by papers printed in an adjoining town, by a neighboring city, or by a paper whose scope is the country or State. The *Indianapolis News,* as an illustration, had a net circulation of 232 copies in a town 113 miles away. The *Chicago Tribune* reported a circulation of over 87,000 outside of its 100-mile radius, while the *New York Times* had over 2,300 paid subscribers in California. It will be seen, therefore, that a paper may be potent many miles from the city printed in its date line. Admittedly, however, the chief value of the individual newspaper lies in its strength as a local medium, of newspapers as a group—of their usefulness in forming a national chain of zone links.

To appreciate the value of newspapers as local mediums, it is only necessary to see how integral a habit their reading has

---

[2] Based on Bulletin No. 496, Bureau of Advertising, American Newspaper Publishers' Association. In addition, there are about 14,000 semi-weeklies and weekly newspapers.

become in the daily life of the people. Eulogies may well be written upon the rôle newspapers have played in moulding public opinion; threnodies may be sung to their habit of stepping between man and wife (at the breakfast table), but advertising contracts are being written because the newspaper, in addition to its personal influence among its readers, is a logical, organized and expedient medium for intensive work in definite localities.

Comparison of morning, evening, and Sunday newspapers. —Of the three groupings of newspapers, morning, evening, and Sunday, the morning papers as a rule have a smaller circulation than evening papers, which as a rule have a larger circulation and offer more local news, as well as more departmental feature articles. Sunday papers, characterized by their bulk and special sections, have the largest circulation in numbers and in territory covered. The morning papers, as a body, carry less advertising than do the evening papers, and have the circulation more widely distributed. Sunday papers offer lower rates in proportion to the number of readers than do either morning or evening. Though the advertiser may choose only a particular section of the Sunday paper, his advertisement has to withstand greater competition of other advertisements.

This comparison is based upon the general qualities of morning, evening, and Sunday newspapers as *groups*. It is well to keep in mind the fact that in actual work, media are not selected as a group but are chosen individually. Therefore, it is not sufficient to select all morning papers or all evening papers, as such, without giving careful consideration to the reading preferences of the prospective buyers. The same rule applies to Sunday papers which are particularly subject to fluctuations in the interest of their readers with the changing of the seasons. In the spring, city dwellers are anxious to get into the open, consequently do less reading on Sunday than they do during the winter months. But the same spring fever may increase their interest in the advertiser's messages if these messages deal with automobile accessories, paints for decorating the house, or vacation resorts. It is therefore well to deal with a product as an individual article and with a medium as an individual medium. Each has its own virtues,

. shortcomings, and usefulness. What is sauce for the goose isn't always sauce for the gander in advertising.

Newspapers: classified and display advertising.—Advertising in newspapers is divided into "classified" and "display." Classified advertising is that which appears in a column especially set aside and labeled by the newspaper for that purpose. When a man turns to the classified section, he is already interested in the subject advertised. Hence the classified insertion may confine itself to a statement of its offer, without undue struggle to attract the notice of people who would be interested in its subject.

Evidence of the usefulness and success of this form of advertising may be seen in the variety of classifications in any paper—classifications under which may be found anything from fountain pens to country manors. The classified advertising sections appear largest in the Sunday and morning papers.

Display [3] advertising in a newspaper may be described as all advertising matter which is not included in the classified section and it is to this form of advertising that the following pages are devoted.

Newspapers: space and rates.—Securing the right to advertise in a publication is called "buying space" in it. Space is sold by the agate line in most newspapers, or by the column-inch in those of lower rates. It will be remembered that the agate line is 1/14 of an inch deep in all cases, and in publication advertising, one column wide. The depth of the column, its width, and the number of columns to the page vary with the newspapers and must be determined from the respective publications. For all practical purposes, the column may be considered as being 2 1/6 inches (13 picas) wide and 280 lines deep, 7 such columns making a page. The small tabloid size newspaper column has a width of 2 inches (12 picas). These are 5 columns to the page, each column being 203 lines deep.

The ideal system of rates is one which guarantees a uni-

---

[3] The term "display" is an obliging hat-rack upon which many meanings are hung. At your leisure look up "display" in the index and study back its different uses.

form charge to all advertisers, regardless of where they are located, how much advertising they do, or how often they insert their advertisements. A number of papers follow this principle and offer a uniform "flat rate" to all advertisers. This plan is not universal, however, for the same considerations of discounts are held to prevail in selling space as in selling merchandise.

Many publications adjust their rates on a sliding scale, the cost per line decreasing as the *quantity* increases. Others offer a scale of rates which decreases with the *number of times* the advertisement is inserted. The former is known as a "quantity" discount, the latter, as "time" discount. Thus a newspaper rate card on a quantity basis appears as follows:

*If the advertiser uses within one year*        *Space is billed at*

| | |
|---|---|
| Less than 1,000 lines | ........32c per line |
| "Base" rate "open," "transient," or "one-time" rate | |
| More than 1,000 lines but less than 5,000 lines........ | 30c per line |
| More than 10,000 lines but less than 15,000 lines........ | 26c per line |
| More than 10,000 lines but less than 15,000 lines........ | 26c per line |
| More than 15,000 | ........24c per line |

According to this schedule, an advertiser using less than 450 lines within the contract year pays 32 cents per line. If he uses more than 1,000 lines in a contract year, but less than 5,000 lines, he pays 30 cents per line for the space he does use; more than 5,000 but less than 10,000 lines, 28 cents, and so forth. For 1,800 lines he would be billed at the 1,000-line rate, since such an amount has not yet earned the next best rate for 2,000 lines, while for 8,500 lines he would be billed at the 5,000-line rate.

The contract year begins with the insertion of the first advertisement.

As an alternative to quantity discounts, time discounts, such as the following, are offered by some newspapers:

| *Quantity Discounts* | | | *Time Insertion Discounts* | | |
|---|---|---|---|---|---|
| Open Rate | .....11 | per line | Open Rate | ....,...11 | per line· |
| 1,400 lines per year | .....11 | per line | 4 times per year | ......105 | per line |
| 2,500 lines per year | .....09 | per line | 13 times per year | ......10 | per line |
| 5,000 lines per year | ....085 | per line | 26 times per year | ......095 | per line |
| 10,000 lines per year | ....08 | per line | 52 times per year | ......09 | per line |
| | | | 78 times per year | ......085 | per line |
| | | | 104 times per year | ......08 | per line |

And here is the rate card of another paper showing how the sliding scale works:

| Quantity Discounts | *per line* | Time Insertion Discounts | *per line* |
|---|---|---|---|
| Open Rate | .....39c | Open Rate | .....39c |
| 2,500 lines within one year | .....37c | 13 times within one year | .....37c |
| 5,000 lines within one year | .....34c | 26 times within one year | .....34c |
| 10,000 lines within one year | .....31c | 52 times within one year | .....29c |
| 20,000 lines within one year | .....28c | 156 times within one year | .....28c |
| 30,000 lines within one year | .....25c | | |
| 40,000 lines within one year | .....23c | | |
| 50,000 lines within one year | .....21c | | |

When an advertisement is to be inserted in a newspaper, a space is ordered the exact size of the advertisement, as for example, 50x1 (read 50 on 1, or 50 by 1, meaning an area 50 agate lines deep by 1 column wide), 140x3, or 303x4, as the case may be. If rates are quoted in inches, the space is ordered by column inches, as 10 inches x 4 columns.

The short rate.—If the advertiser plans to run a number of advertisements, he anticipates the total amount of space he may use within a year, and makes a contract for that space, either on a quantity basis or on a time basis, whichever is less expensive. Space for all his advertisements is then billed, as the advertisements appear at that contract rate. If, at the end of the year, the advertiser has not used all the space he contracted for, he has to make an adjustment for the space which he *did* use, according to card rate. The difference between what he already paid and the higher card rate which he is now obliged to pay is known as the "short rate." Space contracts may be compared to contracts made by users of electricity with electric power companies. There is a sliding scale of rates to take care of all consumers, from the private family to the large industrial company. The user is billed at the fixed rate only for the amount of current actually used. If an advertiser expects to run 15,000 lines the coming year in a publication, and enters his order at 24 cents per line, he is billed at that rate. Should he use only 11,420 lines, he would not be entitled to the 15,000-line rate of 24 cents, but to the next rate (10,000-line rate, at 26 cents). He would consequently have to pay the difference between 26 cents a line and 24 cents for the space he did use. Thus:

```
11,420 lines at 26c per line would cost...........................$2,969.20
For this space he paid only 24c per line or........................ 2,740.80
                                                                   ──────────
He now has to pay the difference or a "short rate" of..............$  228.40
```

A "long rate" is the amount which may be rebated to the advertiser for having earned a better rate (reaching a higher-quantity mark).

A paradoxical situation may arise whereby an advertiser has to pay a short rate if he does not use any further space, but has to pay less if he continues to advertise.

> Assume that the advertiser has contracted for 15,000 lines at 24c per line.........................$3,600
>
> Of this he uses only 14,500 lines which would not entitle him to the 15,000 line rate and for which he would have to pay at the 10,000 line rate of 26c, or 14,500 lines at 26c per line .................................$3,770
>
> If, however, he would run 500 lines extra, he would earn the 24c rate and would have to pay only.........$3,600
>
> Thus by running 500 lines space, and completing the 15,000 line contract he saves....................$170

The foregoing short rate condition may exist when an advertiser does not thoroughly understand the short rate system. One of the first things an advertising man should do in undertaking work for a firm which has already issued space contracts, is to study them all to see what short rate situations, if any, prevail.

**Special rates: preferred positions.**—There is, naturally, competition among advertisers for favorable positions in the paper. The basic rates give the advertisement "run-of-paper" position—anywhere in the paper which the publisher deems best. If the advertiser wishes to be assured of choice position, he may be able to secure it by paying "preferred-position" rates—just as he may purchase grand-stand seats at the ball game instead of buying admission to the bleachers. Certain pages are regarded as preferred positions—such as the front page, back page, and editorial page, when advertising is permitted in the two latter places. Some men's-clothing advertisers seek the sports page, while an advertiser of beauty preparations may desire to appear on the women's page. As

## Record of Position

A RECORD KEPT BY THE CHECKING DEPARTMENT
This department carefully scans each newspaper in which an
advertisement appears and records the above information.
Magazine advertisements are similarly checked.

a paper increases its number of pages. such positions become
more coveted.

The various positions which an advertisement may occupy
on the page itself differ in value. Among the "preferred positions" for which an extra charge may be made are the following:

1. Next to reading.—This means that the advertisement
is to adjoin the editorial reading matter or news text of the
paper.

2. Following reading.—In this case, the advertisement has
the editorial matter above it or below it.

3. **Full position.**—Or next to and following reading matter. Else entirely next to reading at the top of a column.

4. **Top** (of column) surrounded by reading.

5. **Top** (of column) next to reading.

6. **Bottom** next to reading.

An advertisement which occupies the two facing center pages is known as a double-page spread (or "double truck") for which a handsome premium must generally be paid.

Buying preferred positions is an expensive procedure, though it is often found to be thoroughly worth the cost. It may be unnecessary to order such a position if the advertisement is of a character or size which will dominate the page (as an advertisement 11 inches by 4 columns on a 20 inch by 7 column page). Another aid in securing good positions on a run-of-paper contract is to have the advertisement adjoin a preferred-position space. In forwarding the advertisement, it is often helpful to mark on the accompanying order: "Such-and-such position requested" or "Please insert in blank position if possible." It is not wise in regular orders to say, "Blank position only," or "Must appear in certain position," for the latter expressions are equivalent to an order for preferred position, to be billed as such. It can readily be appreciated why publishers are so strict in their requirements, for they strive to satisfy as many as are consistently possible and at the same time to be fair to all.

**Special rates: "classifications."**—Newspapers, especially those in large cities, often maintain a special column, page, or section devoted to certain industries and interests of their readers. A special "classification" rate may then be offered to advertisers who wish to appear there. These sections may be devoted to automobiles, music, hotels, real estate, and so forth.

**Special rates: "reader" advertisements.**—Some publications allow advertisers to have their copy set up in the same type style as the news matter. Such advertisements are run right after the news columns, followed by the abbreviation "Adv." A higher rate is imposed for these advertisements than for the regular run of paper position.

Special rates: foreign and local advertising.—Originally, the sources of newspaper advertising were the local merchants. When concerns outside of the town began advertising, the publisher had to establish representatives in large cities and had to install more elaborate methods of handling the advertisements —all of which involved extra cost. Accordingly, many papers inaugurated two sets of rates: one for local advertising, the other for national advertising—general or "foreign," as it is called. Foreign advertising (not to be confused with foreign-language advertising), is that purchased directly or indirectly by a non-resident manufacturer or distributor. Local advertising is that actually paid for by a local resident or establishment. The double system of rates has been the subject of considerable discussion, being considered by many as decidedly unfair. But the question as to whom it is unfair to is not so easily settled. In recent years, there has been a very healthy tendency to equalize rates. A survey among newspapers shows that approximately 55 per cent of the papers carry equal local and foreign rates; 30 per cent have higher national rates than local; and 15 per cent have higher local rates than national.

This discrepancy is a great problem to outside advertisers in figuring rates in a campaign. If the advertiser expects to share the cost of advertising with his dealer, that fact may boost the rate. The difficulty offered by the double-rate system, and the suspicion of one advertiser that another one is securing a better rate because of it, tend to antiquate this policy. However, it must still be taken into consideration when planning a schedule.

The milline rate.—In calculating the cost of space in newspapers and in magazines also, two factors enter—the rate per line and the quantity circulation of the respective publications. These two variables make it difficult to compare the actual costs of advertising in the several media. Of two newspapers, each charging 10 cents a line, the one with 15,000 circulation would, in truth, be twice as expensive as the other with 30,000 circulation. For although the rates per line are the same, their circulations differ.

Since no two publications will have the identical rate or circulation, the advertiser is constantly obliged to decide between two alternatives, each with a different set of dimensions. The milline rate, an ingenious creation of Benjamin Jefferson, is a unit for comparing space costs, representing the cost per line of space in a publication which has one million circulation. If a publication has several thousand, or several million circulation, its rate can still be measured in units of a milline, just as the cost of a dozen oranges can be determined if the cost of one is known. The milline can be calculated by the simple formula of:

Quantity circulation : rate per line :: 1,000,000 : x

or

$$\frac{1,000,000 \times \text{rate per line}}{\text{quantity circulation}} = \text{milline.}$$

as shown in these problems:

What is the milline rate of a publication having a rate of $5 per line, with a circulation of 500,000? The answer is:

$$\frac{1,000,000 \times 5}{500,000} = \$10, \text{ the milline rate.}$$

What is the milline rate of a publication with a $5 rate and a circulation of 2,000,000?

$$\frac{1,000,000 \times 5}{2,000,000} = \$2.50, \text{ the milline rate.}$$

What is the milline rate of a newspaper with a circulation of 250,000, charging 50 cents a line?

$$\frac{1,000,000 \times .50}{250,000} = \$2 \text{ per milline.}$$

A newspaper has 20,000 circulation and charges 20 cents a line. What is the milline rate?

$$\frac{1,000,000 \times .20}{20,000} = \$10 \text{ per milline.}$$

The milline provides a uniform basis of comparing costs by fixing one of the variables in estimating. It reveals that the newspaper at 50 cents an inch may be more expensive than the paper charging 50 cents a line; that the magazine charging $5 per line may be every bit as economical, as far as quantity of circulation per dollar is concerned, as is the publication whose rate is $50 for an entire column.

The milline does not endeavor, however, to pass upon the comparative value of two different media as far as the desirability of their audience is concerned. It simply places the computation of space rates on a comparable basis, and it does this remarkably well.

**How the space is ordered.**—The placing of an advertisement in a newspaper may involve two steps: first, the signing of a contract agreeing upon the rate (the space contract), and second, the forwarding of the advertisement itself, with an order definitely requesting insertion (the "insertion" order).

When it is not expedient to send engravings and copy with layout instructions, the advertisement may be forwarded either in the form of an electrotype or of a matrix. If no plates are to be used, the advertisement may be taken care of by sending copy and layout. This material is accompanied by an insertion order which states usually:

Date of order.
Name of advertiser.
Publication.
Date or dates upon which advertisement is to appear.
Size (in lines and columns).
Position.
Rate.

It may also tell:

Whether proof is required before insertion.

How advertisement is being shipped—whether material is being sent directly from the advertiser's office or whether the newspaper is to procure it from a neighboring publication.

How to set up or insert the advertisement.

Directions for forwarding checking copy and bill. (A checking copy is an issue of the paper bearing the advertisement, and is sent to the advertiser for his records.)

**Closing dates.**—An advertisement has to be in the publisher's hands before a given "closing date" or "closing hour." The closing time is the latest at which an advertisement will

## Insertion Instructions

Publisher:                                          DATE:

Please insert advertising as follows for

and charge in accordance with contract now in your possession. Unless otherwise noted issues containing advertisements must be sent to *client* and to *this office.*

ISSUE:                          SIZE:

TITLE:

AD. NO.:                        CUTS:

EDITION:                        KEY NO.:

POSITION:

REMARKS:

PROOFS MUST BE SUBMITTED TO US FOR O. K. BEFORE INSERTION

ENCLOSURES:
COPY
LAYOUT
PROOFS

[HOUSE/ORDER] **No._____]**

AN INSERTION ORDER

be accepted for publication in a given issue. It is of the greatest importance that the advertising man know what the closing time for a paper actually is, and get the advertisement in well ahead of it. The early advertiser often gets the choice run-of-paper positions, and his copy also receives more careful attention in the composing room.

**Placing the order through a special representative.**—A local advertiser may be able to walk into the office of a newspaper and hand in his advertisement himself, but a national advertiser has an entirely different task. He may either make a list of all the newspapers he wishes to use and forward an order to each, or he may place his order through the special representatives whom publishers maintain in several of the large advertising centers. One such representative may be the agent for a large number of newspapers in different cities, and the advantages of his services are manifold in the arranging of schedules and contracts. The chief advantage of such service, however, is the fact that the advertiser deals with a few representatives instead of a multitude of offices.

Syndicate sections.—Newspapers in a number of cities may receive supplements and special parts already printed by a syndicate service to which they subscribe. This practice is followed particularly in Sunday magazine sections. The advertiser here deals only with the syndicate publisher or representative in making schedules and contracts, often being entirely relieved of all detail of forwarding and checking.

In small towns, a newspaper may receive a page of editorial matter and advertisements sent as a mat from another form of syndicate. The reverse side of this page and the rest of the paper is filled in by the local publisher with whatever news he wishes. In such cases the advertiser deals only with the news bureau which issues the "boiler plate." This method permits an advertiser to cover a host of small towns with one insertion.

Further customs and suggestions on rates.—Where the rates of a paper are entirely flat, no initial space contract may be necessary. The insertion order bears both the contract and instructions for space.

A short rate provision is not allowed if the contract for space is explicitly marked "Non Cancellable," or if it contains an equivalent clause. The advertiser is then obligated to pay for the full amount of the space mentioned, whether or not he uses it. Otherwise, a "contract for space" is an agreement on rates only. The "short rate" is not figured until the end of the contract year. But the space that has been actually used during the month is billed at the end of each month at contract rates.

When an advertiser agrees to use space on a time basis, namely, so many advertisements a year, his contract will specify the minimum size of advertisement acceptable under the agreement. Usually this is 14 lines x 1 column. The advertiser maý wish to run heavily on some days, while easing up on others. He must not, of course, entirely skip an insertion date, but on "light" days he can conserve his space by running the minimum-sized advertisement allowable—known as a "rate-holder."

A "full-run showing," for which some papers grant a discount, means that the advertiser offers to use as much space in the given paper as in any other paper in that city, the papers being confined to morning or evening publication, as the case may be.

A morning and evening, or Sunday, paper, issued by the same publisher, may be offered at a lower "combination rate" if the two papers are used in conjunction with each other.

A morning newspaper may get out an edition the previous night for mailing to out-of-town subscribers. This is known as the "bull-dog" edition. It is the edition which an advertiser may miss if he does not get his copy and order in on time.

**Further customs and suggestions in ordering space.**—It may be desired to have an advertisement set up in type, ready to run in a newspaper, pending a decision on the exact date. An order known as a "wait order" may then be sent through. It authorizes the newspaper to set up the copy and hold it in readiness for the insertion date. If, however, a newspaper receives a wait order for an advertisement which is not run (within 30 days, as a rule), it may charge the advertiser for the cost of composition.

Some newspapers set up all advance advertisements in which insertion orders have been given before touching the wait orders. Others follow the opposite procedure, setting up wait orders first. It is advisable that a local advertising man determine what the practice of a paper is, so that he may know the quickest way whereby he can secure proof of an advertisement.

Several newspapers in the same city may have a reciprocal agreement whereby one supplies a matrix of the advertisement to the others in which the advertisement is also to appear. This means a saving of time and money to the advertiser, who would otherwise have to issue complete instructions to all of the publications concerned.

An advertisement is often sent with instructions to continue running it until orders to discontinue are issued. This is known as a "till-forbid" order (abbreviated, t. f. order).[4] It is extensively used in classified advertising. When a till-forbid order has been placed, the important thing to remember is that a till-forbid order has been placed.

The appearance of a newspaper is spoken of as its "make-up." The papers maintain certain regulations in this connection. One is that no jet blacks be used in mass, such as an engraving with large black areas. The various papers either define what they regard as too black or maintain the right to determine for themselves whether or not an advertisement appears objectionable. Where such restrictions prevail, it is better for the advertiser to gray down his own plates. Then, at least, he will know how the advertisement is going to look.

To prevent the use of freak-sized advertisements, which cause difficulty in arranging or making-up the paper, publishers require that advertisements have a depth in proportion to their width. One typical newspaper requires that a single-column advertisement be 14 lines deep, but that a two-column advertisement must be at least 28 lines deep, three columns, 50 lines deep, 4 columns, 75 lines, and five columns, 100 lines. Six, seven, and eight-column advertisements must use up the entire 148 lines. An advertisement approaching a full-page depth may be required to occupy the full column, as the remaining space would be of little use for other purposes.

A few newspapers base their rates on advertisements completely set up, charging extra for composition when the latter is necessary; but in most cases, the copy will be set up by the publisher without extra cost. The choice of type faces is, of course, limited, and the effects obtainable vary greatly with the papers themselves.

As an accommodation to advertisers, newspapers may provide the art work and make the plates, including the additional expense in the customer's bill. It is essential in all cases that the advertiser understand at the outset what the rates and charges are to be.

---

[4] "T. f." is also used in printing to indicate the copy is "to fill" a certain space.

**Newspaper supplements in colors.**—The magazine sections of Saturday and Sunday newspapers appearing in colors, and the feature editions in the gala tones, are printed usually either from 2, 3, or 4-color line plates, or Ben Day line plates with a halftone key plate. This part of the paper is of course not dependent upon last-minute news for the editorial and news columns. The printing alone takes longer than does that for the black and white sections; hence the forms close well in advance of the publication date—six weeks being the average. The cost of space is higher than it is in the regular sections of a paper.

Color, especially in a newspaper advertisement, secures quick attention because of its contrast. The colored section itself stands apart from the rest of the paper. The amount of advertising which it can carry is limited, which accounts for the fact that an individual advertisement secures very choice showing when it appears in this section of the newspaper.

**Newspapers: special copy requirements.**—The life enjoyed by a copy of a newspaper is literally a short one. Some copies last the duration of a car-ride. Others may last a week, or a month. The average expectancy of life, as the insurance men would say, is one short day. Therefore, an advertisement in a newspaper must tell its story at the first reading—almost at the first glance. Copy should be concise. If it is not brief in measure of words, it should be so pithy that the reader will not notice its length. The sentences should be short. Their action should be kept moving almost as swiftly as the message of a telegram.

News is the merchandise of newspapers. For it the readers buy the paper. Because of it, they will read the advertisements—if those advertisements tell something new about a product, or give the reader a new thought about it. As a measure of comparison, it is interesting to see if the first three statements in a piece of copy are as interesting as the first three statements in the feature news article on the first page.

Newspaper advertising reaches prospects in a definite locality. Hence the copy can be directed squarely to the conditions and interests which prevail in that particular section. The advertiser is spared the need for generalizing about conditions and events.

**Newspapers: special layout requirements.**—Newspapers are printed by means of high-speed presses on coarse stock. Drawings for the advertisements should therefore be of a sharp, bold nature. Details in the illustrations must not be so fine as to be mashed in stereotyping, or so close to each other as to fill-in when inked. To avoid disappointment when the advertisement is finally published, it is extremely important that all lines in the illustration be kept simple, clear, and open, and be drawn to a scale no larger than twice the desired size.

The general use of photographs for halftones in newspapers should be avoided, but if any are to be employed, they ought to be 65-line screen and retouched for severe contrasts of black and white. The engraver should be told to etch deeply, burnish and tool liberally. Quartertones are a well suited form of engraving to use for photographic effects. Matrices of line plates are good to use, but matrices of halftones should not be used. Advertisers can also learn good lessons from the newspaper editorial illustrations, for which halftones are used very skillfully in combination plates, with plenty of line-cut boldness.

**Newspaper merchandising departments.**—A valuable service is rendered by newspapers through their trade information bureaus known as "Merchandising Departments." The function of these departments is to help the out-of-town or "national" advertiser co-ordinate his sales work with the newspaper advertising in that particular territory. Originally, such departments confined their efforts to making an analysis of the local population, serving, as it were, to introduce the inhabitants to the advertiser so that he, in turn, could intelligently introduce his product to them. Upon this idea, elaborate departments have been developed. Just how they may help the advertiser is indicated by the statement of one leading department—that of the *Indianapolis News*—which says:

"Here are the things the merchandising department will do for any one other than an idle curiosity seeker:

"1. Furnish you accurate and up-to-minute statistics on general conditions, number of retailers, etc., of Indianapolis and the Indianapolis Radius.

"2. Make an accurate investigation of conditions in this market as they pertain to the particular product whose sale you are planning to promote. This will not be a general survey, sent to all your competitors, but will be a specific survey made for you and with confidential information for you.

"This market analysis will include:

—distribution of your product and competing products.

—analysis of number of brands carried by retailers.

—comparative volume of sales per store of your product and competitors.

—retail prices, range and average price of each brand for all sizes of your product and products of competitors.

—study of private branded, unlabeled, or bulk competing lines.

—determination of biggest selling size or product.

—specific information on dealer attitude or criticism of sales policy found in making survey.

—attitude of wholesalers if product is handled through them.

"3. On request the department will work a suggested sales plan for territory.

"4. On entering the market, the advertisers will be given help in organizing a crew of salesmen. When a campaign is placed on a non-cancelable basis, portfolios of the advertising with a letter of introduction to the trade will be furnished.

"Complete route lists of all kinds of retailers are kept up to date at the merchandising offices. In many cases, as with department stores and chain stores, the names of the different buyers will be furnished.

"In addition, there is in the merchandising department a veritable gold mine of information about business in this market, for instance, the number of salesmen traveled by every wholesaler, the approximate number of retailers on each wholesaler's books, and how to cover principal towns of the Indianapolis Radius with train connections. There's hardly a question of this nature which can be asked that cannot be

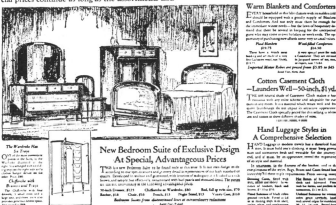

A VIBRANT PAGE

The illustrations for this full-page newspaper advertisement were clearly made for line-plate reproduction. The text is arranged in easily read units. The length of the lines is in keeping with the size of the type. The elements are set off with neat headlines and initial letters. The spacing between the sections is good. Every part of the advertisement is inviting.

answered from the systematized information gathered and collated by a force of trained merchandising experts working in the market for more than five years.

"The merchandising department does not believe that it can serve all News advertisers fairly and equally if it:

Sends out letters to the trade gratis.

Strives to secure display windows.

Prints broadsides gratis.

Sells merchandise.

Gives out highly confidential information promiscuously.

Misleads any one in order to secure advertising."

The statement defining the work which this merchandising department will not undertake to do touches upon the practices regarded unfavorably, but offered by some overzealous merchandising departments who go beyond the pale of news-gathering bureaus into the province of selling. After all, selling is a job for those who make a job of selling; the merchandising department of a paper serves best by providing the real, unbiased facts of the market reached by its paper. An advertiser does well if he makes use of these data.

Foreign-language newspapers.—In the United States, there are approximately 150 daily newspapers printed in foreign tongues; there are about 900 other foreign-language publications appearing, semi-weekly, weekly, bi-weekly, or monthly. Over thirty languages are represented, including Albanian, Arabic, Assyrian, Bulgarian, Chinese, Danish, Dutch, and French; German, Greek, Italian, Japanese, Norwegian, Portuguese, Russian, Spanish, Swedish, and Welsh. The total net circulation reached by this group of media is estimated at 8,000,000 people—an enormous market possessing many opportunities.

The advertisements have to adapt themselves to the tongue, mannerisms and habits of these readers, both in copy idea and visualizing idea. American manufacturers who successfully advertise in foreign countries will go to any amount of trouble in fitting their advertisements to the people. Equal care must be taken in speaking to the foreign language market within our own gates. Advertising space in foreign language publications is usually obtained through the special representatives of the foreign language press. These offices are also equipped to advise upon the appeal and layout requirements for the respective publications. They also translate the copy for the press, arrange the schedule, and supervise the checking of the advertisements.

**The Audit Bureau of Circulation (The A. B. C.).**—At the very heart of any plans for advertising in publications is the question of circulation. Just who gets the paper, and how many readers are there? The advertiser is entitled to know the character and amount of circulation just as surely as he is entitled to see that his advertisement appears in the size of space he specifies. Through the work of the Audit Bureau of Circulation, the A. B. C., as this body is called, an advertiser knows exactly what circulation he is paying for; he may also be confident that he gets all he is entitled to. The A. B. C. covers magazines as well as newspapers, in both Canada and the United States. Although numerous worthy periodicals are not members of the Audit Bureau of Circulation, an advertiser can regard with confidence the circulation statements issued by those publications which do belong to this great organization.

## Chapter XIII

# MAGAZINES

A TRAVELLER journeying around the country sees at all railway stations important enough to have newsstands, the identical magazines on display. He again sees the publications in the homes of the towns visited. He finds not only those periodicals but the very articles advertised in them—a tribute to the magazine's monumental influence in welding innumerable groups of people, each with its own customs, usages and preferences, into a nation of buyers asking for beans of the same brand, cooked in kitchen-ware of the same trade-mark, which in turn is scrubbed with a cleanser whose can bears the same tireless maid in blue chasing herself around its label. The magazines have helped make the whole continent, even the globe itself, the market for the manufacturer whose horizon of sales hitherto had been confined to his local province.

**General magazines: characteristics.**—Magazines are not published with the frequency of newspapers, but their contents retain their editorial freshness longer. Their line cost is higher, and as a rule they are read more thoroughly and enjoy as a medium a longer life.

The magazine permits the use of the finest reproducing effects known. Most magazines use fine screen halftones; nearly all of them have facilities for using colors. But because of the mechanical work involved, advertisements for magazines must be ready well in advance of the closing date, the time required varying from three weeks to three months.

**Space and rates.**—According to the frequency of their issuance, magazines are divided into quarterlies, monthlies, semi-monthlies, and weeklies. It is well to note that a weekly appears 52 times a year and in connection with this fact, 26 insertions and 13 insertions are frequently mentioned.

The usual sizes of magazines are:

Standard Size...........5½ inches × 8 inches type: 112 lines to column, 2 columns to page.

Flat Size................7 inches × 10⅙ inches type page: 143 lines to column, 3 columns to page.

Large Size .............9⅞ inches × 12⅛ inches type page: 170 lines to column, 4 columns to page.

*The Century Magazine* is typical of the standard size, *Good Housekeeping* of the flat size, and the *Saturday Evening Post* of the large size. The flat size has been growing in favor.

When a half-page is ordered in a magazine, it is necessary to know whether the page is divided horizontally, into upper and lower halves, or vertically, into right-hand and left-hand divisions.

The contract and insertion-order procedure employed for newspaper advertising is also used in magazines. Space is mostly sold by the page and fraction thereof. Contracts are usually issued on a definite insertion basis, rather than on a blanket quantity order. Thus, an advertiser will offer to take a certain number of full pages, half pages, or a given number of insertions of whatever other size is specified. In trade papers the practice still prevails of ordering space on a quantity basis, namely, contracting at a 12 full-page rate, the space being used up in 12 full-page insertions, 24 half-page insertions, 48 quarter-page, or whatever schedule is desired.

Most magazines have a minimum space ruling, requiring that all advertisements be above a given size. The smaller advertisements are usually placed towards the back of the book. The larger publications have also enforced a minimum insertion ruling, whereby a weekly magazine, for instance, will sell space only to advertisers who place an order for 13 insertions or more, to be run at regular intervals during the year. Such a provision tends to stabilize the sale of the publication's space. The outstanding reason advanced for its enforcement is the protection of dealers from the misleading claim of "We are advertising heavily in the Blank Magazine," when in fact that company has inserted only one small advertisement. The publications also declare that this proviso enforces a consistent advertising plan resulting in sounder advertising. Some advertisers, on the other hand, regard this stipulation as a form of coercion, and resent the so-called dictation from the publisher's office. However, an advertiser always has the option of omitting a medium if his policy does not coincide with the publisher's terms of contract.

The non-cancellation clauses are necessarily strict in magazines. The advertiser contemplating the use of these publications must therefore definitely plan his schedule well in advance. Compared with the practice in newspapers, this feature tends to make a campaign very rigid, but it is for the very purpose of such rigidity that advertising in magazines should be employed.

Special rates—preferred positions.—The front cover itself is known as the "front cover page." The page formed by the reverse side of the front cover is known as the "second cover page." The inside of the back cover is similarly described or else as the "third cover page." The back cover is referred to as the "fourth cover page."

The pages opposite the second and third cover pages are referred to respectively as the page facing the second cover and the third cover. The page facing the first reading matter and the page following the reading matter (the first advertisement to appear in the back section of the magazine) are considered choice positions. Other positions also may be regarded as preferred, according to the individual magazine. Some advertisers buy the same respective preferred positions in all their magazines during a campaign or over a number of years. This, for instance, was done for Big Ben, which was advertised on the page facing the second cover. Similarly, Campbell's Soup enjoyed the first page following reading matter, and Old Dutch Cleanser the outside cover.

The color pages of many publications are not always printed along with the black-and-white pages, but are run off separately and then inserted. These pages are called "colored inserts." Orders for pages in color are invariably non-cancellable.

New York, N. Y.    **Home Standard**

Monthly
Rate Card No. 2
Issued Oct. 12, 19
In Effect Nov. 1, 19

*("Standard Rate Card" Form. Specimen Card No. 2.)*

**1—GENERAL ADVERTISING**

*a.* Per line agate . . . $5.00
*b.* Time discounts, none.

*c.* Quarter page, 170 lines, $800.00
Half page, 340 lines . . 1,600.00
Full page, 680 lines . . 3,200.00

*d.* PREFERRED POSITIONS

Per Page
2d cover, 2 col. or black  $3,600.00
3d cover, 2 col. or black   3,600.00
3d cover, 3 or 4 colors .  4,000.00
4th cover, 2, 3 or 4 col.   5,500.00
Inserts, when available,
2 colors . . . . . . .   3,600.00

*e.* Minimum size of advertisements, 7 lines.
*f.* Orders specifying positions other than those known as "preferred positions" are not accepted. No cancellation accepted after the 1st of second month preceding date of issue.

**2—CLASSIFICATIONS**

Per line agate
*a.* Publishers . . . . . $4.50

Real Estate . . . . $4.50
Schools and Colleges . . . 4.50

*b.* Advertisements in "Classifications" must not exceed 100 lines.

**3—READING NOTICES**    (Not accepted)

**4—COMMISSION AND CASH DISCOUNT**
*a.* Agency commission 15 per cent.   *b.* Cash discount 2 per cent.

*c.* Cash discount date 20th of month following date of issue.

**5—MECHANICAL REQUIREMENTS**

*a.* Size of plates: All cuts intended for full column width must measure 2¼ in., dbl. col. 4⅝ in.
*b.* Depth of column 175 lines.
*c.* Four columns to a page.
*d.* Center double page, 12½ in. deep x 19¼ in. wide.

*e.* Page, type space, 12½ in. deep x 9⅓ in. wide.
Half page (two columns), 12½ in. deep x 4½ in wide.
Quarter-page, 6⅛ in. deep x 4⅝ in. wide.
*f.* Closing Date – 1st of second month preceding date of issue; for

example: for October number on August 1st.
*g.* To insure the best printing supply original halftones – not electrotypes – 120 screen.
*h.* Original zincs necessary.
*i.* Register marks must appear on all plates for more than 1 color.

**6— CIRCULATION**
*a.* Member of A.B.C.
*b.* Character of circulation: "Household."
*c.* Locality of circulation: national, largely in small towns.
*d.* In circulation 15th of month preceding date of issue.

| *e.* Date of Statement | For Period Ending | Circulation |
| --- | --- | --- |
| . . . . . . . . . . . . . . . . . . | . . . . . . . . . . . . | . . . . . . . . . . . . . . . . . . |
| . . . . . . . . . . . . . . . . . . | . . . . . . . . . . . . . . . . . . | . . . . . . . . . . . . . . . . . . |

**7—MISCELLANEOUS**
*a.* "Stock-selling" advertising not accepted.
*b.* Established 1890.
*c.* Subscription: $1.50 year.

*d.* Also publish "Cookery Journal." No combination rates.
*e.* "Domestic World" consolidated with this publication in 1916.
*f.* Publishers: Thompson Pub. Co. 400 Fourth Avenue, New York.

William Smith, Pres.
John Wilson, Vice-Pres.
Thomas A. Jones, Advg. Mgr.
Mrs. Harriet Thompson, Editor
John B. Johnson, Manager.
Peoples Gas Bldg., Chicago, Ill.

*f Prepared in conformity with "Standard Rate Card" of American Association of Advertising Agencies)*

AN ADVERTISING RATE CARD

A rate card as used by a publisher. The information regarding charges for space is arranged according to uniformly numbered classifications.

**Magazine merchandising and service departments.**—The merchandising collaboration offered by magazines consists mainly of marketing surveys. These reports range from a statement concerning circulation distribution by states to a detailed report on the buying habits of the readers. The magazines of specialized interests are in a position to render surveys which are particularly concrete and informative. In addition, they may be of aid in creating the idea for the advertisement. A moving-picture magazine, for example, may arrange to have an actress pose as a model for its advertisers; a technical magazine may discover an unusual engineering feat performed by the advertisers' product; a millinery trade paper may bring two advertisers together, having one make the hat of the material created by the second. This service is not the function of the merchandising department strictly speaking. Among magazines of special interests, where this aid is particularly helpful, a service department may exist to extend aid in this direction. Or the work may be in the hands of an enterprising space solicitor.

**General magazines: copy requirements.**—In preparing copy it should be remembered that a general magazine is one going to readers whose specific or definite interests are unknown. Included in this category would be readers of such periodicals as the *American Magazine, Collier's,* the *Literary Digest, Liberty,* and the *Saturday Evening Post.* An inspection of this representative list will show that the general magazines may have definite editorial character, as the inspirational tone of the *American Magazine,* the breadth of the *Literary Digest,* and the worldly activity which permeates *Collier's* and the *Saturday Evening Post.* But while the magazines may have a definite editorial personality, their appeal is such that almost anyone can read them. A composite picture of their readers would include all types of people, in all walks of life, and in many by-paths of the journey. These publications are distinctly general magazines.

It would appear an easy task to write copy for general publications. Yet, care must be observed to present ideas which will be of interest to the greatest number of readers.

Then, with regard to the choice of language, provincialisms and colloquialisms should be avoided, for they may not be popularly accepted in all parts of the country. The copy speaks to a huge mixed audience. Hence its language should be simple, clear and explicit. If, however, the advertising of products appearing in general magazines be directed to a specific group of these readers, the copy may become more technical in choice of language (as in the case of an industrial belting advertiser in the *Saturday Evening Post*).

General magazines: mechanical requirements.—Magazines require the advertiser to furnish plates to meet the exact dimensions of the page. Some publishers are very stern in rejecting plates which are over-size even by 1/16 of an inch. A few are equally as strict with under-size plates. Publishers will set up an advertisement if copy is sent to them before the closing date. Copy must be in before the first forms close, in order to secure proofs which may then be revised. All copy coming in after that time, but before final forms close, will go to press without having a proof submitted for O. K. Proofs may be secured, however, for filing purposes if instructions are given: "Send proof for files." When sending in an advertisement, it is best to have it in complete plate form or in lead-mould electrotype.

Before the advertiser sends in the advertisement, he may have his own printer run off several thousand copies for use as reprints of the advertisement, to be sent to dealers or salesmen. Where the magazine sets up the advertisement or where color plates are used, reprints may be ordered from the publisher at a nominal charge.

General magazines of specialized interests.—Among the general magazines there are many which confine themselves to special activities. The reader of such a publication identifies himself as being interested in its particular field. *System, Physical Culture, Radio World, House Beautiful, Harper's Bazaar,* and *Golf Illustrated* are examples of this type.

These publications constitute one of the forms of media used for "cream" campaigns, in which it is desired to reach certain groups of people, regardless of location. The rate per thousand circulation of these magazines is higher than that of the general media, but for many products they reach an audience which includes less waste circulation than do general magazines. (Waste circulation is that which an advertiser gets by going into a medium reaching people for whom the advertisement is not intended.)

In these publications of specialized interest, copy has an exceptional opportunity to adapt itself to the readers, both in substance and in tone. An advertisement for paint could talk in a different vein to readers of *Popular Mechanics* from that in which it would address subscribers to the *House Beautiful*. Shoes would have one story for the readers of *Physical Culture* and another message for those of *Harper's Bazaar*. The extra work involved in preparing separate advertisements for different class [1] magazines is more than offset by their effectiveness.

**Women's magazines.**—The scope of women's magazines can be regarded as wide as the entire province of women's interests. The growth of women's magazines from their "kitchen paper" aspect to their present high character is a true reflection of the broadened fields of women's endeavor. To this development the magazines have helpfully contributed. They have earned for themselves a place as intimate advisers to their readers, moving their decimal point of valuation as a medium far to the right.

Edward Bok has expressed the belief that the general interests of women will merge more and more with those of men. A careful reading of any current issue of a woman's magazine reveals the present wide scope of topics considered —so wide, in fact, that men as well as women find topics of interest. One advertiser in the *Woman's Home Companion* received 64 per cent of his replies from men, and 36 per cent from women. Granting, however, that this was an exceptional case, and that the chief interests of such magazines are directed to women themselves, it should be recognized by adver-

---

[1] A class magazine in its strict sense is one going to a particular class of readers. This term is also used in connection with the technical and trade papers.

tisers that such publications cater to readers whose chief interests are the conduct of the home and the welfare of the family.

**Women's magazines: copy requirements.**—The editorial columns of a woman's magazine are helpful, practical, and pleasing. It would be well to embody, where possible, the same spirit in the advertisements. Direct or indirect ways in which the product may be used are invariably of interest. If vanilla sauce is being advertised, it is better to show what can be done with the sauce than to glorify its merits in adjectives.

Women are observant—particularly in all matters relating to the home. Hence the data and illustrations should be authentic. An advertisement quickly loses the confidence of its readers if they discover a single detail to be erroneous. Pictures, especially, are subject to scrutiny. When a hostess expects guests she will spare no pains to have everything "just so." The advertisement should be prepared with equal care, for it invites all the readers to come in and look around, which they do, as the advertiser is quick to discover if his advertisement is especially good, or if it portrays a breach of etiquette. For instance, a food advertiser pictured a family at the table, with the mother serving the youngest child first. The advertiser was actually reprimanded by a number of readers for his lack of knowledge of family propriety. Another advertisement pictured a housewife working over a washing machine in her afternoon frock. "Foolish young housewife," say the readers when they behold such a picture, or "Ignorant old advertiser." In either case the damage has been done, for anything which detracts from the message itself tends to destroy the effectiveness of the advertisement.

**Farm publications.**—Two-fifths of the population of the United States is agricultural, according to the Department of Agriculture, whose records show that 54 million people live in cities of 2,500 and over. They represent 51.4 per cent of the entire population. Nine million people (8.5 per cent) live in incorporated villages of 2,500 and less, *while 42 million (or 40.1 per cent) live outside incorporated villages,* mostly on farms. This fact conveys some idea of the importance of the market of buyers to be found in the small town and on farms. This market has a character distinct and apart from that of the big city. It has its media, generally referred to as "farm papers," which are suited especially to the interest of its people.

**Farm papers of geographical interest.**—Farm papers may be grouped into those of geographical interest, those of vocational interest, and those of general farm interest. The magazines of geographical interest devote themselves to the problems of farmers of a given section of the country, such as the *Gulf States Farmer*, the *Montana Farmer*, the *Missouri Ruralist*, the *Pennsylvania Farmer*. Readers of these publications have respectively similar interests regarding local crops and welfare. Consequently such magazines are often chosen for zone campaigns in agricultural districts.

**Farm papers of vocational interest.**—Among farm papers of a vocational character may be mentioned the *Breeders' Gazette, Poultry Herald, Wheat Growers' Journal*. These publications have a somewhat different aspect from those referred to in the previous group, in that they are primarily devoted to a particular phase or type of farming, rather than to a definite geographical territory. Accordingly, they are employed for "cream" campaigns.

**Special copy requirements.**—Copy in the farm papers of geographical or vocational appeal must be specific in the sense that it should aim to devote itself to the particular kind of farming in which the reader is engaged. It must recognize the particular nature of its reader's farm and the character of his land. On the subject of automobile trucks, a different presentation would be offered to growers of livestock than to producers of wheat and corn. A farmer in a hilly country would make different demands upon a truck than would a farmer in a flat country, while one making long hauls would be confronted by problems unlike those of the farmer whose journeys to market cover short distances. Hence, it is advisable to divide the farm market for an agricultural product

FARM-PAPER ADVERTISEMENT

This is based on a good understanding of the actual conditions confronting the farmer. The idea is developed in a logical, intelligent way and presented in a clear style.

into as many different characters as possible. Then address each separately.

The laws of work, patience, and cause-and-effect are implanted upon the farmer as upon man in no other endeavor. Consequently the farmer becomes a stolid, logical, steady-moving individual. His copy should reason with him, using straightforward logic simply expressed. It should show what the product has done and for whom. Trial offers, guarantees, testimonials, and references are accorded close attention.

The illustrations in these publications must likewise be authentic in detail. Cattle at the market receive no closer scrutiny than do pictures of cattle in the advertisements. The mode of dress is likewise examined in the advertisement; it too changes with the geography and character of the farm. The same critical attitude will be present when it comes to the construction of buildings. On a dairy farm, for instance, the silo adjoins the barn itself, but on a farm which raises beef cattle, the silo is located in an open place. These details make it evident that farm paper advertisements require a technical portrayal of exceptional accuracy.

**Farm papers of national interest.**—Leaving the magazines of provincial and vocational appeal, we come to the farm paper of national interest—such as the *Country Gentleman, Capper's Farmer, The Farm Journal, Successful Farming,* and *The Farmer.* These publications are in reality home papers with a national following among farmers. They are founded upon the same principles as the general magazines which are identified with the large city. In fact, they are directed to similar interests of enlightenment and entertainment, differing only in their background.

National farm papers with home interests talk to a man when he is in a frame of mind different from that in which he reads the latest crop reports and stock prices. National farm papers also talk to women. If the influence of the automobile, the radio, the introduction of power machinery, and the advent of scientific farming are considered, the reason will be recognized why the modern farm home is as modern in many of its appointments as is the town home. The advertisement must recognize the interests peculiar to the farmer and his

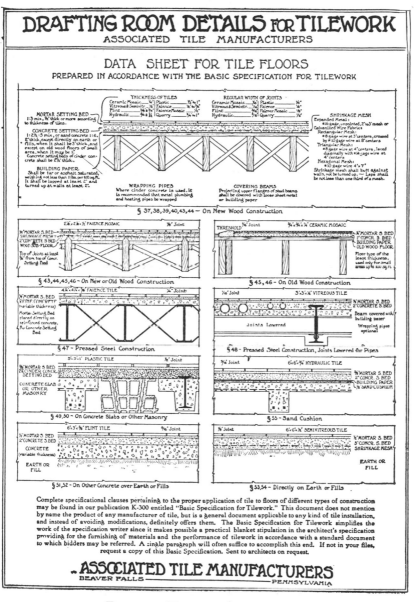

TECHNICAL MAGAZINE ADVERTISEMENT

Designed to be read by the architect. Gives useful information in a manner easily recognized by its intended reader. The same product advertised to a prospective home-buyer would require an entirely different treatment.

family, but it must also appreciate the similarity of the farmer and his aspirations to that of men in other walks of life. *It is well to remember at all times that, though a person may be regarded as one of a group, he still retains the emotions and reasoning power of all other people. His preference as one of a group may dominate his actions. His feelings as an everyday human being may determine them.*

**Technical magazines.**—A man who is actively engaged in a profession, occupation, or vocation can keep informed of the latest developments and news through the journals published in that field. For this reason technical magazines hold an important place among magazines, technical papers being those directed to the engineering-production phase of industry, or to a profession, and differing from trade papers whose readers are essentially interested in the re-sale of commodities. Typical publications among the technical magazines are the *American Machinist, Automotive Industries, The Iron Age, The Mining Congress Journal, Power, The National Petroleum News, Textile World Journal,* and *Oral Hygiene.*

Sloan and Mooney [2] have skillfully analyzed the peculiar features of technical advertising as follows:

1. *In the case of the buyers:*
    a. Buying influences are generally males.
    b. Buying influences are intelligent and critical.
    c. The buying attitude is not a personal attitude, but is a function of a psychology of the industrial or commercial group to which the buyer belongs.
    d. In general, the buyer who can use a product to economic advantage has the money with which to pay for it.

2. *In the case of the market:*
    a. The distribution of the market has no inherent relation to the distribution of population.
    b. The total number of buyers is comparatively small.
    c. The character of one market for a particular product may be entirely different from the character of some other market for the same product.
    d. The character of the market is peculiar to the product to be advertised in that market.

---

[2] "Advertising the Technical Product," by Sloan & Mooney.

e. The character of the market is often determined by the particular *use* to be made of the product.

3. *In the case of the advertisements:*

a. The advertisements depend, in selling the product, exclusively on its utility and economic advantages.

b. The advertisements have peculiarities in form and substance in relation to the peculiar conditions prevailing in the case of the buyers and of the component markets to which the product is being advertised.

4. *In the case of media:*

a. The comparatively small number of buyers, and the peculiar factors that define the distribution of these buyers, demand an entirely special application of the principles of choosing mediums.

**Technical papers: copy requirements.**—The use of these publications offers a splendid chance to picture clearly the man to whom the advertisement is addressed. He has an analytical, logical mind. Have the advertisement give facts. He has the skepticism of the scientist, combined with that of the purchasing agent. Hence the advertisement should give abundant proof and specific details. Testimonials bear unusual weight. They should be used liberally. Records of performance are very acceptable evidence. They should be given in figures or, better, in photographs. To show the product in use is invariably effective in technical advertisements.

**Technical magazines: service departments.**—It is so difficult for an outsider to adjust his copy to a particular industry that many papers have a service department which translates the layman's idea into one appropriate for the publication. These helpful departments gather their facts from the advertiser, from their own experience and files, or from field surveys. With this information they present the subject in a way which will be of interest to the reader. The value of this work, however, diminishes when the department puts all copy into the same hopper and grinds out stock advertisements. This service should therefore be evaluated according to its facilities to acquire all necessary data, and then upon its willingness to exercise creative ability.

# Buying through the wholesaler vs. buying direct

*This simple example in, turnover is one of the strongest arguments your salesmen can give to retailers*

## "Example in Turnover"

### INK, PASTE and MUCILAGE

Typical dealer outlet 12 gross yearly.  Average list per gross $15.00

| BUYING DIRECT<br>184% Profit<br>☞Discount 50%<br>*Buys 6 gross twice yearly*<br>*Two turnovers* | | BUYING of WHOLESALER<br>480% Profit<br>Discount 40%☜<br>*Buys 1½ gross 8 times yearly*<br>*Eight turnovers* | |
|---|---|---|---|
| Cost per gross | $7.50 | Cost per gross | $9.00 |
| Multiplied by | 6 | Multiplied by | 1½ |
| Permanent investment | 45.00 | Permanent investment | 13.50 |
| Multiplied by No. of turnovers | 2 | Multiplied by No. of turnovers | 8 |
| Yearly purchases | 90.00 | Yearly purchases | 108.00 |
| Sells 12 gross $14.40 | 172.80 | Sells 12 gross $14.40 | 172.80 |
| Cost | 90.00 | Cost | 108.00 |
| Profit | 82.80 | Profit | 64.80 |

Or $45.00 (investment) divided into $82.80 (profit) equals 184% profit on in-. vestment.

Or $13.50 (investment) divided into $64.80 (profit) equals 480% profit on investment.

## BUY THROUGH YOUR WHOLESALER

Point out also to the dealer that buying through the wholesaler releases the difference between $45.00 and $13.50 or $31.50 free capital that he can invest in other lines.  He profits all around. This is made possible by the Le Page's Signet policy of full protection to the jobber and by our plan which allows the jobber to compete successfully with the direct selling manufacturers.

**RUSSIA CEMENT CO.**
*Laboratory and Factory,*
GLOUCESTER, MASS.

---

TRADE-PAPER ADVERTISEMENT

Addressed to the retail jobber.  The advertisement concerns itself with the profits to be made in selling the article rather than with its inherent merits.  Strange as it may seem, this manufacturer's advertisement encourages the merchant to buy through the wholesaler rather than direct from the manufacturer.

**Trade papers.**—The trade paper [3] is the "business press" —resembling the technical paper in scope, differing only in the interests of those whom it reaches, namely, merchants and those engaged in the selling end of business. Representative publications in this classification are the *American Grocer, The Automobile Trade Journal, The Boot and Shoe Recorder, The Dry Goods Economist, Drug Topics, The Hardware Merchants' Trade Journal.*

The trade paper is directed to the first line back of the buying line—the dealer. His endorsement of a product is comparable to enlisting the aid of a whole sales staff. His lack of acceptance of a product, or even his non-committal attitude towards it, may ruin the best-laid plans of advertising.

**Trade papers: copy requirements.**—The dealer is engaged in business principally for the resale of products. Hence his chief interest in reading a trade paper is to learn of better ways of selling goods and of better goods to sell. A retailer is not swept away by the grandiloquence of the advertiser, who invites him to participate in a stupendous national effort to impress the glory of the product upon the nation or to make the housewives of the world happy. But the merchant is anxious to learn how he can better serve his customers and realize greater profit. "What is your product?" "Will it sell?" "What are you doing for me to make it sell?" "What profit is there in it for me?" "How can I be sure of all this?" "When can I get it?" These are the questions the dealer asks.

Good copy for trade papers devotes itself to answering these queries. The product should be described in specific terms of the trade. In showing that it *will* sell, the advertisement should prove, if possible, that the product *has* sold, citing the circumstances of such sale.

"What are you doing to make it sell?" is usually answered with a portrayal of the advertising campaign conducted. Very often the advertisements in the trade papers reproduce the consumer advertisements appearing in a national publication, telling the dealer in effect that these advertisements will help him sell his goods. It is desirable, in such a procedure, to em-

---

[3] Also known as a trade magazine or a trade publication.

phasize the local effect of whatever advertising is being done by a manufacturer.

An unusual transforming idea or local advertising plan provides good "meat" for trade paper copy.[4]

Where direct orders are solicited, descriptions should be complete. Sizes, styles, pattern numbers, grades, colors, and similar data which the dealer would wish to know before ordering should be included. Where prices are given, terms of payment are also necessary. Are they net cash, 2 per cent 10 days, 8 per cent 30 days, or what?

The service departments in this field are similar to those in the technical field. As in the technical paper, the main advantages they offer is a knowledge of the problems and needs of their readers.

**Directories and other publications.**—Practically every profession, trade or industry will have its own directory. Some directories confine themselves to a restricted field, such as a list of insurance companies; others embrace a host of classifications, telling whether a name indicates retailer, jobber, manufacturer; if retailer, the size of the store; if jobber, the variety of goods handled; if manufacturer, just what type of goods are produced. The amount of information obtainable from a directory is surprisingly large. One directory alone lists over 47,000 trade classifications and gives several names under each. The value of such a reference book to a buyer is evident. Its usefulness as a medium is accordingly important. Copy in directory advertisements confines itself to describing the type of work in which the advertiser specializes, or else to brief specifications of his product.

There are other forms of media in the field, among which theatre programs deserve special mention. All have their clientele, each its usefulness. That advertiser is wise who recognizes the individual qualities of each and lays his plans accordingly.

---

[4] As described in Chapters XIX and XXI.

## CHAPTER XIV

# ARRANGING THE SCHEDULE

AFTER the advertiser has selected the publications which he wishes to use, he has to prepare what is known as a space schedule. A local retail advertiser may determine the size of his advertisement the day before it is to appear, but a national advertiser, that is, one whose advertisements appear in cities other than his own, or whose advertisements direct inquiries to dealers, must plan his undertaking well in advance. Indeed, it is common to find advertisers anywhere from two months to a year in mapping out a schedule consisting of:

1. A list of the media to be used.
2. Dates upon which the advertisements are to appear (insertion dates).
3. Exact size of the advertisements.

**Newspaper schedules.**—In a simple campaign, we may have one paper, which we shall call the *Morning Dispatch*. Assuming that an advertisement is to appear in it daily for one week, omitting Sunday, the sequence [1] of appearance could be charted as follows:

| Paper | MON. | TUES. | WED. | THURS. | FRI. | SAT. | V = days on which adv. runs |
|-------|------|-------|------|--------|------|------|------------------------------|
| MORNING DISPATCH | V | V | V | V | V | V | |

CHART 1

---

[1] For purpose of illustration, all days are here considered of equal value; all papers of equal importance and of the same rates. In actual practice, however, schedules are arranged in accordance with the importance of the days and circulation of the paper.

Assuming, however, that it is desired also to include the *Evening Gazette* without doubling the appropriation, the schedule of the two papers could be synchronized or "staggered," as in Chart 2, to obtain the greatest effectiveness.

| Paper | MON. | TUES. | WED. | THURS. | FRI. | SAT. | V = days on which adv. runs |
|-------|------|-------|------|--------|------|------|-----------------------------|
| MORNING DISPATCH | | √ | | √ | | √ | |
| EVENING GAZETTE | √ | | √ | | √ | | |

CHART 2

The "staggered" schedules in the selection of media and insertion dates can be worked out to include all the papers in a campaign as indicated in Chart 3.

| Paper | MON. | TUES. | WED. | THURS. | FRI. | SAT. | L = Large adv. S = Small adv. |
|-------|------|-------|------|--------|------|------|-------------------------------|
| MORNING DISPATCH | L | | S | | L | | |
| MORNING STAR | | S | | L | | S | |
| EVENING GAZETTE | S | | L | | S | | |
| EVENING NEWS | | L | | S | | L | |

CHART 3

**What is the cost?**—The cost of a proposed schedule can be ascertained by determining the total number of lines of space considered advisable, and then figuring the line cost of that space in the respective media. Suppose, for instance, it is planned to run three advertisements a week, each 150x3 (150 agate lines deep by 3 columns wide), in the papers whose rates are given as follows:

```
Morning Dispatch..................................22c per line
Morning Star ......................................25c per line
Evening Gazette ..................................20c per line
Evening News .....................................28c per line
```

Then, the number of insertions times lineage times rate per line equals the cost of space, or:

> *Morning Dispatch*
>     3 × (150 × 3) × 22c = $297.00
> *Morning Star*
>     3 × (150 × 3) × 25c = 337.50
> *Evening Gazette*
>     3 × (150 × 3) × 20c = 270.00
> *Evening News*
>     3 × (150 × 3) × 28c = 378.00
>     Total cost of space    $1,282.50

The schedule may be calculated reversely by a second method, extensively used in figuring the size of the advertisements for insertion in a single medium. Here the appropriation divided by the rate per line equals the number of lines. Thus, if an appropriation of $270 was made for advertising in the *Evening Gazette,* whose rate is 20 cents per line, the advertiser would receive a total of 1,350 lines of space.

**What size of advertisements?**—This space could then be used in any of the following arrangements:

```
 1 advertisement  ...................225 x 6
 2 advertisements ...................225 x 3
 3 advertisements ...................150 x 3
 4 advertisements ...................112 x 3  (6 lines surplus)
 5 advertisements ................... 90 x 3
 5 advertisements ...................135 x 2
 6 advertisements ...................112 x 2  (6 lines surplus)
24 advertisements ................... 56 x 1  (6 lines surplus)
48 advertisements ................... 28 x 1  (6 lines surplus)
96 advertisements ................... 14 x 1  (6 lines surplus)
```

It will be seen that a given amount of space may be used in varying quantities. Experience shows that no hard-and-fast rule can be laid down, the policy adopted depending entirely upon the requirements of the individual advertiser. The advantage of the different schedules, however, can be compared as in Chart 4, which represents the fundamental arrangements of advertising according to their size and sequence.

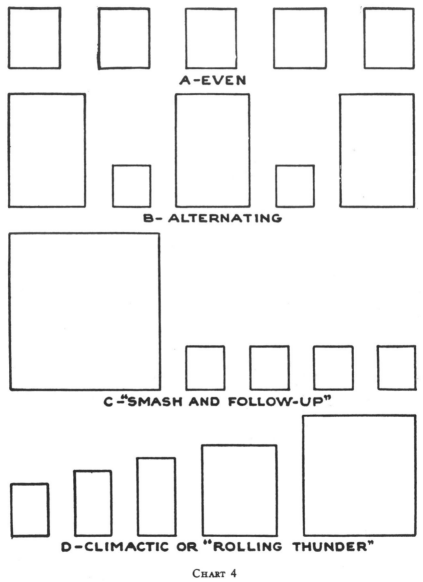

A-EVEN

B- ALTERNATING

C -"SMASH AND FOLLOW-UP"

D-CLIMACTIC OR "ROLLING THUNDER"

CHART 4

METHODS OF DIVIDING A GIVEN AMOUNT OF
SPACE IN A SCHEDULE

A series of advertisements, each of the same small size as those in Series *A*, gives a steady, persistent, uniform effect, while an alternating arrangement, such as exists in Series *B*, gives some of the advertisements greater prominence. To gain this prominence, the space of the intermediate advertisements is reduced in size. The effect is a blow, follow up; blow, follow up; blow, follow up. The third arrangement, Series *C*, makes just one crashing blow which blazes the way for a series of smaller advertisements. The climactic sequence, Series *D*, works up to a point which serves as the grand entree for a campaign or an event.

The arrangements just described may be likened in effect to the various kinds of gunfire—rifle, machine gun, or heavy artillery, depending upon the impression the advertiser desires to make. Contrary to the military analogy, however, it is not always wise to try to enlarge upon the competitor's plan, better results often being possible by adopting one entirely different.

**Magazine schedules.**—The method of staggering advertisements, extensively used in magazine campaigns, is shown by the following schedule of advertisements for a food product to appear in three women's magazines.

MAGAZINE SCHEDULE*

|            | Oct. | Nov. | Dec. | Jan. | Feb. | Mar. |
|------------|------|------|------|------|------|------|
| Magazine A. | 1   | ½    | ¼    | 1    | ½    | ¼    |
| Magazine B. | ½   | ¼    | 1    | ½    | ¼    | 1    |
| Magazine C. | ¼   | 1    | ½    | ¼    | 1    | ½    |

\* Bold Figures indicate color pages.

CHART 5

It will be seen that each magazine carries the same total amount of space, and that a full page advertisement appears each month in one of the publications. Since the appropriation provides for four four-color pages, these are staggered over October, November, January, and March. At the time of this particular campaign, it is deemed best to omit color in the December issues, since they are so well provided with color pages that greater contrast can be secured by using black and white.

Copy and plate schedules. —The different advertisements of a campaign running in several publications do not necessarily require a different piece of copy for each publication with corresponding new illustrations. To make the change would often be uneconomical both in work and plates involved, and in the employment of the ideas created. The advertisements for an extensive campaign to appear in several media are created somewhat in the following manner: The media are chosen, and the schedule is drawn up, a series of key advertisements being prepared. This key series may consist of all the advertisements for the leading medium only, or else it may consist of all the largest-sized advertisements in a campaign, that is, all those which will occupy full pages. Layouts and copy for these key advertisements are then prepared, serving also as guides for the other advertisements. If all the layouts are of the same size, the task may be simply to order an additional set of electrotypes. Where the sizes vary, however, the key advertisement is reduced to the specified dimensions of the other ads. Smaller plates are ordered and the copy is rewritten and condensed. Thus in the campaign presented in Chart 5, a different advertisement is to appear each month in three different sizes, the schedule requiring a total of only six different advertisements in three sizes each.

The desire for simplicity in the layouts of any campaign may now be fully appreciated. Uniformity of standing pictorial detail—whether a picture of the package, trade-mark, or name plate, is advantageous both to the layout man and to the man who pays the bills.

The chief requirement of a newspaper campaign which is to run in conjunction with one in a magazine is that the illustrations be drawn suitable for reproduction on newsstock. Usually the newspaper layout will have less detail, and this statement applies not only to the number of elements contained but to the accessories shown in the pictures themselves. Magazine copy for newspaper use is condensed and introduced by some idea of current news interest whenever possible.

In planning a large campaign, a series of newspaper advertisements will be created to appear just about the same time that similar advertisements are released through the magazines—one set of media thus supporting the other. In following this procedure, it is necessary to time the newspaper schedules to meet the dates upon which the magazines appear on the newsstands.

**Planning the work.**—In the advertising office, all work is timed in accordance with the closing dates prescribed on the publishers' rate-cards. These closing dates vary considerably. The terms in which they are expressed likewise vary. Day, week or month "preceding" means preceding the publication date. By way of example, if the publication date of a periodical is Saturday, November 1, we read on the rate-cards as follows:

|  | *Which means that* |
| --- | --- |
| *Weekly magazine* | *the closing date is:* |
| *A* closing 3 weeks preceding . . . . . . . . . . . Saturday, Oct. 11 | |
| *B* closing Tuesday preceding . . . . . . . . . . . Tuesday, Oct. 28 | |
| *C* closing 3rd Thursday preceding . . . . . Thursday, Oct. 16 | |
| *D* closing 15 days preceding . . . . . . . . . . Thursday, Oct. 16 | |
| *E* closing Saturday, 5th week preceding . . Saturday, Oct. 4 | |
| *Monthly magazine* | |
| *A* closing 25th of 2nd month preceding. . Thursday, Sept. 25 | |
| *B* closing 1st of month preceding . . . . . Wednesday, Oct. 1 | |
| *C* closing 30th of month preceding . . . . . Thursday, Oct. 30 | |
| *D* closing 25th of 4th month preceding . . . Monday, July 25 | |

Morning newspapers usually close the final advertising forms about 6 p. m. of the previous day; evening newspapers, about 9 p. m. of the preceding day. Sunday papers close the various sections at different times. The magazine section, for instance, may close 3 to 6 weeks preceding publication, and the first news section at 10 a. m. the preceding Saturday. To memorize the various closing dates is not necessary, but to consult the rate-card well in advance and carefully note the closing date for a given medium is most important.

**Timing the work.**—In order that creative work and mechanical work may move with the necessary precision, a time schedule is planned. The closing date is the zero hour toward which all calculations are based. Knowing when the complete material must be delivered, the advertiser works backwards

# PRODUCTION ORDER

Client:　　　　　　　　Product:　　　　　　　Req'n:
Medium:　　　　　　　Issue:　　　　Size:　　　　No. Colors
　　　　　　　　　　　　　　　　　Title:
　　　　　　　　　　　　　　　　　Ad. No.:

## PRODUCTION SCHEDULE　 JOB No.____

|  | DUE DATE | DATE MET | REMARKS |
|---|---|---|---|
| Establishment of Idea |  |  |  |
| O.K. of Idea, if necessary |  |  |  |
| Rough Sketch (Estimate $____) |  |  |  |
| Copy |  |  |  |
| O.K. (Rough, Copy and Estimate) |  |  |  |
| *Finished Art Work |  |  |  |
| *Client's O.K. |  |  |  |
| *Engraving |  |  |  |
| *Type Setting |  |  |  |
| *Client's Final O.K. |  |  |  |
| *Electrotyping |  |  |  |
| *Delivery to Publisher |  |  |  |

*These dates established by Mechanical Department when making out order. All other dates established by Production Manager.

Estimate $____ Rough $____ Outside $____ Inside $____ Revise $____

A PRODUCTION SCHEDULE

This form is for use in planning the preparation of an advertisement. The date when it is due at the publishers is first entered (near bottom in form). The date when electrotype is due is next filled out and so on up the column. The work of the entire organization is thus scheduled.

along the calendar, determines when the material must be shipped, when electrotypes of the finished advertisement must be in, when the advertisement is to go to the electrotyper. To be able to ship the type, set-up and plates at a given time, the final O. K. on the advertisement must be secured sufficiently well in advance to permit any changes which become necessary. The dates are then set on which copy and plates are to go to the typographer's; final draft of copy must be ready, plates must come from the engraver, drawings go to the engraver, drawing must be O. K.'d, rough sketch must be ready, layout must be ready, and work on layout and copy must be begun. To take an actual illustration showing how the work is timed:

Advertisement to appear in the *National Monthly*
for ................................... November

The rate card says *Forms Close* 23rd of 3rd
month preceding ...................... August 23

Which means that, according to the time required
for mailing or expressing, the complete advertisement should leave no later than ........ August 19

Obviously, the finished electrotype should be
ready by ............................. August 18

The material for this electrotype (the type set up
and original plates) should go to electrotyper on ............................. August 15

The type set up should be ready sufficiently far
in advance to allow any revises necessary, or. . August 8

The engraving, to be sent to typographer for
set-up, with type should be ready by ........ August 1

The O. K.'d drawing is to be sent to the engraver
by ................................... July 25

Which means that the artist should have his drawing in by ............................. July 18

And rough drawing in (depending on amount of
work necessary. About 3 weeks time is allowed
in this instance) ....................... June 25

Copy and layout should likewise be ready for O. K.. June 25

Which means that creative work should begin
(depending upon individual working on idea). . June 10

In this problem, electrotype of complete advertisement was sent. If the advertisement were to be set by the publication, however, sufficient time would have to be allowed in which to submit proofs to the advertiser. Rate-cards often give two sets of closing dates, one known as "first closing," at which time all advertisements requiring proof must be in, and the other known as "final closing," when all material must be in. Closing date as used in the foregoing instance refers to the final closing date.

The brunt of catching closing dates is usually borne by the engraver and the printer, but the grossest slip-ups in schedules invariably occur in the creative departments; therefore, the time allowed to them should allow for the revisions and changes which are bound to arise in the conception of an idea.

The schedule has to be arranged with enough flexibility to suit the organizations preparing advertisements. Of course, in the case of an advertisement for a weekly magazine, with a closing date ten days previous to the time of publication, the entire schedule would have to be proportionately compressed. In a newspaper advertisement, the work would pass along with even greater dispatch—six hours from idea to O. K.'d proof, if necessary.

In undertaking the preparation of advertising, the important thought to bear in mind is that the work should be so planned, that sufficient time should be allowed the different steps of preparation, and that adherence to the time schedule at every stage of the work is the only assurance of comfortably meeting the closing date.

## CHAPTER XV

# DIRECT-MAIL ADVERTISING

ONE hundred seventy-one nationally known advertisers were asked to state the forms of media in which they would increase their appropriations for the year following, and the media in which they would increase their expenditures. One hundred seven planned to use direct-mail advertising, and 103 of these decided to increase their appropriations for the use of this medium. Any form of advertising which gains favor so thoroughly with its users must offer some unusual virtues—and this one does.

**Untwisting tongue twisters.**—In advertising three terms are often used in a confused sense—direct advertising, direct-mail advertising, and mail-order advertising. *Direct Advertising* is generally known as "circular work," such as letters, leaflets, and folders. Stating it exactly, it is "any form of advertising reproduced in quantities by or for the advertiser and by him or under his direction, issued direct to definite and specific prospects through the medium of the mails, canvassers, salesmen, dealers, or otherwise." [1] *Direct-mail advertising* is that form of direct advertising which is sent through the mail. It is a specific branch of the direct advertising family of which it is the most important, most common, and best known member. If a leaflet is handed out by boys, it is direct advertising; if it is sent through the mail, it is direct-mail advertising—the subject to which this chapter is devoted. *Mail-order advertising,* however, is an old hybrid in the ranks. It represents that method of selling whereby the entire sale is consummated through advertisements and correspondence without the aid of a personal salesman. It is not an advertising medium but employs media such as newspapers, magazines, and direct-mail

---

[1] "Effective Direct Advertising," by Robert E. Ramsay, p. 5.

advertising in its work. Mail-order advertising and direct-mail advertising should be clearly distinguished.

The list.—Direct-mail advertising is based on the names of prospects, or the "list." The term "list" used in describing this compilation, leads one to believe that lists are a ready-made selection of names, which can be bought by the yard like so much gingham or silk, and that all the advertiser has to do is to state what his article is and ask for a list of prospects. There are firms which sell lists, but what they really sell is their ability to gather names of various classes and types of people. Some of the concerns specializing in this field can well advise an advertiser as to what type of names would constitute a suitable list for him. It is the advertiser's burden, however, to determine exactly who his prospects are and what type of person he wishes to place upon his list. Once he has thought this out, he usually finds it possible to compile this list at little expense.

Building the list.—The qualities desirable in the list are: (1) Potentiality of buyers; (2) recency of the record; (3) accuracy of information; (4) completeness of information; (5) avoidance of duplication. The effectiveness of any direct advertising is limited at the outset by the degree to which the people on the list are logical prospects for the product advertised. What would it avail an advertiser to send booklets on world cruises to those who could not afford this luxury, to tell a small retail grocer the advantages of a three-ton truck, or to describe the "satisfaction of making your own clothes" to the woman who is too busy with her modiste to answer her correspondence? The first demand of any direct-mail list is that it shall include only those who are in a position to adopt the idea advertised.

As a list grows in size, the matter of extending credit becomes of increasing importance. The advertiser must look further than the immediate orders, and see that his profit will not be eaten away by poor collections. In a survey conducted by the Class Journal Company among 66,000 automobile dealers, it was found that:

40% had no credit rating (Group A).

20% received credit from their jobbers only (Group B).
40% were rated (Group C).

Of these:

The 40% in Group A had   5% of the buying power.
The 20% in Group B had 15% of the buying power.
The 40% in Group C had 80% of the buying power.

Advertising directed to this list of dealers indiscriminately would be spending 40 per cent of its effort on a group worth only 5 per cent of the advertiser's attention (Group A). From this 40 per cent, the greatest number of initial inquiries would undoubtedly be received, but with this 40 per cent there would be the greatest difficulty in collecting the money. Were the advertising to address only the 40 per cent who were rated (Group C), it would reach 80 per cent of the market. Orders would not be as numerous, but once obtained, payments would be fairly well assured. An analysis of any proposed market will often reveal a similar condition.

The second quality of a good mailing list is that it be in present good health. A list which represented excellent prospects a few months ago is very likely to suffer from changes because of time and circumstances. A list is by no means a fixed quantity, for the needs of people are constantly changing —the people themselves dying with the regularity of insurance statistics.

The third quality desired of a list is that it be accurate. An expensive drain is placed upon many direct-mail advertising campaigns through errors in the address, such as the misspelling of the name of the recipient, or the town. Often the inaccuracy is the result of indefinite information such as Miss for Mrs. and vice versa. Corporation and company names are of little value unless some one person in them can be addressed. Where the name of an individual is not known, the device is usually resorted to of addressing the letter to the attention of some official or department head, as "Purchasing Agent," "Chief Engineer," or "Comptroller," as the case may be.

A fourth quality necessary in any good advertising list is that it be complete. The original list should bear any data which may enable the advertiser better to classify the prospects when the list becomes large and it is desired to subdivide it by groups. The post office address should likewise be given in full.

The final quality of a list is that it be free of duplication. Assume you have an article—paper stock, let us say, that you wished to sell to printers, engravers, lithographers. You duly secure directories listing each of these trades. Each directory in itself may be entirely free of repetition, but if the names in one directory were matched against the other, it would be found that many printers are listed under two, or even three classifications. In building any list from separate sources, caution should be taken so that the names differ, and not merely the capacity in which those people are regarded.

**Securing the names.**—The opportunities for directly obtaining the names of prospects are often so obvious that they are completely overlooked. Present and past customers usually form the best nucleus for a direct-mail advertising program. Also, it may be possible to have the salesmen send in names and addresses of prospective buyers. Another method employed in building up lists is that of watching trade and newspaper clippings for the names of persons who would be interested in the product. Engagement announcements, as an illustration, are a prolific source of names for furniture houses and for insurance agents. Incorporation announcements provide names for office-fixture concerns, while newspaper announcements that a new family has established itself in a community provide an opportunity for local merchants to build up their list. Notes of transfers of property, listings of stockholders in corporations declaring dividends, and lists of maturing mortgages secured from the local register of deeds, provide sources of names for automobile dealers. Then there are the opportunities afforded by directories issued by trade-papers and trade associations as well as by convention rosters, membership lists of commercial, professional, and social clubs, rating books and the classified sections of telephone directories.

Governmental records, if recent, may be fruitful. These records include the Federal reports issued by the respective

Departments of Commerce, Labor, and Agriculture; State and county lists giving tax, incorporation, and industrial data. Municipal records of licenses and permits which have been issued may prove valuable.

No easy solution to all list problems is offered by directories and records; to obtain them is only half of the story. The hard part is to determine what the prospects have in common so that they may be found listed together. In many cases the direct-mail list has to be built up by advertising in periodicals, inviting those readers who are interested to write for further information. Some idea of the extent to which this practice is followed may be obtained by examining current magazines.

The practice of exchanging lists is also followed by advertisers who are in non-competing but allied lines, such as a malted-milk firm and a soda-fountain concern. Each advertiser, by this arrangement, sends his material, ready to mail, to the other for addressing. Another resourceful way of building up a list is that of discovering some names which are easily available in some other field, but which indicate that the people should be good prospects for the given proposition as well. Lists of farmers with automobiles of good make, for example, indicate good prospects for tractors and farm electrical plants.

In buying a list, it is well to determine the age and the source of its information. A simple way in which to judge the accuracy of a directory list is to look up in that list names in a town with which you are thoroughly familiar and then see how close the directory coincides with the facts as you know them. Another way is to use a part of the list on a test mailing, and watch the results. (The method of handling tests is described at a later point.) As a guiding rule, the less thought necessary to secure a name, the less that name is worth for advertising purposes. The ease with which it can be secured invites use by advertisers who give more advertising to their readers than thought to their advertising. Care, diligence, and resourcefulness in compiling a list pay handsomely in any direct-mail work.

**Installing the list.**—Once the names are gathered it is frequently necessary to subdivide them. If only a part of the

list is to be used in any work, classification makes it possible
to choose the desired names. Among the groupings possible,
the following represent some which are most commonly
utilized:

| | |
|---|---|
| Alphabetical. | By credit rating. |
| Geographical. | By buying season. |
| By size of towns. | By frequency of purchase. |
| By departments. | By size of purchase. |
| By lines of business. | By equipment. |

Though lists are spoken of and dealt with as such, it is always well to remember that each name represents a live and
human prospect, not just another name. The successful direct
advertiser always retains his conception of the prospect as an
individual, avoiding the pitfall of regarding the list as a part
of the furniture and fixtures.

Maintaining the list.—It is very important that a list be
kept in a live condition by immediately noting upon it any
changes of data which may occur. After a mailing, a number
of pieces of direct advertising may be returned by the post
office unclaimed. This information should immediately be
checked against the master list, which should also be corrected
from reports coming through the salesmen, or through the
regular information channels of the trade. Large users of
direct advertising scour their lists regularly, separating the
active names from the inactive, prodding the latter until they
are aroused to buy or are proved to be advertisingly dead.
Eternal vigilance is truly the price of a good list.

The forms of direct-mail advertising—letters.—The most
frequently used form of direct advertising is the letter. It
is the first medium to be adopted by many advertisers because
every business house has the facilities and the occasion to use
letters.

Sales letters in quantity may be individually typed, "multigraphed," prepared on automatic typewriters and reproduced
by similar processes. Inserting the salutation of a letter is
known as "filling-in." Instead of going to the expense of
having each letter "filled-in," many advertisers run a caption

across the top of their letters making such fill-in unnecessary.[2]

There is admittedly some prejudice against the use of letters which are reproduced in quantities to represent typewritten letters because "anyone can tell that they are form letters." True enough, but what of it? It is a mistake to believe that letters in quantity endeavor to fool the reader. When printing was first invented, it was hushed up for fear that people would discover that handwriting was being "imitated." The fact was that printing was a new development, and when it was recognized as such it reached its true usefulness. Similarly, the person who thinks process typing is useful only as a surreptitious imitation of hand-typing is likewise overlooking the real significance of this method. People are used to reading advertisements, whether those advertisements appear in periodicals or in their mail. If the copy and message is properly directed to them, they do not even consider the fact that others are likewise reading similar news. Since the distinguishing advantage of the letter is that it can apply itself specifically to the individual reader, the burden of having a "personal touch" is essentially that of the contents. The mechanics of the letter—the reproduction, the fill-in, and the signature serve their purpose if they appear so neat and so appropriate that the reader doesn't pause to notice them. He knows they are there, and goes on to read the letter itself.

**Leaflets.**—A leaflet consists of a single small size sheet, printed on one or on both sides, and folded once. It is an economical form, highly versatile for insertion in a letter or package. If it is to be used in envelopes, the leaflet should be designed to fit the two standard size envelopes:

> No. 6¾ whose size is 3⅜ inches x 6½ inches.
> No. 10    whose size is 4⅛ inches x 9½ inches.

A leaflet must overcome the obscurity of its small size through excellence of copy, visualization, layout and typographic effect. If the leaflet is used to supplement a letter, the letter will bear a timely or personal note to the reader, while the leaflet carries details, specifications and other amplifying data.

---

[2] Multigraphed letters, filled in with the prospect's name and address, may be mailed under third class mail if 20 or more such letters are sent at one time.

**Folders.**—A folder is a grown-up leaflet, usually larger in size, of heavier stock, and with its sheet folded more than once. The variety of folders is endless, but most folders have one trait in common, in that they seek to be read and acted upon at once. Their size permits the telling of a complete sales story.

In selecting the best size of folder to use, it is of importance to learn whether or not the folder can be cut economically from the standard size sheets of paper. In arranging the folds, it is well to keep the idea simple. The copy and illustrations should be arranged so that a person opening the folder in a natural way will be able to follow the copy from part to part easily, as the folder is being opened.

**Broadside.**—A broadside is an enlarged folder, usually about 19"x25" in size, or larger. It is used to give the "smashing" impression of a single idea, or is employed when a lengthy story which lends itself well to pictorial treatment has to be told.

The broadside should not be awkward to handle. Consideration should be given to the distance from the eye at which it will be read. If it is to be hung up by the dealer in his window, the poster treatment is effective; if it is merely to be read at the desk, the copy should be typographically grouped into lines easily read. The size when folded should be suitable for the mailbag, for if it folds into a large size, as compared to the general run of mail, it will be delivered curled up, folded again in half, or with its corners chewed off. Mailing sizes recommended are $9\frac{1}{2}"x6\frac{1}{4}"$ or $9\frac{1}{2}"x4$-$1/6"$, folded from a sheet 19"x25" or 25"x38"; or $8"x5\frac{1}{2}"$ folded from a sheet 22"x32".

The distinction between leaflets, folders and broadsides has never been established with any more precision than the exact size of the three bears; they are only known relatively.

**Booklets.**—When a leaflet alone cannot tell the entire story, it may be amplified into a booklet of several pages. As a booklet becomes larger in its construction, it is duly graduated into the next higher rank and called a book. The purpose of the booklet is to elaborate and to impress a point which refirm was incorporated, and it might even have to render payment to a State in which the corporation maintained a branch office and one-fortieth of one per cent of its assets.

"If the man had stock in a number of such corporations, his executors might be compelled to pay taxes to the Federal Government, half of the American States, and a number of Canadian Provinces. By the time all the taxes were paid, the heirs would be distinctly impressed with the tragedy of the situation.

"Even if a man has not more than $5,000 to leave to his family, it is his manifest duty to make a thorough study of the laws affecting his estate. He should make every effort to see that his own widow and his own orphans are protected as fully as possible from outrageous inheritance taxes and death taxes."

### And what are these taxes?

WHEN A PERSON speaks of inheritance taxes, the thought usually comes to mind: "Oh, they are the taxes which the wealthy have to pay." But, as the editorial above points out, every man with $5,000 is equally concerned about these taxes. Why? Because of the unusual way in which they are imposed, and the exceptional severity with which collection is enforced. The most urgent reason, however, is the fact that a man can take simple precautions to save his estate undue taxation and expense. It is not generally known that:

1 Practically every State imposes an inheritance tax. The State rates run as high as 40 per cent. In addition, the Federal Government also imposes its estate tax (running up to 25 per cent). The Philippine Islands' maximum tax is 64 per cent. The tendency during the past decade has been towards a sharp increase in the rates imposed, and decrease in the exemptions allowed.

2 A man's estate will often be taxed by his State of residence, by the State in which the companies whose securities he holds are incorporated, and by the States in which these companies own property. In-

[2]

deed, a single share of stock may be taxed by six or seven different States. For example, New York Central stock is taxed by:

| New York | Michigan |
| Pennsylvania | Indiana |
| Ohio | Illinois |

In addition to being taxed by the State of decedent's residence, and by the Federal Government. Holdings in the Pittsburgh Plate Glass Company are subject to taxes by Montana, West Virginia, Pennsylvania, as well as by the State of the decedent's residence and by the Federal Government. Stock in the J. C. Penney Company, Inc., is subject to tax in:

| Utah | Montana |
| Arizona | West Virginia |
| Arkansas | |

In addition to the State in which the man leaving the stock resided, and by the Federal Government. Consequently, a single estate often pays taxes to a host of States in which the decedent may never have set foot. When the late Henry C. Jackson, a director of a trust company in Boston, passed away, nineteen different States came in for a share of taxes, and took $690,000 out of a $3,000,000 estate.

3 Inheritance taxes must be paid before estates can be settled—usually within one year. Seldom is there enough cash on hand to pay for the taxes; securities have to be sold. To raise cash immediately, the best holdings have to be offered, invariably at a sacrifice. To quote from Mellon's Taxation: "Particularly is this true where the sales have to be made in large blocks or where the company whose stock is offered is not generally known to the public."

4 So-called tax-exempt bonds are tax-exempt as far as income taxes are concerned, but are hit full force by inheritance taxes. The latter are often larger than the income taxes, as is shown in this illustration. An unmarried man, resident of Illinois, left $400,000 stock in a prominent Ohio soap company as his estate. Illinois taxed it $92,570. Ohio $16,750, the Federal Government $9,500; total inheritance taxes, $138,820. Assuming the stock paid 6 per cent dividends, or $24,000 a year, the Federal income tax would have been $780 per year. If the owner of the stock

[3]

MAKING A BOOKLET INTERESTING THROUGH TYPOGRAPHY

quires considerable space for its presentation. The booklet itself usually serves as a step in a campaign. It provides detailed information which must be appreciated before an order can be expected. In planning a booklet, provision should be made for a suitable envelope, if one is necessary. This detail is usually the step-child of the campaign, neglect of which causes untold disturbance to otherwise well-laid plans.

Catalogues.—A catalogue is a reference book of the merchandise being offered for sale by the advertiser. The catalogue endeavors to tell all there is to be told about a product, in lieu of personal examination of the goods by a prospective purchaser. The purpose of the catalogue is to sell the goods presented over a period of time. The steps in preparing a catalogue may be described as follows:

1. *The merchandise is chosen.*—Only those articles and styles should be selected which will continue in demand during the expected life of the catalogue. The goods should represent the best offers a firm can make, for the man compiling the catalogue acts as the buyer's representative. He must recom-

mend the most worthy and desirable items, choosing those of which the greatest quantity can be sold.

2. *The catalogue size is determined.*—There has been a movement to standardize catalogue sizes to 7½"x10⅝" and 8½"x11"; or else to 5-5/16"x7½" if the catalogue will open flat when placed in a file. The number of pages depends largely upon the appropriation. This, in turn, depends upon the amount of business which the catalogue may be expected to secure. The amount of space necessary properly to present the merchandise also influences the amount of space.

3. *The paper stock is selected.*—Provision must be made for envelopes and cover stock, as well as paper for text pages. The quality of the paper must be good enough to accommodate the engravings which are to be used, the weight of the paper light enough to keep the postage cost down.

4. *The layouts are drawn.*—Space is assigned in proportion to the profit which a given article may secure. Products are arranged in logical sequence. Hardware will be together in one section, clothing in another section, and jewelry in still another. In the jewelry section a page may be devoted to brooches and pins, another to watches and clocks, a third to table silver.

5. *The illustrations are made.*—Pictures are made with a view to their engraving requirements. Shall halftones be used? If so, how much detail in the background shall be included? Shall separate photographs be made and then stripped into a halftone background, or can all the products be photographed together? These are the more important questions which must be answered.

6. *The copy is written.*—The copy must be concise, and the description of styles, colors, and sizes, complete. The catalogue must sell, and towards this end all questions must be anticipated. Provision must also be made for explicit ordering instructions, blanks of "fool proof" simplicity are usually included, as well as return envelopes.

7. *The plates are made.*—The screen and finish of halftones are very important. If space is very limited, the half-

tones can be cropped close, permitting the type to be set almost up to the edge of the picture itself.

8. *The copy is set up and O. K.'d.*—The pages may be crowded with type, for space in a catalogue is closely measured, but at all times the copy must be distinct and readable. Judicious use of bold-face, upper and lower case, italics, and indentations may prove helpful.

9. *The catalogue is printed and mailed.*—Complete provision is made in advance for the distribution and mailing of the catalogue, as it represents a heavy investment which is worthless on the shelves.

A catalogue is a costly piece of advertising. It is printed as a rule to span a long period of time. During the life of a catalogue many changes may take place in the content. To avoid this disadvantage, advertisers often plan less elaborate catalogues, of fewer pages, and issue them more frequently. This method has particular merit for use in selling products subject to constant changes in price and style, or to addition of new numbers.

A second plan is to issue departmental catalogues, these being smaller catalogues devoted to one particular type of merchandise. This plan permits a greater degree of selection of prospects in the issuance of the catalogue. A third method is that of using a loose-leaf catalogue with supplements showing changes, while a fourth idea is that of using a portfolio, consisting of a folder or envelope in which loose sheets are conveniently held. It verges on the nature of a catalogue, but does not, as a rule, present so much merchandise, seeking to present that which it does offer in a more elaborate way. A fifth plan is to issue new catalogue information regularly throughout the year, in conjunction with the house organ, which will be described later.

**The technical catalogue.**—Catalogues of machine parts and other mechanical equipment differ in several respects from the usual catalogues of household merchandise. Technical catalogues give their detail and data in the tone of an engineering handbook. Space in a technical catalogue is used more liberally, illustrations are more skillfully treated, and even the paper stock itself is of a finer quality than is used for general merchandise catalogues. Furthermore, these catalogues include tables, statistics, and other useful information very much like an abridged encyclopedia, the purpose of this data being to secure for the technical catalogue consideration as a helpful reference book.

House organs.—A house organ is a publication issued periodically by a firm for the furtherance of its own interests, inviting attention on the strength of its editorial content. House organs are also known as "company magazines" and "company newspapers." The house organ serves as the mouthpiece of a concern, either directly or through implication, expressing its ideals, policies, and wishes.

The branches of the house organ family are four in number, each representing a different activity. First we may consider the house organ addressed to the salesmen of a house. Such an organ is usually the development of the regular letter which the sales manager finds advisable to send to his representatives. It gives suggestions for making further sales and offers inspiration to offset the effects of sales which did not materialize. Any firm engaging a large number of salesmen, agents, or representatives will find this a useful medium. The second type of house organ is written in similar vein but goes to the dealers of the product. It usually presents better methods of storekeeping and cites the experience of other dealers, showing how the article advertised contributed to the successes pictured. The third form of house organ is created for the buyer, or prospective buyer of the product, showing at length in an interesting manner how the product advertised could be used to fullest advantage. It is designed to create a favorable attitude toward the house so the reader will give preference to its products as well as to increase the use of those products. The fourth classification of a house organ is that issued for the employees themselves, to develop the big-family spirit within any organization.

The issuance of a house organ is especially feasible when the advertiser is confronted with the danger of losing touch with his own personnel, when the sale of the goods could be aided both by better knowledge on the part of consumers, and good-will among the sales outlets, or when repeat and replacement business depends upon the satisfactory use of the original article over a period of time. The success of a house organ lies in its definiteness of purpose, the consistency of its editorial content, its abundance of interesting and helpful information, and the regularity with which it is published.

**First class mail cards.**—A first class mail card is one which bears an individually written message. The most popular member of this line is the post card which the Government itself issues. A private mailing card can likewise be used if it consists of an unfolded piece of cardboard about the same weight as the government card, with dimensions as follows:

Minimum—2¾ inches x 4 inches
Maximum—3 9/16 inches x 5 9/16 inches

Under the Postal Act of 1925, private post cards require 2c postage. *On first class mail cards the right half of the address side must be clear of printing; the left half may be used for the message.* The words "Post Card" should appear on the address side.

**Third class mail cards.**—An unfolded sheet of cardboard sent through the mails without envelope is known as a mail card. If it contains printed matter only and bears no individually written signature, it may be sent under third class postage. The minimum size of a third class mail card is 2¾"x4"; no maximum size is specified. *On all third class mail matter, a 3½" panel on the address side must be left clear of all printing. The panel is measured from the right edge and extends from the top to the bottom of the card.*

**Return cards.**—A return card is a first class mail card which the reader is asked to sign and mail to the advertiser for whatever purpose is expressed. Return cards form an adjunct to many of the other forms of direct advertising described. They may be used (1) as a part of the folder, or booklet, from which they may be detached for mailing; (2) enclosed loosely or "thrown in" the folder, or booklet; (3) fastened by means of a seal; or (4) held by means of slits in the paper, like a picture in a postcard album.

Return cards can be livened considerably through attention to their layout. The copy on the card should tell the entire story of its purpose and offer. Then, should the card become separated from its advertisement, it will still convey a complete message. In its final appearance the card should be attractive, simple and complete with plenty of room for the signature and address.

A host of novel forms of direct advertising have been created. Those described embrace types used most generally. Improvements upon these will undoubtedly be made, but ample opportunity awaits the advertiser who puts better thought into the preparation of the forms that are already known.

**Figuring costs.**—The basis of all direct advertising plans are the cost estimates. Upon these figures the appropriation is based, the extent of the campaign is gauged and the elaborateness of the individual piece determined. The "cost per inquiry" in advertising is the pro rata expense of securing each inquiry. Thus, assume that a mailing of 10,000 folders costs $60 a thousand to send out, or a total of $600. In response, 500 replies are received asking for further information. The cost per inquiry then would be 600 divided by 500, or $1.20 a piece. Assume further that 50 finally purchase the product. The cost per order then would be 600 divided by 50, or $12 each. The percentage of returns which may plausibly be expected serves as a basis for gauging the appropriation. A basis is then created for determining the plan and elaborateness of the individual pieces. Experience has shown that direct orders to the amount of 4 per cent in a direct-mail campaign is an excellent showing for products costing $10 and less. In a new undertaking, however, one is optimistic, if he counts on more than 2 per cent orders on the strength of any one mailing.

Knowing how the cost per order is computed, and the number of replies per mailing that may be expected, an advertiser may calculate the direct-mail appropriations by either of the following methods:

ON THE QUESTION
or
DOING BUSINESS
IN OTHER STATES

PRENTICE-HALL, Inc., 70 Fifth Ave. New York
*publishers*, The State Corporation Tax Service

*Please send a copy of this Manual, without cost or obligation to us.*

*Name*_____

*Title*_____

*Firm*_____

*Address*_____

_____

*Actual Size 5x7¾ inches*                              SCB

A SIMPLE RETURN CARD

This card proved quite effective. It tells the whole story by itself and shows its subject up to advantage. It leaves plenty of room for signing. Note the initials ("key") in the corner to aid in keeping a record of the replies.

1. Determine the amount of business expected, the maximum selling costs, and see what can be done with that appropriation, as in these simple instances:

*Example A:*

Article sells for $4.50
Selling cost allowable is 33⅓% or $1.50 per article.
Product can be sold to list of 25,000.
Returns expected are 2% or 500 orders.
At $1.50 each, the selling cost on the 500 orders, makes an appropriation of $750.
This allows 3c per name. Consequently the mailing will have to be a simple one.

*Example B:*

Article sells for $18.00.
Selling cost allowable is 20% or $3.60 per article.
List of 25,000.
Returns expected are 2% or 500 orders.
At $3.60 each the selling cost on the 500 orders makes an appropriation of $1,800 which can be invested.
This allows 7.2c per name.

2. Determine what must be done, then prepare the necessary material, as economically as possible. Usually this is the practice followed with products sold through salesmen or

dealers, such products, for instance, as automobiles, bonds, machinery, and office equipment. This method is also used by retail stores which invite the reader to call at the store to buy.

**Creating the plan.**—The amount of the appropriation fixes the maximum expenditure; the length of the message fixes the minimum physical size of the mailing. The different forms of direct-mail advertising can then be organized for consistent selling purposes in accordance with any of three plans known as continuous plan, wear-out plan, or climactic plan.

**The continuous plan.**—By the continuous plan, advertisements are sent throughout the year to the same list of people. Each advertisement deals with a different offering, there being no relation between them except for the fact that they come from the same house. We can take the case of a retailer who has a list of active customers. Throughout the year he may run sales, or conduct seasonable "merchandising events" which he wishes to call to the attention of his clientele. Accordingly, he sends out a direct-mail piece, requesting these people to visit the store for the occasion.

In some industries buyers come to market only at given seasons of the year. A manufacturer wishing to keep in touch with his prospects during the year can do so by direct-mail advertisements bearing some item of news or some offer of interest. The continuous plan is well suited for use by any advertiser who has a definite limited list of customers or prospects, and who has a staple article which is in constant, or in recurring, demand. It also may be used if he seeks the replacement and parts business of these people. Letters, leaflets, folders, mailing cards, and house organs are the most popular form for use in continuous campaigns. Their choice depends upon the length of the story and the need for distinctiveness.

The total amount of business which any one advertisement in a continuous plan secures should prove profitable. Otherwise a weakness in the planning and preparation of that particular mailing is indicated. But though a given person does not respond to any given advertisement, his name is still retained on the list for subsequent advertisements, because it is known that the reader is a logical prospect. Viewed in another light, the advertisements are sent more or less sporadically throughout the year; they are changed from mailing to mailing, but the list is retained.

**The wear-out plan.** .—In the wear-out plan we come upon an advertiser who has a single product which he is interested in selling, but which would appeal to a diversified list. He accordingly concentrates on one section of his list at a time, leaving the others to be used after he has exhausted that division. He tells about his product completely in one mailing piece and addresses that advertisement to a specific list of prospects. He sends to them one mailing piece after the other, each one making its own complete sales appeal and each responsible for its own immediate sales. The series is continued until the list is "worn out" and the total returns on any one mailing no longer pays for the mailing to the entire list. The advertiser then repeats the series on another list.

Thus, assume that 10,000 letters were sent out, and it is figured that the cost would be defrayed if only 2 per cent of the people purchase the product. The first piece of wear-out campaign copy is planned for a list of 10,000 names, and receives a return of 5 per cent, which pays a profit;

The second mailing to 9,499 names again receives 5 per cent returns, which pays profit;

The third mailing to 9,024 names receives 4.5 per cent returns, which pays profit;

The fourth mailing to 8,619 names receives 3.5 per cent returns, which pays profit;

The fifth mailing to 8,315 names receives 2 per cent returns. At this point the list is regarded as worn-out and the performance is repeated on another list.

The wear-out system resembles the continuous system in the completeness of the individual units. However, the wear-out series must be valuated after every mailing, whereas in a continuous series, lack of immediate response is not necessarily a signal for dropping the list.

In the wear-out method, the forms most frequently used are letters and folders. The wear-out plan is extensively used by publishers of "special edition" sets of books which are used as premiums by those who have some novel article selling for less than $10.

**The climactic or campaign plan.**—An advertiser with a high-priced calculating machine to sell can choose a definite list of prospects. But there are so many technical features to explain that he may not think it best to present the entire message in one mailing piece. Instead, he can plan a series of pieces which *together* will tell one complete story. Every mailing is designed not to produce the result ultimately desired, but merely to serve as a wedge to the next mailing. Each advertisement then acts as a wedge leading to the final piece which will seek the order. All the mailings are planned with a view to their effect as a complete campaign, not as independent units.

The climactic plan is employed in selling a new device requiring considerable pioneering work. The appeals are arranged in climactic order and the forms are chosen to suit the message. Letters may be used exclusively—the first making just one point; the second making another point, paving the way for the third; and so on until the last letter. But until then, all attempts to "close the order" would be held in abeyance. Letters may be used in conjunction with a booklet and folders. The letter announces the booklet which does most of the explanatory work, followed by a series of folders, each stressing a detail of the product. Finally another letter inviting the order would be sent.

It will be seen that the climactic system of direct advertising can be made to dovetail splendidly with publication advertising and personal selling.

As is the case in most other plans, these three methods are often combined to suit individual conditions. Where they are so consolidated, one usually follows the other, but every successful direct-mail advertising experience employs one of the triumvirate—the continuous plan, the wear-out plan, or the climactic plan.

**The follow-up.**—That advertising which is sent in response to an inquiry is known as the follow-up. It may consist of a single letter giving the desired information, or it may be an entire series of direct-mail advertisements.

The doctrine of successful follow-up is a simple one: The inquiry should be answered promptly and completely; the inquirer should be made to feel that he granted a courtesy to the house in directing his inquiry to them, and that it is a pleasure to the house to have the opportunity of providing the information asked. The query sent to the house should be read twice before being answered, to make sure that the reply covers the doubt in the writer's mind. Everything in his letter should be scrutinized to see what it reveals about the possible need or use he may have for the product. Once the inquiry is understood, the answer should completely cover the question asked. It should not be too forward in presuming that the inquirer is ready to order; far better is it for the reply to close by asking whether there is anything which has not been made perfectly clear, or whether there is any further information of any nature which the writer seeks. Then it may be opportune to indicate a readiness to enter his order. The best success in turning inquirers into purchasers is obtained, not by seeking to rush them into buying, but by patiently cultivating their interest in the product from the day they write in.

Effective letters which are sent after the first one is mailed in response to an inquiry usually possess several features worth noting. First, in their opening they indicate the reason why the writer is addressed again (as "In our previous letter we did not mention the fact that," or "Perhaps you have been wondering, since our last letter, just how you can use this piece of equipment in your own work"). Second, the letter makes one outstanding point; third, in passing it summarizes the information previously given; fourth, it makes a stronger bid for the order than did the first letter. As the series progresses, the tone of the letter becomes more insistent, culminating in a direct request for a decision.

Often an additional incentive to order is included in the final letter of the series. This incentive may be in the form of a premium such as a pair of book ends, if the prospect orders the set of books before a given date; attachments for a vacuum

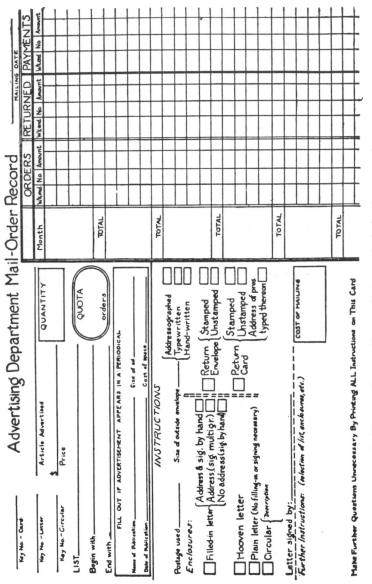

A USEFUL RECORD FORM. Note particularly the quota box.

cleaner if the cleaner is promptly ordered; or an allowance in the price, or in the terms of payment—a practice to be followed with considerable caution.

Before any advertisements inviting inquiries are issued, all follow-up material should be ready for issuance.

**Keying advertisements.**—When a direct-mail advertisement is sent to a number of lists, or when several different advertisements are sent out, it is important to know which of the lists, or advertisements, is to be credited with the replies that come in. This information can easily be procured by placing a code letter or number (known as a *key number*) on the reply card.

The methods of keying are numerous. In publication advertising, department numbers are commonly employed, likewise booklet numbers. "Write to Dept. 14," or "Send for booklet LS" are examples. Another plan used is that of varying the street address to which replies are to be made. In direct-mail advertising, return cards and coupons may also bear number or letter in the corner which serves as an identification mark.[3]

**Keeping the records.**—It is of utmost importance for the direct-mail advertiser to keep accurate records of all mailings Only in this way can he tell whether he is using the right method. He may also discover that he has a better opportunity with some list or direct-mail piece than he realized. The only procedure to follow at the outset is to key every advertisement issued and keep a thorough record of all replies, and an absolute check on costs. Many advertisers have built their success by making every piece of advertising they prepare teach them something, as well as cost them something.

**Making tests.**—The possible results of direct-mail advertising can in a very fair measure be predetermined by "test mailings." The test may be of advertisements, or of lists, or

---

[3] In general advertising where no written reply to the advertisement is solicited, keying is unnecessary. The effectiveness of the campaign may be gauged by the increase of business in the period of time following its appearance or in the zone in which the advertising is being conducted. Department stores test newspapers by advertising a product in that medium alone. By the sales of that article they can judge the value of that medium as compared to the demand created for a similar product by another paper.

of any elements entering into the mailing. Testing simply involves taking a representative fraction of the proposed list, and sending out the advertisement in question. If the test names are picked at random, are fairly representative of the other names on the list, and if other conditions remain unchanged, the same percentage of replies may be safely expected of the whole list. Suppose we wish to find out which of two letters, A and B, is the better. They are to go to banks and are designed to secure inquiries. A list of 20,000 banks in the United States is secured. The first 10 per cent of the names in every state are addressed, selected alphabetically— an arbitrary device to insure a fair choice. There is now a stack of 2,000 envelopes. These envelopes are then divided into two stacks of 1,000 each, by picking the alternate envelopes for each stack. Into one stack we insert letter A; into the other, letter B. Both letters are thus given the same chance. In response to letter A, twenty-two replies are received, let us say; letter B brings in sixty-five replies. Letter B has shown its superiority and would be chosen for use on the rest of the list. It is possible to base mammoth mailings on these tests.

Conversely, if two lists were to be tested, it would be necessary to take an equal part of each, chosen from the same geographical territories, and send a mailing piece identical in every respect to both. The comparison of replies would tell the story.

If an advertiser wishes to send letters to a list of 1,400,000 people, he will send out twenty tests of 1,000 each, trying out different pieces of copy, also comparing postage or two-cent postage. He will next take the three pieces which prove best and send out 10,000 of each. Of the best two letters on these tests he sends out 50,000 each, and he sends out the best of those two letters to the remaining names; in this way he can definitely anticipate the exact number of orders.

Tests of the different units in a campaign should be conducted on a part of the total list. The conclusions then will hold true as a rule when the remainder of the list is used. The conclusions drawn from one complete mailing, however, do not necessarily hold good for another product, another list, another season, or another offer.

On seasonable products, tests have to be arranged well enough in advance to have the big mailing arrive just on time.

**Other suggestions.**—A profitable idea may be found in writing to the customers who have not bought within the past year. "We have not had the privilege of serving you lately," a letter of this style may read, or "We hope that you have been satisfied with our product, but we are writing to make sure. If there is anything which has displeased you we want you to let us know of it. And if you are still one of our satisfied patrons, as we believe you are, will you not let us know by checking the enclosed assortments you wish us to send you, as in past years?

If a concern has salesmen out, direct-mail advertising may profitably be employed to reach the small towns at which the men do not stop. Present customers may help build up a valuable list by sending the names of their friends who would be interested. The creditors and stockholders of the company which is advertising also represent good mailing lists often overlooked.

When space is used in publications, it may be a good idea to reprint the advertisement, send it out to dealers or prospects with a notation, "You may have seen this in the 'Blank' monthly. I am sending you this reprint in case it escaped your attention, for I know you will be interested in it." To dealers, the message may be, "By the way, this may be a good reminder to look over your stock and let us know what to send you."

Cards, leaflets, folders, broadsides, and other direct-mail going out as third class mail cost one and one-half cents for each two ounces. A bound booklet, book, or catalogue of less than twenty-four pages and cover likewise costs one and one-half cents postage for each two ounces. *But if it is above twenty-four pages and cover, providing the total weight with envelope does not exceed eight ounces, the postage rate is only one cent for each two ounces.*

On any postal question which would affect the direct advertising it is a very good practice to get a ruling from the local postmaster, before the material is produced.

If there is any question as to the best method of using direct-mail advertising, send out tests; if the effectiveness of a mailing cannot immediately be ascertained, take a small list of your best prospects and pound away at them.

**The advertising file.**—Users of direct advertising find an invaluable aid in a file of samples. To start such a collection, it is best at first to save every piece of direct advertising that may come to your attention. Subsequently these should be classified in accordance with your own interests. Many subdivisions of samples are possible, of which the following are typical groupings. They may be classified according to:

1. Forms,
    as letters, leaflets, folders, and so forth.
2. Color effects,
    as 1-color, 2-color, 3-color.
3. Paper stock,
    as writing, book and cover paper, effectively used.
4. Typography,
    as pleasant effects, bold effects, economical use of space.
5. Business,
    arranged by subject.
6. Novel ideas,
    in appearance; miscellaneous odd effects.

The value of any file of advertisements rests solely upon its usefulness. It should be a source of new suggestions and not a mere storehouse of used ideas. Hence it is well to observe everything, preserve that which is good according to your own standards, consult frequently, and overhaul regularly.

# CHAPTER XVI

## SUPPLEMENTARY MEDIA

**The package insert.**—A very useful medium of advertiseing is afforded by the package insert. This is an enclosure in the package itself bearing the advertiser's message. Like many other ideas, this one was the evolution of a need. Manufacturers found that a product would arrive in poor condition when inserted loosely in its container; accordingly they enclosed a stuffer of paper to keep the article snugly in place. One of these manufacturers, who was alert to the possibilities, used this stuffer to carry his advertisement. From this humble origin a mighty medium has sprung up. The package insert enables the advertiser to reach every one of his customers at a time when they are most interested in his product, with no extra space charge or postage expense. Moreover, the advertiser enjoys an exclusive circulation, since no competitor has an advertisement appearing with his.

The insert itself may be used to introduce other members of the sales family, to increase the use of the product, and to gain the goodwill of the buyer. Recipes are generously distributed as package inserts. An entire cook book or other instructional reading matter may be mailed upon receipt of coupons sent as package inserts. The insert may also endeavor to secure additional names for the mailing list by offering some sort of bonus to the purchaser who will take the trouble to fill out the insert with the names of friends who might be prospects for the article. This form of advertising may even invite a direct order, although it is more useful as a supplementary medium than as a complete mail-order advertisement itself. The uses of the insert are many, and the possibilities for employing it are more.

The limitation on package inserts is largely mechanical. When placed in coffee packages, they sometimes absorb the oils and become greasy. Also, where a product is being produced in large quantities, the device for enclosing an additional article in the package without interfering with the speed of packaging the product requires attention.

Blotters.—Blotters provide many opportune uses. The one requirement of a blotter, which is apt to be overlooked, is that it shall be able to blot. Blotters should furthermore be distributed with a definite plan. They may be sent by mail in a manner similar to that of sending direct-mail advertising, they may be distributed by hand in offices, or—as is the practice of local shoe stores—they may be distributed by hand to children in the schools. Blotters may also be given away through dealers or they may be inclosed in packages. In any event, a plan for their distribution should be worked out in advance. An advertiser would not have an advertisement set up in type unless he had some idea of how the advertisement was to be used. Yet it has happened time after time that blotters are ordered without the slightest conception of what is to be done with them.

Calendars.—Calendars range in size from those which curl around the top of a pencil to the "jumbo" masterpieces which can be read from across a large room. The usual calendars are in the form either of a mounted pad with separate sheets, or of a single sheet bearing all the months. The calendar may show one month at a time, or present the month preceding and the month following as well. These are known as three-months-at-a-glance calendars, and are very popular with manufacturers who buy them for distribution by their dealers. Calendars bearing notification of tax dates have been popular with banks and accountants, and present one of the many possibilities in this field.

Calendars have followed the tradition of being printed to span twelve-month periods and most of them are issued the first of the year. The result is that the New Year brings with it to most offices a flood of calendars, only one or two of which attain the honor of being used. A few alert advertisers have therefore issued their New Year's presents in July, when the calendar of the past winter is just beginning to appear shabby.

Others have given out eighteen-month pads to lengthen the stay of their calendars. These instances are cited not as a recommendation blindly to follow suit, but to show that even a staid form of advertising offers possibilities for better thought.

Specialties.—Advertising specialties constitute the unconventional form of media described as novelties, souvenirs, gifts, and favors. The following examples are but a few of the inexhaustible variety that have been used in advertising:

| | | |
|---|---|---|
| Aprons | Cups | Paper cutters |
| Aluminum novelties | Diaries | Pencils |
| Buttons | Drinking cups | Pocketbooks |
| Bill folds | Fans | Pocket mirrors |
| Banks | Kitchen reminders | Puzzles |
| Book marks | Knife sharpeners | School bags |
| Card cases | Letter openers | Telephone indexes |
| Check book covers | Match safes | Thimbles |
| Cigar cases | Memorandum tablets | Tobacco pouches |
| Coin cases | Mirrors | Watch fobs |

The essential difference between a specialty and a direct-mail advertisement is the usefulness which the specialty possesses for the reader. A direct-mail advertisement secures consideration because of what it says; a specialty, because of what it is.

The specialty is essentially a device for securing goodwill. The prince of ancient India heralded his visit by sending a caravan of gifts to his prospective host. The modern prince takes with him on his Wednesday evening visit to his princess a box of candy, a book, or a similar token, to express his esteem. It is to this spirit of goodwill on a little different scale that the specialty owes its success. It is a gift from the advertiser to one who may influence a decision.

The specialty is used to effect an entrance into provinces which the more conventional media do not economically cover. Haberdashers have distributed baseball league schedules to men entering and leaving the large office buildings near their shops; shoe stores have distributed rulers and school bags to school children. Soda fountains have given fans to moving picture patrons; savings banks have distributed small coin banks among factory employees. The value of a specialty in each case depends upon its acceptability as a gift, and upon its careful distribution.

**Samples.**—The sample is the nearest approach of media to the actual merchandise. It has been found useful for low-cost products having a high repeat sale, such as tooth paste and chewing gum, and for more expensive products in which a mere fraction can prove the value of the article itself, such as perfumes. In these instances, the sample method serves as a good entering wedge.

**Methods of distributing samples.**—There are many methods of distributing samples. One method, where the product is one of general use, such as tooth paste and after-dinner mints, is to have specially costumed girls give them away at busy street corners in large cities. Newspaper advertising can then be used to feature these girls with their baskets of samples.

Another method is that of house-to-house distributors. This plan is conducted by "crews" who are specially employed for the purpose. The two types of house-to-house service are known as "front door service" and "rear door service," the sample being left in the vestibule or otherwise assured an entrance into the house. "Hand-in service" is the method whereby the sample is delivered personally to the resident. A third method of distributing the sample is through the dealer, who is supplied with a quantity of samples which he can hand out over the counter. In practice, however, dealer distributions of samples has proved unsatisfactory because of the unchecked waste. To overcome the waste of indiscriminate giving away of samples, a plan can be worked out whereby coupons, redeemable in merchandise, appear in newspaper advertising. This practice may invite a number of abuses, but it is generally well regarded. An improvement on the general coupon idea is to mail coupons with an explanatory letter to lists or prospects supplied by the dealer. The person who receives the coupon may then redeem it at the dealer's store for the sample itself.

Still another method of distributing samples is that of featuring them in advertisements and inviting the reader to send for them. By this method the reader writes directly to the advertiser for the sample. The advertiser may thus build up a valuable mailing list, if he wishes, and individually follow up prospects. A nominal charge is often made for the sample to eliminate curiosity-seekers and to defray in part the costs involved.

The sample may also be distributed as regular merchandise. Many advertisers have found their samples such a popular feature that they have accordingly introduced them into their regular stock as a low-priced line of merchandise. The 5-and-10-cent stores may be regarded in a sense as a huge natural outlet for selling sample merchandise.

There are still other ways of letting the public try a product, such as enclosing trial packages in shipments of other goods or enclosing in the same manner a coupon entitling the recipient to a sample of the goods advertised.

**Motion pictures.**—The services of a number of industrial motion picture producing concerns are available to the advertiser who contemplates the use of the screen. Where the film has any educational value, its distribution may be arranged through any of three channels: a professional industrial film exchange, the governmental agencies, or direct company promotion. In the first group are those commercial bureaus which organize and direct the showing of a film at a definite rate per showing, or else are paid so much per reel; they are often supported by subsidies. In this group there are also the institutional exchanges which provide clubs, churches, and schools with the pictures at a nominal cost. The institutional exchanges are largely supported by outright donations. The government bureaus, which offer a second channel of distribution for films, handle those pictures which contribute directly to the national welfare. Thus the individual advertiser who wishes to avail himself of the government's help must have films of a decidedly altruistic nature. Finally, if an advertiser does not wish to use the private film exchanges, or is unable to use the governmental facilities, he may direct his own staff in having a film shown to the people he wishes to reach. In this connection the portable projector comes in handy. A salesman can arrange showings in the stores of dealers, at fairs, at club meetings, or wherever else motion picture publicity is needed.

Radio broadcasting.—The radio industry is still too unorganized at this writing to have broadcasting regarded as a full-fledged medium. That it will provide an important medium of the future, however, there can be but little question. The elements in its favor are several: at the outset, it is novel —and will continue to be so for an entire generation. It appeals through a sensory organ different from that through which the printed advertisement appeals, namely, the ear; its circulation is profoundly large. On the other hand, there is this thought to bear in mind regarding the possible importance and influence of radio advertising: All things, as has been observed before, are a matter of proportion. The total value of all radio advertising will compare to the total value of published advertising in the same measure as the amount of time a person spends listening-in on the radio compares to the amount of time he spends in reading. Advertisers interested in using all media to their best advantage will simply recognize in radio an additional occasion on which to reach their clientele and a new method for doing so.

As this is being written, broadcasting from established sending stations is in vogue. Perhaps overnight this system will be scrapped and broadcasting will become more confined, or more general. The practice of selling broadcasting privileges will, no doubt, be continued and enlarged, for private broadcasting concerns eventually will have to resort to advertising income for their maintenance and profit—just as publishers have found it possible to sell their magazines at a ludicrously low price only because of the advertising revenue. How, then, can advertising use this medium appropriately? All plans will have to be based on a willingness to enlighten and to entertain the listeners. Talks will have to be on topics of significant interest to the public. "Different ways to prepare coffee," for example, may be appropriate in an afternoon program, while "Why you should never accept a substitute for our coffee" can have little place in the air. The talks will have to be of a strong pioneering flavor. As for the entertainment—such as dance music and the like—that will undoubtedly be popular. By his orchestra will the advertiser become known, which isn't a bad method at all, in view of the fact that he *is* becoming known. The greatest ingenuity will have to be shown in co-ordinating radio advertising with the other parts of a selling plan. Contests have been successful in that they have required entrants to secure blanks, issued by the dealers in the respective products.

If those most interested in the welfare of radio take steps to keep it from being abused during the early years, the broadcasting station will be able to attract to it the advertisers who can make of this medium a useful, permanent institution.

## CHAPTER XVII

## OUTDOOR ADVERTISING. CAR CARDS

NOBLE indeed is the ancestry of the modern outdoor advertisement. The Romans named streets in the Eternal City after signs which appeared on the respective highways, such as the *vicus Ursi Pileati,* meaning "The Street of the Bear with the Hat On." Pliny bestowed upon a certain Lucius Mummius the credit for being the first to put a picture outside his house, the picture serving not only as a street name but as a house address as well.

Early in the thirteenth century the old English inn-keepers borrowed the idea and vied with one another in composing attractive signs. These usually took the form of a symbol or simple illustration, such as "The Three Crows," "The Flying Dutchman," "The Hand and Lock of Hair," "The Major's Wig," "The King's Head," "The Dancing Bears," "The Man Loaded with Mischief," "The Goldfish," "The Bush," "The Cat and Fiddle," "The Goat in Boots," "The Pig and Whistle." In the familiar tea room signs of the twentieth century, the picturesque heritage of these names may be recognized.

The derivation of some of these names is very interesting.[1] "The Cat and Fiddle" is believed to have originated with the sign of a certain *Caton fidele,* a staunch Protestant in the reign of Queen Mary. "The Goat in Boots" is probably a corruption of the latter part of the Dutch legend, *"Mercurius is der Goden Boode,"* "Mercury is the messenger of the gods." "The Pig and Whistle" is held to be a popularization of "The Pig and Wassail Bowl." There was also an inn known as "The Maggoty Pie," the name of which was inspired by a line in a play, "I do by at the signe of Dona Margaretta de

---

[1] "History of Signboards," by Larwood & Hotton (written in 1866).

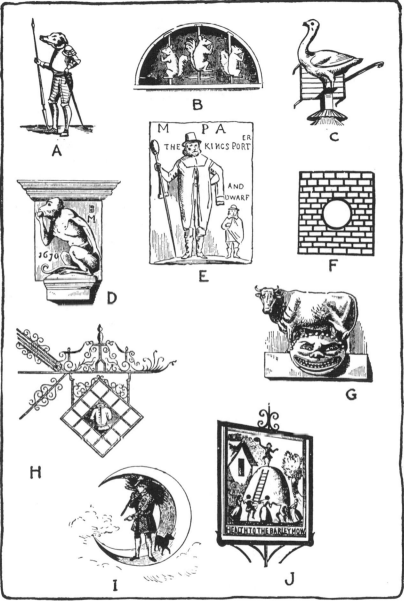

OUTDOOR SIGNS OF THE SEVENTEENTH CENTURY

These signs appeared over inns:

A. Hog in Armour.
B. Three Squirrels.
C. Goose and Gridiron.
D. The Ape.
E. King's Porter and Dwarf.

F. Hole in the Wall.
   "A Guide for Malt Worms."
G. Not Bull Durham but the Bull and Mouth.
H. Harrow and Doublet.
I. Man in the Moon.
J. Barley Mow.

Pia in the Strand." Many names had their derivation in historic and commemorative events, heraldic and emblematic devices, animals, flowers, trades and professions, and comic situations.

At first, signs were hung boldly outside of the buildings themselves—usually over the doorway. In the seventeenth century, the idea of planting a sign-post before the building seems to have made its first appearance. The success of this plan inspired in some unknown genius the idea of erecting duplicate signs on the road itself, down the road, and in adjoining towns, so that the name of the inn would receive widespread attention among travelers. And there we have the progenitor of modern outdoor advertising.

**Modern forms.**—It has been a long step, indeed, from the Roman street boards to the modern elaborate signs which seem almost to grow along the country highway and climb the city skyscrapers. In the maze of present-day outdoor advertisements, three specific forms may be discerned: First are those signs in which electric bulbs themselves form the words or the design of the advertisement. These displays are known as *electric spectaculars*. The second general group consists of signs which are individually painted on their respective backgrounds. These are referred to as *painted displays*. Third come the advertisements consisting of large sheets of paper, which are pasted on mounts. These are called *posters*.

**The electric spectaculars.**—The electric spectaculars are primarily night displays, consisting of electric lights on steel frames, without any background. During the day they may not appear in their full impressiveness, but at night they are true to their name. Electric spectaculars are the most costly form of outdoor advertising, measured in terms of unit price. They are erected only at very heavy traffic centers, especially in the famous districts of large cities, such as Michigan Boulevard, Chicago; Campus Martius, Detroit; the Public Square, Cleveland; on the piers in Atlantic City; Canal Street, New Orleans; and Times Square, New York, whose Gay White Way owes its sobriquet to its brilliant electric spectacular signs.

ELECTRIC SPECTACULARS (*top*).—The lights themselves form the sign.

POSTERS (*center and bottom*).—The advertisements are printed on sheets of paper, then pasted on mounts. The size of the posters is uniform.

Electric spectaculars are designed, erected, and maintained by the outdoor advertising companies. Space upon them is usually sold for a period of from one to five years. Advertisers pay a flat monthly rate for maintenance and are rendered credit pro rata for loss of service which occurs for any reason whatever. Such displays are sold individually. An advertiser may order as many or as few as he wishes, choosing the specific signs in each case.

**Painted displays.**—Painted displays, upon 'a closer examination, reveal two subdivisions, namely, bulletins and wall panels; these in turn may be either illuminated or non-illuminated.

A bulletin is a panel of wood or sheet steel erected at street level, on roofs of buildings, or along highways. A wall panel utilizes the side of a building which is already standing. Where the night traffic warrants the cost, bulletins and wall panels are illuminated by having lights made to shine upon them. When this is done, the passerby sees the sign illuminated, but does not see the actual lights. Illuminated bulletins and wall panels are erected by the outdoor advertising company which repaints them every four months, with a change of copy at that time, if desired.

Unilluminated bulletins and wall panels are of many types and are found on roofs, at street level, along motor roads, and on the sides of store buildings. These displays are placed freely along the thoroughfares — especially at busy intersections.

Painted displays, whether bulletins or wall panels, illuminated or unilluminated, are bought selectively. The advertiser may order one display or he may purchase space on a thousand. The price varies with the size of the display and the position of the individual sign. While most advertisers using painted displays do so for an extended period (one year or more), space may be obtained for any length of time desired. Copy may be changed every four months. The price of unilluminated displays in smaller cities ranges from $7.50 per month to $30 per month; in metropolitan sections the price runs from $15 per month to $75 per month. Illuminated displays vary in price from $40 per month in smaller cities, to as high as $2,000 per month in the larger centers of population.

**Posters.**—The third form of outdoor advertising, and the one in most extensive use, is the poster, which, it will be remembered, consists of the advertisement lithographed or otherwise printed on sheets which are pasted on a background. Unlike the electric spectacular and the painted display, which appear in unstandardized sizes, the poster has a definite unit of measurement known as a "sheet," measuring 26 by 39 inches—very useful figures to remember in advertising.

A one-sheet poster is 26 by 39 inches; a three sheet, 39 by 78 inches. An eight-sheet poster is 8 feet 8 inches high and 78 inches across the base, while a twenty-four-sheet poster is 8 feet 8 inches high and 19 feet 6 inches wide. There are intermediate sizes, but three, eight, and twenty-four sheets are the popular sizes. Three-sheet posters are used principally on the sides of retailers' stores. Eight-sheet posters are used mainly for theatrical signs, while the twenty-four sheet variety is truly the standard poster on which advertising may be placed in over 12,500 cities, towns, and villages. Posters are not as a rule illuminated except in heavy traffic centers where there is considerable night traffic.

**Poster "showings."** Poster locations are scattered throughout a city, depending essentially upon the character of the neighborhood and the resourcefulness of the outdoor advertising plant in obtaining the right to erect the sign. Space is sold on the basis of "showings"; varying with the size of the town. A "full" or intensive showing is one including sufficient postings to dominate a town. A "half" or representative showing is one in which the posters are as evenly distributed but with one-half the intensity of the full showing. Similarly, a "quarter" or minimum showing means that the number of posters used is one-quarter of the number employed in a full showing. *The poster size remains the same*—merely the number of posters varies. A half-showing in any town is regarded as quite a formidable campaign and is comparable in dominance to a full page in a magazine. A full showing may be compared to a double-page spread. Different towns require a different number of posters to constitute a full showing, depending upon the density of the population and its distribution within a city.[2] As an illustration:

| City | Population | No. of 24-Sheet Posters in Full Showing |
|---|---|---|
| South Bend | 70,000 | 30 |
| Spokane | 105,000 | 40 |
| Houston | 138,000 | 44 |
| Atlanta | 230,000 | 64 |
| Minneapolis | 380,000 | 88 |
| San Francisco | 650,000 | 120 |
| Chicago | 2,701,000 | 280 |
| New York City Manhattan and the Bronx | 5,620,000 | 300 |

Poster showings are bought by the month; copy can also be changed once a month. Unlike electric spectaculars and painted displays, which may be chosen individually, posters afford no choice of location to the advertiser when he buys them. He may choose the town in which he wishes to advertise, and may determine the extent of the showing (whether full, half, or quarter), but he does not pick the individual stands where the posters are to appear.

The advertiser must supply the lithographed posters which are to be mounted by the posting company. Usually 20 per cent more of the posters are sent than the number of showings calls for, the additional posters being used to replace and mend those displays which become torn during the contract period. The cost per poster averages about $8 per month for space. The cost of the lithographs is about $1.30 per poster.

How selling outdoor space is organized.—There are three different channels through which an advertiser may buy outdoor advertising: through the operating "plant," through the outdoor advertising company, or through his advertising agency. An operating plant is the local firm which maintains outdoor advertising positions in the town in which it is located.

---

[2] The exact number varies from time to time. The latest data can always be secured through the local outdoor advertising plant.

The plant leases from land and house owners the right to erect signs, or else to use the outside of their buildings for advertising purposes. Usually the contract for this privilege runs for a period of years. The plant erects at its own cost whatever fixtures are necessary; it handles the actual work of painting the sign, or mounting the posters. It then rents that space.

An outdoor advertising company is an organization which sells the space of many operating plants with whom it has made necessary arrangements. The headquarters of these companies are in the large cities. Through them, an advertiser can buy space of the plants all over the country. An outdoor advertising company is thus enabled to "control" space in any of 12,500 towns and cities in which the plants operate with them.

Advertising agencies are likewise able conveniently to buy positions from various plant owners by purchasing membership in the National Outdoor Advertising Bureau, which acts as a clearing house for all their outdoor advertising orders. An advertiser may go directly to his local operating plant, if he wishes to advertise in one town alone; he may go to the specialized outdoor advertising companies; he may go to his advertising agency if that agency is equipped to handle this work.

In reality, the advertiser is relieved of all detail. The outdoor advertising companies, or the advertising agencies:

1. Submit a schedule of space and rates in towns desired.

2. Suggest and prepare designs.

3. Give an exact report of the locations of various signs.

4. Supervise painting of signs and maintain them in good condition.

In the case of posters, the advertiser can have his own lithographer prepare the sheets. The outdoor advertising company completely supervises the shipment of posters to the operating plants and their proper display, in accordance with the list of towns and size of showings agreed upon.

In buying a spectacular and painted display in his own city, an advertiser and the plant representative will travel around town, selecting the most favorable positions from among those available. For electric spectacular and painted bulletin advertising out of town, the advertiser depends upon the outdoor selling company or his own representative to pick the choice locations for him.

National advertisers frequently prepare posters on which the dealer may have his individual imprint placed. These are offered to dealers by the manufacturer without cost, provided the merchant is willing to pay for the poster space in his own town.

**Outdoor advertising: characteristics.**—Outdoor advertising is flexible in that the advertiser can choose the area of his effort. Outdoor advertising is also intensive on a broad scale. It can be made to appear in whatever volume desired at the very point where it is most desirable to leave the impression. Every position in outdoor advertising is a preferred position; otherwise it would not have been chosen for the erection of a display.

Outdoor advertising is striking. As a visitor declared when he beheld the famous old Wrigley electric sign at Times Square, "Yes, it is a remarkable sign. But really, itsn't it exceedingly conspicuous?" Outdoor advertising *is* that, first, because its large dimensions permit the product to be shown in its natural colors and in a magnified size, and secondly, because, in the case of spectaculars, there is an unlimited opportunity for brightness, action, and unconventional effects.

The fact that outdoor advertising reaches transients adds to its value as a medium, as does its very important effect upon the dealers, in whose neighborhood it appears. Especially for products in every-day use by a large part of the population, the outdoor advertisement is effective. Such products are usually in an advanced competitive or in a retentive stage. The chief duty assigned to their advertisements is to reiterate the name or the trade-mark, or to show the package, for to each of these tasks outdoor advertising lends itself well.

**Outdoor advertising: copy and art requirements.**—Advertisements in publications pass before the reader at a rapidity determined by the attractiveness of the advertisement. Out-

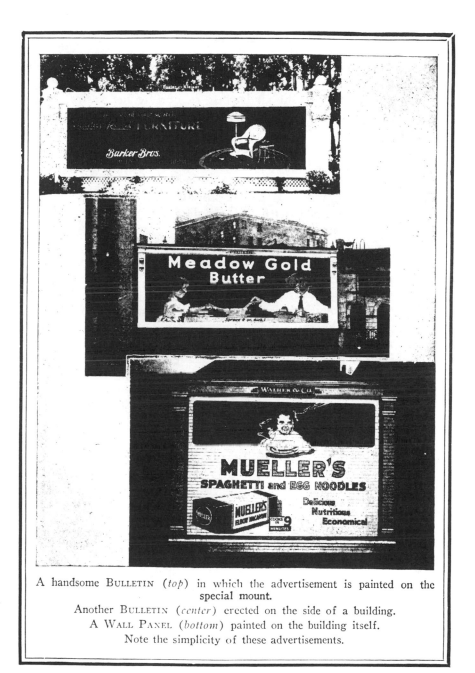

A handsome BULLETIN (*top*) in which the advertisement is painted on the special mount.
Another BULLETIN (*center*) erected on the side of a building.
A WALL PANEL (*bottom*) painted on the building itself.
Note the simplicity of these advertisements.

door advertising stands still—the reader passes before it. His rate of travel is not determined by the attractiveness of the different outdoor billboards, but rather by his desire to get to his destination. Hence the outdoor advertisement must tell its story in a flash. The copy should be very short—less than a dozen words, all together. It should express a simple statement of fact. It should be able to deliver its full message in the length of time it takes a man to walk or ride by, as the case may be. Often the slogan alone furnishes the outdoor advertisement with its complete copy, assisted perhaps by an epigrammatic secondary slogan.

The greater emphasis in outdoor advertising is given to the art work. Painters of theatrical scenery have the knack of painting a canvas which looks, at close range, like a batch of daubs and streaks of colors, but which appears to the audience as a finely painted background. Similarly, in outdoor advertising the small preliminary sketch is deceptive to the person who is not familiar with the technique of outdoor illustrating. It is well, therefore, to leave the preparation of the sketch entirely to the outdoor advertising company which engages artists thoroughly trained in outdoor advertising designing. There is another reason why this is advisable. Posters are printed in separate sheets, which are pasted together to form the entire design. In most cases there are 24 of these sheets to every full size poster. An artist who knows his work can so arrange the design that all the highly colored effects appear on but a few of the sections, saving the extra press work on the remaining sheets. The final effect should be judged, however, by the degree in which it succeeds in giving an instantaneous picture of a complete idea—the idea being the one it is sought to convey.

## Car Cards.

Like outdoor posters, car cards are bought on the basis of showings. The showings may be limited to given cities, and in the largest cities may further be confined to certain lines of cars within those communities. A card is placed in every car, when a full-showing is ordered; in every other car when a half-showing is called for, and in every fourth car in the case of a quarter-showing.

**Characteristics to consider.**—The cards are of uniform size, 11″x21″—giving to all advertisements equal prominence of space, regardless of the power of the advertiser or the importance of his product judged by other standards. The advertisement of the small local baker attains the same dignity of bearing as does that of the baking company whose bread is on the table of homes all over the country. In the communities through which the cars pass, the advertisements reach that large mass of people representing what is estimated as 60 to 90 per cent of the adult population. Consequently, the cards enjoy an audience wide in the range of its buying preferences and in its ability to purchase the things it wishes. The products which can best use car advertising are those for which practically all riders are prospects, products such as are sold in the grocery stores, drug stores, hardware and house furnishings stores, haberdashery shops, dry-goods stores, and hosiery and shoe stores. Success has also been attained by advertisers who find among the masses of car riders those people who seek and can afford a higher enjoyment of living, through furniture, automobiles, bond investments, real estate, and homes.

Car cards offer great latitude in the reproduction of illustrations. The number of colors in which the card may be printed can run from black and white to seven colors; the technique used may run from that used in line plate drawings, through drawings suited for Ben Day plates, process halftones, direct lithography, and offset lithography, to the embossed and varnished cards which have made their appearance, with novel effect. This freedom is especially conducive to the reproduction of small products in their natural color and in their approximate size—products such as preserved fruits, crackers, oranges, apples, cold cuts with their accompanying condiments, gloves, shoes, and cosmetics; also those products of everyday use, in a highly competitive field depending for their individuality upon distinctive techniques in reproduction, such as face-creams and collars. The only limitation to the combination of colors used in car cards is the difficulty of seeing certain colors in the artificial light of cars. The colors which have the greatest visibility at a distance are yellow, orange, and green. Then follow red, blue, and purple, in the order named. The greater the area of any color used, the more readable will that color be at any distance; yellows, oranges, and greens, if properly used, can generally make their cards dominate. The choice of colors used on a card is influenced by another factor besides visibility; namely, contrast with the color of cards by others in the field. Before designing a card, advertisers, therefore, study the colors prevailing at that time in car cards, especially among others in their field, and then strike an individual color note. The simple, rugged, poster style of art work with its strong, contrasting colors is better adapted for use in car cards than is the magazine type of colored illustration with its delicate lines and subtle gradations.

The distribution of car cards is elastic in that the advertiser can fairly choose the neighborhood whose people he wishes to reach, without necessarily addressing the entire city and paying for his folly. This characteristic should be a valuable consideration for merchants such as furniture dealers who wish to secure the trade of an outlying or neighborhood shopping section of their own. Also the intensity with which car cards are used can be varied to suit a given requirement. Where a product is subject to everyday purchase, where its cost is low and the occasion for using it is frequent—as in the case of the five-cent packaged candies, preserves, fruits, bread, soaps, tooth pastes, chewing gum, cold creams, and so forth, a full showing can be used to advantage. The product is then constantly before the largest possible number of persons, each of whom may be considering purchasing it at any time. When more lengthy deliberation is given to the product by a prospective buyer, as in the case of stoves, furniture, automobiles, bond investments, and homes, a half, or even a quarter, showing may suffice. Whether a full, half, or quarter showing should be used can best be determined by judging the number of times a card may be seen between pur-

WELL-DESIGNED CAR CARDS

Observe how few elements are introduced into each card, their unified composition, and the dominance in each card of a single feature; also the conciseness of the copy.

chases. The longer the period preceding purchase, the smaller the size of the showing need be; the shorter the period between purchases, the larger the showing should be. The size of the showing is also affected by the intensity with which competing brands use space.

The best use of car cards is made when they can tell their story boldly and in very few words. They provide an ideal medium for the impressing of a name (with perhaps a slogan or secondary slogan), of a trade-mark, or of the picture of a package. Where considerable explanatory matter has to appear in a campaign, publication and direct-mail advertisements can best carry the burden of the copy. But the entire story can constantly be brought back to the mind of the reader by means of car cards, either through their distinctive illustrations, similar to the publication advertisements, or else by means of pithy copy, summarizing the text.

Buying space.—The cost of cards averages about 70 cents per card per car per month; the contract period runs from 12 months to 5 years. The cards must be supplied by the advertiser, and cost from $5.00 to $25.00 a hundred. The companies selling space in cars (a few concerns control most of the available space, one firm alone owning or controlling through its subsidiaries the cars in over 3,500 cities) offer excellent service, both to the small local advertiser and to the national advertiser—the one who sells the idea or the merits of his particular merchandise to the public and leaves to the local merchant the opportunity of supplying the demand of the public for that merchandise

For the local merchants these companies have prepared an extensive assortment of attractive cards, suited to the particular season in which their respective products sell best. The merchant's imprint can be placed on these cards at nominal cost. Syndicate stock cards usually present the merchant's message far more attractively than could his own card and cost no more than the imprint charge. The one objection to the use of stock cards—their failure to reflect the personality and distinctiveness of the different advertiser—is not as serious as may at first appear, not merely because many small stores are utterly devoid of personality and never present any distinctive atmosphere until thrust upon them, but also because the car-card concerns reveal an amazing fecundity of ideas in constantly creating new designs for the advertisers.

In the largest cities, the car-card companies offer a "merchandising service" to those advertisers who wish to enter the respective markets. The staff responsible for this service consists of a corps of men who are intimately acquainted with the drug, grocery, and other retail-store merchants of those cities. When an advertiser is ready to introduce his wares, the representatives help him secure local distribution for his product in the various stores, in a manner similar to that in which the newspaper "merchandising" departments function.

## CHAPTER XVIII

## DEALER DISPLAY ADVERTISING

"WE find our grocers enshrined in temples whose columns are of canisters," wrote John Ruskin in his essay on the English Villa, "and whose pinnacles are of sugarloaves." Were the shop which he described a typical grocery store of modern time, little homage would have been paid to the columns of canisters without mentioning the advertisements of Del Monte Peaches which were probably leaning against them. In front of the pinnacles of sugarloaves there would have appeared elaborate cardboard signs telling about the many uses of Crystal Domino Sugar. For the modern retail store is no mere warehouse or trading post. Rather it is a shop which skillfully invites the buyer, by means of signs varied in color and form, to consider all its wares, making a pleasing suggestion to try some Gulden's Mustard with cold cuts, or offering emphatic advice not to go home without a package of Tetley's Tea. The retail shopkeeper is no longer satisfied to present mute exhibitions of merchandise; he advertises them so that all who enter may want them and buy. This practice has been encouraged by the manufacturers who, selling the goods to the retailer, have assumed much of the responsibility for the resale of those products to the dealer's own customers—for which purpose there has been evolved a form of advertising known as dealer display.

What dealer display advertising is.—Dealer display advertising is spoken of in part as "store card" advertising, "window display" advertising, "store display" advertising, and similar terms. More exactly, dealer display advertising is that form of advertising issued to the retailer by the manufacturer, producer, or selling agent of an article for the purpose of increasing the sale of that product, and intended to be

366

A WHOLE WINDOW AROUND ONE IDEA
The Nestlé's Display unselfishly promotes a "Better Babies Window." The strips pasted on the window and the panel in the center constitute the actual display. The druggist himself supplied the merchandise from his stock.

shown in or about the store itself. Dealer display advertising should not be confused with "display advertising" as applied in the newspaper sense, where there is a division into display advertising and classified advertising.[1] Dealer display advertising should furthermore be distinguished from "trade advertising," which is essentially planned to sell goods *to the merchant,* whereas dealer displays are created to sell the advertised product *for him.* A distinguishing feature of this medium is the fact that its circulation depends upon the people who pass or enter the merchant's store in which the goods advertised are being sold.

**Characteristics as a medium.**—Dealer display advertising appears "on the spot when the goods are sold." It is the advertiser's final word before the buyer makes up his mind to purchase or alters his intention of buying a certain article. Dealer display advertising is a flexible medium in that it lit-

---

[1] See p. 273.

erally follows the distribution of the product from store to store. It permits showing the actual merchandise in a setting of advertising, a fact which gives the advantage of novelty in construction, color, size and shape, along with the possibility of motion and flash effects in electric lighting. There are some forms of dealer display advertising, soon to be described, which also enjoy unusual permanency.

The disadvantage of this form of advertising is the difficulty which a manufacturer has in securing the proper showing for his display. Or, viewed from the dealer's side of the counter, the chief trouble in the past has been inability to create effective displays which are in keeping with everyday requirements.

**Planning the forms.**—The particular nature of any display is based upon a careful consideration of:

1. The character of the product itself.
2. The importance of the product compared with the other merchandise sold in the same store.
3. The particular requirements of these retail stores.

**Display as affected by character of product.**—Generally, the power of dealer displays is greatest when the price of the commodity is a low one. This is true because a person is more disposed to act upon last-minute suggestion in making a small expenditure than in making a large one. Dealer displays are especially helpful in marketing merchandise in the "convenience" class, bought because it is near at hand, rather than in marketing "shopping" merchandise for which a person looks around among competing articles, weighs their respective advantages, ponders, and then purchases. In the case of ten-cent items, the sales resulting from dealer displays may be directly apparent. For high-priced articles, such as kitchen cabinets and even automobiles, displays may, however, justify themselves because they create inquiries which may culminate in sales.

The displays designed for a product in the pioneering stage ought to show vividly the need for a product such as this one; for a product in the competitive stage, the display ought to emphasize those features of merit possessed in the given product not obtainable in similar ones. Or, in the latter case, the display may help make that product distinctive in the way it is presented. To illustrate: if a display were planned to sell shoe-trees (which are not in extensive use) it would be better to show the advantages of having shoes properly kept, with trees, than it would be to focus attention upon the details of construction possessed by the article. Perhaps it would simply be necessary to show a pair of shoes, one with a shoe-tree, the other without, to convey the idea. But a display to sell shoe-laces would do better to direct attention to some feature of the lace—such as the beaded tip. Shoe trees are largely in a pioneering stage, but shoe laces are in a competitive stage.

**Display as affected by importance of product.**—When a merchant is asked to erect a dealer display, he is really being asked to give to the advertiser the space necessary for the display at the expense of his other merchandise. The merchant is in business to sell all his wares. He naturally gives attention to the various lines of merchandise in proportion to their respective sales, and consequent profits; the advertising for a product in an established field generally follows in importance.

If an automobile accessory dealer makes 50 per cent of his sales in tires, it could safely be assumed that he would be willing to devote about 50 per cent of his total advertising space to featuring the different tires he sells. If only 2 per cent of his revenue comes from the sale of piston rings, a dealer display of that product would have to recognize the comparative value to him. It would not be feasible to plan a permanent display requiring the entire window. An exception to this principle arises when the retailer is shown that he is getting only a fraction of the business possible in a given article, in which case he may temporarily offer a much larger share of the advertising space than the product generally warrants. After the special displays have been removed, increased sales may have raised the percentage of importance sufficiently to warrant giving future displays of the product more prominence. Another plan for increasing the amount of allotted display space is that of using other forms of advertising to bring more customers into the store, thus increasing the importance of the product. It is always well to recognize, however, that the total importance of a display to a dealer varies directly with the importance of the article compared with that of the other items sold in that store.

**Display as affected by nature of store.**—Successful dealer displays conform to the dealer's own ideas of what he would like to create for himself had he the manufacturer's facilities. Different dealers have different requirements; hence, different ideas. In the haberdashery field, little glass signs on wooden mounts have proved quite effective, whereas metal signs are more popular in the automobile accessory field, probably because metal signs are able to withstand rough handling and do not show the oiled fingerprints of the garage man's hand. Grocers prefer hanging cards because of the generally crowded condition of their stores. Department stores are reluctant to use any manufacturers' display material and, as a rule, do so only when they have an exclusive agency, or else where the display is in keeping with the dignity of the shop. A concern in the knit-goods field, as an illustration, successfully gained department store display by offering small mahogany and glass trade-mark signs.

Because competition for display space in the drug field is keen and the number of products sold is great, the matter of dimensions is very important. Counter display material for these stores should be higher than they are wide, to economize on the counter space required. The same requirement prevails also in cigar stores and in other shops in which the counter space is equally as crowded.

In the optical and jewelry fields, felt counter-pads bearing the product's name have been effective. In stationery stores and on cigar counters, glass stands from which it is easy to scoop change receive a welcome position near the cashier's desk. And in the shoe repairing trade, it is not at all unusual to have metal advertising signs nailed right against the counter itself.

Some products have distribution through many retail channels. Metallic pencils are commonly sold through stationery stores, optical stores, jewelry, and drug stores; and flashlights may be bought in electrical shops, sporting goods stores, drug stores, stationery stores, and paint and hardware stores. To prepare an individual display for each type of store, would prove an expensive plan. Consequently, more economical methods have been evolved. For articles of such versatile selling nature, it is possible to create one large general display, and issue with it supplementary units of smaller size designed especially for the respective trades. Another plan is to standardize a number of different displays for use in stores having similar requirements. For example, in showing metallic pencils, colored card displays may be used in stationery and in drug stores, while for jewelry shops and optical shops, neat small metal signs might be issued.

As a matter of general principle, it is also well to distinguish between the dealer in a small town and the one in the large city, when planning their requirements for displays.

**The forms of dealer display advertising.**—The inside of the store, with its counters and shelves, offers an opportunity for dealer display advertising entirely different from that afforded by the windows of the store, valuable as that location may be. Likewise the outside of the store itself has its own advantages and shortcomings to which this medium seeks to adapt itself. Of the many ingenious forms that are possible, the following groupings are fairly inclusive:

**Inside the store—on the counters.**—The simplest form of counter-showing is a card with an easel mounted on its back, so that it will stand erect. A variation of this form is a folded card standing like an open book-cover on edge. Another form is the three-wing screen which consists of a center panel and a leaf on either sire. The simple three-wing screen construction, incidentally, is perhaps the most widely used motif in dealer display advertising. These displays are merely advertising posters in miniature form, with perhaps novel die-cut effects to avoid the monotony of the rectangular shape.

The next form of counter display to consider is likewise a card, but one which holds an actual sample of the merchandise being advertised. To secure this effect, it may be necessary to die-cut a hole in the card, enabling the insertion of the article, or else arrange a special slit in the display to hold the object firmly in position. This type of display is especially popular for handy-sized packages or merchandise.

*Merchandise containers.*—When selling a packaged commodity which is both low in price and small in size, it is desirable to keep a constant supply neatly arranged on the dealer's counters. The display now becomes a merchandising container. These "silent salesmen" are extensively used for five-cent candy, hair-nets, drug tablets, notions, and other small-packaged merchandise. Ingenious shipping boxes have been designed, which, when opened, become counter display containers for the merchandise. In the experience of many advertisers, merchandise so displayed will outsell to a marked degree the identical product placed inside of a glass counter. A number of specific tests have shown that the sale of flavoring extracts increased from 68 bottles to 154 bottles, when placed in merchandise containers; dental cream sales rose from 160 tubes to 417 tubes; spark-plug sales from 72 to 125. On candy, the sales mounted from 358 to 1,047 packages.[2]

The merchandise display container is especially popular in a field such as that of automobile accessories, because the store shelving is not adapted to small items of spark-plug size.

A more substantial display of wood or metal may be furnished by the advertisers and refilled by the dealers from bulk stock (on the style of the post-card rack). These displays often become so large that they receive floor space rather than counter position. Occasionally a utility idea may be embodied in the display, such as a mirror on a hair-net stand, or a testing bulb in a flashlight-battery rack.

In the five-and-ten-cent products which are displayed openly, the loss to dealers through pilferage is negligible. But to avoid loss in items of greater value, a number of displays have been specially designed. The principle upon which they are constructed permits the customer to see the article itself, but

---

[2] A. T. Fischer, "Window and Store Display," page 159.

the opening for the merchandise faces the merchant's side of the counter.

**Inside the store—miscellaneous forms.**—Looking up from the counter, we next behold the shelf and its opportunities for dealer display advertising. It is not always practicable to have a large sign hang over the merchandise as this may hide the actual wares. Shelf-strips, however, have been in favor, these being strips of cardboard or metal tacked along the edge of the shelf. Instead of being tacked on, these strips may be so designed that the merchandise will hold them in place. In the grocery field, the upright partitions of shelving are utilized either by these strips or by vertical self-service merchandise racks. In the soda fountain and candy trade, the mirror space is often utilized by cementing signs on the mirrors. Even overhead space is sought, so that the advertiser's sign may dangle from a string attached to electric lights.

A survey of stores will show that not much display space is being overlooked or neglected, but resourcefulness may reveal methods superior to those already utilized.

**Store window displays.**—Passing from the interior of the store itself, we come to the grand parade ground of dealer display—the windows, whose sole purpose is to advertise the store and the goods. The window invites the very best ideas that are possible in this field.

The lithographic or cardboard display which is placed in the background as a setting for the rest of the window display is usually referred to as a "window screen." Its size and importance cause it to be an expensive piece of equipment—perhaps the most costly unit of all. Seasonability and freshness are important virtues in such a display, a fact which makes frequent changes imperative. To offset the cost of changing the display, a number of semi-permanent trims have been evolved. For its Rexall Stores, the United Drug Company has developed a very successful method, whereby new lithographed sheets are readily slipped into a permanent wooden frame screen which is provided at the outset. To further help "dress" the window, other units of unnumbered variety have been created, as a tour of inspection among retail stores will reveal.

Dealer displays: miscellaneous forms.—Glass signs featuring a well-known product often find a secure resting place on the outside of the dealer's window—secure because they must be cemented to the glass itself. Light metal and celluloid products may be used instead of glass.

Window transparencies and decalcomanias are about one-quarter as expensive as glass signs. They are pasted directly on the glass (preferably inside, for the sake of protection from the weather). They last for years, with perhaps a few wrinkles and scratches at most, to show for their wear.

Glass signs are popular in clothing, optical, and jewelry stores because of their dignified bearing. On the other hand, transparencies, because of their economy, warrant broad distribution through grocery, hardware, cigar, and drug stores.

Window banners to protect the goods from the sun's rays have been successfully issued by candy manufacturers. Enlarged magazine advertisements possess a news element which makes them valuable as a form of window display. "Streamers," "cut-outs," metal signs for attachment outside the store, and electric display signs are among the other forms used in dealer display work. Painted bulletins and posters on the side of the dealers' stores also offer opportunity in this field of advertising.

Traveling displays.—If an advertiser knows that one display will be shown to five dealers in succession, he can afford to spend five times as much for each display. The new avenue of possibilities thus opened has made possible the "traveling displays," also descriptively called educational or scenic exhibits. With such an exhibit, a shoe manufacturer showed the historical development of shoes, a linen house showed the steps in the growing and manufacturing of the flax, a phonograph advertiser showed the anatomy of his machines, while another produced a series of miniature opera settings for use in selling more records. The traveling display is an exceptional presentation. It has received showing in the windows of department stores and has gained distinction for dealers with exclusive territories, even when they handle a highly competitive product.

The success of traveling displays depends upon their informative ideas and the interesting manner whereby these are dramatized. Careful provision must also be made to route the display from dealer to dealer.

**Planning the issuance of material.**—Manufacturers have thrust displays upon the dealers so indiscriminately and with such profusion that the average dealer is about ready to demand a bonus for showing the display. To ask him to pay for any material issued may seem out of the question, yet may be feasible where the volume of business done on a well-advertised line justifies the cost of the material. Instances in which a small charge might not be out of order may be found in the tire, men's clothing, talking machine, and electrical fields.

If the selling plan calls for exclusive agencies, that is, the rule of having the goods sold through one dealer only in a restricted locality, conditions are also favorable for securing payment on dealer-display advertising. In such a case the advertiser usually has a more personal contact with the dealer than when selling an article of general distribution. Whether or not the dealer will be allowed to continue as the exclusive agent invariably depends upon his ability to meet a certain quota of sales. The manufacturer's advertising under these circumstances is accorded a very favorable reception.

A manufacturer selling through exclusive agencies and asking payment for the advertising material furnished, usually points out to the dealer that a certain appropriation has been set aside for national advertising. That serves to make the product more popular and the dealer's franchise more valuable. If the retailer will pay for his own share of local advertising, he can directly capitalize on the reputation of the manufacturer's general advertising. The cost of the individual dealer display is furthermore much lower when the material is secured from the manufacturer than it is when the displays are prepared by the merchant himself, due to the economy of quantity production.

In several industries, far-sighted manufacturers offer to

their dealers a complete window display service, functioning regularly throughout the year and designed from the dealer's own viewpoint. The displays feature his store and the general line of merchandise being sold, introducing in a subordinate manner the manufacturer's products. Retail merchants have shown themselves willing to pay for services of this kind, if properly worked out. It relieves them of the bother of planning their displays, saves the annoyance of experimenting with different arrangements, and provides the suggestions of expert window trimmers whom the merchants individually could not afford to hire.

**Where the material is issued free.** —When material is to be distributed free, a most important consideration is that of deciding how much per dealer should be spent. If the article is sold without the aid of a jobber, the amount of sales per average dealer may serve as a basis for the individual display appropriation. In the tire field, for instance, the manufacturer will look up the account of a deal requesting certain material, to be sure the volume of business he does or can do is in keeping with the cost of the displays.

On the basis of such calculation, "deals" may also be worked out, as is frequently done in the drug and stationery trade, whereby with a $25 purchase, let us say, the retailer gets Display *A* costing $1.30; with a $40 purchase, Display *B* costing $2.00; with a $50 order, Display *C* costing $3.00. A salesman may also use such material as a rational inducement in encouraging the merchant to place a larger order.

One manufacturer in the drug field, selling through jobbers, succeeded in the deal plan by packing the displays with the merchandise, together in a corrugated box. Pasted on the outside of each case, a label told in big type what merchandise was being shipped and listed the display material included. These cases were then sold by jobbers as a complete unit of sale.

Where a new product is being offered or a special zone campaign being launched, it may be necessary to disregard the amount of display that can be afforded per sale, since the potential sale may warrant the excess. An important consideration to bear in mind in all dealer display advertising is to keep the expense of the material in proportion to the value of securing initial sales and consistent with the profits of the sales which may follow.

Getting free material used.—The natural assumption of "cost nothing, worth nothing" makes it particularly trying to give away dealer displays successfully. The only merit which a dealer will recognize in a display is its ability to bring business to his door—both for the product advertised and, more important, for his other wares. The best rule to follow in designing a display is that of having it serve the dealer, through appropriateness to his needs, through character that will help the prestige of his store, and through ideas that will be of immediate practical value to him. The mirror signs at many soda fountains earn their position by saying, "Please get checks at desk." The National Biscuit Company was able to secure the coveted hanging-from-the-ceiling position by issuing a sign which boldly stated "Cracker Department," and in a smaller type carried the National Biscuit Company's message; and clothing manufacturers have issued "How to Dress Well" charts for similar use in haberdashery shops.

The intrinsic value of the display helps greatly in securing its use. In addition, the advertiser's salesman can be of great assistance in presenting the dealer display, erecting it, or securing authorization to have a special crew of window-trimmers put in the display. On subsequent trips, the salesman may also be able to replace soiled cards with new ones.

The manufacturer's salesman can enter a formal requisition to have the material sent with the merchandise or under separate cover. Or else, the request for material may come direct from the dealer. The actual shipment of material presents an important phase of dealer-display work. It can be carried by the salesman and installed by him, size permitting, or it can be erected by special crews where feasible. In some cases a display may be included in every shipment of goods, for which purpose it is necessary to plan its size and nature to fit the package in which the merchandise is to be shipped.

Jobbers' salesmen have to devote their attention to a number of lines; their commission is measured in terms of sales rather than the goodwill they create for any one manufacturer.

Hence they will seldom undertake the detailed work just described. Dealer display work through jobbers is made still more difficult by the general aversion of jobbers to handling this service for their customers.

**Further suggestions for securing use of free material.**— An advertiser of tire chains offered to dealers special signs, such as "Rain Predicted for Tomorrow, Have You Your Chains?" Dealers were told how to secure the daily weather reports without cost from the Government. The displays of this advertiser received many preferred positions. Manufacturers' house organs to dealers usually give special attention to displays, showing what effects other stores obtain, encouraging better use of displays already issued, and announcing new material.

Prize contests with cash awards for the best displays are often held among dealers. This plan offers many possibilities, especially if the contest is announced in trade papers, and pictures of the winning displays are shown with perhaps the photograph of the man who received the award.

Window and store displays are frequently designed to repeat the message of the other advertising *at the time that advertising appears.* The dealer displays then capitalize on the general advertising; the similarity or "tie-up" serves as a final reminder of the message which may already have interested the public, thereby naturally increasing the value of the display in the eyes of the dealer.

Many concerns make it a rule not to issue material without a distinct request from the merchant, and then check its use carefully. The small advertiser will do well to plan very modestly at the outset in the creation of material, and see personally, if possible, that it is installed. His display may have to compete with the very attractive ones of the large advertiser; hence the character of his material should be especially worthy of the dealer's attention.

**Suggestions in designing displays.**—The dealer display seldom is beheld alone and is often obscured by surrounding displays and merchandise. Consequently, the important copy should not be placed along the bottom of cards or signs, but well up toward the top where there is less danger of having other displays or merchandise cover up the message.

The display should be able to stand firmly. Top-heavy designs and weak bases are especially to be avoided, as are cards which curl and‚warp easily. For general purposes, 12-ply cardboard or heavier is desirable.

A good display is simple to erect. Complicated devices for putting the display together are not practical. The dealer seldom has the patience or time necessary to erect a display which its creator failed to simplify.

In designing the display, it is also well to keep in mind that the size and shape of the typical merchant's window may be far different from that of the window of the large city store, with its deep setting, its high front, its model, light interior—and its weekly changes of merchandise. The chief danger in conceiving displays is that of idealizing the merchant's store and his altruism.

**Precautions in dealer displays.**—An advertiser would also do well to heed these common weaknesses, reported by Fischer:[3]

1. Too hard to put together.
2. Too large for the space the dealer has.
3. Too small for the purpose.
4. Not enough profit in the probable business to justify the amount of space.
5. Display was received in wrong season for sales.
6. Small appeal of product to dealer's class of trade.
7. Display was not distinctive enough to attract attention.
8. Display was out of keeping with character of store.

An authoritative résumé of the entire field may be obtained by constant observation of the displays to be seen in any store.

**Other dealer helps.**—Dealer displays provide only one of the devices whereby a manufacturer may address the consumer through the merchant in whose store the product is sold. Other media which enable the retailer to obtain the immediate benefit of the manufacturer's advertising are generally spoken of as "dealer helps"—typified by the following forms:

---

[3] A. T. Fischer, *op cit.*, pages 43-47.

THE MATERIAL in this complete *Dealer Campaign* was designed by the Westinghouse Electric Co. to aid the storekeepers selling their fan in advertising the fact. Through these "dealer aids" retailers can dovetail their own advertising with the manufacturer's extensive advertising to the general public.

**1.** This advertisement is the same as the advertisement to the public except that the text is addressed to merchants.

**2.** Copy paragraphs about the fan, suggested for use by retailers in writing their own advertisements.

**3.** Samples of complete, ready-made newspaper advertisements of which electrotypes are supplied to dealers. Each merchant has his own name and address inserted. (Note—advertisements are numbered for convenience in ordering.)

**4.** Illustrations which the manufacturer will furnish in plate form, for use in the dealers' own advertising.

**5.** Direct advertising bearing dealer's imprint to be distributed by mail or over the counter.

**6.** Lantern slides (name of dealers to be inserted at bottom) to be flashed in local movie houses.

**7.** A distinctive window display (size greatly reduced). The breeze of a fan placed on the pedestal in the foreground would cause the "cool-off" semaphore to rotate.

**8.** Booklet of suggestions for clerks to aid in selling more fans by showing how to make effective sales presentation.

**9.** The requisition blank for the material.

1. *Advertising in local newspapers.*—This may consist of advertisements which do not list the dealer's names, those which list names of all dealers of a town in a piece of copy, or those which are to be inserted by the dealers over their own name. Advertisements which appear without listing any dealers' names are practically straight consumer advertising; those which list names of all dealers are, as a rule, more effective for their moral effect upon the dealers themselves than for their aid to the consumer. Where the merchant has the exclusive agency for the product, his name alone is usually signed to the advertisements.

It must be borne in mind that many retail merchants appreciate and would use the aid of manufacturers' advertising if that advertising played fair with the dealer. "See what pretty advertisements we are giving you" will be the tone assumed by the manufacturer, when in fact the advertisements are wholly designed to further the sale of that product alone, ignoring the feelings, problems and wishes of the dealer whose greatest asset is the goodwill he has earned among his neighbors. This heedlessness has resulted in a flood of "slotted advertisements"—advertisements prepared ostensibly for the dealer but featuring the advertised product exclusively and leaving just a slot at the bottom for "dealer's name here." To avoid this common deficiency it is necessary to determine the size of the store for which the advertising is to be prepared. If the store is a large one, it is well to learn its exact policy regarding manufacturer's advertising. For large stores the product generally has to be well known, and the amount of space required small. The exception exists when a special merchandise sale transaction is made with the retail store, in which case the manufacturer's name may be displayed prominently. On the other hand, if the stores are comparatively small, the advisable procedure is that of securing samples of their advertising, seeing how it could be improved generally, and then suggesting to them a layout and copy plan for their entire advertising. In the appropriate place, the copy and plate for the manufacturer's article can be included.

The manufacturer can furthermore forward electrotypes of the advertisement to the retailer. These electrotypes may consist of the complete advertisement, or else of the illustration and trade-mark only, accompanied by copy and layout. In preparing electrotypes and layouts for the dealers' use it is advisable to design plates in various sizes to meet different requirements. (The usual tendency is to make them too large for practical purposes.) A "Book of Cuts" or "Portfolio of Proofs," from which the dealer may select the plates, is often provided. This book may also include advertisements with copy and layout suggestions. The opening pages of a "Dealer Book" are generally devoted to selling the merchant on the value of the accompanying advertising ideas. Numbers are usually assigned to the illustrations for reference purposes, and a standard return order or "request" card is inserted in the back of the book for use by the dealer in ordering the plates.

2. *Direct advertisements.*—These may consist of letter-heads, folders, leaflets, or booklets bearing the dealer's name and address imprinted on the cover and similar material for mailing or for counter distribution. Here again the precaution should be taken of designing all material in such a way that the dealer will want it, and want to use it.

3. *Salesmanship instruction for retail clerks.*—After advertising has brought a prospect into a store, it steps aside and lets the retail clerk complete the sale. The effectiveness of all the previous advertising may depend upon the ability of this salesman and in his training advertising has a keen interest. Manufacturers have accordingly endeavored to show store clerks how to serve customers in a manner which will improve sales. The training may be given by the advertiser's salesmen, or by specialists where the product warrants the extra expense. For kitchen cabinets and linoleums, by way of illustration, advertisers have had special instructors travel from store to store.

A few concerns offer mail courses in instruction while others use their trade paper advertisements for an educational series. An advertiser does not require an ambitious program to conduct this work, for he can invariably suggest selling ideas for use in conjunction with his own product.

4. *Storekeeping instruction for merchants.*—The shoe dealer, the grocer, or the druggist must know more than shoes and groceries or drugs to become a successful merchant. They

must know accounting, to determine where profits lie and where money is tied up; they must know the principles of sound credit to avoid loss on accounts; and they must know how to sell goods at a rapid turnover.

Carrying out the instruction idea one step further, advertisers have successfully instituted courses in store management for dealers. They endeavor to "help the grocer to groce," quoting Thomas Russell. They pass on to him some of the experience which has come to them through their contact with thousands of other storekeepers.

It is only logical that national advertisers, having become teachers in the use of their product to the public at large, should also assist merchants to develop better business methods. The growth of firms such as the United Drug Company and Beech Nut Packing Co. is largely attributed to their work in helping merchants make more profits through better storekeeping methods.

\*     \*     \*     \*

With the exception of Packages (which, in a sense, are advertising media), we have completed the discussion of media, as the term is understood. Newspapers, magazines, outdoor advertising and car cards, direct-mail advertising and dealer display advertising have each their subdivisions and specialized classifications. The advertiser who wonders which is "better" on general principles can learn a lesson from the very men who publish and produce the media. A newspaper will advertise for readers in a magazine; a magazine, in the newspaper; both will employ outdoor advertising; and the merits of outdoor advertising will be advertised in both. Publishers use direct-mail advertising, while printers and direct-mail agencies will use publication space; magazines will use counter-display stands and dealer-display organizations will use magazines. If the chief sponsors of one medium so appreciate the value of other media for their purpose, then the advertiser can well recognize that the only way to choose media is to find out who his prospects are, where they are, and what constitute the best media as far as they alone are concerned.

CHAPTER XIX

PACKAGES

WITHIN five weeks of the time that the little box of Sun-Maid raisins made its débût, orders were received for 333 million packages, having a retail value of over 16½ million dollars, disposing of over 16 thousand tons of raisins. All because of a package—and a five-cent package at that!

Evidently the modern package is far more than a humble receptacle for a product; it is a device which changes the very buying custom of a people. In advertising, the package is not only an advertisement in itself, but it is a source of ideas upon which entire businesses have been built. Uneeda Biscuits, Kellogg's Corn Flakes, Colgate's Tooth Paste, Yuban Coffee, Charms, Old Dutch Cleanser, Lux—how can one think of them without thinking of their containers? Packages have literally moulded the character of these products.

The advent of the package and the improvement in package machinery have done even more; they have brought about more sanitary methods of selling merchandise. They have largely displaced bulk selling with trade-mark selling. The package bestows upon its product a reputation which the consumer can recognize, which the retailer can depend upon, and which the manufacturer is obliged to maintain.

Choosing the package.—But to leave the general discussion of the package to take up the actual work of choosing the container for a given product, a package, as the term is here used, refers to any container or wrapper of a product. It may be a cardboard box or a glass jar; a tin can or a sheet of tissue, a soap wrapper or a finely ornamented perfume bottle. The styles of packages are so many, the forms, shapes, sizes, and materials so varied, that an intelligent choice requires a careful study of the three factors given on the next page.

385

1. The requirements of the consumer.
2. The requirements of the trade.
3. The special requirements of the product.

Requirements of the consumer.—How do people expect to buy the product? An advertiser may discover that people have become accustomed to certain ideas which he must recognize. There was a time, by way of illustration, when cold cream could be sold directly from the jar. With his spatula the druggist would fill a little wooden box, clamp on the cover, wipe off the excess cream with a towel, and slap on a label to complete the sale. The wooden box gave way to the tin can, and today milady the fashionable woman demands a pretty jar or a tube when she buys cold cream. It isn't for the advertiser to decide arbitrarily upon what type of container he shall give; his choice is affected at the outset by the type of container his clientele will require.

The tendency in modern business has been to go from bulk selling to package selling; from one form of package to a superior type of package. Before the new advertiser makes his plan, he must inquire as to the degree of package-expectation purchasers of that article have attained.

Requirements of the trade.—The second factor to consider in deciding upon a package is its disposition in the retail store in which the product is to be sold. Is the product one that is displayed on the shelves, or buried under the counter? How is it placed on the shelf? In the grocery field, the front or large side is given display position. (Note that Aunt Jemima's Pancake Flour and Kellogg's Toasted Corn Flakes have their pictorial effect on the front. Biscuit boxes have their names across the long edge.)

In the drug field, where shelf space is more crowded, packages will either be stood up on end or else displayed with only the small end (the bottom) showing. An advertiser of medicinal crackers ran into a perplexing situation when he sought to design a single package which would be effective both in the drug and grocery fields. He had the alternative either of making two different boxes or of making a package to suit one trade and taking a chance of its acceptance by the other. Instead he ingeniously compromised by making a cube-shaped box. In canned goods the precaution must also be taken of having the label so designed that it can be identified regardless of the way in which the can faces the buyer. The type matter on the label should be readable without the necessity of turning the can backward and forward.

**Requirement of the product.**—The third factor in considering the choice of a package involves a very interesting phase of the subject. Until this point, we have been subservient to the demands of precedent. "These are the conditions, and you must conform to them," we were warned. But the package is in close competition with all other packages around it in the dealer's store, and we are now free to seek distinctiveness in its behalf, either through construction, design, or label. Individuality in construction may be obtained through change of shape, of size, or through the introduction of utility devices.

**Distinction through shape.**—To see the extremes to which advertisers have gone in their quest for the odd-shaped container, it is only necessary to examine an array of perfume bottles in any drug store. Shapes? There are shapes without number! Some are as graceful as a Grecian urn; others otherwise. Bottles with straight sides, concave sides, convex sides; bottles with wide bases, bottles with narrow bases; bottles which rise from the counter like a steeple; bottles shaped like the face of a steeple-clock—there is no dearth of shapes here!

Obviously, it is best to take a few precautions in planning a unique-shaped package. The container should at all times be practicable for its purpose. If it is a bottle, it should be steady on its base so that it will not be tipped readily. On the other hand, a bottle which has a very wide base, like a pyramid, proves equally objectionable to merchants for it may require an undue amount of room on the shelves. The size and shape of a container are often restricted by the use to which the package is put—as for example, tooth powder cans and mouthwash bottles, which must fit into medicine chests. No matter how unique the package may be, it should be convenient to grasp. A talcum powder can of rectangular shape proved unpopular because of its squared edges, which the can made less comfortable to hold than did the customary oval-shape.

The container should be inviting to use. Some cosmetic jars have openings so narrow that it is difficult to extract the contents, and are so deep that it is a trying task to reach the bottom.

An advantage can sometimes be obtained in the dealer's store by employing a unique device, such as the one on the familiar package of CN. The well-known gable is more than a means of identification; it secures top display position for the package, since its shape precludes having other merchandise rest upon it.

The package must be structurally strong. "Angles, shoulders, and other irregularities in bottles' surfaces create weak spots and cause increased breakage in the process of washing, filling, capping, labeling, packing, and shipping," says George P. Nelson, who goes on to show that, for glassware, the straight-edged round tumbler is the ideal container from the standpoint of strength.[1]

Again, the demands of the shipping room may well be heeded in designing the odd-shaped package, for the shape of the container has an important bearing upon the cost of shipping the product. A round container requires approximately 20 per cent more room in packing than does a square one. If a business grows to the point where many thousand packages are shipped, a decrease of one-fifth the shipping cost is well worth considering.

**Distinction through size.**—A student of modern social tendencies may be able to discover the reason why smaller packages have become so very popular. The five-cent box of raisins and of prunes, the ten-cent box of dates, the miniature perfume tubes, are all unmistakable evidence of a distinct mode. Perhaps they represent the spirit of the sample product, or else reflect the cramped kitchenette age in which we live; but whatever the cause, they have undoubtedly opened new channels of sales for their respective commodities.

The economics of package sizes is a subject unto itself. If her household uses only a few ounces of bicarbonate of soda a month, a woman would rather pay ten cents for a four-ounce

---

[1] "Package Facts," by George P. Nelson, page 25.

Mobiloil in Quart Cans!
New! Ideal convenience—and
protection—while touring.
Put 2 or 3 under the seat of
your car.

Ask for
Gargoyle Mobiloil
"A", "Arctic", "E",
"B"or "BB"— the grade
specified for your car in the
Chart.

VACUUM OIL COMPANY

DISTINCTIVENESS THROUGH METHOD
OF "PACKAGING" A PRODUCT

box than twenty-five cents for a pound carton. A man will
pay one cent for twenty-four matches rather than two cents
for a hundred. Not price alone, but speed of using a product
and convenience of carrying it are deciding elements. If an
advertiser seeks to improve the sale of a packaged product,
he may advantageously make some investigations on this score
for himself. It may be more profitable to establish a precedent
here than to follow one.[2]

A word of caution is opportune here regarding the choice
of a new package size. Sometimes an unexpected surprise will
greet the advertiser who adopts a size not generally identified
with the product. A soap flake was offered in a very large box
similar to the type in which breakfast foods are sold. Surely
enough, when the packages were displayed on the grocer's
counter, people repeatedly mistook it for a new brand of
breakfast food.

---

[2] In Chapter II, packages were mentioned for their usefulness in increasing
the unit of purchase. It was pointed out that a "family" or "gift" size could
be introduced, or else a box containing an assortment or combination set could
be offered.

Distinction through a utility device.—Where the product is used directly from the container, another opportunity in package construction is offered—that of adding a feature which will make the product more convenient to use. Le Page's Paste has a "spread tip" which does away with the brush; the tube of Kolynos Tooth Paste and Williams Shaving Cream have caps hinged to the tube to prevent loss; Colgate & Co. offer a refillable holder with their shaving stick; Shaker Salt provides a box with a simple spout, a special buffer bottom distinguishes the container for Griffin's Suede Shoe Powder, while Van Ess Liquid Scalp Massage provides a rubber-pronged cap.

An improvement in the package through a utility feature increases the purchaser's satisfaction with the use of that product. It also increases the amount of the product used, by making its consumption more inviting. The improvement offers a point of individuality that can be featured in the advertising. For a competitive product especially, a new note in package construction is an asset to be highly treasured—and advertised. It will be remembered that an improvement in package construction is not eligible for registration as a trademark, but such an improvement may obtain patent protection if it meets the requirements here imposed.

A novel package idea may furthermore be found in the very name or nature of the product; animal crackers were never so popular as they were when they were herded in a real cardboard Noah's Ark, and who could mistake Log Cabin Syrup with its can shaped like a log cabin to suit the name? The value of these unconventional ideas lies not in their sheer cleverness, but in the touch of imagination which lifts the products from the commonplace.

Distinction in label design.—Up to this point the package has been considered essentially as a carrier of goods. But the package is a carrier of an advertisement as well; its area is small but the space on the label belongs exclusively to the advertiser. It reaches people interested in buying the article by resting on the shelves of the very stores which they enter; its circulation is available without extra cost to the advertiser

Buy the new package

LORD SALISBURY
NOW 20 for 18c

One of the famous brands of Turkish cigarettes—
always celebrated for its quality and economy. Now
try the new packing—still economical—20 in the
package for 18cts. And notice this novel feature, the
slide tabs in each corner. Something new and better
cigarettes come out easily as wanted; the rest keep in
good shape. We recommend LORD SALISBURY cigarettes.

A. SCHULTE
248 CIGAR STORES —— and growing

DISTINCTIVENESS THROUGH NEW
FEATURE OF USEFULNESS IN THE
PACKAGE

who sells his wares in packages, and upon its appearance the
sale of the product often depends.

The appearance of a package can be such a good advertisement that it creates a sale for itself though the purchaser
had not previously considered buying the article. The design
may suggest the use of a product, or it may distinguish the
product from its competing neighbors; it may help secure recognition for the article as being the one advertised in other
media, or as belonging to a well-known family of products.
Furthermore, whenever the package is seen on the table, desk,
or dresser of its buyer, it serves as a testimonial of that purchaser's approval, and a good-looking label does much to
secure favor for its wares. A package is on constant display
before a critical though hasty audience. Consequently, the

search for a good package design must continue until one is created which is both attractive and unique.

Testing packages.—The order-of-merit method, whereby various packages are put to a vote of preference among the people who would be expected to buy the article, is a simple way in which to pick out a good container The prospective customers really choose their own package. An advertiser who had two proposed packages for face powder, let us say, could arbitrarily select one, fill it with powder, and offer it to his clientele. But if he could by some means find out which of the two boxes was more attractive to purchasers of face powder, his product would gain the immediate advantage of having a package capable of helping its sales. If the advertiser could get the opinion of only a representative group of prospective buyers, he would still be choosing his package more scientifically than if he based his selection upon his own personal whim; he would have some idea as to which box was actually better, and would not be compelled to make an expensive guess.

Steps necessary in making a test.—An advertiser may determine the feature upon which the success of a package depends by conducting a scientific test of packages in the following manner:

1. Create a sample package of each of the designs considered (or secure a package in each of the different shapes or styles contemplated).

2. Arrange to ask the judgment of a representative number of probable customers. A representative number consists of a group of people sufficiently large to permit a conclusion to be drawn—usually not less than 50. On nationally distributed articles, it is necessary to pick random groups from different parts of the country, which may involve questioning several thousand prospects. The actual number, of course, depends upon the variance in judgments and opinions. Generally, the inquiry keeps up until one package is obviously the choice and further investigation would serve only to increase its lead.

DESIGNS TESTED IN CHOOSING A PACKAGE

*Prepared by the Robert Gair Co.*

3. Determine the elements in question about the package. These may be size, shape, structure, and design. Instead of asking simply, "Which package do you like best?" it is often more helpful to inquire, "Which size of package do you like best?" or "Which shape?" Likewise, "Which color scheme?" "Which illustration?" "Which lettering?" and so forth. A division of questions such as these enables the advertiser to combine the best features of the several packages.

4. Hold a vote. Usually a test by personal investigation, conducted in a retail store where most of the prospects may be conveniently approached, is most satisfactory. The answers to the specific questions are written on paper, so that all the reactions may be studied and proper conclusions drawn.

A typical example.—The Wheatsworth Cracker package offers an interesting application of the order-of-merit method used in selecting from several designs the best one for a cracker package. This particular test was an unusually thorough one, but its method could be followed even for a very modest-sized business. Seven dummy packages were designed. These cartons were marked *A, B, C, D, E, F,* and *H* (*G* was omitted because it could easily be confused with the letter *C*). The cartons were considered for the pleasing effect of the entire box, of the color combination alone, and finally of the designs alone. The designs on the ends of the box were separately considered for their respective color combination and pictorial design.

The first step was to determine the type of person whose judgment had any value as far as the purchase of crackers was concerned. The use of crackers is so general that any member of the family might qualify as judge. Arrangements were made with a number of dealers to have investigators stationed in their stores and the packages were laid out on a table near the entrance. After a customer had completed her purchase at the counter, the investigator would explain to her the purpose of the test and invite her judgment of the box she liked best. Then she was asked for her second choice, and so on through the seven, the investigator making a record of the judgments. The customer was also asked which color she liked best, disregarding the design, then which design, and finally which end-design. Altogether 202 consumers were asked for an opinion. If a package ranked first in a test it was ranked 1, second choice 2, third choice 3, and so forth. Thus, if 202 people ranked the same box in first place, its total rating would be 202; if 202 people ranked a box in seventh place, its score would be 202x7, or 1,414; therefore, the smaller the total numerically, the higher the rank of the package. According to the tables which are here shown, box F received the decision.

| Box | General Appropriateness | | Color | | Design | | Ends | |
|-----|-------|------|-------|------|-------|------|-------|------|
| | Score | Rank | Score | Rank | Score | Rank | Score | Rank |
| A | 716 | 3 | 712 | 4 | 654 | 4 | 619 | 5 |
| B. | 931 | 7 | 763 | 5 | 816 | 5 | 617 | 4 |
| C. | 977 | 6 | 868 | 7 | 918 | 7 | 696 | 7 |
| D. | 725 | 4 | 612 | 2 | 614 | 3 | 476 | 3 |
| E. | 966 | 5 | 784 | 6 | 865 | 6 | 658 | 6 |
| F. | 652 | 2 | 587 | 1 | 574 | 1 | 399 | 1 |
| H. | 648 | 1 | 679 | 3 | 591 | 2 | 430 | 2 |

In order to see how this package compared with the old box, also with the packages of competing brands, another test was made, the same procedure being followed. The new box F, the old package, and five competing packages were used as the subjects. In this test box F again received the decision.

**Suggestions for conducting a test.**[3]—Many incidental difficulties may arise in conducting an order-of-merit test of packages. "Another one of those demonstrations," a merchant says when first approached on the subject; or a housewife

---

[3] The suggestions here given show how research is applied specifically to packages. The next chapter is devoted entirely to methods of conducting researches and investigations.

may answer the inquiry with, "I have no time; my children are waiting," or else, "Here's my choice for the best; I don't care for the others at all." Such objections can only be met and overcome by the patience and tactfulness of the investigator.

Since the entire test is performed to secure others' judgments, the investigator must avoid giving *his* judgment, either to the consumer or to the manufacturer. Giving judgments to the consumer may consist merely of a leading manner of questioning, as, "Don't you prefer this box?" instead of "Which box do you prefer?"

Precautions should be taken to have the conditions of every examination constant; a comparison, to be of value, must be a comparison of like with like. Otherwise, effort may be wasted, as in a perfume test in which an advertiser arranged ten vials of perfumes for investigation. The corks of these containers were removed for each individual test, and as they were not marked in any way, were replaced indiscriminately. Because of the interchanging of the corks, the scents were not the same at the end as at the beginning of the experiment. The test had to be repeated after the corks were marked to correspond with the bottles.

The questions to be asked and the factors to be tested should be planned to meet the particular problem; furthermore, the test should seek only the information in doubt. It is obviously unnecessary to conduct any investigation of features already determined or monopolized, such as the relative merits of three different can openings when each of them is already patented by a competitor, or the advantage of a color combination which is impractical to use because it fades too quickly.

**Concluding suggestions on packages.**—For the sake of the consumer, the package should be convenient to handle, attractive to behold, and of a character which meets popular expectation for such product. Trade requirements demand that the package be strong enough to handle, economical to ship, and of a size and shape suited to the retailer's shelf display space. For its own sake, the package ought to be more distinctive in some respect than the neighboring packages. This distinction may be obtained through size, shape, some utility feature, general conception, or through the appearance of its label. The degree of merit attained by the distinctive feature may be judged by testing the package before adopting it. If the package has an individuality which can be featured in the advertising, that is an advantage. If the package can inspire an entire selling plan on behalf of its product, then it is a most valuable contribution to the advertising idea.

# PART IV

# THE MACHINERY IN MOTION

## Chapter XX

# ADVERTISING RESEARCH

An advertising research is an investigation based on the scientific method, in which there are five steps as follows:

1. Determining the problem.
2. Gathering all available data.
3. Securing additional data.
4. Compiling the facts in orderly form.
5. Drawing the conclusion.

**Determining the problem.**—The purpose of an investigation is to secure facts. The facts desired in this work are those which would help to anticipate the best course of action to follow, or to overcome any difficulties which have been met. The first step in a research, therefore, is to define the questions whose answers would serve as a basis for the plans.

The questions usually arise before the research is undertaken in actual procedure, and are, therefore, quite apparent. Some of the problems among the more common queries for which researches have provided answers are the following:

1. *Determining the use of a product.*—This is especially important in the case of a concern which is equipped to produce goods if a market of buyers can be found for the output. It is also useful in finding new uses for the products in the competitive stage. After the war, many companies sought peace-time products which could be made with their war-time equipment. One shell manufacturer produced an improved "cartridge" radiator. Research thus finds new uses for equipment as well as for products.

2. *Determining extent of consuming market.*—Who are the users, where are they and what are the possible requirements?

A survey of the electrical field by Livermore & Knight reported the percentage of electrically wired homes as follows:

| *1% to 15%* | Kentucky | Oklahoma | *50% to 75%* |
|---|---|---|---|
| North Dakota | West Virginia | Texas | Washington |
| New Mexico | Virginia | Missouri | Colorado |
| North Carolina | *25% to 50%* | Iowa | Minnesota |
| South Carolina | Arizona | Wisconsin | Michigan |
| *15% to 25%* | Nevada | Pennsylvania | Indiana |
| South Dakota | Oregon | Vermont | Ohio |
| Arkansas | Idaho | New Hampshire | New Jersey |
| Louisiana | Montana | Rhode Island | Maine |
| Alabama | Wyoming | Delaware | Connecticut |
| Georgia | Nebraska | Florida | Mississippi |
| Tennessee | Kansas | Maryland | |

*75% to 100%*

| California | | Illinois |
|---|---|---|
| Utah | | New York |
| | Massachusetts | |

An advertiser of electric equipment could well choose his territory from the data given above.

3. *Determining stage of product among its different prospects.*—Is the product in the pioneering stage or in the competitive stage? A research by the *Milwaukee Journal* showed that the percentage of families in Milwaukee owning the following electric appliances to be:

| Electric ranges | .9% | Electric washing machines | 27.1% |
|---|---|---|---|
| Electric vibrators | 9.1% | Electric toasters | 29.2% |
| Electric percolators | 12.6% | Electric vacuum cleaners | 51.2% |
| Electric heaters | 20.7% | Electric irons | 75.7% |

These figures indicate the proportion of pioneering work and competitive work that should be done in each case. To illustrate: in this territory electric ranges are 99.1% in the pioneering stage, and .9% in the competitive; electric heaters are 79.3% in the pioneering stage, and 20.7% in the competitive; vacuum cleaners are 48.8% in the pioneering stage and 51.2% in the competitive stage.[1]

---

[1] Repeat sales on the above electrical appliances are comparatively few, as contrasted with the repeat sales on grocery products. The question arises that, since we consider those who have not yet bought the equipment as our market, why do any competitive work among them at all? They apparently have to be sold on the idea of using electrical equipment and that would require pioneering work exclusively. We may properly assume that each person owning

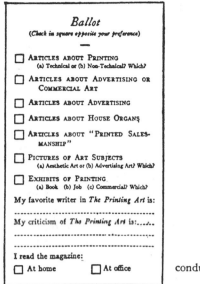

*Ballot*

(Check in square opposite your preference)

☐ ARTICLES ABOUT PRINTING
   (a) Technical or (b) Non-Technical? Which?

☐ ARTICLES ABOUT ADVERTISING OR
   COMMERCIAL ART

☐ ARTICLES ABOUT ADVERTISING

☐ ARTICLES ABOUT HOUSE ORGANS

☐ ARTICLES ABOUT "PRINTED SALES-
   MANSHIP"

☐ PICTURES OF ART SUBJECTS
   (a) Aesthetic Art or (b) Advertising Art? Which?

☐ EXHIBITS OF PRINTING
   (a) Book (b) Job (c) Commercial? Which?

My favorite writer in *The Printing Art* is:

------------------------------------------------

My criticism of *The Printing Art* is:........

------------------------------------------------

------------------------------------------------

I read the magazine:

☐ At home    ☐ At office

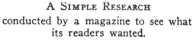

A SIMPLE RESEARCH
conducted by a magazine to see what
its readers wanted.

4. *Requirements of stages.*—If the product is in the pioneering stage, what particular custom, habit, method, or impression must be overcome; if in the competitive stage, who are the competitors and wherein is their strength? Referring to the foregoing figures, the survey also showed that 93.2% of the families in Milwaukee used gas ranges. Pioneering work on electric ranges would consequently be based upon the advantages these ranges afford over gas ranges. An advertiser of electric ranges would be very little concerned to know wherein the other makers of these ranges had an advantage over him. Not so in the case of electric irons, however. Here the product is three-fourths (75.7%) in a competitive stage and only one fourth (24.3%) in a pioneering stage. An advertiser would be deeply interested to learn all

---

one of these accessories is responsible for at least one other person becoming interested in it. Neighborly experiences are one of the most potent forces performing pioneering work. That newly interested prospect still inquires what the relative advantages are of the various makes offered. The product thus enters the competitive stage as far as he is concerned. The degree to which a product is in the pioneering stage and competitive stage is invariably in the same proportion as the total number of non-users is to total number of users.

about the others in this field. He would find out that 64 different makes of electric irons were sold in that city; of these the American Beauty made 32.9% of the sales, Hot Point 32.3%, G-E 9.9%, and Westinghouse 7.6%. That is to say, four brands had been sold to 82.7% of those who owned electric irons, while 60 brands shared between them 17.3% of the market. A new advertiser should proceed here, only if he learned what made the four leaders so successful, and why the other 60 brands trailed so far behind; then he could decide what he could offer in his iron that would insure a better success than is enjoyed by the 60 "trailers" in this field.

5. *Determining the trade requirement.*—In the drug trade, for example, the method of selling on consignment and offering free deals of merchandise (giving an extra quantity of goods without cost if a stipulated quantity is ordered) is common. A new advertiser in this field would have to be familiar with its trade customs, expectations and demands. Likewise in other fields as well.

6. *Determining change in the stage, and in the trade requirements.*—With ukeleles popular one season and saxophones the next, with "standard" size tires being supplanted by balloon tires, with the habits of the world changing overnight, an advertiser must be constantly alert to changes affecting the sale of his product. Even trade customs change. An investigation was made to learn through whom automobile owners had their repair work done—whether through the dealer or whether through a general repair shop. Four years later the research was repeated and a complete reversal in the choice was found to exist. The conclusions of a research are lasting only so long as those conditions continue under which the research was made.

7. *Choosing the best trade-mark and package.*—This can be done by the order-of-merit method, putting the suggestion to a vote as described in the previous chapter.

8. *Judging the comparative value of different ideas in advertisements and of different methods of presenting them.*—This plan offers a comparative basis for judging the relative effectiveness of the various advertising elements.

9. *Judging the comparative effectiveness of various media.*
—This type of research is particularly necessary in the case
of advertisements calling for a direct answer.

In brief, the problems of advertising research are the questions of advertising itself. "What do you want to know before going ahead?" is the crux of the entire question which a
research endeavors to answer.

**Gathering available data.**—The questions which may confront an advertiser for the first time may have been answered
long since by others. "Never undertake anything new," said
a steel man, many years ago, "until your managers have had
an opportunity to examine everything that has ever been done
in that department." What more rational step could an advertiser, likewise, take than that of scouring around for all information and experience on the point in question? This is particularly true when it is desired to introduce a new type of
product or an apparent innovation in the distributing plan.

The best information for most purposes is often closest
at hand. The internal records of an organization may supply
the very facts sought. Sales records, for instance, show units
of sales, fluctuations of sales, geographical spread of customers, amount of repeat business, and so forth. The following
sources can also provide information on questions arising in
advertising:

1. Trade associations and societies.

    It is surprising to discover the amount of sterling ma-
    terial obtainable by writing to the secretary of the trade
    organizations in a particular industry.

2. Trade publications.

    These are usually well equipped with data on their re-
    spective fields and are interested in properly directing
    inquiries in cases where they are not in possession of the
    material required.

3. Newspapers.

    The merchandising departments of these publications of-
    fer analyses of their respective cities.

4. Magazines and directories.

5. Information bureaus at public libraries.

6. Bulletins of banks and chambers of commerce.

7. Governmental reports and bureaus.

The Superintendent of Documents, Washington, D. C., will send upon request a catalogue of government publications.

State governments and municipal offices, as well as chambers of Commerce, can often be of assistance.

8. Clipping bureaus.

9. Study of competitors' advertising.

From these it is possible to learn, for example, what features are being emphasized by others in the field, and what media they use.

10. University and private research bureaus.

These institutions have made prominent surveys in various fields.

At all times, the search for information should be planned from the inside out—beginning with that which is most readily available, and gradually widening the search as more facts are desired. A little thought will often tell where to go for desired information. Ask yourself exactly what data do you want, then ask who would be most likely to have gathered that information before. Finally, with as little delay as possible, apply there and get it.

**Securing additional data.**—Any information which is already available is of necessity old. Age does not vitiate its usefulness in many cases, but where new information on the subject is desired, where more specific knowledge is needed than is offered in the existing material, or where it is advisable to substantiate existing reports, further inquiry is made directly of the person concerned—whether he be consumer or dealer, or person who influences the sale, as engineer, architect, or physician. At first thought, it would appear a stupendous undertaking personally to call upon all the people interested. Imagine trying to interview two and a quarter million people before running an advertisement in the *Saturday Evening Post,* or to measure tendencies as uncertain as public whims. The task appears still more impossible when it is considered that the very people whose likes are to be measured may not even know the reasons for their prejudices and preferences—may not even be aware of the fact that they have such preferences. Thanks to two obliging statistical principles, however, it is possible to gather all the facts desired without a research as exhaustive as the census. The first of these principles is that of mass similarity. This law holds in an investigation because most people are startlingly alike. Of course, some individuals are decidedly different, but taken *as a group,* they resemble each other in many ways.

**Principles of statistics.**—If you were to stop a thousand men at random, Fred C. Kelly tells us very interestingly in his "Human Nature in Business," and asked these thousand men what size of shoe they wore, then repeated the question to another thousand men on another street, the chances would be that almost exactly the same percentage in each thousand would be found to wear number nine. Army quartermasters, he tells us, know that 230 men out of every thousand wear hats the size of which is $6\frac{7}{8}$. Only one man in a thousand wears size $6\frac{1}{2}$. One man out of three wears a fifteen collar, but hardly one man in ten could get into a size fourteen. This similarity among people in groups makes it possible to think of them in terms of thousands with a fair degree of accuracy.

The entire structure of the insurance business rests on the fact that people, in the aggregate, are pretty much alike. Actuarial experts [2] have figured out that of 100,000 boys at 10 years of age:

96,285 will be living at 15 years of age
92,637 will be living at 20 years of age
89,032 will be living at 25 years of age
85,441 will be living at 30 years of age
81,822 will be living at 35 years of age
78,106 will be living at 40 years of age
74,173 will be living at 45 years of age
69,804 will be living at 50 years of age
64,563 will be living at 55 years of age
57,917 will be living at 60 years of age
49,341 will be living at 65 years of age

---

[2] This is from the American Experience Table of Mortality, compiled from "Practical Lessons in Actuarial Science," Vol. II, page 7.

38,569 will be living at 70 years of age
26,237 will be living at 75 years of age
14,474 will be living at 80 years of age
5,485 will be living at 85 years of age
847 will be living at 90 years of age
3 will be living at 95 years of age

Closely allied with the law of mass similarity, is the second principle, the law of sampling, based on the statistical regularity of quantities. This law states that a moderately large number of items chosen at random from a very large group is almost sure to have the characteristics of the larger group. Buyers of fruit judge entire train shipments by opening a few barrels in each car and examining their contents. They do not endeavor to go over every piece of fruit, but their judgment is as good as though they did.

A bacteriologist depends upon the same principles in making tests of drinking water. He will take cupfuls of water from various parts of a reservoir, and from these draw one test-tubeful for one part of his investigation, finally using a single drop upon his microscopic slide. The result of this test will apply to the entire lake of water. Advertisers, also, by making a fair investigation of a part of a representative market, may reach conclusions which apply to the entire market.

**Essentials of a fair investigation.**—What are the requirements for a fair investigation? The first essential in any research is that it be approached with a view to getting the true facts, whatever they may be. The research should be as impartial as a banker's survey of the financial affairs of a company. The research bureaus of advertising agencies, of the universities, and of private research organizations have their value not only because of their familiarity with methods, but because they are disinterested outsiders as far as final results are concerned. Their interest lies mostly in getting at the facts. Anyone doing research work should approach it in a similar spirit.

The second essential for a fair research is that it deal with comparable things. Like must be compared with like. Some time ago an investigation was conducted among banks. Surely, everybody knows what a bank is, and that label would seem definite enough. But there are banks with deposits of only $250,000 and banks with deposits of $250,000,000—each bank having different sets of problems. The research accordingly divided the banks into groups according to the amounts of their deposits and considered the groups separately. A research among retail grocery stores would classify them with even greater care. The stores could be grouped according to location, or according to the population of the towns in which they are located, such as 2,500 to 5,000; 5,000 to 15,000; 15,000 to 25,000; 25,000 to 100,000; 100,000 to 250,000; 250,000 and up. Or else the stores could be grouped according to the amount of gross business handled, if that information were obtainable, and again, according to credit rating. The purpose of such division would be to secure homogeneous groups and avoid generalities in the conclusion.

The units and definitions in any research must be clearly understood. Suppose the number of passenger and freight cars on a railroad were to be counted. The questions arise, What is a passenger car? What is a freight car? How would the cabooses be counted? What is the dining car? It is necessary to define at the outset of every research the exact meaning of the terms used.

That the fraction chosen for the research must be representative of the whole, is the third requirement for fair research. Obviously, the facts which provide the sample of the whole must be fairly chosen. There must be no "jockeying" of instances whereby they are chosen willfully rather than at random. A magazine issued to advertisers an analysis of its circulation. The report sought to show the high buying calibre of its readers by listing the financial standing of 100 "typical readers." The inference was that the rest of the circulation was built up of a similar clientele. Close examination, however, showed that the "representative readers" represented the cream of the subscription list and not a fair cross-section of all the readers. Error in selection of "typical" examples, though it may not be intentional, is common. The instance most frequently encountered is that of the man who says, "Take my case; I'm an average man." Few men are "aver-

age." Or else there is the case of the investigation which
confines itself to the home city of the advertiser instead of
considering other cities and towns where the product is extensively used. In examining the results of any research it is
a good plan to ask, "How was the sample group chosen?"
In conducting a research it is doubly important that this matter be fairly treated.

The group selected for the research must be representative
not only in calibre, but in numbers. The question often arises,
"How many cases is it necessary to investigate in order to
provide convincing evidence?" Statisticians have a mathematical formula whereby they answer this question. For general
purposes, investigate the number of instances beyond which
point further investigation merely corroborates the conclusions and does not alter them.

Percentages are serious offenders in investigation. Just
how serious they may be is well illustrated by the anecdote of
the college of which it is said that 33-1/3 per cent of all the
women students marry their instructors! This statement contains the customary grain of truth, but fails to reveal the fact
that when there were only three women attending that college (just opened to co-eds) one became the wife of her
teacher—which state of affairs assumes a different aspect
entirely.

The fourth essential for a fair research is that all the facts
having a bearing upon the case be included and that all others
be excluded. If the object of an investigation is to find out
how many tire-chains could be used in a given district, it would
be necessary to determine how many automobiles there are
in that district; how many of them have tire-chains and the
number per car, and the frequency with which they are replaced with new sets. It would furthermore be important to
determine how often the owners use the chains; what brands
of chains are in favor and why; and what local prejudice exists against the use of chains; also, how are the local roads
paved? The answers to these questions may give an insight
into the potentiality of the market. Such a research would
have little use for figures on bank clearances, number of home

owners, or number of voters in the last election. Yet these extraneous figures are present in many reports.

Figures alone mean little unless they serve as a basis of comparison. In one State the fact that $143,455,545.20 was paid in income taxes alone was declared to show how prosperous that State was and how advisable it was to use the media circularizing within the State's borders. Consider $143,455,545.20 in taxes! Just think of the enormous market offered by these people. Think how much they must be spending. Think of the share of the income from which the $143,455,545.20 was paid. Advertise here and partake of the riches—so the argument ran. The fact that about 143½ million dollars were paid in income taxes alone in a certain State was interesting enough, but it did not necessarily indicate a wealthy State. How much was paid in an adjoining State of about the same population? How did the tax one year compare with that for the previous year? Was the difference due to a boom, to a change in price level, or to a new tax law? There must be two points to determine the direction of a line. Mass figures must likewise be presented in pairs so that a comparative picture can be drawn to show tendencies and to establish the relative significance of a fact.

It hardly bears saying that the comparison should be a logical one. At a convention of wholesale men's hatters, the statement was made that whereas women spent $75,000,000 in one year for corsets alone, men spent only $83,000,000 for hats, the inference being that men were not spending enough for hats. Yet wherein are the expenditures comparable?

**The questionnaire—methods of issuing.**—To record the various interviews, a questionnaire will undoubtedly be found convenient. The nature of the questionnaire will depend in large measure upon the method whereby it is to be issued. The two most common methods are: (1) sending out field men or enumerators, to call upon the people, make the inquiries desired and record the answers; (2) mailing the questionnaires to the people from whom the information is desired with the request that they fill out the sheets and return them. The advantage of the personal interview is its ability

to reach the correct individual from whom the necessary
information is desired, and the opportunity it offers of securing detailed comment on points which are not clear—which
means, of course, more complete information. The personal
interview has the disadvantage of being expensive, limited in
scope, and slow. Furthermore, it requires experienced investigators, whose own errors or prejudices may seriously alter
the value of the investigation.

Sending questionnaires by mail is less expensive. Furthermore, the answers are more expedient and cover a larger geographical territory. Finally, this method gives a person time
to think before answering. The mail questionnaire, however,
often has the disadvantage of reaching the wrong person and
of obtaining only limited information, since it cannot ask the
reader to explain himself after he has answered. Indeed,
there is no assurance of any answer at all, since it is easier
to toss away a sheet of paper than it is to turn away a person
who calls upon you.

**Preparing the questionnaire.**—The questionnaire serves to
define the investigation, standardize the questions, record the
information, and facilitate compiling the data. The ideal to
strive for in a questionnaire, whether it is to be sent by mail
or filled in upon personal inquiry, is to get all the information
wanted with the smallest expenditure of effort and time. It
should be as short as possible. The skill in making out these
forms lies in breaking up a general question into its parts. As
many of the questions as possible should be answerable by
"yes" or "no" or else by a simpler number. It is easy to
count up "yes's" or "no's," whereas it is difficult to tabulate
a heterogeneous collection of adjectives such as "excellent,"
"very good," "rather nice," "fair," and "pretty good."

The questions should be as clear, definite, and separated as
possible. They should invite answers. Queries delving into
family relationships, religion, health, and income are likely
to meet with resentment. The questionnaire must not suggest
ignorance on the part of the person who is answering. It is
better to ask, "Have you been informed that so-and-so is the
case?" rather than "Did you know so-and-so to be the case?"
A man may be unwilling to confess that he does not know of

**D'ARCY ADVERTISING COMPANY**

INTERNATIONAL LIFE BUILDING

**ST. LOUIS**

WOULD YOU BE KIND ENOUGH TO
GIVE US SOME INFORMATION ---

Your answer will help us to solve a perplexing
problem relating to the marketing of a product of
interest to automobile owners. There are just two
questions we would like to have you answer.

I - Who does your repair work when certain
parts of your motor wear out?

The dealer from whom you purchased
your car ☐
OR
A general repair shop ☐

II - When it is necessary to have certain
parts of your motor replaced, such as piston rings,
pistons, bearings, etc.

Do you let the repairman select the
material or parts ☐
OR
Do you specify the particular make of
part desired ☐

Please indicate your answer to the above
questions by placing a check-mark in the square
a pencil will do.

There is no need to sign this letter and you
will not obligate yourself in any way by giving
us this information.

We thank you for your kindness and co-operation.

Research Division,
D'ARCY ADVERTISING COMPANY.

P.S. A stamped, addressed envelope is enclosed
for the convenience of your reply.

A COMPLETE SHORT QUESTIONNAIRE

This page contains (1) the note asking for the information, (2) the
questions proper, and (3) the instructions for filling and returning.
A good percentage of answers may be expected from such a well-
planned form.

a fact, but he is perfectly willing to admit that he has not been informed of that fact.

The very nature of the questionnaire sometimes biases the answer. If a newspaper were to send out an inquiry over its own name asking, "What paper do you prefer to read?" the majority of the replies would unquestionably elect that paper —first, because only people who were friends of the paper would take the trouble to answer, and second, because people are at heart good-natured and would consider the request an opportunity for harmless flattery. This difficulty illustrates the need for having the investigation conducted by an impartial body, or else for creating a pseudonym such as "The Research Bureau," or "Housewives Help Co.," and conducting the research under that name.

It is well to have the answers to the questions depend as little as possible upon the personal judgment of the investigator, if one is sent out. His prejudices and opinions should not be permitted to enter the research. He should be strictly cautioned against volunteering the answer or supplying his own opinion as to what the person queried may have meant. If he cannot secure an answer to any one question he should indicate, "Does not know," "Does not wish to answer," or "Omitted," as the case may be. Every question must be accounted for to maintain accuracy in tabulation.

Salesmen by temperament are poor investigators. They had rather get a person to accept their ideas, than to learn what the persons ideas are upon the same subject. Their enthusiasm for their house is commendable in selling but disconcerting when it comes to investigating facts. Several years before soap flakes were placed upon the market, one of the largest soap manufacturers considered the advisability of selling flakes in box form. It had not been done to any extent before and the numerous salesmen for this concern were told to "sound out the market." After lengthy "ground investigation," the report came back practically unanimous that the venture was inadvisable. Subsequently, another company obtained information to the contrary, used the idea, and has capitalized most profitably upon it. The very doubt which existed in the mind of the former organization failed to in-

spire confidence in the salesmen; that the plan was not successfully tried before served to convince the men that all was not
well with the proposal. The so-called investigation merely
showed their attitude—and a sterling idea was tossed into the
discard merely to be used by another.

Suggestions on questionnaires.—It has been found that an
investigation proceeds best if the purpose of the research is
clearly and candidly stated at the outset. If the questionnaire
is to be sent through the mail, it should be accompanied by
a frank, courteous explanatory note and a stamped return
envelope. If it can be shown that the research is endeavoring
to establish some facts which may have been puzzling the person addressed, and if an offer is made to advise him of the
completed reports, the replies will be surprisingly numerous.
Of the total number sent out, replies may be expected from
5 to 20 per cent in general investigations, and from 30 to 80
per cent in limited investigations among people who know you.

The questions should be grouped in logical sequence, and
numbered to expedite handling. Their proper arrangement
on the sheet will aid in picking off the answers quickly. The
instructions should clearly state whether the rejected alternatives in a question are to be indicated by checking, underlining,
or crossed out, or whether only the accepted items should be
treated in this manner. When investigators are sent out, it is
advisable to prepare a specimen return showing exactly how
the information is to be supplied. A sheet or booklet of
instructions may furthermore be advisable. Thus every question that may arise on the correct definition or on the method
is anticipated. The investigator should be firmly directed to
write legibly. This caution might appear trivial, but in an extensive research poor handwriting may prove one of the most
exasperating, time-consuming elements.

Compiling the data.—After the answers to the questionnaires have been assembled, they are edited, as a preliminary
step to actual tabulation. The purpose of editing is to check
the schedule against the qualities sought in a questionnaire,
especially accuracy, uniformity and completeness. Errors
which need further investigation may develop, or a difficulty
which was experienced by all investigators, such as inability to

| JOSEPH RICHARDS COMPANY | ENTERED | BY |
| ADVERTISING | EDITED | BY |
| | COPIED | BY |

Consumer—Field

**A. IDENTIFICATION**

1. Name of Individual:

   ....................

2. Address:

   No..................... Street

   City................ State....

3. Approximate age:

   30 years or under ...............
   21 to 30 years....................
   31 to 40 years....................
   41 years or older.................

4. Occupation of individual:

   Chief executive ..................
   Office employee ..................
   Factory executive ................
   Factory foreman or assistant .....
   Factory employee .................
   Teacher ..........................
   Farmer ...........................
   Miner ............................
   Professional man .................
   Artisan or mechanic...............

**B. SHAVING**

1. Ordinarily, how many times a week

   Do you shave yourself....:.....
   Are you shaved by barber.........

2. Is your beard tough:

   Yes ..............................
   No ...............................

3. When shaving yourself, what make of razor do you use:

   Auto-Strop .......................
   Ever Ready .......................
   Durham Duplex ....................
   Gem ..............................
   Gillette .........................
   Straight Razor ...................
   ..................................
   ..................................
   ..................................

4. Which of the following forms of shaving soaps have you used in the past:

   Cake .............................
   Cream ............................
   Powder ...........................
   Stick ............................

5. Which form are you now using:

   Cake .............................
   Cream ............................
   Powder ...........................
   Stick ............................

6. What caused you to decide to use this particular form:

   Advertising ......................
   Dealer's recommendation ..........
   Dissatisfaction with other forms .
   Experience .......................
   Friend's recommendation ..........
   Price ............................
   Sample ...........................
   More convenient to carry .........
   ..................................
   ..................................

7. Which form of shaving soap do you like best:

   Cake .............................
   Cream ............................
   Powder ...........................
   Stick ............................

8. Why do you like this form best:

   Produces better lather ...........
   Produces quicker lather ..........
   Lasts longer .....................
   Easier to handle .................
   More sanitary ....................
   More convenient to carry..........
   Requires no rubbing ..............
   Massages face ....................
   Other forms unsatisfactory........
   Other reasons ....................
   ..................................

9. Which of the following brands of shaving soap have you used in the past:

   Barbasol .........................
   Colgate's ........................
   Daggett & Ramsdell................
   J. & J. ..........................
   Krank's ..........................
   Melba ............................
   Mennen's .........................
   Molle ............................
   National .........................
   Palmer's .........................
   Palmolive ........................
   Rexall ...........................
   Williams' ........................
   Woodbury's .......................
   Others ...........................

10. Which brand are you now using:

    Barbasol .........................
    Colgate's ........................
    Daggett & Ramsdell................
    J. & J. ..........................
    Krank's ..........................
    Melba ............................
    Mennen's .........................
    Molle ............................
    National .........................
    Palmer's .........................
    Palmolive ........................
    Rexall ...........................
    Williams' ........................
    Woodbury's .......................
    Others ...........................

11. What caused you to start using this particular brand:

    Advertising ......................
    Barber's recommendation ..........
    Dealer's recommendation ..........
    Friend or relative's recommendation ..................
    Sample ...........................
    Liked other products made by this manufacturer .............
    Cheaper than other brands.....
    Liked holder top or refill
    Idea .............................
    Dissatisfaction with other brands ..........................
    Other reasons ....................
    ..................................

A MORE EXTENDED QUESTIONNAIRE

Illustrating a thorough, logical investigation. The questions are put in a manner to invite answer. The questionnaire is arranged for convenience in answering.

12. What particular brand do you like best:

Barbasol ..........................
Colgate's ..........................
Daggett & Ramsdell ...............
J. & J. ..........................
Krank's ..........................
Melba ..........................
Menaen's ..........................
Molle ..........................
National ..........................
Palmer's ..........................
Palmolive ..........................
Rexall ..........................
Williams' ..........................
Woodbury's ..........................
Others ..........................

13. Why do you prefer this particular brand:

Produces better lather ...............
Produces quicker lather ...............
Lasts longer ..........................
Like scent or odor best ...............
Cheaper in price ..........................
Like holder top or refill idea ...........
Requires no rubbing ...................
Does not irritate skin ...............
Gives smoother shave ...............
Gives quicker shave ...............
Lathers better in cold water ...........
Lather remains moist longer ...........
Other reasons ..........................
..........................
..........................
..........................

14. When buying shaving soap do you always insist on getting the particular brand you ask for:

Yes ..........................
No ..........................

Note: The following six questions are to be asked only of men using shaving stick.

15. Do you use the holder top or handy grip type of shaving stick:

Yes ..........................
No ..........................

16. If "yes," which type do you prefer:

Colgate's Handy Grip ...............
Williams' Holder Top ...............

17. Do you buy refills for your holder top or handy grip:

Yes ..........................
No ..........................

18. Does a feature of the shaving soap container, which adds to its convenience—for example, the handy grip or holder top principle, influence you in your preference for some particular brand:

Yes ..........................
No ..........................

19. Does the fact that you can purchase a refill for the handy grip or holder top style of container at less cost than a new stick of shaving soap, influence you in your preference for a particular brand:

Yes ..........................
No ..........................

20. In your selection of shaving soap in stick form, are you influenced by the fact that the handy grip or holder top style of container makes it more convenient to apply the soap to the face:

Yes ..........................
No ..........................

21. When preparing your face for a shave, do you, or do you not rub the lather in:

Do ..........................
Don't ..........................

22. If you do rub the lather in, what are your reasons for doing so:

Softens beard ..........................
Permits easier shave ...............
Massages face ..........................
Other reasons—give them ...............
..........................
..........................

23. In what quantity do you buy your shaving soap:

.......................... Cake
.......................... Cream
.......................... Powder
.......................... Stick

24. For approximately how many weeks does shaving soap last you:

.......................... Weeks
10c Stick ..........................
Standard Stick ...............
Extra large stick ...............
10c Cream ..........................
Standard size tube ...............
Double size tube ...............
Cake ..........................
Powder ..........................
Could not estimate ...............

25. After shaving, what brand of face lotion do you use: (Write in particular kind of odor preferred).

Colgate's ..........................
Listerine ..........................
Pinaud's ..........................
Rexall ..........................
Williams' ..........................
Witch Hazel ..........................
Others ..........................

26. Why do you prefer this particular brand:

Like scent or odor best ...............
Does not smart ...............
Cheaper in price ...............
Like other products made by this manufacturer ...............
Makes face feel cool ...............
Makes face feel smooth ...............
Other reasons ...............
..........................
..........................
..........................

27. After shaving, what brand of talc powder do you use:

Colgate's ..........................
Djer Kiss ..........................
Hudnut's ..........................
J. & J. ..........................
Mavis ..........................
Menaen's ..........................
Rexall ..........................
Squibb's ..........................
Williams ..........................
Others (give name) ...............

28. Why do you prefer this particular brand:

Like scent or odor best ...............
Cheaper in price ...............
Like other products made by this manufacturer ...............
Because of antiseptic properties ...............
Other reasons (give them) ...............
..........................
..........................
..........................

Note how the questionnaire is arranged, how the questions are grouped according to topic and how simple and direct each question is: A well conducted research provides valuable information for use in preparing advertisements.

secure answers to a given question, may appear. A difference in interpretation may crop up despite all precautions. The policy in handling all these considerations must be decided upon before actual compilations begin.

It is desirable to secure as much information as possible from the questionnaire. Frequently, some valuable information will reveal itself though it was not directly sought. To insure gleaning all the possible data from the questionnaires, the answers should be tabulated by classes. If a research were conducted among men and women, for instance, the answers from these two classes should be recorded separately, though they may have no apparent bearing on the question. Likewise different groups, ages, and geographical sections should be listed separately in making the tabulation. It may be discovered that the information so arranged may provide the answers to other questions later.

**Drawing the conclusion.**—The last step in the research is to extract the conclusions that have been made evident. If the questionnaire was simple, this part of the work will be equally so; where the research went into many questions, it is advisable to establish the answers to the most important matters first.

**Final suggestions on research.**—To insure the usefulness of any research, handle each step carefully. Define clearly the questions which must be answered, search diligently for the experience of other men with that problem, be unbiased in obtaining new data, and be observant in compiling the facts. Watch out for misleading instances. Give to all things weight in keeping with their importance; remove all question of partiality in gathering the facts. Avoid generalities if it is specific facts you seek; valuate exceptional instances if it is general conclusions you wish. Beware of the flaw of averages—the fallacy of considering yourself an "average" person, or accepting a fact as an "average" instance without determining how that average was determined. At all times remember that the purpose of a research is to secure necessary facts; its value lies in its honesty and completeness. The skill lies in securing the desired information as accurately, as directly, and as economically as possible.

CHAPTER XXI

THE TRANSFORMING IDEA

A HABERDASHER made sets consisting of a necktie, a shirt, and a pair of hose, in well-matched colors. Then he advertised the idea of being dressed in good taste—and sold neckties, shirts, and hosiery. A manufacturer of air rifles instituted boys' rifle clubs, prepared plans for their organization, supplied membership forms and targets, then advertised for membership in the local clubs—and sold rifles. A chewing gum manufacturer conceived the idea of making gum in tablets rather than in sticks and built an entire new business on that idea. In each of these instances there was an *idea* which helped sell the goods. The haberdasher evolved this idea by grouping his wares; the rifle manufacturer by creating an incentive for the use of rifles; the chewing-gum manufacturer by altering the character of his product. Truly, these were transforming ideas through which the product was converted into one having a new point of interest or of usefulness for its prospects. Likewise they served as the basis for all the advertising itself. It is not necessary to catalogue the variety of possible transforming ideas, for the fact that they vary with the stages of a product offers a working basis upon which they may be originated.

**For products in pioneering stage.**—When first we discussed the origin of pioneering products, we said they sprang from one great source: a man observing a shortcoming, proceeded to overcome it with his invention or discovery. Industry, however, does not wait for the occasional inventor for its suggestions; it is often forced to institute search for these ideas. Factories are already standing. Machines are already equipped to produce a certain type of goods. Something must be done to keep those machines moving. Increasing the demand for that product, of course, serves the purpose in most cases. But suppose a change in custom, requirement, style, or

419

public taste is too strong a tide to be pushed back by the advertising of one manufacturer, or by a whole association of them. What can be done? Or assume that a great waste of by-products is going on, and to sustain profits it is necessary to convert that waste into a useful article. What shall the next move be? The answer to both questions lies in finding a new product to make. Such a product may be found by an experimental department specially conducted for the purpose; by an organized research among users, by contests inviting suggestions, by observation on the part of the manufacturer, or by his alertness in heeding the comments and requests of consumers, dealers, and of salesmen.

If, upon the discovery of the article, it proves to be in the pioneering stage, the best method for introducing it is through the use of indirect suggestion. The advertiser proceeds to popularize an idea which by its nature will find a quick response with the public, and the fulfillment of which involves the use of the product. Radio has been introduced by giving broadcasting programs; asbestos boards have been sold by advocating the building of attics into spare-rooms; nail polish was introduced by popularizing home manicures. For the time being, the advertiser really goes into the business of selling the idea and apparently lets the sale of his product take care of itself.

Advertisements which sell products as such, build a business by addition; after they sell the article to a man, they have to repeat the performance and sell it to him the second time, then the third time, and so on. The effort to secure the order may be somewhat decreased after each successive purchase, if the product gives satisfaction. Nevertheless, the advertiser has to go after every order and, sale by sale, build the total volume of business. But advertisements which sell ideas, build their business by multiplication. They implant an idea; ideas spread quickly among groups. Before long a host of people have adopted the idea, and use the product as a matter of course. Therein lies the opportunity for advertisers of a product in the pioneering stage.

**For products in competitive stage.**—In a conversation between an advertising man and a manufacturer, the latter will frequently describe his article as being "as good as any on the market, but there is nothing particularly different about it." Such an opinion is usually founded upon only a production acquaintance with the article. To the selling mind this statement means, "There may be nothing different in the way the product has been made, but a point of difference may be found in the methods of marketing the article, or a difference in the esteem in which it's held by the possible buyers." The task then resolves itself into a search for distinctiveness, either in the article itself, in the way it is distributed, or in the manner it is advertised.

The best form of individuality that a competitive product can possess is that which gives more value to the purchaser or renders him greater satisfaction from the use of the product. The first step in any competitive undertaking, therefore, is to see how the product itself can be improved, for unless the heart be sound, as Disraeli has philosophized, the whole body must suffer, and the heart of every advertising plan is the product. Let there be no doubt about that. It has been shown time upon time that advertising can be no better than its products. To improve the advertising of a competitive product, improve the product, then let the advertising tell about these improvements. When a new brand of an article is to be introduced, and the competition in that field is strongly intrenched, it is advisable to proceed only if the new brand offers some decided physical superiority.

**Getting distinctiveness.**—A distinctive idea may be obtained through the following investigation and preparation:

1. Finding the distinctiveness in the product.
2. Creating distinctiveness for the product.
3. Creating distinctiveness in method of distribution.
4. Partaking in performance or demonstration.
5. Improving the advertising strategy.
6. Creating distinctiveness in the advertisements.

The quest for the idea, it will be noted, starts with an intimate inspection of the product, gradually becoming more remote as the search for distinctiveness is widened. The closer to the product the idea is embedded, the better will the undertaking be.

**Finding difference in the product itself.**—Structural differences in the article itself offer a basis upon which the advertising idea may well be founded. The distinction may lie in the *principle of construction or operation,* as that of the Caloric Pipeless Furnace, the Noiseless Typewriter, the Ansonia Gravity Clock, or Barbasol, the shaving cream which requires no rubbing-in. The distinction may be chiefly one in *detail of construction,* as it is in Hoosier Kitchen Cabinets, which are featured for their tool compartment tray, and in O'Cedar Mops, for which seven such distinctive details are recorded.[1]

The distinction may not be of vital structural character, in which case a discerning eye and an appreciative sense may be necessary to recognize the important differences which exist. The "outside viewpoint" is here valuable, for the manufacturer of a product is apt to overlook his best advantages. He is so familiar with the appearance and history of his article, that when he beholds it he views only the effort, the machinery, and the men necessary to build it. But the purchaser is not interested in a portrayal of these facts. If anything, he wants to know what he can obtain from the advertised product that he does not already secure. In searching for the true distinguishing points of a competitive product, it is necessary carefully to inspect the article itself for the fundamental distinctions, so that the advertising may direct attention to an idea literally imbedded within the product itself.

**Creating distinctiveness for competitive product.**—Whether or not physical differences are evident in the product, additional distinctiveness may be created to serve the same purpose. *Color* is useful. To give a fountain pen a distinguished appearance, the handle was made red, though it could just as well have been black. The colored wire in the Yellowstrand wire rope likewise was designed for individuality; for the same reason Beaver Board was given a red border. *Design* of product helps. Life Savers are known by their hole; Octagon Soap, by its shape. *A change in packaging method* may strike a note

---

[1] Technical details may not be as impressive to housewives as to the engineer. When a product intended for housewives is to have its details featured, it is advisable to emphasize the significance of those details as well as the existence of the details themselves. It is also advisable to concentrate on one or a few of the features instead of presenting an uninteresting array of them.

TRANSFORMING IDEAS IN UNDERWEAR ADVERTISING

Underwear, being in the competitive stage, requires points of distinction for its transforming idea. Sealpax has twin buttons, Hatchway none at all. Topkis secures individuality through its price, Wright's through its loop stitching and absorbent texture, presented by a startling visualizing style.

of individuality. The change may be a conversion from bulk selling to package sales, the creation of a superior method of packing, of a better container opening, a unique package, a different package size, or any of the other devices previously discussed on the subject. "We couldn't improve the product, but we improved the package" is a sound idea, for any improvement in the container invariably provides an article in the competitive stage with a transforming idea of merit. The feature of individuality is all the more valuable if it can be registered as a trade-mark, or patented for its mechanical design.[2]

Distinctiveness for a product may be established by a *fourth* possible method—that of associating it with a distinguished personality. Oldfield converted his status as a race-car driver into that of a tire manufacturer, while Mary Garden became the godmother of a line of cosmetics. The namesake of the distinguished personage thus shares some of his or her halo. An endorsement written by a popular character, such as a moving picture actress, is at times effective for the same purpose; it expresses the opinion of one whose legion of admirers will follow her example—when they can.

Before using the picture of some living individual, it is necessary to secure written permission from that model to publish the picture. Though the personal publicity offered may be sufficient inducement, a "release" protecting the advertiser against all claims for using the picture should nevertheless be secured.

A *fifth* device for giving a product distinctiveness is that of presenting with it something of value—a premium. The premium may be of an entirely extraneous nature, as the novelty in the boxes of Cracker Jack, or the household utensils given for cigar coupons and trading stamps.[3] The premium may be created to accent the virtue of the commodity, as the insurance certificates against forgery, issued with check protectors. Finally, the premium may be for merchandise itself,

---

[2] See the Comparison Chart, Legal Protection of Ideas in the chapter on The "A B C" of Trade-Marks.

[3] Some states enforce laws affecting the issuance of tokens and require payment of a license fee. This question treads upon delicate legal ground for guidance over which an attorney should properly be consulted.

**The £500 name**

## CLOSING DATE
## 14th AUGUST

J. S. FRY & SONS, LTD. (BRISTOL & LONDON).
NAME COMPETITION.

After almost 200 years in Bristol FRY'S now find that their well-known business of Cocoa and Chocolate Manufacturers has grown to such dimensions that the old city can no longer accommodate it. A site of nearly 300 acres has, therefore, been bought at Keynsham, five miles from Bristol, to afford scope for the larger developments necessary.

The site, bordered by the River Avon, lies in the green and pleasant county of Somerset, and there is ample room, not only for factories, wharves, and sidings, but also for playing fields, bathing pools and sports grounds.

The erection there of the first of the great factories is nearing completion and now the Company want a NAME for the new site itself. A prize of £500 is offered for a suitable name, which should preferably be brief, easy to pronounce, striking and unique, and which might for example, suggest the ideal surroundings of the new site. There will also be awarded boxes of Chocolates as 1,000 Consolation prizes.

Read the Conditions of Entry and send in suggestions as soon as possible and so as to arrive not later than twelve noon on Tuesday, 14th August, 1923.

### CONDITIONS OF ENTRY
(WHICH MUST BE STRICTLY COMPLIED WITH).

NOTE TO THE TRADE.—An award of £50 will be made to the Retailer who sold the "Belgrave" Chocolate to the winner of the £500 prize, and whose name and address are entered on the sheet bearing the winning name (see Condition 3). In the event of two or more Retailers being entitled (see Condition 1), the £50 will be divided.

A CONTEST AS A TRANSFORMING IDEA

Contests often absorb all the attention of the advertising at the expense of the product. Here, however, is a contest skillfully handled, in that it focuses attention upon the product itself. What is here said about the chocolate will be remembered long after the contest is over.

as the coupon from a bar of soap entitling the bearer to a box of cleanser, and vice versa.

A premium is a bonus for buying. Under no circumstances should the premium be given as a compromise for quality which the customer expects in the product. It should, furthermore, not become the tail that wags the dog, as happens when the advertising continuously sells the gifts rather than the product. If any premiums are to be used, those are best which help the buyer appreciate the merits of the article or which cause increased consumption of the advertised wares.

A *sixth* device for making a product distinctive is the contest. A contest may be designed to secure a trade-mark idea, or a slogan; its purpose may be to familiarize the reader with the product, by having him write an essay on its merits, usefulness and service; or else the contest may be launched to discover new uses and appeals for the article. Many contests require that the reader go to the dealer's store, either for a form or for further information; or the contests are planned for use in building a mailing list.

Several considerations will arise in holding a contest which may not be apparent at the outset. First, and most important, come the post office regulations which prohibit lotteries in any form. The local postmaster should accordingly be consulted before the advertiser embarks on any contest which will require the use of the mails. Individual publications likewise impose certain requirements which should be known in advance, if the use of their media is contemplated. Contests should have some useful intellectual value and not be freakish time-wasters.

Provisions should be made for maintaining the goodwill of those participants who do not win—and there are usually quite a number of them. The rules of the contest should be clearly stipulated; the method for determining the winners given particular mention. Contestants ought to be told when the results will be announced, and how the winners will be advised of the news. Contests are usually planned to excite the interest of the public in a product; more often than not they leave the advertiser more excited than the public.

A *seventh* method for lending distinctiveness to a product

is by means of additional "service work" rendered by the advertiser for the benefit of the purchaser. An entire advertising campaign was designed for Gillette Safety Razors when the representatives were stationed in drug stores, and Gillette users were invited to bring their razors in for examination. Parts which were damaged were generously replaced and the user was also shown how to shave in the easiest way. The Multigraph Company has likewise devoted its attention to "service" work among users of its machines. The "service" plan offers an avenue of ideas open to any product, especially of a technical or of a mechanical nature. There is a double advantage to this method—that of satisfying present customers and of influencing future sales, for as Norval A. Hawkins of the General Motors Advisory Staff said, in speaking of this point, "As a product attains a wide distribution, the prospective purchaser becomes more or less immune to our advertising and sales activity and more and more under the influence of his friends who have had experience with the product in question. Whether the product receives an endorsement or condemnation, depends largely upon the efficiency of the service that has been and is being rendered." [4]

The foregoing methods for creating a point of distinction in the product itself are essentially suggestive of the possibilities which exist. The ideas conceivable are quite unlimited, the methods used quite interesting, as an examination of current advertisements will reveal.

Creating distinctiveness in method of distribution. —Besides finding the difference in the product itself, or creating individuality for it as just described, better methods of selling it than prevail in an industry may be developed. Razors at one time were a hardware store item, but safety razors are now to be found in drug stores and men's furnishing shops. Candies were at one time sold through confectionery stores exclusively; raisins through grocery stores. Not so any more. The Oliver Typewriter Company withdrew its main sales force and sold its machines upon direct inquiry. The Fuller Brush Company, on the other hand, arranged to sell to the

---

[4] "Car Owner Is Boss of Automotive Industry," by Norval A. Hawkins, in Automotive Industries, Nov. 24, 1921, p. 1021.

housewife through personal house-to-house representatives exclusively. The effort in these cases was expended in organizing more expedient distributing channels. Two precautions demand observance when such tactics are considered: first, merely "being different" is not enough. The plan must be an improvement over the established distributive system as well. The second precaution to heed is that a more general character of distributing agent involves the corresponding task of helping sales over a more diversified range of trades and industries—thereby increasing the cost of selling.

**Partaking in demonstrations or performance.**—Products, like men, can earn distinction through accomplishment. An advertiser may purposely arrange that his product show its mettle in some performance, after which advertisements may be devoted to that accomplishment. These demonstrations may range in elaborateness as follows:

1. Personal demonstration.
2. Private demonstration.
3. Public demonstration, local.
4. Public demonstration, national.

**Personal demonstration.**—A confirmed skeptic could not ask for better proof than that of a demonstration which he has given himself. For this reason, the issuance of samples and testing equipment, or the offer of a trial often serves as the idea around which campaigns are woven. The advertisements can then invite inquiries for the material, these inquiries serving as opening wedges to be followed by salesmen or by correspondence, or by the suggestion to visit the merchants selling that goods. All purposes may be served by simply illustrating the test in an advertisement, with an invitation for the reader to try it himself. Vulcanite advertisements show "6 daring tests"—the heat test, the ice test, the water test, the acid test, the fire test, the scuff test. The reader is urged to perform these experiments in his own home. Even if the suggestion is not acted upon, the point gets over.

Opportunity for personal demonstrations may be provided in the form of a counter display, placed in the dealer's store. The advertising can then encourage readers to see the demon-

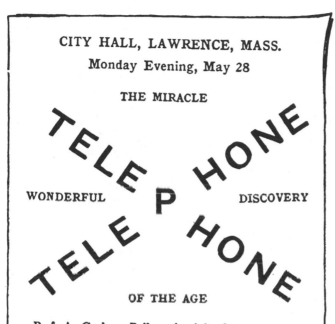

CITY HALL, LAWRENCE, MASS.

Monday Evening, May 28

THE MIRACLE

WONDERFUL
DISCOVERY

TELEPHONE
TELEPHONE

OF THE AGE

Prof. A. Graham Bell, assisted by Mr. Frederic A. Gower, will give an exhibition of his wonderful and miraculous discovery The Telephone, before the people of Lawrence as above, when Boston and Lawrence will be connected via the Western Union Telegraph and vocal and instrumental music and conversation will be transmitted a distance of 27 miles and received by the audience in the City Hall.

Prof. Bell will give an explanatory lecture with this marvellous exhibition.

**Cards of Admission, 35 cents**
**Reserved Seats, 50 cents**

Sale of seats at Stratton's will open at 9 o'clock.

A Transforming Idea of 1877

Even the telephone required a local public demonstration to transform it from a toy to a public utility. Do you recognize any similar instances in more recent times?

stration at their local merchant's store, at which time the retailer continues the selling success.

**Private demonstration.**—If it is not practical to have the prospect try out the article for himself, the next best thing may be to have the persons of technical authority witness the demonstration or performance. The results of such laboratory tests, field tests, or official performances, conducted before an impartial body, then provide the basis of the advertisement. An alert advertising man often finds his product being subjected to tests, or performing under unusual conditions, and, as a result of such performances, he is able to conduct an extended campaign. The advertising which is based upon a private performance depends upon the vividness whereby the conclusion is made evident, as well as upon the stamp of authenticity given to the demonstration.

**Public demonstration, local.**—Even more impressive than a private performance arranged by the advertiser is one which the public can witness. An automobile towing a steam roller was driven through the streets to demonstrate the strength of the special friction drive. Photographs of this feat were used in the advertisements and were quite as impressive as an actual observation of the performance. Another instance of an opportune local public demonstration was that of a sectional bungalow manufacturer who had one of his houses erected before the public at a fair. Food advertisers have made excellent use of local public demonstrations by establishing special displays in retailers' stores. These demonstrations usually consist of a booth in which a woman, well versed in domestic science, shows housewives how to cook or bake the advertised food properly. In all such instances, the manufacturer has really created traveling service stations which the advertisements can subsequently feature.

Local public performances often take advantage of some timely event, under which circumstance a camera can play a useful part. Provisions should always be made to follow up the interested prospects.

**Public demonstration, national.**—A local demonstration may profitably assume national interest as did the first concert given by Leo Ornstein upon the Ampico Reproducing

Piano. The artist alternated his own playing with that of the piano itself. The fidelity of reproduction was a revelation to its select audience, with the result that the event received nation-wide comment. Advertisers of automobiles and automobile parts have been noteworthy users of national demonstrations, at first to prove certain qualities of the motor car, then to show the prowess of their own makes. The day of the spectacular automobile races and endurance trips has not passed as yet. In their zeal for a noteworthy performance, however, some advertisers have overlooked the inference that the layman has drawn, namely, that the cars used were stock cars, when in fact they were specially built models, and that the cars were designed mainly for speed demons. Special performances must be watched to see that they do not overplay their parts.

In planning any performance of demonstration or of a product, it is well to anticipate the task of the advertisements which are to be prepared. They will seek to show, first, what the product did, second, what that fact proves, and, third, what the conclusions really mean to the reader (presented in the opposite sequence to give the advertisements their entering wedge). Every endeavor should accordingly be made to have these points of the demonstration convincingly apparent.

Improving the advertising strategy.—In the second chapter of this book we saw the many purposes to which advertising can be assigned. Every purpose considered, every additional one conceived—and there is little doubt but that many additional ones could be enumerated—may offer a suggestion for an entire plan of advertising. The following specific purposes mentioned in the second chapter will now be reviewed with an eye to their strategic worth:

1. *Increasing the frequency of a product's use, by direct suggestion, indirect suggestion, or altruistic suggestion.*—This offers opportunity for constructive original work which will lift the advertising out of the competitive class. It may also serve to stabilize production by eliminating seasonal depression. The plan is almost an unfailing source of ideas.

2. *Reaching the person who influences purchaser.*—This

plan takes it for granted that the purchaser himself is being reached.

3. *Dovetailing with sales force and with dealers.*—Improved and intensified efforts in this direction offer an unfailing idea upon which a whole selling campaign can be based.

4. *Linking one product with another.*—This method involves resourcefulness in getting a product which can rationally be advertised in co-operation with the given product.

5. *Securing acceptance for subordinate product.*—Acceptance for a subordinate product may generally be obtained if the money necessary in advertising to the consumer is available. If the money is not available, effort should be concentrated on selling to the trade.

6. *Bringing family of products together.*—This helps capitalize on the goodwill already created. It should be seriously considered whenever a family of products is being sold.

7. *Attracting new generation.*—This is a farsighted plan which may be introduced in conjunction with any of the other plans.

8. *Dispelling mal-impression.*—Research can be used to find out if any erroneous impression exists regarding a product. If one exists, it should be recognized, corrected and counter-attacked.

9. *Meeting price cutting and substitution.*—Meeting price cutting and competition involves one of the serious matters of corporate selling policy. The alternatives which each firm must decide for itself are: "Shall we counter-attack in the price-war of our competitors or shall we ignore them and follow the path upon which we are set?"

10. *Obtaining recognition as a leader in the field.*—In a highly competitive industry such a course may be an unduly expensive undertaking. In many branches of business, however, the advertising has been so undeveloped that an aggressive and consistent advertiser could easily gain leadership.

11. *Increasing strength of entire industry.*—This plan is offered with the heartiest endorsement as to its general efficacy. Every advertiser can do something in this respect by dedicating a part of his own advertisements to raising the

standards of the industry and arousing better appreciation of its usefulness.

Creating distinctiveness in the advertisements.—A product which has no inherent distinctiveness, and which has had no individuality created in its behalf by the methods described, still has at its disposal the distinctiveness obtainable through the actual advertisements—a privilege which is open to all articles even though they already have "points of distinction."

Originality in the advertisements themselves may be obtained through:

1. Changing the appeal.
2. Better use of media.
3. Creating an individual style of advertisement.

Improving the appeal.—A prospective buyer expects a product to render him a certain amount of satisfaction which, in turn, prompts him to make the purchase. The more accurately these satisfactions are discerned, the more effective will the advertising be. It is for this reason that researches are undertaken to investigate the value of different psychological appeals.

When a new campaign appeal is discovered, that appeal will serve to individualize the product. Where no better appeal can be found than is already being used by others, the competitive advertisements may still be able to show how the product fulfills its purpose in a better way.

The desired individuality for an article in the competitive stage is at times attainable by refraining from any unusual note in the appeal. Dentifrices illustrate this possibility. One brand prevents acid mouth, another pyorrhea, while a third removes the film from the teeth. Such a keen endeavor for distinctiveness made it possible for still another advertiser to come along and say: "It just cleans your teeth—that is all." The moral is this: If a product is competing with a large number of other brands, each of which has emphasized an individual feature, the desired contrast may be obtained by reverting to the elementary idea. But the very simplicity of the idea creates the individuality necessary in a competitive product.

Instead of letting himself be drawn into a battle of competitive terms, an advertiser should find his own keynote and stress that consistently. Simply to say that a product is better than others is an amateurish attempt to prove distinctiveness, but let the advertising actually demonstrate wherein that superiority arises, and better results are almost inevitable.

**Distinctive use of media.**—There are so many forms of media, so many classifications in each, so many ways of utilizing each classification, that an advertiser need seldom feel that he must enter a race with his competitors for space or for position in any one of them. The tactics of cigarette advertisers serve as a good illustration. One used painted bulletins as the backbone of his campaign; another, small preferred space in newspapers; a third, color pages in magazines—each endeavoring to attain his end through the use of media which the others had neglected.

**Distinctive illustration and copy.**—Every advertiser has a wide latitude in the manner of expressing his ideas, and thus is at liberty to develop his own style of illustration or of copy with all the possibilities which individuality implies. The advertisements of Douglas Shoes, Mennen's Shaving Cream, Edgeworth Tobacco, have a personality of their own in each case. These advertisements would be recognizable though every mention of their name were to be dropped, because their style is distinctive. A similar individuality is even more desirable for the small advertiser. He needs all the distinctiveness he can obtain—for which reason he should specially avoid aping the style of others.

On upper Fifth Avenue there stands St. Thomas' Church, considered one of the finest modern replicas of Gothic architecture. It is only natural that all buildings in the vicinity pay homage to this beautiful edifice. Across the street, it was planned to erect a building to house one of the very exclusive Fifth Avenue shops. Nine architects out of ten would have proceeded to design a building in the Gothic style, vainly trying to outdo the Gothic gem. But the architect who conceived the Cammeyer Building (for that is the one) proceeded along different lines. He evidently knew that a building after the

Gothic would merely be a humble shadow of the beautiful structure. He therefore planned a building, the simple square lines of which are quite unlike the arched curves of the Gothic era, with its trefoils, quatrefoils, and spires. The result is one of the most charming buildings on the Avenue, worthy of the Street and a distinctive monument to its possessor.

The lesson to advertisers is obvious. Imitate the other fellow and you simply invite attention to his superiorities. Play your own game and everything you do will reflect credit on your own product.

**Securing distribution.**—When the transforming ideas are being worked out, provision must also be made for securing distribution—for having the dealers order the merchandise. We have not endeavored to decide upon any policy towards jobbers and the respective middlemen, but it is our task in planning the advertising to provide for the idea and the method which will secure the cooperation of the desired distributors.

**Making the proposition.**—The new advertiser often assumes that the so-called marketing channel is already organized into a smooth-running machine, awaiting the pleasure of the producer; that all he has to do is to tell the dealer what he is offering and how good it is, and then ship a carload to him as quickly as it can be produced. The truth offers a far different picture. That which we speak of as the "distributive" system is a system in the economic sense rather than concrete sense. It consists of Tom Smith, the grocer, Fred Jones, the garage man, and Wallace James, the owner of the general store; it consists of thousands of such merchants. The jobbers consist of Tom Smiths who have grown into larger organizations now selling to the merchants in their respective territories, and so it goes all along the scale of business. To secure the cooperation of these distributors, it is necessary to appreciate the attitude which they naturally assume, epitomized in the classical query, "What's in it for me?" This can best be answered by presenting reasons to the distributors which will convince them that the product will sell quickly and profitably. An advertiser of a new product is also met with the retort, "All right, create the demand and I'll stock your article." Here the seller opens his advertising portfolio. The dealer is shown just what advertising is being done, special emphasis being placed on the local work, the effect of which will be most immediate. The presentation may furthermore rest upon a plan for local direct advertising—a sampling campaign, an unusual store display or store exhibit, or a noteworthy demonstration which is to take place. Merchandise "deals" may furthermore be made, whereby the merchant gets so many packages as a bonus with every order of a stipulated size.

It is also common for the advertiser of a new product to have his own salesman call on a number of retailers in a town and secure their orders. These orders are then turned over to the respective jobbers, both as proof that the product will sell and as an inducement to multiply the quantity with their own orders.

**Method of approaching campaigns.**—The general courses that may be followed in securing distribution and advertising the product are numerous. The manufacturer may devote his efforts to selling his dealers only, leaving to them the entire burden of selling to the consumer; or he may advertise to the consumer exclusively, expecting him to ask for the article with such insistence that the merchant will demand the goods from the wholesaler, the wholesaler then coming to the manufacturer. Because these two plans are extreme, their effectiveness is seldom as great as that of a third plan which aims primarily to secure distribution in retail stores, making provision at the same time for advertising to help move the goods off the merchant's shelf.

**Summary of methods.**—The following as a résumé of the methods of securing useful distinctiveness for a product in the competitive stage.[5] The most valuable ideas are those which enhance the worth of the product itself; next in order are those which increase the purchasers' satisfaction or pleasure in the use of the article. As the plans followed become

---

[5] The sequence of the methods differs somewhat from that followed in the chapter. They are here arranged to serve as a convenient reference.

removed from the goods themselves, the possible effectiveness in proportion to the energy and money spent become less. As a product advances further and further into the competitive stage, however, the choice of distinction becomes more restricted. In the case of men's collars and men's hats, for instance, style demands a uniformity in the product. The advertiser is forced to look towards layouts, illustrations, and perhaps engraving effects, for distinctiveness in his advertisements. The reader will find it interesting to find examples illustrating each of these methods, choosing the instances either from this book or from current advertising. Another suggestion would be to take some product with which he is particularly familiar, and indicate which method would serve it best.

1. Making product distinctive in one of the following:
   a. Purpose.
   b. Principle.
   c. Detail.
2. Creating novel trade-mark.
3. Creating distinctive package by means of one of the following:
   a. Method followed in trade.
   b. Size.
   c. Shape.
   d. Utility feature.
   e. Design.
   f. Novelty.
4. Choosing distinctive method of distribution.
5. Doing service work among purchasers.
6. Attaching distinctive personality to product.
7. Offering premium.
8. Holding contest.
9. Planning demonstrations for the product by:
   a. National public demonstration.
   b. Local public demonstration.
   c. Private demonstration, personal direction.
   d. Simple visualization of self-evident demonstration.
10. Improving advertising strategy.

 *a.* Increasing the use of the product.
 *b.* Reaching person who influences purchaser.
 *c.* Linking one product with another.
 *d.* Strengthening support of trade.
 *e.* Securing acceptance of subordinate product.
 *f.* Bringing family of products together.
 *g.* Attracting new generation.
 *h.* Dispelling mal-impression.
 *i.* Meeting price cutting and substitutions.
 *j.* Becoming leader in field.
 *k.* Strengthening entire industry.
11. Choosing different media.
12. Changing size of advertisement.
13. Changing copy style by:
 *a.* Approach.
 *b.* Method of development.
 *c.* Tone and structure.
14. Creating distinctive method of visualizing ideas.
15. Designing distinctive layouts through
 *a.* Shape.
 *b.* White space.
 *c.* Technique.
 *d.* Color.
16. Using distinctive engraving effects.
17. Obtaining distinctive printing effects, through
 *a.* Type style.
 *b.* Type layout.
 *c.* Paper.

In striving for competitive distinctiveness, the opportunity which always awaits the advertiser who does pioneering work should not be overlooked.

# CHAPTER XXII

## THE COMPLETE CAMPAIGN

**The first step—The product.**—All our operations are going to evolve from the product; hence we shall place that before us so that we may never lose sight of it. The product may be a commodity, bread or butter for instance; it may be a service such as that rendered by a bank; it may be an ideal such as that fostered by the advocate of a League of Nations. A definition and declaration of that which we have to offer constitutes the first step in our work.

**The second step—The use of the product.**—An electric public utility concern generates and distributes electric current, but it is not current that customers want; rather is it light, heat, and power for use in the home, the factories, the office, and the store. The entire gamut of products can similarly be examined and distinctness found between that which a product is, in a technical sense, and that for which it can be used in an applied sense. Advertising is chiefly concerned with the use of the product. To find the use of widest application represents the second step. Of course, many uses may suggest themselves, but we are not interested in any of them at the present time except the most promising one.

**The third step—The buyers.**—Knowing for what purpose the product can be used, it is a short step to inquire who its possible users may be. If the use of the product is limited to a small group, the search will have to be a diligent one to discover every possible member of that group. When the product is one in extensive use (as in the case of soft drinks and candies), the task is less to discover who the possible users are than it is to limit the number whom the advertising shall try to reach at the outset.

**The fourth step—What stage?**—After the possible buyers for the product are established, it is desirable to divide them

439

into groups. Instead o. trying to handle everybody at one time, we can confine ourselves to the group which looks best to us and then proceed to the next group, making each pay as we go along. To each body of prospects the test is then applied: "Is the product in the pioneering stage, as far as the given group is concerned, or in a competitive stage?" If the people have to be shown their need for the product, what habits or prejudices must be overcome? If they have to be switched from one brand to another, what features must be improved and emphasized?

The fifth step—The transforming idea.—On the one hand we have a product and a use for it, on the other hand we have a market of those who logically may be prospects for the product. We now have to inject some idea which will suggest the need for the product, if it is in the pioneering stage, or lend it distinctiveness if it is in the competitive stage. To sell raisins, the growers prepared recipes of raisin bread, for use by bakers throughout the country; then they advertised to housewives the advantages of getting raisin bread on Wednesdays. That was a transforming idea. It changed raisins to a sales aid for bakers, and to a variation in the menu for the housewife.

For a pioneering product, the idea will need to be one the nature of which strikes the public fancy and the acceptance of which involves the use of the product, subsequently its sale.

For a product in the competitive stage, the search for the idea is directed along lines which will provide a feature of distinctiveness to the product. Tipper has said that the selective process on the part of the buyer makes it necessary to provide in a product a difference in value, so that the buyer may make a comparison of all the products in a field and select one on justifiable grounds. Where a product is to enter into a struggle with others for the business which has already been created, it must possess some unusual feature of merit if it is to secure consideration. Of all the methods described previously, those are most desirable which provide better value in the product than is now obtainable, and a distinctive physical appearance. Better value in the product itself is necessary to bring "repeat" business, and to invite word-of-mouth commendation. Distinctive physical appearance is desirable in attracting attention to the individual product, and in assisting in its identification.

The following analysis may be helpful in differentiating between the product as such, and the aspect of it, which the advertising is to present. The reader will find it valuable practice to continue this list for himself, drawing the instances from his own observation.

*Product.*                     *Transforming Idea.*

Filing cabinets ...............................Institute a service which installs filing systems in offices, then recommend suitable file.

Shaving stick ...............................Provide a new package in the form of a refill stick.

Bank ...............................Help organize employees' saving clubs.

Automobile Oil ...............................Recommend the grade of oil to be used for the given cars.

Cosmetic ...............................Hold local beauty contests, then a national contest of local winners.

Asbestos ...............................Make boards of it for partitioning.

Check protector ...............................Issue insurance policy.

Laundry machine ...............................Stimulate the business of laundries, who are users of the machines.

Aluminum wear ...............................Provide convenient store displays for dealer.

Breakfast food ...............................Provide recipes.

Bottles ...............................Make hygienic toothbrush holder of bottle.

Andrew Carnegie was known as a steel man and a philanthropist. Respect goes to him also, however, because he was a past master in the art of applying transforming ideas, for he made steel but sold bridges. And to sell bridges he fostered railroad construction, incidentally selling the steel for the rails. For that matter, if we want to go back into history, and into other than advertising spheres, we find that the "Canterbury Tales" were built around a transforming idea. The innkeeper at Tabard Inn gathered the travelers around him and staged a contest to see who could tell the best tale of adventure. As a reward, the winner was to be the guest at a feast given by all those present, at their expense, at the Tabard Inn. The modern hotel keepers are just as alert in utilizing transforming ideas. When they want to rent their rooms do they advertise the size of the rooms and the details of the woodwork? Not quite. They bring a convention to town. Then heaven help the delegate who did not get his reservations in early enough.

The sixth step—The distributing plan.—We next consider the methods of distributing the actual product itself. All wares entering upon the business field today have an advantage in finding the more-or-less organized forms of doing business through wholesaler, jobber, retailer, consumer, and the numerous variations in which the middlemen are organized to reach the consumer.[1] Several realities must be faced in establishing any policy here. In the drug field, for example, the jobbers are very influential, owing to the great variety of wares handled by the druggist, who certainly could not deal direct with the many manufacturers. The drug chains also offer a problem since they are manufacturers as well as distributors of their wares. In the grocery field the jobbers are strong because they help finance so many of the stores from the "shoe-string" days up.

These jobbers are extensive packers under their private brand names; that is to say, they will buy a product, give it their own label and enter it into competition with the national

---

[1] For a clear discussion of trade channels see Chapter V "Marketing Methods and Policies," by Paul D. Converse. For a comprehensive report of the condition in any one industry, refer to Crain's "Market Data Book."

advertising manufacturer's brand. Despite this fact, the national advertiser is often obliged to entrust his brand to that jobber. Depàrtment stores offer a different problem. Generally, they buy direct from the manufacturer. As a class they do not like to have the manufacturer's name appear on the product, unless his trade-mark is so well known that it will undoubtedly attract trade. In the case of a new product that is seldom the case, and where it is the case—where an advertiser has thoroughly intrenched himself with the public —he naturally resents the demand for price concessions made by department stores, large buyers that they are. The jobber is again strongly intrenched in the hardware trade, so strongly, in fact, that a manufacturer can pursue no middle ground. He either sells through them or pits himself directly against them. In the ready-to-wear trade, on the other hand, the jobber is not nearly as strong. An insight into these situations is given here to indicate the nature of the practical considerations which enter into a decision upon the distributive system.

A different line of attack is followed in the case of raw materials, which are sold by one industrial firm to another, or in the case of equipment, or building material. For most of these, methods of distribution have been organized to a greater or lesser extent. A man coming upon the market with his product may accept these forms or reject them; in any event, he will wish to understand them before deciding upon the means to be used in distributing his product. After this the question of advertising itself can be considered.

The seventh step—The media.-We now enter the domains of advertising itself. Which of the three plans for using advertisements shall we use, the zone, the cream, or the national plan? If our funds are limited, we shall put to one side the national plan. That involves an attempt to secure all the business whenever it may be found all over the country in one effort—a most ambitious plan for an advertiser to embark upon at the outset. We shall therefore confine ourselves to using either a zone plan of attack or a cream plan. If our product is one in wide use by the general public (such as flour, stoves, underwear, crackers, cigars, hosiery, dentifrice, breakfast food, tires), we can choose a typical "test" city for our zone of action. An ideal test city is one whose population represents closely the population of that section of the country, and whose numbers are not so large as to make the cost of advertising to them prohibitive for a trial undertaking.

Where a product requires the use of a plan in which the effort can be concentrated upon certain classes of people, or types of audience (as in the case of ocean journeys, dental equipment, or residence organs) we can decide upon a cream plan in which we choose the clientele whom we are most anxious to reach, regardless of their geographical location.

The eighth step—The appropriation.—The amount to be set apart for advertising may be decided by:

1. *Devoting a certain part of the past year's sales to advertising.*

> Hosiery jobber, selling under his own brand name,
> with sales during the past year of..............$1,500,000
> It is decided to spend 2% of this amount for adver-
> tising during the coming year, or................    30,000
> The advertiser has fair distribution well scattered
> over the country. The best showing is made in
> the Middle-Western States. It is desired to
> strengthen the sales in these States. Local news-
> paper advertising is planned as the backbone of
> the program. This medium is to receive 50% of
> the appropriation, or........................    15,000
> For trade-paper advertising 25%..................     7,500
> For dealer displays and dealer helps 10%..........     3,000
> For direct advertising to dealers 15%.............     4,500
>
> Total ......................................   $30,000.

The percentages set aside for the respective media are based on a proportion according to the comparative value of the different media in the plan.

2. *Devoting a certain part of the anticipated sales for the coming year to advertising.*

The method of dividing the appropriation is the same as in the foregoing instance. The difference between the two plans lies in the fact that one is based on past sales, the other on anticipated sales. The second plan is regarded as more logical than the first one, in that the criterion is the increased business which is sought, and not the lesser amount of business of past years. Since the appropriation is to be used for the coming year's business it seems more rational to let all calculations be on the anticipated amount of sales, just the way production plans are based on the probable amount of business. Furthermore, the conditions under which last year's sales were made may differ from those of the coming year—a difference which the advertising appropriation would not recognize according to the first plan. If all concerned in the advertising realize the fact that the appropriation has been based on anticipated sales, they will feel their responsibility for helping to achieve that quota much more keenly than they would if they are called upon to spend an appropriation founded on work already performed.

Both plans 1 and 2 are useful when business on staples has been established long enough to provide a guide in the calculations of sales. Retail stores use the foregoing methods, in setting both the entire appropriation and the departmental allowances.

3. *Making an assessment on a certain unit of the objects, the units being sold either in previous years or anticipated for the coming year.*

This is the method used by the advertisers of soap who make a cake the unit of measure, set aside a fraction of the selling price per cake and, by multiplying this amount by the total number, reach the appropriation to be set. A similar practice is followed by fruit growers who assess a certain amount per case. The method in this instance is specially practicable when a number of advertisers enter into associated efforts. Each invests an amount to the advertising in proportion to the relative benefit he will obtain from it.

4. *Defining the work to be done, determining the forms of advertising necessary, and figuring the cost of producing that form, and determining the space.*

Where the work to be performed can be defined and accomplishment seems possible, this plan is good by way of securing a certain amount of distribution in a given city or securing the specification of a product as a standard part equipment.

5. *Putting all the money that can possibly be obtained into*

*advertising and reinvesting a part of the profits again in advertising.*

Here we have the method followed by most of the large advertisers today at the time they first began. The smaller the advertiser in volume of business handled, the greater percentage of their capital have they invested in advertising; as their sales grew in dollars and cents, their advertising was placed upon one of the first four plans. As the amount of their advertising increased, the percentage selling cost grew proportionately smaller, the profits per dollar of sale larger.

When the business advertised is a corporation which is run on fixed policies, the matter of appropriation has a different aspect than when the policies of a business are decided upon the spur of the moment by the owner. In the former instance, the appropriation usually means what it says. The board of directors invests a given sum in advertising. The general manager and subsequently the advertising manager are responsible for the execution of the plan. Where the head of a concern decides upon the daily policy of the business, the appropriation is a highly flexible matter. The impersonal corporation gives to an appropriation the advantage of definiteness with perhaps a corresponding handicap of inflexibility to meet a special occasion. It is the task of the man in charge of advertising to consolidate these two conditions, to see that a definite plan is set and carried out, and yet to be able to capitalize on unforeseen opportunities by setting up a reserve fund in the appropriation.

**The ninth step—The schedules.**—We have three schedules to keep in mind—the space schedule, the copy schedule, and the art and plate schedule. In the space schedule we determine upon the media, the publication date, and the size of the advertisements. Space contracts are then entered into with the respective publishers. When the advertisements are ready, they are forwarded with the insertion orders. In the copy schedule, we determine how many pieces of copy will be required and the length of the copy. We establish the approach to the idea to be used in the respective advertisements. Where two or more publications are being used, we also try to employ a piece of copy in as many media as feasible, to save unnecessary work. In the art and plate schedule we determine how many different drawings will be required and their sizes, and we endeavor to adopt one illustration to as many different advertisements as possible. As a case in point, suppose an advertisement were to appear in a consumer's magazine in full colors, in a newspaper and trade paper in black and white, and in a two-color folder to be distributed by dealers. One oil painting could be used for all. This painting may be reproduced by a four-color process (133-screen halftone) for the magazine; then photographed on a panchromatic plate for reproduction in a 110-screen black-and-white halftone in the trade paper; a silver print made of the panchromatic plate for a reproduction in line plate in a newspaper; finally a tint block run back of an electrotype of that line plate for use in a two-color folder. As a campaign assumes large proportions, money can also be saved by so planning the schedule that a set of plates can be forwarded from one publication, in which the advertisement is to appear, to the next.

The tenth step—The preparation.—We are now ready actually to prepare the advertisement. The copy theme and visualizing ideas are established. The layouts are drawn up. While the copy is being written, the illustrations are being made. As soon as the illustrations are finished, they are sent to the photo-engraver and plates made of them. The plates and copy go to the typographical shop, where the copy is set up together with the plates as a completed advertisement. Then if it is necessary, electrotypes are made of the entire set-up, and each electrotype is sent on its way in accordance with the schedule. Finally, the media in which the advertisement is to appear are examined by the advertising department to see that the advertisement is satisfactorily inserted. This being the case, the accounting department puts through the bill in payment.

Summary of the steps.—The steps in the work of advertising may be summarized in the following manner:

1. Secure product which offers good value.
2. Find out what it can be used for.
3. Determine who can use it and pick biggest market.
4. Determine stage of product to them.
5. Create or decide upon the transforming idea.
6. Decide upon plan of distribution.
7. Choose advertising plan—zone, cream, or national.
8. Fix appropriation.
9. Choose media.
10. Arrange space, copy, art and plate schedule.
11. Prepare advertisements.
12. If publication advertising:
    a. Prepare space schedules.
    b. Order space.
    c. Prepare layouts.
    d. Order art work.
    e. Write copy.
    f. Have plates made.
    g. Forward to publication.
    h. Receive checking copy.
13. If direct-mail advertising:
    a. Gather names of prospects into a list.
    b. Decide form of advertisements, whether letter, folder, or booklet.
    c. Prepare dummies and layout.
    d. Choose stock and ink.
    e. Order art work.
    f. Write copy.
    g. Have plates made.
    h. Order printing.
    i. Have folded, addressed, and mailed.

Under any circumstance, an advertisement should not go to press unless all plans are completed for properly following it up.

CHAPTER XXIII

THE ADVERTISING ORGANIZATION

TO handle the work of advertising, there has been developed an industry with many divisions. At one end there is the advertiser himself; at the other end, the publisher and the printer. Then there is a unique entity known as the advertising agency, important because of the part it plays, interesting because it gives a cross-section of the entire advertising structure.

## The Advertising Agency.

The work of the advertising agency has often been compared with that of the lawyer. Both render a personal service, the lawyer concerning himself with the legal affairs of the client, the agency looking after matters in any way affecting the advertising. Each requires a certain amount of specialized training, experience, and skill for the performance of his work. Both act as outside counsel to a number of clients with whom their relationship is a professional one, requiring access to intimate information and a high degree of confidence if the service is to be worth anything. A point of divergence is soon reached in the comparison, however, for a lawyer is paid his fee directly by his client, whereas an advertising agency, in addition to such a retainer payment which it may or may not receive, is granted a commission by the publications in which it places advertising. An advertiser could purchase in a magazine a page of space costing $1,000, pay that amount and prepare the advertisement. Or he could employ the services of an agency to prepare the advertisement, the agency receiving from the publication a commission representing partial or total remuneration.

This arrangement at first may seem a most unusual one but

449

in its existence lies the remarkable story of the development
of the advertising agency—a development which in large
measure is responsible for the progress advertising itself has
made since 1870.

The genesis of agencies.—"In the early days of advertising and advertising agencies, no one knew much about newspapers or periodicals that were published in any other than
their own immediate locality. Advertising agents were mostly
space brokers. Such lists as they did have were considered
their chief stock in trade and guarded with great care. Among
advertisers, that agency or organization was deemed most
successful, or the most profitable, with which to do business
which possessed the most extensive lists of media.

"One of these pioneer agents was George P. Rowell of
Boston, who placed advertising in the newspapers of Boston
and its environs—in what they called their 'New England
List.'

"When they came to place this advertising they found that
the list was only about 60 per cent correct. Many of the
papers had ceased to print, others had been absorbed, and
others had changed their rates. This was hardly surprising
in view of the fact that they had secured their information
from former residents who had been away from their homes
at least five years and were depending upon their memories
for the facts supplied.

"This experience soon proved to Mr. Rowell and his associates that if the agency was to thrive it would have to build
up a set of lists of newspapers and magazines for the use of
advertisers . . . and at a little later period they determined
to make up a list of newspapers in New York State. There-
after lists in various States and sections of the country were
slowly compiled and added to the general list already in possession of the agency.

"In 1870 Mr. Rowell determined to issue a directory of
newspapers. When the advertising agencies of New York,
Boston, and elsewhere learned of his intention, they protested
vigorously, for they believed that he was undermining their
business by giving away their chief 'stock in trade.' They all

felt that if advertisers could procure from this directory the names of media in such localities as they desired to cover with advertising, the advertising agents would all lose their business. What actually occurred was that the agencies were slowly forced to become something more than mere *space brokers*, and established a higher reputation as *space buyers*." [1]

The modern agency emerges.—The advertising agency of the nineteenth century (the advertising agent, rather, as it was a one-man affair) would either buy entire blocks of advertising space and sell it piecemeal to advertisers at its own rates, or else be awarded by the publisher a commission varying from 25 to 50 per cent of the space sold. How the advertiser used the space was none of the agent's concern. It was a time when running a card was considered the height of good advertising. Researches and appeals were as yet unborn; the need for judging the effectiveness of advertisements was little appreciated. According to St. Elmo Massengale, some of the first agencies were not enthusiastic even about checking advertising. [2] Gradually the agent's responsibility in the substance of the advertisements became greater, and from broker of space he passed not merely to the seller of space but to its purchaser, for the use of his clients. The agency then assumed a new character—that of an organization responsible for the most effective use of the advertising appropriation, and responsible also for the sales-welfare of its clients. Today the modern agency is not only a creator of advertising but a business counsellor as well.

Functions of a modern agency.—The function of the advertising agency is to increase the sales and profits of clients whom it serves through advertising. The broader scope of the agency's work requires that it understand the financial and production problems of its clients' businesses, be familiar

---

[1] From "Scientific Space Selection," Chapter V, published by the Audit Bureau of Circulation. This book traces the beginning of newspaper lists showing the gradual recognition of accurate circulation figures which culminated in the splendid Audit Bureau of Circulation of the present day.

[2] "Agency Origin and Development," by St. Elmo Massengale, appearing in the *Advertising Year Book for 1921-22*.

with the selling customs and the trade conditions in the clients' field, and know how to obtain additional information through research so that the selling policies of the business may be soundly directed. With this equipment, the agency is ready to help determine the best ways of increasing sales of a product, including the questions of uses to which a product may be put, potentiality and location of market, package and price, the selling appeal, and the methods of securing distribution. The agency will then create the advertising plan, determine the appropriation, recommend media, arrange the schedule, and secure the space under the most advantageous conditions to which the advertiser is entitled.

The agency prepares the advertisement, buying the necessary art work and plates, and forwards complete material to the publications. It also checks the advertisements, to see that they all have appeared in the desired position, in keeping with the schedule; and then submits itemized bills for expenses to the client. The agency will furthermore work with the client's advertising department, serving as counsel and assistant to the advertising manager.

Types of agencies.—The nature of the work with which advertising agencies occupy themselves varies considerably. An agency may do nothing more than place classified advertising. It may simply "clear" the advertising for its clients, that is, place the advertising but not create it—a practice which is regarded with disfavor. The agency may devote itself to direct-mail work, in which case it may not even seek recognition, or else apply itself to specialized trade paper work. It may be a "general" agency in that it uses any form of media best suited for the given purpose. The advertising agency may develop the merchandising plan and, stepping into the province of the sales agency, raise a staff of salesmen for its clients. In this group of "general" agencies most agencies are grouped, their chief distinction being in the size of their business and personnel. This may vary from three men to over three hundred. In terms of business "handled," that is, the cost of the advertising which an agency creates and "places," the agency may handle advertising costing from a few thousand dollars per year up to sixteen million dollars, which is the attainment of one of the very large firms.

**The organization of an agency.**—To understand the organization of an agency, let us take a single instance and watch its development from the time the establishment consisted of only one man, whom we may call the agency founder, until the day its branch offices were spread all over the continent, and the advertising of its clients, all over the world.

The founder of this concern may have had his start in the advertising world in several ways: He may have been on some newspaper, where he revealed his ability and eagerness in suggesting copy ideas to smaller advertisers who were neglected by the professional expert; he may have been on the sales force of some firm or he may have worked in a retail store where he wrote effective sales letters or designed good counter-cards; he may have been an "idea man" in a print shop or else, like Topsy, he may just have "growed" into the business.

At first, he probably did not call himself an agency, nor did he function as such in' the complete sense. Undoubtedly he merely prepared the incidental advertising for anyone within his acquaintance who required that such work be done. Probably his first clients were local retail stores, small manufacturers, local jobbers, or neighboring printers. With the successful execution of his earlier advertising, he was called upon to prepare more advertisements, simple direct-mail advertising, no doubt, or copy for a trade paper or for local newspaper advertisements.

Upon the spirit of the start, and not upon its splendor, rests the success of men, as the biographer of George Westinghouse observed; it is the diligence of our agency embryo which is worthy of watching, rather than the grandness of his surroundings, for his work carries him along successfully to the next point in our narrative where he has opened his own office and requires the assistance of an associate.

**The agency staff.**—What the work of this associate will be depends largely upon the phase of advertising for which the agency founder has shown a particular aptitude. The founder may have been a very successful "business getter" (by knowing the details of various industries so well that he can offer constructive advertising suggestions, thereby gaining "accounts"). If he is of this salesman type, he will probably seek an inside man to handle the execution of the advertisements and their mechanical production.

He may be exceptionally strong on copy, in which case he will prefer a visualizer and layout man, or vice versa. Or he may be so thoroughly versatile that he merely requires a secretarial assistant whom he duly employs and who, as often happens, proves to be one of the most important members of the staff. The chances are, however, that the agency founder will continue to be essentially an "outside" or "contact" man and that he will seek an associate who will complement his own abilities. Some of the happiest combinations of men in agencies exist where the principals thus complement each other in ability. This condition will be found to exist in other professional fields also, as in law and accounting.

Let us assume, therefore, that the head of this agency was the "outside" man with a good sense of merchandising and copy, and that his associate is a capable visualizer and mechanical production man—truly a valuable combination of talents.

The complete organization.—From this point on, the growth of the organization was rapid. The "inside" man became the *service manager.* He in turn added to his staff a *research man,* a *copy man* who subsequently was appointed *copy chief;* a *layout man* who became the *art director;* one who ordered the engraving and printing (later head of the *mechanical department*); and a *space buyer* who handled the selection of the media and checked space. The accounting and billing work made a *bookkeeper* necessary early in the history of the business. To keep the work progressing steadily from department to department, the duties of *traffic manager* or *accelerator* were relegated to a member of the staff, who also served as chief of files.[3] Meanwhile the "outside" organization had also grown, not so rapidly, to be sure, for one man outside

---

[3] There usually is a correspondence file, data file, and proof file. The latter will be divided according to clients and may be subdivided into printers' proofs, publication proofs, black-and-white proofs, colored proofs, and engravers' proofs.

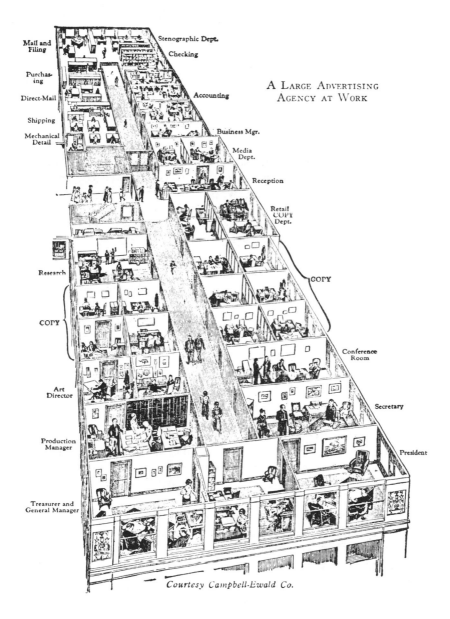

A LARGE ADVERTISING
AGENCY AT WORK

*Courtesy Campbell-Ewald Co.*

could keep many people inside very busy. And so, after a number of years, there emerges a full-fledged, well-manned advertising agency.[4]

Not every agency grows along these lines. Not every agency has as sharp a line of demarcation between the work of the members of its personnel, for it is truly remarkable to see how many titles some agency men earn. And there may be many more titles than here indicated, such as a "plan board," consisting of the department heads, or a "merchandising board." There is one man (or one group of men) however, from whom all work emanates, namely, the account executive. He is the man on the agency staff who is assigned to "handle" an account. He is the one who represents the agency to the advertiser, and looks after the advertiser's interests in the agency. No grandeur of agency machinery can ever replace the need for the applied attention of at least one man—the account executive. He has to lead in the thinking. He must see that the plan as decided upon is properly carried out. He must also secure the O. K. on the advertisements, as they are created.

The account executive may have obtained his knowledge through actual work in the client's industry. The former advertising man for a drug company, upon joining an agency, becomes account executive for their clients selling drug products; similarly many prominent men often come into the agency world equipped with ripe experience in some particular field, as the electrical goods, grocery, hardware, financial, or automobile—yes, even in the field of social welfare work. The account executive of another type may not have had this specialized experience, but having risen from the agency ranks, he is able to offer a fund of advertising knowledge to the clients he serves.

The account executive is the center of the agency's operation. He will direct the creative departments through the research director, art director, copy chief; the media department through the space buyer; and the mechanical department

---

[4] Because different organizations call the various positions by different names, it is well in entering an organization to index a position by its function and not by its name alone.

through the department head in charge of the buying of printing and engraving. Furthermore, his cooperation is always sought by the accounting and collection departments.

**Agency "recognition."**—There are approximately twelve hundred organizations in the United States and Canada which render an advertising service and which may be regarded as agencies. Of these, about half are "recognized" agencies. Recognition means that an organization is granted commission by the publishers in whose journals space is sought. Recognition is obtained by meeting certain requirements set by these publishers. This does not necessarily imply that an advertising organization which does not seek recognition may not be thoroughly competent and worthy in its work. The fact that recognition has been obtained, however, does indicate that a certain standard has been met by the agency. Some publications do not grant commissions to agencies, hence do not "recognize" them. This condition is frequently met among the trade papers which may feel that a general agency cannot serve the interests of their advertisers in their specialized field. These trade papers will often have their own "Service Department" to take the place of the agencies.

What are these requirements for recognition? Briefly, the agency must not be a tool which an advertiser may have set up to secure a rebate for himself, nor may it rebate a part of its commission to advertisers whose accounts it handles. The agency must be capable of rendering a constructive advertising service as evidenced by the experience of its men and its accomplishments over a period of one year, during which time the agency has to be in existence as an entity. The agency must be sound financially. If a newly formed agency wishes to place advertising in publications during its first year before recognition is granted it may enter into an arrangement with the publisher to be credited with its commission for the year if recognition is obtained at the end of that time.

The first direction in which a new agency will turn for recognition is toward the local newspaper; then toward other neighboring papers in which space is to be bought, or toward a trade paper or general magazine. But instead of asking recognition from each publication individually, the agency may apply for recognition to the American Newspaper Publishers' Association (A. N. P. A.), the Association of Business Papers (A. B. P.), or the Agricultural Publishers' Association (A. G. P. A.) or the other associations of publishers. Recognition from these organizations is generally honored by their respective members.

**How the agency operates.**—An agency may work with many clients but an advertiser will need only one agency to handle his work. Exceptions will be found in the case of huge concerns producing a number of similar lines. Examples of such concerns are the American Tobacco Company which employs different agencies for its various brands of cigarettes, and the General Motors Company, whose diversity of products is handled through a number of agencies.

The confidential relationship of agency and client tends to preclude the agency from handling accounts which are in competition with each other. The list of accounts handled by an agency accordingly will appear quite varied—one agency handling a writing paper account, a residence house organ, a tire, an insurance account, and a paint account; another agency handles the advertising of ginghams, linoleums, cutlery, watches, chocolates, shoes, biscuits, bicycles, and batteries. To these advertisers, the agency supplies a new fund of ideas and thorough familiarity with aggressive advertising methods.

On the other hand, an agency may have specialized in a given field to such an extent that it confines itself to noncompetitive accounts in that and allied lines only. An organization of this type advertised a thresher and a seeding machine, a pleasure car, a motor truck, a piston ring, a disc clutch, an automobile bearing, an ignition system, and a tractor transmission—all of these products being of a mechanical nature. One agency in the textile and wearing apparel trades handled a high grade of summer clothing, knitting yarn, and boys' clothing, as well as a cap and a hosiery account.

**Methods of payment.**—The publisher bills the agency for the space it orders, the agency, in turn, billing the advertiser.

In reality, the agency assumes a financial risk which often runs into hundreds of thousands of dollars.

A recognized agency will receive a commission from the various publications in which it orders space. The rate is fixed by the individual periodical and is usually 13 or 15 per cent of the card rate. In addition, an extra 2 per cent is allowed on the net payment for cash, as is common in any trade. The arrangement is spoken of as "13 and 2" or more frequently as "15 and 2."

Of the several bases of remuneration upon which an agency may undertake work in behalf of a client, the following are the methods in general use:

*The straight commission plan.*—In the straight commission arrangement, the agency accepts in payment for its services the commission granted by the publisher upon the client's advertising. The client merely pays the card rates for the space bought.

Thus:

```
For  space  costing  $1,000  the  publisher  bills  the
  agency ...................................................  $1,000
Less 15% .........................................     150
                                                      _____
                                                       $850
Discount for cash 2% ............................      17
                                                      _____
Agency pays ......................................              $833
Agency bills client .............................  $1,000
  and passes on cash discount if client pays promptly...   17
                                                           _____
Client pays agency ..............................              $983
```

If any art work, engraving, or typographical set-ups are required for the advertisement, the agency bills these to the client either at cost (price paid by agency) or at cost plus 15% for the agency's service. The latter arrangement is the one generally accepted. Thus:

```
                    MECHANICAL COSTS
Art Work ........................................  $150.00
Plates ..........................................    60.00
Setting-up  Advertisement  ......................    15.00
                                                   _____
                                                    $225.00
Plus 15% ........................................     33.75
Charges to client for mechanical costs...........            $258.75
```

*Plus 15, less commissions.*—Another method used with satisfaction by a number of agencies is that of charging for their services a flat fee representing usually 15 per cent of the card rates (and of expenditures for art work or mechanical charges), crediting the client with whatever discounts they receive, thus:

| | |
|---|---:|
| There is spent in | |
| Publication *A* | $10,000 |
| Publication *B.* | 20,000 |
| Publication *C.* | 2,000 |
| There is also spent | |
| Art work | 500 |
| Type set-up and plates | 145 |
| Total expenditure | $32,645 |
| Agency fee for its services is 15%, or | $ 4,896 |
| Assume that agency commissions on publications *A* and *B* were 13% each, and 2% for cash on net amount, and assume that publication *C* granted no commission to agencies; the total commission would be | $4,422 |
| which would be credited to the advertiser. He would actually be debited | $37,541 |
| and credited | 4,422 |
| leaving his total bill | $33,129 |

This method of "plussing" a flat 15 per cent (or whatever percentage, as agreed) and crediting all commission, is fair to the agency, which often has to do considerable work among media where the amount of commissions vary. Another advantage is its comparative simplicity of bookkeeping.

**Retainer and commission.**—The chief value of an agency to a client may consist of its research counsel and ideas, though little publication advertising be used. A "retainer-plus-commission" plan has been introduced to provide for this situation, and offers a method which is rapidly coming into wide acceptance. By this plan, the agency is assured a definite income of, let us say, $5,000 for the year. Towards this amount the agency will credit whatever commission it receives. The client pays a monthly retainer which is to make up for the difference between the income from commission and the set fee. If the commissions exceed the fee, the client need pay no retainer and the agency continues on its straight commission basis. Thus:

Instance *A*:

Retainer fee set for the year .................................. $5,000

Commissions from publications amount to ....................... 1,500

In addition to the cost of the space, the client pays a fee of....... $3,500
in monthly instalments, adjustments made every six months.

Instance *B*:

Retainer fee set for the year .................................. $5,000

Commissions from publications amount to ....................... 5,500

Client need pay no further retainer, but only the card-rate cost of
the space used.

The agency is not allowed to rebate its commission and accordingly cannot agree to a flat fee which represents less than a 15% commission.

The retainer and commission basis provides a solution to the quixotic situation whereby an agency serves one master but apparently receives its payment from another. The retainer plan, as its name implies, retains the agency to serve the client without preference towards any form of media. There is no incentive to rush the client into advertising.

**Initial fee.**—The better agencies will not undertake to prepare any advertising without thoroughly probing into the feasibility of the effort. Neither will they offer suggestions or ideas before they are definitely engaged by a client. The reason for this is evident—an idea without thought is worth little, and thinking is worth money, especially when thoughts are the entire assets of a profession and the nucleus of entire industries. Before the agency will even begin work for the client, it will conduct a preliminary investigation, charging for the actual cost of such an investigation.

The prospective advertiser does not buy an advertising plan but something even more important—an authentic survey into the practicability of going into advertising. The same research may provide the information for subsequent advertising, if advertising be used. In either case, the arrangement is fair, both to client and agency. If the agency is called upon to prepare the advertising, it may operate in accordance with any of the plans outlined, crediting the initial fee to the retainer payment.

The question of equitable payment for agency service has been receiving considerable attention by advertisers, publishers, and agencies themselves.

**Judging the agency.**—To see the qualities desired by an advertiser in an agency, strip away all the stage-setting of elaborate offices and handsome portfolios, look past the rituals of soliciting the account and look right to the men of the organization. What has been their training and experience? What businesses have they helped develop? What successes can they point to—successes being measured in terms of effective handling of all things they have undertaken? Would they be able to secure for you facts and thoughts about your business of which you were not previously aware? Are they financially stable?

How sound are their ideas? What is their creative initiative? Upon what plan or idea did the advertising of their clients succeed? What part did they play in originating the plan and in developing it? How completely did the agency execute the plans discussed? How long has it had its respective accounts? Which has it lost and why? Exactly how is the handling of an account conducted? These queries probe deeper into the agency service than would a perfunctory examination of its sample file or its organization chart.

## The Internal Advertising Department.

After our trip through the advertising agency, we call upon the internal advertising department, which may vary in size from the small department occupying the upper right hand drawer of a desk to one covering several floors of office space.

**The retail store's advertising department.**—In the small retail store, the advertising department (or the man in charge of advertising) is occupied usually with the dressing of the windows, the preparation of the store cards, the issuance of direct-mail matter, the preparation of the local newspaper copy. Retail stores, as a rule, deal directly with the newspapers. They use agencies on magazine advertising.

In the large retail 'store, the work of the advertising department is greatly increased. At the very head of the business and above the advertising manager (unless the man be the advertising manager) is the functionary known as the merchandising manager. He decides upon the general sales policy of the store and of its respective departments. In conjunction with him and the respective departmental buyers, the advertising manager helps create the various sales events throughout the year.

To each department a definite appropriation will be allotted, based upon sales. The department buyer and the advertising manager determine on the exact space schedule, four to six weeks ahead of the publication date. Different days of the week upon which the different departments will appear are generally chosen by the departments themselves. Sunday and Wednesday, for example, are usually devoted to wearing apparel; Tuesdays and Thursdays to furniture, rugs, and house furnishings; Friday to men's clothing and haberdashery. The buyers, knowing exactly when their advertisements will appear, will then determine which items in the stock to feature. Often the advertising man will be called in on this most important question.

The advertising department is then furnished with the technical facts 'necessary to describe the goods properly. One of the copywriters delevops these data into copy suited to the layout requirements of the advertisement; the art work is prepared and submitted to the buyer to make sure that the details of the product are correctly portrayed. The plates are then made and the advertisement put into type. Meanwhile, a staff of "comparison shoppers" have been out comparing the offers of other stores with the offers contemplated. Prices may then be adjusted to meet competition, after which advance prints of the advertisement are distributed among the sales force and the advertisement is duly published.

There is far more romance to retail store advertising than a description of its mechanics would indicate. The excitement of an opportune purchase, the tension of watching the competing market to go it one better, the speed with which the advertising group gathers its material and prepares its ideas—

finally the pleasure of seeing the advertisement appear and the merchandise sell the very next day—these things make vibrant the work in retail advertising.

In addition to the newspaper advertising, as above outlined, a retail store may employ a considerable amount of outdoor advertising and direct-mail advertising. There is invariably an excellent list of customers awaiting the advertising department; the task resolves itself simply into segregating them according to the character of the prospects (married women, heads of households, juniors, etc.) and according to the amount of purchase, frequency of purchase, nature of purchase, and credit standing. Once the list is in order, the opportunities will be quite apparent to the alert advertising man.

The manufacturer's advertising department.—There is another advertising department to consider—that of the manufacturer. Even those concerns using an agency will often have an internal advertising department to handle that work best done by someone in intimate and continued contact with the firm. The work of the manufacturer's advertising department includes:

1. Issuance of direct-mail advertising, created by member of staff, by agency, by printer, or by special direct-mail agency.

2. Issuance of dealer-display advertising, likewise created by member of staff, by agency, by printer, or by special dealer-display service.

3. Handling of trade paper advertising, unless agency is specially equipped to do this.

4. Working with salesmen (sales-promotion work), sending them advance prints of advertisements; securing sales-leads, following up their calls with suitable direct-mail advertising.

5. Directing the advertising agency in preparation of publication advertising.

The exact management of the internal advertising department varies considerably with the requirements of the respective institutions. Anyone establishing such a department would do best to follow the recognized principles of management; in other words, determine exactly what must be done, assign the work to the proper individuals, define the responsibility, and clearly indicate how the work is to flow, finally employing the simplest possible system to insure the prompt completion of the work.

"Breaking into advertising."—The question is repeatedly asked, "How can I actually get into advertising work?" Many are the ways, humble, perhaps, but nevertheless befitting one who seeks a career. There are records which have to be kept in an advertising office. They require the attention of one who is thorough and who appreciates the significance of figures. Then there is the production phase of advertising work—ordering printing, engraving, supervising the mailing. That is another beginner's opportunity—seeing that all material is where it ought to be when it is supposed to be there, if not sooner. This work involves calling up the printer, phoning the engraver, and keeping track of the work until it is finally completed. To one entering advertising through this department, experience comes in rich measure.

Another record-keeping task which affords opportunity is that of checking the advertisements to see that they appear according to schedule. This work puts one on the road to space buying.

Moving towards the creative departments, we find opportunity for the "copy cub." The cub may come to the attention of the advertising department through a suggestion on existing copy. At first he may be furnished with an advertisement and asked to write more like it. Or he may be assigned to some piece of copy which may not appear important to him, compared with the other jobs being turned out, but which may prove the sesame to his future in advertising. The layout man similarly may get his start in the art department or art studio where he cleans up drawings, keeps records, and prepares the borders and pastes up dummies.

Among publishers and printers, there is the work of selling space and securing customers. The advertising man here is an outside man, selling the merits of his product to prospective advertisers. Perhaps research work is being done by these organizations, in which case someone is needed to compile the data and handle the reports. Here again is an opening. (In a publication office, the advertising manager is concerned with the *sale of space*. The circulation department may have its own advertising staff to secure new subscribers, but this is usually referred to as the "promotion" department.)

Once given an opportunity to do some work in an advertising department, the novice must apply himself with enthusiasm and thoroughness. Isn't there some work which has been passed around and buried? Isn't there some task which no one considers important enough to touch, but which everyone wishes were done? Are any customer's inquiries being lost in the crevice which may exist between sharply drawn lines of responsibility? Everybody may be doing his "share" as was the case in Buckingham Palace, described in Strachey's "Queen Victoria." The Department of Lord Chamberlain had charge of the rooms, and was responsible for the cleaning of the windows on the inside, while the outsides were left to the Officer of Woods and Forests, with the result that the windows were never as clean as they could have been. So in organizations, work which is half-done by two people is often not done at all. There is always opportunity for the man who takes a task in hand and cleans it up with thoroughness—that being one quality cordially welcomed in any calling—advertising included.

# CHAPTER XXIV

## IMPROVING THE PROCEDURE

ANY discussion of advertising procedure would not be complete if it provided merely a working knowledge of advertising practice without indicating the manner in which the advertising of the future may be improved. To valuate the true opportunities and needs of advertising, it is necessary to turn back two centuries and appreciate the circumstances which brought modern advertising into being.

Considering the age of the human race, a few hundred years is, admittedly, a brief lapse of time over which to trace any evolutionary process. The study of contemporary advertising problems, however, began in the eighteenth century; and in the changes which have been brought about since, the forces influencing the advertising of the future may be discerned.

**Dipping into history.**—Industry, as we know it today, really began when machinery was ushered in, with the aid of which it extended its influence far and wide. After this scramble was over, industry sought to intrench itself in its various fields, finally striving to grow two blades of business grass where one grew before. If the years of transition were to be divided into definite periods, we would have four eras, the first extending roughly from 1760 to 1830. These years witnessed the Industrial Revolution in which machinery first supplanted hand labor. The second era, from 1830 to 1887, was one of rapid expansion; here man spread his domain through the use of machinery. The third period, in which industry settled itself into a more competitive roll, lasting from 1887 to 1905, witnessed the birth of "big business," the struggle to gain production superiority, and the groping for new avenues of expansion. The fourth period, beginning about 1905 and extending to the present time, is characterized by the ascendency of marketing.

467

Up to 1760 the industrial structure in England, where we may begin our survey, was a comparatively simple one. The population was engaged chiefly in agricultural pursuits.[1] The towns were small and quite self-contained. Each had its own bootmaker, blacksmith, and candle-stick maker. Practically everything needed by the townsfolk was made right in their midst. Even the individual households were in large measure self-contained, each with its own spinning frame on which the cloth for raiment was patiently woven. People lived unto themselves and spent most of their time in making the goods which they themselves used.

**The Industrial Revolution: 1764-1830.**—Then came the Industrial Revolution in England—the birth of machinery for manufacturing. The spinning-jenny of James Hargreaves in 1764, the textile machines invented by Arkwright and Crompton and Cartwright, Watt's steam engine in 1782, and Whitney's cotton gin in 1794 (this last in the United States) were among the conspicuous inventions destined to alter the very character of industry. They were the beginning of quantity production.

About the same time when machinery for manufacturing purposes was being introduced, the canal systems were greatly extended. Then came the railroads. The locomotive of Stephenson, the moulding of iron rails in Coalbrookdale, the improvement by Newcomen of mine-pumping machinery which made coal more accessible—all these marked the dawn of rapid transportation. It was more than a coincidence that railroads came into existence at about the same time as did manufacturing machinery. The circumstance was in keeping with a fundamental principle of industry, a principle which we shall again meet when we analyze the problem of the twentieth century, namely, that mass production entails a corresponding need for speedy channels of distribution. If goods

---

[1] In England, even as recently as 1850, only 33.3% of the population lived in towns of over 20,000; while in 1911, 78.1% lived in urban areas. This shifting of the population towards cities is still going on, though to a lesser extent, shown by the fact that in 1921 the urban areas held 79.3% of the population— "Industrial History of Modern England," by George Herbert Perris, p. 105; also communication from British Embassy, Washington.

**B**EFORE the Industrial Revolution the maker of the goods and the user were personally acquainted.

**T**HEN machinery came; towns grew. Goods were made in quantities. The distance between consumer and producer began spreading.

**G**OODS were produced in still greater quantities. Transportation improved. The distances became greater. Advertising was introduced to bring producer and consumer together.

**P**RODUCER and consumer are now far removed. Goods are made in enormous quantities. Advertising is required to tell the widespread public about the goods. Distribution of goods made possible through speedy transportation and extensive marketing facilities.

*Specially drawn for* ADVERTISING PROCEDURE *by George L. Hollrock.*

THE ECONOMICS OF ADVERTISING

are to be made in quantity, they must be quickly disposed of or else the facilities for making them become clogged.[2] On repeated occasions this relationship will show its importance.

The era of expansion: 1830-1887.—Passing from the England of the Industrial Revolution to America of the nineteenth century, we again find the invention of machinery and the development of transportation keeping abreast of each other in their rapid strides.

The introduction of farm machinery in 1833 was epoch making. In that year the name of Cyrus McCormick first became known through his "automatic mower" by means of which one man with a team of horses was able to cut as much grain as twenty men swinging a cradle. Throughout the half century which followed McCormick's invention, further improvements were made in farm equipment. The bushel of wheat which took three hours of labor to produce in the early part of the century was produced in ten minutes by the end of the century. Machinery alone decreased labor costs by 80 per cent.

The manufacturing inventions also were many in the decades following 1830. The electric telegraph came in 1838, revolutionizing communication. A further impetus was given to large-scale production in 1845 by the invention of the sewing machine by Elias Howe (on whose machine over 7,000 patents for improvements have since been issued), followed by the McKay shoe-sewing machine which was the forerunner of the boot-making industry with its present output of a million pairs per day in the United States alone. The spinning, weaving, knitting, and other wearing-apparel industries were especially benefited by the inventions in the period 1830-1887; the new Bessemer process for making steel (England, 1859) likewise was a boon to the metal manufacturing trades.[3]

Transportation too was enjoying increased progress. In

---

[2] "The application of steam power to mechanical devices for production of goods extended the market, necessitated better means of transportation which were provided through the invention of the locomotive and the application of steam to marine transportation." "Modern Industrialism," by Dr. Frank L. McVey, p. 28.

[3] "The Progress of Invention in the Nineteenth Century," by Edward W. Byrn.

1830 one of the first steam locomotives was built for use on the South Carolina railroad. By 1833 the road had 133 miles of trackage and was known as the longest continuous line of railroad in the world. The Mohawk and Hudson, and Baltimore and Ohio railroads also came into existence in the early years of the eighteen-thirties. Railroad building progressed steadily until the Homestead Act, whereby the Government encouraged settlement across the Mississippi, was passed in 1862. "The West is open" was the cry, and into the West went the railroads.

Interrupted but not hindered by the Civil War, the railways then began their historic expansion. The roads which had first linked nearby Eastern cities thrust their fingers through the Alleghanies into the Middle West, finally pushing boldly through the Rockies into the springtime land of the Pacific Coast. Golden pages in railroad history were written in the years preceding 1887; in that year more mileage was laid than during any other year in the history of the railroad. What did all this invention and construction indicate? Simply that industry had been endowed with a new power of multiplying its products. The barrier or distance was being reduced from months to days, and from days to hours.[4]

The struggle of production: 1887-1905.—Actually, however, the world had been moving into a new house, making great changes at the outset, and gradually coming down to the finer details. Towards the latter part of the nineteenth century the improvements in machinery were many but their individual nature was not as radical as heretofore; their savings not as large. There was greater saving in the change from hand production to machine production than in the improvement of one detail of a machine over its predecessor. Railroads eased up in their race to span the countryside, for the good reason that the important highways already had their tracks of steel. For, while 12,876 miles of railways were laid in 1887, only 5,162 miles were laid in 1889, and 1,895 miles in 1895.

Since new railroads were not being built at their former

---

[4] Until this point the railroads represented the "distributive" or "marketing" system. The personnel of distribution, the "middlemen," come into greater prominence at this juncture.

rate, new markets were not suddenly opened. Since new machinery did not startlingly decrease the production costs, new demand for goods was not suddenly created. Consequently, the attention of industry began moving from the machinery of production to methods for the economical use of the machinery, and to that which was even more important—a means of keeping the machinery employed steadily. Through mergers and consolidations, characteristic of the closing years of the nineteenth century, and through the introduction of scientific management, industry sought to reduce the expense of making goods. It might be added that production costs have ever since then been subject to the closest study. To meet the second problem—that of keeping manufacturing facilities in continual use, industry looked in a new direction. Until that time it had been satisfied merely with producing; demand took care of itself. But a fierce competition developed to control the existing demand for goods, and to create among consumers additional requirements which would keep the factory wheels moving.

A manufacturer was a manufacturer in the strict sense of the word. He simply made the goods and left to the wholesaler the task of disposing of the merchandise to the retail store. Strenuous competition prompted the manufacturers to establish their own sales force whose duty would be to interest merchants in the goods produced by that concern only. From this step onward, the manufacturer became increasingly concerned with the sales of his goods. Into this intensely competitive arena there entered a new force, designed to inspire the desire for goods and influence the sale of commodities—advertising.

Enter advertising.—Modern advertising was born amid strife and competition. Its introduction on a commercial scale in the latter part of the nineteenth century was a casual but unfailing recognition by industry that the reputation of a product was as vital as its construction, the good name of its maker as important as its price. Advertising helped a product to become known for a certain standard of quality which the buyer could depend upon securing when he again desired to make a purchase. Advertising further helped a product to establish a character for itself so that a purchaser might choose it from among the nondescript brands. During the years preceding 1900 advertising was primarily used to identify the product, and it did so by presenting the manufacturer's name to the public.

The spirit of competition soon invaded this field. An advertiser was not satisfied merely with presenting his name. He told the world how good his product was, in terms quite outspoken. His neighbor, not to be beaten, tried to outdo his claims. Nothing in the way of adjectives was too blatant to use; no strain upon the imagination was too severe until the sheer incredibility of statement was on the verge of destroying the very thing which the advertising set out to earn—the respect and confidence of the public.

The old order of exaggerated advertising was basically wrong; it never can be extenuated. The only consoling feature of the entire delusion lies in the fact that the very men who created such advertising were the first to see that its salvation, its strength, and its future lay in absolute truth. The Associated Advertising Clubs of the World first met in 1904; it has carried the symbol of TRUTH around the world and its light into the offices and shops of almost every nation.

**The advent of marketing: 1905.**—With the recognition of the higher ideal in industry, the fourth period was opened. In 1905 the Trade-mark Act was passed, enabling a man better to protect the reputation of his products. In the same year the Pure Food and Drug Act was also passed. This law required that contents be stated on all packages; and it fixed the responsibility as to the truth of such statements upon the producer. Both these enactments are cornerstones of truth in the structure of advertising. In 1911 the State Statute known as the Printers' Ink Model Statute directed against misleading advertising was passed. The Federal Trade Commission was furthermore created (1914) to aid in fair methods of doing business.

Once the truth in advertising movement began making headway, a better conception of advertising arose—that of inviting attention to a product through a simple statement of the advantages attendant upon its purchase and use. Advertising since 1905 bears witness to this wholesome change.

The existence of different appeals in advertisements came into recognition, the possibilities of copy were grasped and the requirements of layouts were better understood. Furthermore, the necessity for honest circulation figures was acknowledged, the need for getting facts through research gradually appreciated, and the importance of dovetailing advertising with the other departments of the business seriously regarded. These questions still need to be fully appreciated; nevertheless advertising is certainly thriving on the principles, whose importance came to light during this period.

**Immediate problems.**—It will not be sufficient for advertising merely to continue perfecting its technique; advertising will have to assume its share of the burden imposed by industry upon the entire work of marketing, of which advertising is only a part.

From the very beginning of quantity production we have seen that the marketing system must be capable of distributing these huge quantities of goods. Production comes first; marketing must be equal to it. Yet what do we find? Attention has been given almost entirely to production; marketing has been left to take care of itself. Engineers and cost accountants have made a fine study of production. Marketing is nobody's child. Ask a manufacturer how much it costs him to make a pair of shoes and he will tell you to a cent the cost of every operation in the construction. But ask him exactly where the money goes in selling the shoes—well, that is another matter entirely.

It may cost $1.85 actually to make a pair of shoes. The consumer pays $10 for them. The spread between the production cost and the price the consumer pays represents the "distributing cost" out of which the respective distributors are expected to meet their expenses and realize their profit.[5] Comparatively few manufacturers know their exact distributing costs, know which member of their line of products is

---

[5] The Harvard Bureau of Business Research made an investigation of costs in the retail shoe field, offering one of the first thorough investigations of distribution charges.

paying best, know where their selling expenses are unduly heavy, or know what they can afford to pay to sell an article. Consequently they seldom know how much money, if any, is being wasted at this point. So long as they secure a residue of profit from production, they are satisfied. When profits are low or sales are few, production bears the brunt of criticisms. "We must reduce the cost of making that article," manufacturers will declare when effecting a picayune economy in the factory, while marketing costs outside are allowed to soar as they please, apparently immune from scrutiny.

What does it avail industry to shave costs in production if big chips of the capital are scattered to the winds in selling? What purpose is served by advertising which increases the sale of a product if the other factors of distribution are permitted to run costs up beyond all reason? As one member of the National Association of Cost Accountants, said at a meeting of that society, "I presume several of you men present at this meeting have heard their superintendents remark that every time they increased the efficiency of their plant, which consequently means a lower manufacturing cost, they feel highly elated over their success, until they are informed of the net results, and then only find out that the economies effected have been swallowed up by the selling expenses."

The Joint Congressional Committee of Agricultural Inquiry conducted an exhaustive investigation of the matter, and in a report which is remarkable both for its thoroughness and for the understanding manner in which it was prepared, showed just how much more it costs to sell, transport, and deliver commodities in the United States at the present time, than it does to produce them. The fact apparent to any observer of industry, that knowledge of distribution is in its medieval days compared with that of production, makes it evident that great economy and great improvement in the manufacturing industry will come through a study of marketing.

Even agriculture has reached the point where the development of better distribution methods is more important to the farmer than the acquisition of new machines. The decrease in production costs through the use of new implements is overshadowed by the cost of that machinery. "Payment for these increase costs," reports the Joint Agricultural Committee referring to purchases of new equipment for farms, "is dependent for the most part upon better organization and more efficient marketing of farm crops." [6]

So here we are, with lower marketing costs the paramount issue for the manufactured products and the rising hope for agriculture also. The question that confronts all industry is, "How can the costs of selling and distributing be reduced?"

How can the costs be reduced?—Perhaps no suggestion has been offered more frequently as a panacea for all distribution ills than that of "decreasing the number of middlemen." The middlemen represent the wholesaler, the jobber, the retailer, and all others through whom a product must pass from producer to consumer, by whatever name they may be known.

Many miles often separate the producer and consumer. We recognize that vehicles are necessary to transport the goods. But who is there to supervise the local distribution of the goods after they have been delivered at the depot? The middleman. Who takes the goods in quantity and sells in smaller units to the neighborhood grocer? The middleman. To whom does the housewife go when she wants some soap, or shoes, or carpet tacks? The middleman. To whom does her husband go for a collar-button or a lawn-mower? The middleman. We would not have middlemen if we ourselves did not call upon their services. By and large, they are just as important and as economically justified as the roads upon which the vehicles pass. To decrease marketing costs by "decreasing the number of middlemen" would offer just about as effective a remedy for reducing present marketing costs as would the reduction of present freight charges by removing some of the ties from the railroad track. In laying new tracks, better ties may be used, better methods for laying them invented; or, a system devised whereby fewer ties will be needed between stations, and whereby unnecessary curves and grades will be removed. But a more immediate approach

---

[6] "The Agricultural Crisis and its Causes," Report of the Joint Commission, of Agricultural Inquiry, Part III, p. 201.

to the question of marketing costs lies in the better use of the existing channels of distribution.

**Clear definitions.**—Before even endeavoring to formulate a solution to any problem, it is necessary to define the terms used. In the case of manufactured products, we have visualized production as representing the various steps in industry from the time the raw material is extracted from the ground until the time it is converted into its manufactured form. Distribution covers all steps from the completion of manufacture until the product is used by the consumer. In the case of farm products, distribution begins with the packing of the produce for the market. These definitions barely serve the present elementary discussion; obviously they are too vague for cost-finding purposes.

An example of the limitation of definitions is close at hand: Upon the suggestion of the Hon. Sydney Anderson, the report of whose Joint Committee of Agricultural Inquiry has previously been referred to, the writer endeavored to prepare a table which would make a comparison of the amount of money and the number of people engaged in the work of production and distribution respectively over a period of thirty years. To measure the activity of the manufacturing industries, a copy of the Government census of manufacturers was consulted. This lists, among other things, the number of proprietors, firm members, and salaried employees engaged in manufacture which at first glance appear strictly as production items. The question naturally arises as to whether the salary of the vice-president in charge of sales would go to production or selling (distribution). What other internal charges at present grouped under "manufacturing" would be allocated to "distribution"? Where shall the line be drawn? We said that the expense incurred in the gap between factory and consumer roughly represented distribution. If a concern maintains distant warehouses for shipment of material which is sold in that territory, would the cost of transportation from factory to warehouse represent an expense of production, or of distribution? If instead of the warehouse there were an assembling plant, how would the answer be affected? The question becomes still more involved in tracing the costs of raw materials which are sold to a manufacturer who, in turn, sells the finished product to the final user. The definitions will have to be clearly stated and a common basis of understanding established before any headway can be made in bringing distribution to the same degree of perfection attained by production.

Definite cost information.—Once the definition of terms is established, the next step is to secure exact data, for which purpose accurate systems of keeping selling costs must be introduced. The value of exact figures has been recognized in finance and in production. More accurate methods of securing cost figures must also be introduced in marketing, for unless these costs are known they cannot very well be reduced. The selling mind is prone to think in terms of adjectives rather than figures; without specific data, however, it cannot learn by its own experiences, nor can it safely draw any conclusions. What percentage of selling price can be allowed to sales costs? If several different products or else varying styles or sizes of the same product are being sold by the one concern, which are the paying numbers? Which ought to be eliminated? Is it profitable to increase the territory in which a product is being sold? These questions are random instances of those which may be answered only when a knowledge of selling costs has been acquired.

The need for actual figures on distributing costs is not entirely unheeded. O. D. Street, while general manager of distribution for the Western Electric Company, told as follows the headway made through a knowledge and analysis of marketing costs:[7]

"Prior to the date of these studies," said Mr. Street, "and owing to the methods we had employed in computing expenses, we had shown on one line, a loss on sales of about 1.5 per cent, and a loss on investment of more than 10 per cent. Since then, knowing more about how to figure distribution costs, we have shown a profit on sales of about 8 per cent.

"On another item, we had shown a loss on sales of 3 per

---

[7] "How the Western Electric Company Is Analyzing Its Distribution Costs," by O. D. Street. Address before A. N. A., reported in *Printer's Ink*, December 7, 1922, p. 33.

cent and a loss on investment of more than 15 per cent. Now we show a profit on investment of about 35 per cent. We had always made money on all these items, but we did not know it because of the unsound methods used in figuring distribution costs. On still another line we had been showing a profit on sales of 15 per cent, and a profit on investment of 38 per cent, but now on that same item, the gross profit rate being about the same as before, we are showing a loss on sales of about 2.5 per cent and a loss on investment of about 8 per cent. This was one of the items we had been pushing hard, because, since the gross profit rate was 30 per cent, we had thought we were making a great deal of money on it, but instead our new system of computing expenses proved that we were really losing money on every sale."

Is it worth while to study distribution costs? There can be little question about it. Exact definitions and accurate cost figures are the basis of all solutions to lower distribution costs. Advertising itself may then be of help by eliminating production depressions, and by speeding the course of goods in their sales journey.

**Eliminating seasonal depressions.**—Before the Industrial Revolution, depressions in their present sense were unknown. People lived largely on farms. They were dependent upon the soil for their livelihood. A draught or poor crop in one part of the country affected the people in that part only; the suffering was purely local, the inhabitants of another locality often enjoying their feasts of plenty. Not until 1816, when England was gripped by its first national depression, did the nation come to realize the significance of the new order of things—the interdependence of distribution and production.[3] In that year the refusal of people, several hundred, even several thousand miles away, to buy the wares of the local manufacturer, threw the workers in domestic plants out of employment. Rather a new experience this, of having remote influences vibrate throughout the land and even the world, affecting most vitally the nation's productive usefulness. His-

---

[3] "The First Overproduction Crisis," in "Industrial Depression," by G. P. Hull, p. 7.

tory with its depressions unfortunately has repeated itself on numberle·s occasions. Even more unfortunate has industry overlooked a chronic condition which in the aggregate is a greater drain upon the public than any single depression has ever been, namely, the wastes of seasons and slumps causing an organization to be rushed one month, idle another, have overtime work one season and half-time work the next.

In any month of even the "best" years, it is possible to discover some industry with its equipment idle and awaiting orders, or else with more orders on hand than goods—usually a short-lived experience confined to the height of seasons only. Even when demand exceeds the output, the apparent benefit of the boom times is lost in the slumps which inevitably follow, slumps in which workmen are laid off, machines stand unused, and overhead expense continues.

Advertising can here enter upon the scene to make production more continuous, as it did for the Walnut Growers' Exchange by increasing the season in which people used their product from six weeks to eight months out of every year; as when it lengthened the season for cranberries and canned fruits, lemons and oranges, water heaters and ice, underwear and jewelry, enameled ware, concrete and motor cars, and an endless host of products upon whose continuous production depends the welfare of communities of producers and nations of purchasers who secure the benefit of the lower costs brought about by sustained production. Even retail department stores have put advertising to use in keeping the sales from taking their big slumps in "off" days. Monday was formerly the day of lowest sales. Through advertising it has become one of the leading days.

**Quickening the passage of goods through trade channels.**— Thousands of dollars will be spent on a machine to hasten its output by ten seconds; the traffic manager will arrange his shipment of goods to catch a through train to save a half hour in the delivery of the goods. But goods may rest for weeks and weeks on the shelves of the dealer's store before being resold. Here we have another day-and-night contrast between the effectiveness of production and the laxity of distribution; moments are saved in making a product, months are wasted in selling it. The retailer pays for this slowness; the manufacturer pays; the consumer pays. It is the speed of selling a certain consignment of goods, as well as the total quantity sold, or its price that determines the profits of a business. Quickened "turnover," as the rapidity of selling goods is termed, decreases selling costs; and advertising is one of the most effective weapons for quickening the sale of goods. It does so by spreading information about the product's usefulness, thereby bringing more customers to the store; by rapidly spreading its reputation, thereby decreasing the time necessary for the public to become acquainted with the article; and by causing the commodity to live up to a standard, thereby inspiring repeat orders. Since it is apparent, furthermore, that quantity production tends to lower the cost of a product, it must then be granted that anything which makes quantity production possible contributes to the decrease in the cost of that commodity. Besides the actual machinery of multiple production, what is the most essential requirement for bringing this economy about? Advertising. Quantity production uniformly spread over all months of the year serves to reduce costs; advertising sustains quantity production. This, in a nutshell, is the reason for the success of advertising.

We have here dealt with four fundamental steps necessary in the lowering of distribution costs: first, the coming to an understanding as regards definitions; second, the gathering and comparing of accurate marketing cost data; third (with the aid of advertising), the eliminating of slumps and depressions; and fourth, the speeding of the passage of goods through the dealers' stores.

In addition, other methods deserve consideration, both for agricultural products and for manufactured goods. These are: the standardization of production of crops by the farmer so as to permit better selection; the grading and preparation of goods in the producing centers; the providing of more adequate central wholesale markets for farm products so that less time will be lost in the selling of perishable foodstuffs; the standardization of styles, sizes, shapes, and grades of manufactured wares, so that a dealer will not be obliged to handle thirty different styles of an article when four would suffice; the self-restriction of sales territory by a manufacturer or wholesaler to that area which he can cultivate intensively for business; in brief, the developing of all those measures which will insure a continuous flow of goods.

Advertising is not an exclusive device for reducing expenses, because advertising alone is not the only element which enters into the question. Good production management, sound financing, economical transportation—each of these plays an important part in industry. However, advertising does provide a sound, practicable, and expedient method for bringing about that which is desired by all—lower costs.

**The future.**—The future of advertising lies in a clearer understanding of the part it plays in marketing, and of the relation between marketing and production. The same study that has been given to production will have to be given to distribution. The same exact standards and precise thinking will have to be applied. Advertisements will find improvement through more consistent planning; through more intelligent understanding of why people buy; through better knowledge of the effectiveness of different media for a given proposition; by the giving of more creative thought to the advertisements and by a better expression of those ideas. Advertising itself will become greater as it is applied to the more important problems of the day.

# IN CONCLUSION

Make your product a useful contribution to the life of the public. Make the product bearing your name represent the highest quality attainable at the price. Once you have done this, keep the product bearing your name fresh in the public mind.

Know exactly what you hope to achieve through advertising before you set out to prepare it. Define or create the idea which the advertising is to convey. Then express it as clearly and as directly as you can.

Do not regard copy as a matter of phrases; consider it in terms of ideas. If these are sound, simple language will make the advertisement eloquent.

Present your advertisement in a manner that will cause the reader to remember the *thought* and not the mere advertisement. Let the reader say, "That must be an excellent product!" Beware of the advertisement which prompts him to declare, "That is an excellent advertisement!" His saying so does not bear out that statement; only if it leads him to act in accordance with its wishes is an advertisement really good.

Avoid the abstract question, "Which is the best medium?" Rather inquire who are your best prospects, where are they, through which of the media can they best be reached.

Get your facts before you start. Spending money on plans based on mere hunches is a costly form of experiment. Spending a fraction of that money in investigating all the facts which can be determined in advance represents the soundest form of advertising investment.

Know your costs.

Have every member of your advertising campaign assigned to a definite part of the work. Then see that all phases of the campaign are actually carried out as planned.

The purpose of an advertisement is to spread the truth

about a product, belief, or idea. Advertising itself must be Truth, even unto the adjective.

To all your undertakings apply yourself with the zest of the artist who finds a pleasure in beholding an idea well carried out, and with the zeal of the craftsman who earns a generous measure of happiness in bringing a task to its completion.

Where there is work to be done, there opportunity may be found, opportunity for a career in advertising, opportunity for the use of advertising, opportunity for advertising itself.

# GLOSSARY

AND

# ADVERTISING ABBREVIATIONS

# GLOSSARY OF PROCEDURE

**F**OLLOWING is a list of the advertising terms most frequently used, whose applied meaning may not be self-evident. The definitions have either been drawn from authoritative sources, or else are based upon general acceptance. In many instances the glossary does not confine itself to a definition of a term, but indicates the practices connected with it as well. For more extended information, the index should be consulted.

Abbreviations are appended in a separate listing.

**Account Executive.**—That member of an advertising agency staff who directs the handling of a client's advertising. He serves as the liaison man between the agency and the advertiser—one of the highest positions in an agency. Known also as *Contact Man.*

**Advertising Agency.**—A professional organization rendering advertising service to two or more clients.

**Antique Finish Paper.**—Book or cover paper which has a rough uneven surface. Can reproduce illustrations from line plates but not from halftones.

**Author's Corrections.**—Alterations or changes made in proofs, not due to the printer's errors and chargeable to whoever is paying for composition—advertiser or publisher, as the case may be. Unnecessary expense for this item can be reduced by carefully editing copy before sending it to printer.

**Backing Up.**—A term used by printers to indicate that one side of a sheet has been printed and its reverse side is now being printed.

**Basic Weight.**—The weight of a ream of paper if cut to the standard or basic size for that class of paper. The basic sizes are: Writing Papers, 17x22; Book Papers, 25x38; Cover Stocks, 20x26.

**Ben Day Process.**—The process invented by Benjamin Day whereby an engraver can produce a great variety of shaded tints and mottled effects in line plates.

**Bleeding Off.**—When printed matter is trimmed so that the type or plates run over the edges, it is said *to bleed.* Colored tint blocks are often made to bleed off, making a solid background without any margin of white space.

**Blue Prints.**—In the course of making a photo-engraving, it is possible to have a blue print made and delivered several hours before the completion of the plate, enabling the advertiser to prepare type layout while the engraving is still being made. Good to know about when time is short.

**Boiler Plate.**—Pages that publishers of small newspapers buy with the editorial matter and the advertisements of national advertisers already printed. Provides economical space rate for advertisers wishing to reach many small towns. Also known as *patent inside* and *patent outside*.

**Body Type.**—The type commonly used for reading matter as distinguished from *display* type used in the headlines of advertisements. Usually type 14 points in size, or smaller.

**Bold-face Type.**—A type which stands out strongly and prominently.

**Bond Paper.**—The writing paper most frequently used in commercial correspondence. The weight in most extensive use for letterheads is 20 lbs. (17x22-20).

**Book Paper.**—A paper which is frequently used in printing books, as well as for light-weight leaflets and folders, distinguished from *writing papers* and *cover stocks*. Basic size, 25x38.

**Breaking for Color (Separating for Color).**—When an advertisement in two or more colors is to be printed from type, it will first be set up in its entirety. The printer will then separate the type to appear in one color from that to appear in the other colors; this is said to be *breaking for colors*.

**Bull-dog Edition.**—That edition of a morning paper which is printed early the preceding evening and sent to out-of-town readers on the night trains. If an advertiser does not get his copy in early, he misses this edition.

**Burnishing.**—An engraving term. The mechanical act of making the dark areas in a halftone appear still darker. Accomplished by smoothing over the dots in a halftone with a tool, causing those dots to spread and fill up the areas between them.

**Buying Space.**—Buying the right to insert an advertisement in a given medium, such as in a periodical, a program, or on an outdoor sign.

**Caps.**—(1) Capital letters. The large, or upper case letters, SUCH AS THESE, as compared to lower case letters. (2) Paper covers for protecting the edges of a book while it is being covered and finished.

**Coined Word.**—An original and arbitrary combination of syllables forming a word for which the advertiser prescribes the meaning. Extensively used for trade-marks, as *Kodak, Moxie, Mazda*.

**Center Spread.**—The space occupied by an advertisement when it appears on the two facing center pages of a publication. Also known as *Double Page Spread* and *Double Truck*.

**Checking Copy.**—In order that an advertiser may see that his advertisement appears in a periodical as specified, the publisher forwards a copy of the issue containing that advertisement; this copy is known as the *checking copy*.

**Closing Date (Closing Hour).**—The day or hour, respectively, when all copy and plates must be in the publisher's hands if the advertisement is to appear in a given issue. The closing time is specified by the publisher. If proof is to be seen, all material has to be in when *first forms close*.

**Column-inch.**—A unit of measure in a periodical one inch deep and one column wide. The width of the column is not fixed.

**Combination Plates.**—The joining of halftone and line plate in one engraving.

**Combination Rate.**—(1) Often one publisher issues two papers, such as a morning paper and an evening paper; he may then offer a special rate if the two papers are used in conjunction with each other. Applies also to any other special rate granted in connection with two or more periodicals. (2) The rate paid for a combination photo-engraving plate.

**Competitive Stage.**—The advertising stage which a product reaches when its general usefulness is recognized but its individual superiority over similar brands has to be established

in order that it secure the preference. Compare with *Pioneering Advertising, Retentive Advertising.*
See *Spiral.*

**Consumer Advertising.**—Advertising
directed by a manufacturer to those
people who will finally use his
product.

**Contract Year.**—The period of time
in space-contracts, running for one
year beginning with the insertion of
the first advertisement under that
contract. It is usually specified that
the first advertisement appear within 30 days of the signing of the
contract.

**Conversion Table.**—Tables showing
what the equivalent weight of paper
stock of a given size would be if
the sheet were cut to another size.

**Copy.** (1) The text of an advertisement. (2) Matter for a compositor
to set. (3) Illustrations for an engraver to reproduce. (4) Any material to be used in the production
of a publication.

**Copyholder.**—An assistant who reads
copy aloud to the proof-reader who
reads and corrects the proof itself.

**Copy Approach.**—The method of
opening the text of an advertisement.
In the *Imaginative Approach* the
satisfaction which the product can
give is featured; the *Interpretive
Approach* says commonplace things
in a new manner; the *Initiative Approach* places the reader in such a
position that he naturally falls in
line with the advertiser's suggestion.

**Copy Writer.**—A person who writes
the text of advertisements.

**Copyright.**—Legal protection offered
to an original intellectual effort.
Registration fee, $1. Application
blank is procurable from the Copyright Office, Library of Congress,
Washington, D. C.

**Cover.**—The front cover of a publication is known as the *first cover;* the
inside of the front cover is the *second cover;* the inside of the back
cover is the *third cover;* the outside
back cover is the *fourth cover.*

Extra rates are charged for cover
positions.

**Cover Stock.**—A paper made of
heavy, strong fiber, used for folders
and for booklet covers. Some cover
stocks run into the low weights of
the paper known as *books,* but most
cover stocks are heavier. Basic
size is 20"x26".

**Crash Finish.**—A surface design on
paper simulating the appearance of
cloth.

**Cream Plan.**—The tactics of directing the advertising to the most potential class of buyers first, then to
the next best market, etc., "taking
the cream off first." Used in selling specialties. Compare with the
*Zone Plan, National Plan.*

**Cropping.**—An illustration is cropped
when part of its foreground, background, or sides are trimmed off to
enable the reproduction to fit in a
specific space. Cropping is done
either to eliminate non-essential
background in an illustration, or
else to change the proportions of
the illustration to the desired size.

**Cut.**—The commonly used term meaning a photo-engraving, electrotype,
or stereotype. Derived from its use
in the term *wood-cut.* Also known
as *block* (English)

**Cut-out.**—A window or store counter
sign with a design literally cut out
of it.

**Cylinder Press.**—A press which prints
from flat sheets. Has a rotating
cylinder under which a flat bed
containing type or plates moves forward and backward. Used for
large-quantity work, or for advertisements of large size.

**Decalcomania.**—A transparent gelat-
inous film bearing an advertisement,
which may be gummed into the
dealers' window. Also known as
*Transparency.*

**Delete.**—"Omit." Used in proof-
reading.

**Deckle-edge.**—The untrimmed ragged
edges of a sheet of paper.

**Depth of Columns.**—The dimension

of a column space measure from top of the page to bottom. Cited in number of agate lines, or in inches.

**Direct Advertising.**—Any form of advertising reproduced in quantities by or for the advertiser and by him or under his direction issued direct to definite and specific prospects through the medium of the mails, canvassers, salesmen, dealers or otherwise—as letters, leaflets, folders or booklets.

**Direct-Mail Advertising.**—That form of direct advertising sent through the mails.

**Double-decker.**—Outdoor advertising stands in which one stand is erected above another.

**Double-leaded.**—See Leaded.

**Double Truck.**—Same as *Double-page Spread.*

**Dummy.**—Blank sheets of paper cut and folded to the size of a proposed leaflet, folder, booklet or book, to indicate weight, shape, size, and general appearance. On the pages of the dummy the layouts can be drawn. Useful in designing direct mail advertisements. A dummy may also be made from the proof furnished by the printer.

**Ears of Newspaper.**—The boxes or announcements appearing at top of the front page, alongside the name of the paper, in the upper right and left-hand corners, respectively. Sold for advertising space by some papers.

**Electric Spectaculars.**—Outdoor advertisements in which electric lights are used to form the words and design. Not to be confused with illuminated *Posters* or illuminated *Painted Bulletins.* Space on electric spectaculars is sold by the individual stand.

**Electrotype.**—A metal plate which is a fac-simile of another plate, and made by the electrotype process. When several identical plates of a reproduction are required, one original can be made, and then electrotypes from that original. Elec-

trotypes cost less than original plates. They are made from a wax mold unless otherwise specified; a lead mold is more costly. Sometimes faced with steel for long runs.

**Enameled Paper (Enamel-coated Stock).**—A book or cover paper which can take the highest screen halftone. Is covered with a coating of China clay and a binder, then ironed under high speed rollers. This gives it a hard, smooth finish too brittle to fold well. Made also in dull and semi-dull finish.

**Equivalent Weight of Paper.**—The weight of a given paper stock in terms of its basic weight.

**Extended Covers.**—A cover that is slightly wider and longer than the pages of a paper-bound booklet or catalogue; one that extends or hangs over the inside pages. Also called *Overhang* and *Overlap.* Compare with *Flush Covers.*

**Facing Text Matter.**—Placing an advertisement in a periodical so that it is opposite to reading matter.

**Family of Type.**—Fonts of type faces related in design, as Caslon Bold, Caslon Old Style, Caslon Bold Italics, Caslon Old Style Italics.

**Fill-in.**—(1) In letters, the salutation and any other data which is inserted in the individual letters after those letters have been printed. (2) In printing, the blurring of an illustration due to the closeness of the lines or dots in the plate.

**Flat Proofs.**—Ordinary rough proofs taken of type when it is on the compositor's work bench, or "stone" in contrast to *press proofs* which are made after the type has been carefully adjusted to take the best possible impression.

**Flat Rate.**—A uniform charge for space in a medium, without regard to the amount of space used or frequency of insertion. When *Flat Rates* do not prevail, *Time Discounts* or *Quantity Discounts* are offered.

**Follow Style.**—When it is desired to have a piece of copy set up in accordance with a previous advertisement or proof, it is merely necessary for the advertiser to send that specimen to the printer, with the copy marked *follow style*. Saves work of making a new layout.

**Following, Next to Reading Matter.** —The specification of a position for an advertisement to appear in a publication. Also known as *Full Position*. This is a *Preferred Position* which usually costs more than *Run-of-paper* position.

**Font.**—An assortment of type in one size and face. Includes numerals and punctuation marks.

**Font, Wrong.**—A type letter of a different face from that of the rest of a set-up, erroneously inserted. On proof marked *w.f.*

**Foreign Advertising.**—(1) Advertising which appears in a newspaper paid for directly or indirectly by the non-resident manufacturer or distributor, as contrasted with *Local Advertising*, which is paid for by the local resident or establishment. In many cases, the local rate is lower. Also known as *National Advertising*. (2) Advertising in another country.

**Foreign-language Advertising.**—Domestic advertising printed in a language other than in English.

**Form.**—(1) Pages of type locked into place in a strong, rectangular iron frame known as a *Chase*. Usually holds 1, 2, 4, 8, 16, 32 or 64 pages (hence it is uneconomical to print booklets with 10, 12, 20, 26, or 50 pages). (2) The general style of a book, as opposed to its subject.

**Forms Close.**—All copy and plates for a periodical advertisement must be in when its forms close for press.

**Free Lance.**—An independent artist or copy-writer. Takes individual assignments from different accounts but is not in the employ of, or associated with, any of them otherwise.

**Foundry Proof.**—The proofs of a typographical set-up just before the material is sent to foundry for electrotyping; can be identified by its heavy, funeral-black border (the foundry rules).

**Four-color Process.**—The photoengraving process whereby color illustrations are reproduced by means of a set of plates, one of which prints all the yellows, another the blues, a third the reds, the fourth the blacks (sequence variable). The plates are referred to as *Process Plates*.

**Full Position.**—A special preferred position of an advertisement in a newspaper. Means either (1) that the advertisement both follows a column, or columns of the news reading matter, and is completely flanked by reading matter as well, or else (2) the advertisement is at the top of the page and alongside of reading matter.

**Full Showing.**—(1) In outdoor advertising, the number of poster positions necessary to make a thorough presentation; an arbitrary sum, which varies with the cities. Half-showing includes every other such position; quarter-showing, every fourth position. (2) In car cards, a full showing means one card in each car of a line, or of the city in which space is bought.

**Galley Proof.**—Proofs on sheets usually twenty to twenty-two inches long, printed from type as it stands in the *Galley Trays* before that type is split up into pages.

**Ghosted Views.** — An illustration showing an X-ray view of a subject.

**Half Showing.**—See *Full Showing*.

**Halftone.**—A photo-engraving plate, photographed through a glass screen (in the camera) which serves to break up the reproduction of the subject into dots, makes possible the printing of halftone values as of photographs. Screens must be adapted to the surfaces on which the engraving is to appear. They vary from 45 to 300 lines to the inch. The most common are 120 and 133 line screens in magazines; 65 to 85 line screens in newspaper.

**Halftone, Coarse Screen.**—A halftone with a comparatively low, or coarse, screen; usually applies to 60, 65, 85 lines to inch.

**Halftone, Direct.**—A halftone made by photographing an object itself instead of a picture of it. Is possible where the product is flat or nearly flat as a rug, lace, or table silver.

**Halftone, Highlight (Drop-out).**—A halftone plate in which the white areas are "dropped out" *in the making of the plate.* An ordinary halftone has a fine screen over the white areas, which may cause trouble in printing on papers like newsstock.

**Halftone, Shallow.**—Inferior halftones in which the dots have not been deeply etched. Consequently the detail of the illustration is lost. When halftones have been over-developed they may have their dots undermined.

**Halftone, Silhouette.**—One in which all background is eliminated, the product alone appearing. Also known as *Outline Halftone.*

**Halftone, Square Finish.**—A halftone in which the background has been left in, but trimmed by the engraver to a definite shape, usually rectangular. Can also be trimmed to an oval or circle.

**Halftone, Vignette.** — Halftones whose backgrounds fade away in a cloud effect. For use in very high-class work only.

**Hand Composition.**—Type set up by hand, as distinguished from type set up by machine. Compare with *Linotype Composition* or *Monotype Composition.*

**Hand-lettering.**—Any lettering that is drawn by hand (such as that in a name plate), as distinguished from type regularly set.

**Hand-tooling.**—Hand work on an engraving or plate to improve its reproducing qualities. Charged for by the hour. Hand-tooling is neces-

sary if it is desired to have pure whites appear in a halftone unless that plate is a *Highlight Halftone.*

**Head-on Position.**—An outdoor advertising stand which directly faces traffic on a highway.

**House Organ.**—A publication issued periodically by a firm for the furtherance of its own interests, inviting attention on the strength of its editorial content. Also known as *Company Magazine* and *Company Newspaper.*

**Imaginative Approach.**—See *Copy Approach.*

**Inch.**—The term as used in advertising is not a square inch but a space one inch deep and one column wide. The unit therefore varies in accordance with the width of the column. See *Column Inch.*

**Individual location.**—The location of an outdoor advertisement in which there is but a single panel, and not several adjacent ones.

**Initial Letter.**—The first letter in a piece of copy, set in a size of type larger than that of the rest of the copy. Useful in getting the eye started on the message.

**Initiative Approach.**—See *Copy Approach.*

**Insertion Order.**—Instructions from an advertiser authorizing a publisher to print an advertisement of specified size on a given date at an agreed rate. Accompanied or followed by the copy for advertisement.

**Inserts.**—(1) In letters or packages —An enclosure usually in the form of a little slip bearing an advertisement. (2) In periodicals—A page printed by the advertiser, or for him, and forwarded to the publisher who binds it up in the publication. Usually in colors, and on heavier stock (where publisher permits). Charged for at preferred space rates.

**Island Position.**—Position in a newspaper entirely surrounded by reading matter. Not generally procurable.

**Intaglio Printing.**—Printing from a depressed surface, such as from the copper-plate or steel plate which produces *engraved* calling cards and announcements. *Rotogravure* is a form of intaglio printing. Compare with *Letterpress Printing* and *Lithographic Printing*.

**Interpretive Approach.**—See *Copy Approach*.

**Job Press.**—A press which takes sizes up to 25 x 38 inches. Best known types are called the *Gordon Press* and the *Universal Type*.

**Job Ticket.**—A sheet, or an envelope, which accompanies a printing job through the various departments, bearing all the instructions and all records showing the progress of the work.

**Justification of Type.** — Arranging type so that it appears in even lines, with its letters properly spaced.

**Keep Standing.** — Instructions to printer to hold type after it has been used on a job, for further instructions. Where it may be necessary to hold type for any length of time, it is better to have an electrotype of the set-up made.

**Keying an Advertisement.**—Giving to an advertisement a code number or letter so that when people respond, the source of the inquiry can be traced. May be found in the address, or corner of most advertisements embodying return coupons.

**Laid Paper.**—Paper showing a regular water-marked pattern, usually of parallel lines.

**Layout.**—A working drawing showing how an advertisement is to look. *A Printer's Layout* is a set of instructions accompanying a piece of copy showing how it is to be set up.

**Leaders.**—A line of dots or dashes used to guide the eye across the page, thus :.............................

**Leading (pronounced ledding).**—The insertion of metal strips

(known as leads) between lines of type, causing greater space to appear between these lines. Usually means the insertion of a 2-point lead. Type can often be made more legible by generous leading between the lines. Leaded type necessarily requires more room than type which is not leaded (which is set *solid*).

**Ledger Papers.**—A high-class writing paper of tough body and smooth plated surface. Used for accounting work and for documents.

**Letterpress Printing.**—Printing from a raised or relief surface, like that of a rubber stamp. Most advertisements are printed by the letterpress method. Exceptions are *Lithographic (and Offset); Intaglio (and Rotogravure)*.

**Lineage.**—The total number of lines of space occupied by one advertisement or a series of them.

**Line Plates.**—A photo-engraving made from a drawing composed of solid lines or masses which can print on any quality stock. Less expensive than halftones but cannot be used to reproduce photographs, wash drawings or similar illustrations.

**Linotype Composition.**—The Linotype is a machine which sets type by moulding a line of type at a time. Operated by a keyboard resembling that of a typewriter. Compare with *Hand Composition; Monotype Composition*.

**Local Advertising.**—Advertising which appears in a newspaper paid for by the local resident or establishment and for which a *local* or lower rate is often charged than for *National Advertising*.

**Locking Up.**—When a printer tightens the type matter put into a chase preparatory to going to press, he is said to be locking up the type.

**Logotype.**—(1) Two letters cast on one block of type, fi, ct, ff. (2) The name-plate of an advertiser.

**Lower Case (l.c.).**—The small letters in the alphabet, such as those in which this is printed, COMPARED WITH UPPER CASE OR CAPITAL LETTERS. Note that the difference lies in the formation of the letters. The term is derived from the lower case of the printer's type cabinet in which the type is kept.

**Lithographic Printing.**—The process of printing from a flat surface; usually a stone on which the design has been drawn. Invented 1796 by Alois Senefelder of Munich. Used for color work of large quantities, such as labels and package inserts. See *Offset Printing*. Compare with *Intaglio* and *Letterpress Printing*.

**Machine-finish (M.F.) Paper.**—The cheapest of book papers that take halftones well. A paper which has had its pores filled ("sized") but which is not ironed. Thus it possesses a moderately smooth surface. Smoother than *Antique*, but not as smooth as *Sized and Super-Calendered Paper*.

**Mail-order Advertising.**—That method of selling whereby the complete sales transaction is negotiated through advertising and the mails, and is consummated without the aid of a salesman. Not to be confused with *Direct-mail Advertising*.

**Make-ready.**—The process of finely adjusting the form of type or the plates for the press to insure good printing. A preliminary proof of the form on the press is inspected for those letters or plates which appear lighter than the rest of the material. *Overlays* and *Underlays* of paper are inserted under the printing surfaces to secure the uniform pressure necessary to obtain even effects. The skill and care in this work represent one of the hidden elements which serve to make a good printing job.

**Make-up of a Page.**—The general appearance of a page. Generally refers to the arrangement of the editorial matter and advertising material to appear.

**Matrix, "Mat."**—(1) A mould of paper pulp, or similar substance, made by pressing a sheet of it into the type set-up, or engraving plate. Molten lead is poured in, forming a replica of the original plate. This is known as a stereotype. (2) The brass moulds used in the linotype.

**Matter.**—Composed type, often referred to as: (1) *Dead Matter*—of no further use; (2) *Leaded Matter*—having extra spacing between lines; (3) *Live Matter*—to be used again; (4) *Solid Matter*—lines set close to each other; (5) *Standing Matter*—held for future use.

**Medium.**—(1) The vehicle which carries the advertisement, as newspaper, magazine, letter, car card, etc. (2) The tool and method used by an artist in drawing illustrations, as pen and ink, pencil, wash, and crayon.

**Milline Rate.**—A unit of measuring the rate of advertising space in conjunction with circulation. Represents the cost of having one agate line appear before one million readers. Calculated by multiplying the cost per agate line by 1 million, and dividing by the circulation of the newspaper.

$$\text{Milline Rate} = \frac{\text{Actual line rate} \times 1{,}000{,}000}{\text{Circulation}}$$

**Modern Type.**—See *Old-Style Type*.

**Monotype Composition.**—Type set by a machine in which the individual letters are separately moulded and automatically assembled into lines, as distinguished from *Hand Composition* and *Linotype Composition*.

**Month Preceding.**—First Month Preceding publication means that the closing date falls on the given day during the month which immediately precedes the publication date of a periodical. If the rate card says closing date is on the 5th of the first month preceding, it means the forms for the March issue, for instance, would close February 5th. *Second Month Preceding* would mean forms close January 5th; *Third Month Preceding*, December 5th.

**Mortise.**—The section of an engraving plate sawed out to make room for type or another plate. When a border is engraved, the inside or white area will be mortised.

**Natural Fold.**—That method of folding a direct advertisement whereby the continuity of the copy is preserved as the advertisement is opened.

**National Advertising.**—(1) Advertising which appears in media with circulation in all parts of the country. (2) More exactly, advertising conducted by a manufacturer, producer or wholesale distributer of a product for the purpose of creating a demand for that product and thereby directing purchasers to the retail stores in which it is sold. (3) Advertising which appears in a newspaper paid for directly or indirectly by the non-resident manufacturer or distributer. Also known as *Foreign Advertising*.

**National Plan.**—The tactics, used in advertising campaigns, of trying to get all the business that can be secured from all over the country at one time. When rightfully used, the outgrowth of numerous *Zone Plans*. Compare also with the *Cream Plan*.

**Next to Reading Matter.**—The location of an advertisement immediately adjacent to editorial or reportorial matter in a publication.

**Offset.**—(1) The method of lithographic printing whereby the impression is not transferred directly to the paper but to a rubber blanket and then to the sheet. Gives a softer effect than direct lithography. Makes possible the use of rough surfaced stock in reproducing lithographic illustration. (2) The blotting of a wet or freshly printed sheet against an accompanying sheet. Can be prevented by slip-sheeting. When a job is wanted in a hurry, antique paper should be used if possible. It absorbs the ink and thus prevents offsetting.

**Old Style Type.**—Originally the face of Roman type with slight difference in weight between its different strokes, as contrasted with *Modern Type* which has sharp contrast and accents in its strokes. Its serifs are oblique; Modern serifs are horizontal. An Old Style type also refers to the Old Style member of a family of types, usually the lighter face.

**On Speculation.**—An offer to create an idea which, if used, is paid for, but if not used, is not to be paid for.

**One-time Rate.**—The rate paid by an advertiser who uses less space than that necessary to earn a time or rate discount, when such discounts are offered. Same as *Transient Rate*.

**One-Way Screen.**—A half-tone with the screen in one direction only; has not the cross-screen which gives the dot effect. Good for odd effects. Makes tooling difficult.

**Order-of-Merit Method.**—Putting a piece of copy or an illustration, advertisement, trade-mark, design, or package to a test, giving first place to the one with the highest vote.

**Overlapping Circulation.**—The extent to which two or more media duplicate each other in reaching the same prospect. Sometimes this is a desirable feature, providing an immediate cumulative effect.

**Overrun.**—The number of pieces of advertising printed in excess of the specified quantity. According to the trade custom, an advertiser agrees to accept an overrun of no more than 10 per cent at pro rata cost.

**Page Proof.**—A proof of type matter and plates arranged by pages, as they are finally to appear. Usually is made ("pulled") after *galley proof* has been shown and corrections made.

**Patent Inside.**—Same as Boiler Plate.

**Pica-em (The pica).**—The unit for measuring width in printing. There are 6 pica-ems to the inch. Derived from pica, the name of the 12-pt. type (1/6" high) and the letter M of that series, whose width likewise is 1/6" wide. There can be 10-point ems, 14-point ems, etc., but when the term *em* is ordinarily used, it refers to the pica-em. If a page of type is 25 picas wide, it is 4 1/6 inches wide ($25 \div 6 = 4\,1/6$).

**Pied Type.**—A type set-up which has become deranged.

**Pioneering Stage.**—The advertising stage of a product in which the need for such product is not recognized and has to be established, or when the need has been established but the success of a commodity in filling those requirements has to be evidenced. See *Competitive Stage, Retentive Stage, Spiral.*

**Plated Stock.**—Paper which has been pressed between metal sheets. Has hard, smooth surfaces.

**Point (Pt.).**—(1) Referring to type—the unit of measurement of type 1/72 inch in depth. Type is specified by its point size, as 8 pt., 12 pt., 24 pt., 48 pt. (2) Referring to paper—the unit of which there are 1000 to an inch for measuring thickness.

**Poster Plant.**—An organization which provides the actual outdoor advertising service.

**Preferred Position.**—When an advertiser wants to make sure that his advertisement appears in a given position in a periodical, he may be able to obtain that space by paying a higher preferred position rate for it. Otherwise the advertisement appears in *run-of-paper* position, that is, wherever the publisher chooses to place it. Certain pages are preferred in publication advertising, just as are the positions on that page.

**Printer's Ink Model Statute.**—The act prepared and sponsored by

*Printer's Ink Magazine,* the popular advertising journal, directed at fraudulent advertising.

**Process Plates.** — Photo-engraving plates for printing two, three, or four colors, one over the other to produce the final desired effect.

**Process Printing.**—Letterpress color printing in which one color is printed over the other (by means of a set of process plates).

**Production Department.**—The department of an advertising agency responsible for the mechanical production of an advertisement, dealing with printers and engravers. In some agencies it includes the copy and art departments.

**Progressive Proofs.**—A set of photo-engraving proofs in color in which the yellow plate is printed on one sheet and the red on another. The yellow and red are then combined. Next the blue is printed and a yellow-red-blue combination made. Then the black alone is printed and finally all colors are combined (sequence varies). Used by the printer in matching up his inks when printing color plates.

**Proof.**—(1) An inked impression of composed type or of a plate taken for the purpose of inspection or for filing. (2) In engraving and etching, an impression taken to show the condition of the illustration at any stage of the work. Taking a proof is known as *pulling a proof.*

**Proof for Files.**—When a corrected proof of an advertisement is returned to the periodical too late to secure a revised proof for final O. K., the corrected proof is marked *"OK with C"* (approved, with corrections) and proof for files is requested. The advertiser will then receive copies of the final advertisement for his records or for future use in preparing other advertisements.

**Publisher's Statement.**—The statement of circulation issued by a periodical publisher.

**Quads.**—Blank pieces of metal used by the printer to fill out lines where the amount of type does not do so.

**Quarter Showing.**—See *Full Showing.*

**Quartertones, or double - process halftones.**—A development of the halftone plate for use in reproducing illustrations on newspaper and other rough stock. Made in a coarse screen by a process which retains more detail than does the ordinary coarse-screen halftone.

**Railroad Showing.**—An outdoor advertisement conspicuously placed so that it can be seen by passengers on trains.

**Rate Book.**—A compilation of the periodical rates charged by periodicals for space.

**Rate Card.**—A card giving the space rates of a publication, and additional data on mechanical requirements and closing dates.

**Rate Holder.**—The minimum-sized advertisement which must appear during a given period if an advertiser is to secure a certain time or quantity discount. Takes its name from the fact that it holds a lower rate for an advertiser.

**Reading Notices.**—Advertisements in newspapers set up in a type similar to that of the editorial matter. Must be followed by "Adv." Is charged for at rates higher than those for regular ads. Many publications will not accept reading notices.

**Ream.**—In the publishing and advertising world, 500 sheets of paper (not 480). 1,000-sheet reams are proposed.

**Recognized Agency.**—An advertising agency recognized as such by the various publishers or their associations and granted a commission for the space it sells to advertisers. The commission is usually 15 per cent on the gross with 2 per cent on the net for cash, expressed *"15 and 2."*

**Reducing Glass.**—The opposite of a magnifying glass. Used in looking at illustrations to judge how they will appear when reproduced in smaller size.

**Register.**—A term used in printing to indicate that the type, or the plates, print exactly where desired on the sheet. In color work, correct registration of the different colors is especially important.

**Registering Trade Mark.**—In the United States, the act of recording a trade mark with the Commissioner of Patents.

**Release (on Photograph).**—A statement by a person photographed authorizing the advertiser to use that photograph. In the case of minors, the guardian's release is necessary.

**Retentive Stage.**—The third stage of a product, reached when its general usefulness is everywhere known, its individual qualities thoroughly appreciated, and when it is satisfied to retain its patronage merely on the strength of its past reputation. See *Pioneering Advertising; Competitive Advertising; Spiral.*

**Reversed Plate.**—(1) A line-plate engraving in which whites come out black, and vice versa. (2) An engraving in which right and left, as they appear in the illustration, are transposed.

**Ripple Finish.**—Paper having a regularly uneven surface.

**Roman Type.**—(1) Originally, type of the Italian and Roman school of design, as distinguished from the Black Face Old English style of type. The Old Style and Modern are the two branches of the Roman Family. (2) Type faces which are not italics are called Roman.

**Rotate.**—When a series of advertisements is to be published several times and the publisher is to begin again with No. 1 after all have been run and repeat the original order of insertion, the series is said to rotate.

**Rotogravure.**—The method of *Intaglio Printing* in which the advertisement is chemically etched out of a copper roller. (In photo-engraving the area not to appear in an illustration is etched away.) Useful in large runs of pictorial effects.

**Rough (noun).**—The first pencil draft of an illustration executed in crude style. An artist submits a rough of an illustration to the advertiser for O.K. before proceeding, in order to insure correctness of the general conception and composition.

**Routing Out.**—An engraving term meaning to tool out dead metal on an engraving plate.

**Run of Paper.**—Position of an advertisement in a publication wherever the publisher may deem fit. Unless space is ordered for a preferred position, it is given run-of-paper showing.

**Saddle Stitching.**—The method of binding a booklet by stitching it with wire through the center. The stitching passes through the fold in the center pages and backbone of the booklet. Enables the booklet to lie flat. Where booklet is too thick to permit of this method, *Side Stitching* is used.

**Sales Promotion Department.**—The department which acts as a liaison between the sales department and the advertising department. Concerns itself with matters such as investigating for new markets, following-up inquiries resulting from advertisements, and following up salesmen's visits with proper letters and literature.

**Scale Rate.**—In photo-engraving, the standard cost rate.

**Scaling Down.**—Most illustrations are drawn larger than they are to appear. The artist thus has more freedom in developing details. When the illustration is reduced to the desired size, in the making of the plate, it is said to be *Scaled Down.* Drawing the illustration in larger size also serves to reduce crudities when the drawing is reduced.

**Self-Mailer.**—A direct-mail advertisement folder, booklet, or book which requires no envelope for mailing.

**Sheet.**—The unit of a poster size, 26"x39". The standard size poster has 24 sheets.

**Short Rate.**—When an advertiser signs a contract to use a certain amount of space in a given time and thereby secures a lower rate, and subsequently fails to use the specified amount of that space, he must pay for the space he did use at the higher rate for the lesser amount. The actual difference in dollars and cents is called the short rate.

**Shoulder of Type.**—The space between the upper end of a type letter as mounted on its block and the letter itself. The shoulder does not print. The type size, as given in points, includes the shoulder, thus accounting for the fact that a 36-point type letter, for example, does not appear exactly ½" in size.

**Sized and Super-Calendered Paper (S. & S. C.).**—Machine-finish book paper, which has been given extra ironings, to insure a smooth surface. Takes halftones very well.

**Side Stitching.**—The method of wire stitching from one side of booklet to the other. Wiring can be seen on front cover and on back. Used in thick booklet work. Pages do not lie flat. See *Saddle Stitching.*

**Signature.**—(1) The name of an advertiser. (2) A sheet folded ready for stitching in a book, usually 16 pages, but with thin paper 32 pages; a mark, letter, or number is placed at the bottom of the first page of every group of 16 or 32 pages to serve as a guide in folding.

**Sized Paper.**—Paper which has received a chemical bath to make it less porous. Paper sized once and ironed (calendered) is known as *Machine Finish.* If it is again ironed, it becomes *Sized Super-Calendered (S. & S. C.).*

**Slip-Sheeting.**—To prevent the sheets of a printing job from smudging as they come from the press, a sheet of paper (usually tissue or a cheap porous stock) is placed between them.

**Sniping.**—The mounting of an outdoor advertisement wherever space and opportunity permit, as against rocks, barrels, fences, etc.

**Space Discount.**—A discount given by a publisher for the amount of lineage which an advertiser uses. Compare with *Time Discount.*

**Space Schedule.**—A schedule showing the media in which an advertisement is to appear, the dates on which the advertisement is to appear; the exact size of the prospective advertisement, and the cost.

**Special Representative.**—An individual or organization which represents a certain publisher in the selling of space outside the city of publication. Really space salesmen. One special representative may serve two or more publishers of different cities. Also known as *Foreign Representative.*

**Spiral.**—The Advertising Spiral is a graphic representation showing the evolution through which a product passes in its acceptance by the public The stages are the *Pioneering,* the *Competitive,* and the *Retentive.*

**Staggered Schedule.**—A schedule of space to be used in two or more periodicals arranged so that the insertions alternate or otherwise synchronize with each other.

**Steel Die Embossing.**—Printing from steel dies engraved by the *Intaglio Process,* the sharp, raised outlines being produced by stamping over a counter die. Used for monograms, crests, stationery and similar social and business purposes. When part of the detail is to be brought out in contour, the die is counter-sunk.

**Stereotype.**—A plate cast by pouring molten metal into a matrix. One of the least expensive forms of duplicate plates. Lacks the strength and sharpness of detail of an electrotype. Newspapers are printed

from stereotypes. Should not be used in magazine advertisements.

**Stet.**—A proofreader's term—"Let it stand as it is; disregard change specified." A dotted line is placed underneath the letter or words to which the instructions apply.

**Stock Cuts.**—Photo-engraving plates of standard or conventional illustrations, sold by the dealer.

**Stone-Proof.**—See Flat Proof.

**Style Manual.**—A compilation of typographical rules to be followed in a publication, codifying the method of treating spelling, abbreviations, and other questions of uniformity in editing.

**Substance No.**—(Usually followed by figure as *Substance No. 16, Substance No. 20, Substance No. 24.*) In specifying paper stock, the equivalent weight of a given paper in the standard size.

**Surprint.**—(1) A photo-engraving in which a line-plate effect appears over the face of a halftone, or vice versa. (2) To place printing over the face of an advertisement already printed.

**Tail Piece.**—A small typographical ornament or illustration placed at the end of a piece of copy.

**Till Forbid (Run T.F.).**—Instructions to publisher: "Continue running this advertisement until instructions are issued to the contrary."

**Time Discount.**—A discount given to an advertiser for the frequency or regularity with which he inserts his advertisements in a publication. Compare *Quantity Discount.*

**Tint Block.**—Usually a solid piece of zinc, used to print a light shade of ink for a background.

**Tip In.**—To paste a leaf, or leaves, on a page or on a mount. Halftones are often printed on a smooth stock which will be pasted into place in a book printed on a stock which will not take halftones.

**To Fill (T.F.).**—Instructions to printer: "Set this copy in the proper size necessary to fill the specified space indicated in the layout."

**Trade Advertising.**—Advertising directed by a manufacturer or distributor to the retail merchants through whom the product is sold.

**Trade-mark.**—(In the U. S. A.)—Any device which identifies the origin of a product, telling who made it or who sold it. (A word can be a trade-mark.) Not to be confused with *trade name*.

**Trade Name.**—(In the U. S. A.)—A name which applies to a business as a whole and not to an individual product.

**Traffic Department.**—The department in an advertising agency responsible for the prompt execution of the work in the respective departments and for turning over the complete material for shipment to the forwarding department, in keeping with the schedule. Where one person handles this work he is popularly known as the *Accelerator*.

**Transient Rate.**—Same as *One-time rate* in buying space.

**Transparencies.**—Same as *Decalcomania*.

**Traveling Displays.**—An elaborate exhibit prepared by a manufacturer of a product and loaned by him to each of several dealers in his product in rotation. Usually based on the product and prepared in such a way as to be of educational or dramatizing value.

**Trimmed Flush.**—A booklet or book trimmed after the cover is on, the cover thus being cut flush with the leaves. Compare with *Extended Covers*.

**Type Face.**—The design of a type letter. Type faces are usually named after men, as Caslon, Della Robbia, Jensen, Goudy. In machine composition, the faces are known also by numbers.

**Type Page.**—The area of a page which type can occupy; the total area of a page less the margins.

**Up.**—Number of times a cut or page is duplicated in a form; one page two "up" is a two-page form; four pages two "up" is an eight-page form.

**Wait Order.**—Instructions to a periodical to set up an advertisement and hold it in readiness to run upon the issuance of the subsequent insertion order.

**Wash Drawing.**—A brush-work illustration, usually made with diluted India ink or water color so that in addition to its black and white, it has varying shades of gray, like a photograph. Halftones, not line plates, are made from wash drawings. Wash drawings are extensively used to picture merchandise as they can emphasize details better than photographs.

**Wax Engraving.**—The process of coating a plate with wax upon which the design is drawn, photographed, or impressed. The wax is then cut through to the metal base. Used in the making of maps.

**Wedge Ladder.**—A graphic representation of that method of action whereby each step is planned to lead directly to the next and so on to the conclusion. In copy, refers to coherence; in campaigns, refers to method of using media in such a way that all dovetail in accordance with a complete plan.

**Window Envelope.**—Mailing envelopes with a transparent panel in front, permitting the address on the enclosure to serve as a mailing address as well.

**Wove Paper.**—Paper having a very faint, cloth-like appearance when held to the light.

**Wood Cuts.**—Wooden printing blocks upon which the design is carved by hand. These preceded the use of metal for type plates.

**Writing Paper.**—Paper made to accommodate pen-and-ink writing, varying from *flat writing paper*, as used in cheap memorandum pads, through *bonds* of various grades to *ledger paper.* Basic size is 17x22 inches.

**Zinc Etching.**—A photo-engraving in zinc. Term is usually applied to line plates.

**Zone Plan.**—The tactics, used in advertising campaigns, of concentrating on a certain limited geographical area rather than trying to cover the entire country at once, as in the *National Plan*, or picking the choice prospects from different. parts of the country at the same time, as in the *Cream Plan*. Valuable for effective use of limited appropriations devoted to advertising a product in common use, as soap, dentifrices, cigarettes, and shoes.

# ADVERTISING ABBREVIATIONS

THE following list gives the meaning of abbreviations common in advertising. The use of abbreviations is not to be recommended. They allow too easily of errors which may prove very costly.

**A.A.C. of W.**—The Associated Advertising Clubs of The World. The senior organization composed of the local advertising clubs and the departmental organizations.

**A.A.A.A. (The 4 A's).**—The American Association of Advertising Agencies. An organization of leading advertising agencies.

**A.B.C.**—The Audit Bureau of Circulation. The organization sponsored by publishers, agencies, and advertisers for the securing of accurate circulation statements.

**A.B.P.** — The Associated Business Papers.

**A.N.P.A.**—The American Newspaper Publishers' Association.

**A.N.A.**—The Association of National Advertisers.

**c.**—(1) Column; (2) Capital letter.

**d.**—Daily. Refers to an insertion in a publication 6 days a week, excluding Sunday.

**d. and s.**—Run advertisement daily and Sunday.

**D.M.A.A.**—The Direct-Mail Advertisers' Association.

**e.d.**—Run advertisement every day.

**h.t.**—A halftone photo-engraving.

**l.**—An agate line, 1/14 of an inch deep, as 14 l., 56 l., 140 l.

**l.c.**—Lower-case letters.

**m.f.**—Machine-finish paper.

**n.r.**—Next to reading.

**O.S.**—Old Style type.

**P.P.A.**—The Periodical Publishers' Association.

**P.A.A.**—The Poster Advertisers' Association.

**p.**—Page. **pp.** pages.

**pt.**—Point, or 1/72 of an inch. The unit of measuring type depth; also paper thickness, 1/1000 of an inch.

**s.c.**—(1) Single Column. (2) Small caps.

**s. and s.c.**—Sized and super-calendered paper.

**t.**—Time, such as 1-t, 5-t. Refers to the frequency with which an advertisement is to appear.

**t.f.**—(1) Till forbid. (2) To fill. (3) Copy is to follow.

**t.c.**—Top of column.

**tr.**—Transpose type as indicated.

**U.N.S.**—United News Service.

**U.P.**—United Press.

**U.T.A.**—United Typothetae of America.

**w.**—Weekly.

**w.f.**—Wrong font. Used in proof-reading to indicate that a letter of an incorrect type face has been used.

**15 and 2.**—Used by advertising agencies to indicate the terms in which they secure space from the publishers. Means that they secure 15 per cent commission from publishers on the gross amount of space used, plus 2 per cent on the net for cash payment. Similarly 13 *and* 2, 10 *and* 2, etc.

**25 x 38 — 80.**—Read *twenty-five, thirty-eight, eighty.* The method of expressing paper weight, meaning that a ream of paper 25 x 38 inches in size weighs 80 lbs. Similarly 25 x 38 — 60, 25 x 38 — 70, 25 x 38 — 120; 17 x 22 — 16, 17 x 22 — 24 20 x 26 — 80, 38 x 50 — 140.

# READING SUGGESTIONS

### AND

# BIBLIOGRAPHY

# READING SUGGESTIONS AND BIBLIOGRAPHY

CURRENT developments in this field are as rapid as they are interesting. It is particularly fortunate that the journals dealing with advertising are exceptionally alert in reporting new methods and experiences. These periodicals offer much that is worth reading.

## Magazines on Advertising.

There is a group of publications which frequently treats advertising in its relation to the rest of business—a wholesome viewpoint to cultivate. The following list, while not exhaustive, gives the magazines of this type:

Nation's Business. Chamber of Commerce of the U. S., Mills Building, Washington, D. C.

System. A. W. Shaw Company, Cass, Huron & Erie Sts., Chicago.

Harvard Business Review. A. W. Shaw Company, Cass, Huron & Erie Sts., Chicago.

Management & Administration. Ronald Press Company, 20 Vesey Street, New York.

Forbes Magazine. B. C. Forbes Pub. Co., 120 Fifth Avenue, New York.

Sales Management. Dartnell Corporation, 1801 Leland Avenue, Chicago.

Now we come to the advertising magazines themselves. A number of them cover the field in all its aspects. Each issue of the following publications will be found rich in campaign reports, recommended for study in conjunction with the chapters on The Advertising Spiral, The Specific Purposes of Advertising, and The Transforming Idea:

507

Printer's Ink Weekly. Romer Publishing Co. Inc., 185 Madison Avenue, New York.

Printer's Ink Monthly. Romer Publishing Co. Inc., 185 Madison Avenue, New York.

Advertising & Selling Fortnightly. M. C. Robbins, Inc., 9 East 38th Street, New York.

Judicious Advertising. Lord & Thomas Publishing Co., 400 N. Michigan Avenue, Chicago.

Western Advertising. Ramsay Oppenheimer, 564 Market Street, San Francisco, Calif.

Marketing. Market Publishers, Ltd., Toronto, Canada.

A number of publications are devoted to specific departments of advertising, as follows:

### Technical Advertising.

Class. G. D. Crain, Jr., 537 So. Dearborn Street, Chicago.

### Direct-Mail Advertising, Sales Correspondence.

Postage. John Howie Wright, 18 East 18th Street, New York City.

Mailbag. Mailbag Publishing Co., Caxton Building, Cleveland, Ohio.

### Printing, Typography, Direct-Mail Advertising.

American Printer. Oswald Publishing Co., 239 West 39th St., New York.

Printing Art. University Press, Cambridge, Mass.

Inland Printer. Inland Printer Co., 632 Sherman Street, Chicago.

Ben Franklin Monthly. 306 S. Canal Street, Chicago, Ill.

National Lithographer. National Lithographer Pub. Co., 150 Nassau Street, New York.

### Newspaper Advertising.

Fourth Estate. Fourth Estate Publishing Co., 232 W. 59th Street, New York.

Advertisers Weekly. 30 Church Street, New York.

Further publications devoted to media are:

Poster. Poster Advertising Ass'n., 307 So. Green St., Chicago.

Package Advertiser. 326 W. Madison St., Chicago.

National Advertising. John Howie Wright, 18 East 18th Street, New York.

Novelty News. Waukegan, Ill.

Other publications on advertising are:

Advertising World (Retail Advertising). 33 West Gay Street, Columbus, Ohio.

Associated Advertising (Official Organ, A. A. C. of W.). The Associated Clubs of the World, 383 Madison Ave., New York City.

The Dartnell Service (1801 Leland Ave., Chicago), has issued a set of valuable reports, each covering some particular question of advertising. Methods of advertising specific industries and trades are covered by the business press. To find out just which of these publications to consult, address the Secretary, Associated Business Papers, 220 West 42nd Street, New York City, stating on which trade the information is sought.

## Books on Advertising.

In addition to the periodicals on advertising, numerous books offer their help. For the convenience of the reader who wishes to acquaint himself with the different texts treating the subjects described in the present work, the following bibliography is arranged, as far as possible, in accordance with the respective subjects treated.

### General.

We first examine the books which discuss advertising in its general aspects. In each, a section will be found dealing with the more familiar topics covered in the present work—especially copy, layouts, and media.

Advertising, Its Principles & Practices, by Tipper, Hotchkiss, Hollingworth & Parsons. New York: Ronald Press Co.

Principles of Advertising, by Daniel Starch. Chicago: A. W. Shaw Company.

The Advertising Handbook, by S. Roland Hall. New York: Mc-Graw-Hill Book Company.

Advertising Campaigns, by Tipper & French. New York: D. Van Nostrand & Company.

Introduction to Advertising, by Brewster & Palmer. Chicago: A. W. Shaw & Company.

A Short Course in Advertising, by Alex. Osborne. New York: Chas. Scribner's Sons.

Essentials of Advertising, by Frank Le Roy Blanchard. New York: McGraw-Hill Book Company.

Advertisers' Handbook. Scranton, Pa.: International Correspondence School.

## *Markèting.*

The entire study of advertising is based on a knowledge of economics in its applied branch marketing. This question is discussed in the following books:

The Economics of Marketing and Advertising, by W. D. Moriarty. New York: Harper & Bros.

Marketing Methods and Policies, by Paul D. Converse. New York: Prentice-Hall, Inc.

Principles of Marketing, by Fred E. Clark. New York: Macmillan Company.

Readings In Marketing, by Fred E. Clark. New York: Macmillan Company.

Elements of Marketing, by Paul T. Cherington. New York: Macmillan Company.

Marketing, Its Problems and Methods, by C. S. Duncan. New York: D. Appleton & Company.

Principles of Marketing, by P. W. Ivey. New York: Ronald Press Company.

Some Problems in Market Distribution, by A. W. Shaw. Cambridge: Harvard University Press.

The Marketing of Farm Products, by L. H. D. Weld. New York: Macmillan Company.

Co-operative Marketing, by H. Steen. New York: Doubleday Page & Co.

Marketing Agricultural Products, by H. B. Hibbard. New York: D. Appleton & Co.

Organized Produce Markets, by J. G. Smith. New York: Longmans, Green & Co.

Marketing Problems, by Melvin T. Copeland. Chicago: A. W. Shaw & Company.

Efficient Marketing for Agricultural Products, by Theodore Macklin. New York: Macmillan Company.

### Psychology of Advertising.

A number of books consider advertising in the light of a mental problem. Included in these psychological discussions are:

Advertising and Selling, by H. L. Hollingworth. New York: D. Appleton & Co.

Principles of Advertising, by Daniel Starch. Chicago: A. W. Shaw & Co.

The Psychology of Advertising, by Walter Dill Scott. Boston: Small Maynard & Co.

The Theory of Advertising, by Walter Dill Scott. Boston: Small Maynard & Co.

Productive Advertising, by Herbert W. Hess. Philadelphia: J. B. Lippincott Company.

Advertising—Its Mental Laws, by H. F. Adams. New York: Macmillan Company.

Manual for the Study of the Psychology of Advertising and Selling, by Harry D. Kitson. Philadelphia: J. B. Lippincott Company.

### Sales Correspondence.

The subject of copy is but one step removed from the study of sales correspondence, on which subject the following books will be found helpful:

Handbook of Business English, by Hotchkiss & Kilduff. New York: Harper & Bros.

Advanced Business Correspondence, by Hotchkiss & Kilduff. New York: Harper & Bros.

Handbook of Business Correspondence, by S. Roland Hall. New York: McGraw-Hill Book Company.

Commercial Correspondence, by Butler & Burd. New York: D. Appleton & Co.

Effective Business Letters, by E. H. Gardner. New York: Ronald Press Company.

English Manual for Business, by Winternitz & Cherington. Chicago: A. W. Shaw Company.

Better Business English, by Manly & Powell. Chicago: F. J. Drake & Co.

Applied Business Correspondence, by Herbert Watson. Chicago: A. W. Shaw Company.

Business Letter Practice, by John B. Opdycke. New York: Isaac Pitman & Co.

## Copy.

Good discussions of copy will be found in the general books mentioned in the first group. Other works which may profitably be read in conjunction with copy are:

Advertising Copy, by G. B. Hotchkiss. New York: Harper & Bros.

Writing an Advertisement, by S. Roland Hall. New York: Houghton Mifflin & Co.

Thirty Practical Lessons in Advertising & Selling, by Guy Hubbart. New York: The U. P. C. Book Company.

Business Writing, by James Melvin Lee. New York: Ronald Press Company.

Imagination in Business, by L. F. Deland. New York: Harper & Bros.

Making Advertisements and Making Them Pay, by Roy Durstine. New York: Chas. Scribner's Sons.

Influencing Men in Business, by Walter Dill Scott. New York: Ronald Press Company.

The Mind of the Buyer, by H. D. Kitson. New York: Macmillan Company.

Human Nature in Business, by Fred C. Kelly. New York: G. P. Putnam's Sons.

For reference purposes, it is well to have the following works available in the working library:

Webster's New International Dictionary.

Roget's Thesaurus.

Fernald's Synonyms and Antonyms and Prepositions.

Encyclopedia Britannica or a similar encyclopedia.

## Trade-Marks.

Numerous works are available to anyone who is interested in trade-marks, and the law on unfair competition. Many of the following authorities were drawn upon for the chapter dealing with the subject:

Law of Unfair Competition and Trade-Marks, by Harry D. Nims. New York: Baker, Voorhis & Co.

Law of Trade-Marks, Including Trade Names, by A. C. Paul. St. Paul: Keefe & Davidson Co.

American Copyright Law, by A. W. Weil. New York: Baker Voorhis & Co.

Good-Will, Trade-Marks & Unfair Competition, by E. S. Rogers, Chicago: A. W. Shaw Co.

Patents, Copyrights and Trade-Marks, by W. H. Elfreth. New York: Baker, Voorhis & Co.

Law of Trade-Marks, Trade Names and Unfair Competition, by J. L. Hopkins. Cincinnati: W. H. Anderson Company.

Trade-Mark Power, by Glen Buck. Chicago: Munroe & Southworth.

Trade-Marks of the Jewelry and Kindred Trades. New York: Jewelers' Circular Publishing Company.

Business Competition and The Law, by G. H. Montague. New York: G. P. Putnam's Sons.

Manual of Federal Trade Commission, by Harvey & Bradford. Washington: John Byrne & Co.

Law of Trade-Marks and Designs in Canada, by R. S. Swart. Philadelphia: Crowmarty Law Book Company.

Law of Trade-Marks, by T. B. Sebastian. London: Stevens & Sons, Ltd.

Trade-Marks, by J. S. Salamon. London: Kegan Paul, French Trubner & Co.

A Book of American Trade-Marks and Devices, by Joseph Sinel. New York: Alfred H. Knopf.

Psychological Study of Trade-Mark Infringements, by R. H. Paynter, Jr. New York: The Science Press.

Statutes Concerning the Registration of Trade-Marks (in the United States). Washington: Commissioner of Patents.

Circular of the Patent & Copyright Office (in Canada). Ottawa: Commissioner of Patents.

Instructions to Persons Who Wish to Register Trade-Marks (in the United Kingdom). London: The Registrar, Patent Office.

## Visualizing.

Practically nothing had previously been said in book form on the subject of visualizing as distinguished from layout. The publications which offer the nearest approach to it are: The Annual of Illustrations for Advertisements in the United States. New York: Art Directors Club.

Charts & Graphs, by K. G. Karsten. New York: Prentice-Hall, Inc.

## Layouts.

On the subject of layouts, and the illustrative treatment of advertisements, we have:

The Art Appeal in Display Advertising, by Frank Alvah Parsons. New York: Harper & Bros.

Principles of Advertising Arrangement, by Frank Alvah Parsons. New York: Prang Educational Company.

Light & Color in Advertising & Merchandising, by M. Luckiesch. New York: D. Van Nostrand Company.

## Printing.

Of the books on printing, those which apply most immediately to advertising are the following:

Making Type Work, by Benjamin Sherbow. New York: The Century Company.

Effective Type Use for Advertising, by Benjamin Sherbow. New York: The author.

Typography of Advertisements that Pay, by Gilbert Farrar. New York: D. Appleton Company.

Art & Practice of Typography, by E. J. Gress. New York: Oswald Publishing Company.

Typography of Advertising, by F. J. Trezise. Chicago: Inland Printer.

Manual of Style. Chicago: Chicago University Press.

Among the works in which the history of printing is unfolded and which have supplied much of the historical data in the chapter dealing with the subject, are these:

John Guttenberg, First Master Printer, translated from the German. London: Kegan Paul, French Trubner & Co.

Typographia, by J. F. Adams. Philadelphia: L. Johnson & Co.

Guttenberg and The Art of Printing, by E. C. Pearson. Boston: D. Lathrop Company.

Early Printed Books, by E. G. Duff. London: Kegan Paul, Trench Trubner & Co.

A History of Old English Type Founders, by T. B. Reed. London: Elliot Stack.

Two Centuries of Type Founding, by J. F. MacRae. London: G. R. Jones.

Origin of Printing, by Middelon & Meerman. London: Bowyer & J. Michaels.

Paper, Its History, Sources and Manufacture, by H. A. Maddox. New York: Isaac Pitman & Sons.

Chronology of Paper and Paper Making, by Joel Munsell. London Kegan Paul, Trench Trubner & Co.

Essential Facts About Paper, by W. B. Wheelwright. Boston: Stone Andrew & Co.

## *Media.*

*Regarding publications*—the tendency has been to consider publications in the light of their markets. Considerable information is, consequently, issued by the publishers of media regarding the markets they serve. These survey reports are full of information. Applications for them should be made direct to the newspaper and magazine publishers.

On the technique of advertising in newspapers, few works published are better than the monographs issued by the American Newspaper Publishers' Association (headquarters, World Building, New York). The New York *Times* has issued a stylebook which contains many suggestions for use by newspaper advertisers.

## *Direct-Mail Advertising.*

The following books will be of interest in conjunction with the chapter on direct-mail advertising:

Year Book of Direct-Mail Advertising Conventions. Detroit: Direct Mail Advertising Ass'n.

Effective Direct Advertising, by Robert E. Ramsay. New York: D. Appleton & Co.

Selling by Mail, by V. E. Pratt. New York: McGraw-Hill Book Company.

Effective House Organs, by Robert E. Ramsay. New York: D. Appleton & Co.

The House Organ, by G. F. Wilson. Milwaukee: Washington Park Publishing Company.

Intensive Selling, by Flint McNaughton. Chicago: Selling Aid.

More Business Through Post Cards, by Flint McNaughton. Chicago: Selling Aid.

Mailing List Directory, by Dana, Morely & Kight. New York: McGraw-Hill Book Company.

Putnam's Directory of Mailing Lists, by W. S. Thompson. New York: G. P. Putnam's Sons.

Building Your Business by Mail, by W. G. Clifford. Chicago: Addressograph Company.

Effective Postal Publicity (British), by Max Rittenberg. London: Isaac Pitman & Sons.

Marketing by Mail, by Homer J. Buckley. New York: B. C. Forbes & Co.

## Research.

A study of Research carries one through a wide field, in which these books will be found helpful:

Principles of Advertising, by Daniel Starch. Chicago: A. W. Shaw & Co.

Marketing Analysis, by Percival White. New York: McGraw-Hill Book Company.

Business Research and Statistics, by J. George Frederick. New York: D. Appleton & Co.

Commercial Research, by C. S. Duncan. New York: Macmillan Company.

Elements of Statistical Method, by W. F. King. New York: Macmillan Company.

Business Statistics, by Melvin T. Copeland. Cambridge: Harvard University Press.

Statistics in Business, by Horace Secrist. New York: McGraw-Hill Book Company.

Source-Book of Research Data, by Lewis H. Haney. New York: Prentice-Hall, Inc.

Monthly Catalogue of U. S. Public Documents. Washington: Superintendent of Printing.

## For Beginners.

Three books offer guidance for those who contemplate entering the work of advertising:

The Advertising Man, by Earnest Elmo Calkins. New York: Chas. Scribner's Sons.

Training for the Business of Advertising, by Charles Hoyt. New York: G. B. Woolson.

Advertising as a Vocation, by Frederick I. Allen. New York: Macmillan Company.

## Economics of Advertising.

He who sees in the closing chapter of the book—treating of the evolution of industry—the importance of the subject it covers, will find new vistas opened for him in these books. Included in this list are the historical sources cited in the final chapter.

The New Business, by Harry Tipper. New York: Doubleday Page & Co.

Modern Industrialism, by F. L. McVey. New York: D. Appleton & Co.

The Economics of Marketing and Advertising, by W. D. Moriarty. New York: Harper & Bros.

Industrial History of the United States, by Katharine Coman. New York: Macmillan Company.

Industrial Depressions, by G. H. Hull. New York: F. A. Stokes Company.

Industrial History of Modern England, by A. H. Perris. London: Kegan Paul, French Trubner & Co., Ltd.

Progress of Invention in the Nineteenth Century, by E. W. Byrne. New York: Munn & Co.

Business Forecasting, by David F. Jordan. New York: Prentice-Hall, Inc.

## Other Books.

The following will also prove helpful to the reader seeking information on the subjects they discuss:

Advertising for the Retailer, by L. D. Herrold. New York: D. Appleton & Co.

Retail Advertising & Selling, by S. Roland Hall. New York: McGraw-Hill Book Company.

Manual of Successful Storekeeping, by W. P. Hotchkin. New York: Doubleday Page & Co.

Advertising the Retail Store, by B. H. Namm. New York: U. P. C. Book Company.

Export Advertising Practice, by Carl F. Propson. New York: Prentice-Hall, Inc.

Export Merchandising, by Walter F. Wyman. New York: McGraw-Hill Book Company.

Advertising for Trade in Latin America, by W. H. Aughinbaugh. New York: The Century Co.

Exporting Advertising, by D. L. Brown. New York: Ronald Press Company.

Constructive Merchandising, by Robert E. Ramsay. New York: D. Appleton & Co.

Bank Advertising Plans, by T. D. MacGregor. New York: Bankers Publishing Company.

Church Publicity, by C. F. Reisner. New York: Methodist Book Concern.

Automobile Selling Sense, by Cliff Knoble. New York: Prentice-Hall, Inc.

Commercial Engraving & Printing, by C. W. Hackleman. Indianapolis: Commercial Engraving Publishing Company.

The Process and Practice of Photo-Engraving, by H. A. Groesbeck, Jr. New York: Doubleday Page & Co.

Outdoor Advertising, by Wilmot Lippincott. New York: McGraw-Hill Book Company.

Window & Store Display, by A. T. Fischer. New York: Doubleday Page & Co.

History of Signboards, by Larwood & Hotten. London: Chatto & Windus.

A History of Advertising, by Henry Sampson. London: Chatto & Windus.

The Advertising Year Book (Reporting the A. A. C. of W. Convention), by E. T. Praigg. New York: Doubleday Page & Co.

Commercial Advertising (British), by Thomas Russell. New York: G. P. Putnam's Sons.

Textbook of Advertisement Writing and Designing (British), by B. C. Woodcock. New York: E. P. Dutton.

Scientific Distribution, by C. F. Higham. New York: Alfred Knopf.

Advertising—Selling the Consumer, by John Lee Mahin. New York: Doubleday Page & Co.

Advertising to Retailers, by R. T. Burdick. New York: Ronald Press Company.

Leadership of Advertised Brands, by Hotchkiss & Franken. New York: Doubleday, Page & Co.

Advertising Response, by H. M. Donovan. Philadelphia: J. B. Lippincott Co.

Creative Selling, by C. H. Mackintosh. New York: D. Appleton & Co.

Advertising as a Business Force, by Paul T. Cherington. New York: Doubleday, Page & Co.

More Sales through Advertising. Chicago: A. W. Shaw Company.

The Business of Advertising, by Ernest Elmo Calkins. New York: D. Appleton & Co.

Better Advertising, by J. M. Manly. Chicago: F. J. Drake & Co.

The Actline & Milline System, by Benjamin Jefferson. Niles, Mich.: H. M. Jefferson & Co.

First Principles of Advertising, by W. D. Nesbit. New York: Gregg Publishing Co.

How to Advertise, by George French. New York: Doubleday, Page & Co.

Advertising and Selling Practice, by John B. Opdyke. Chicago: A. W. Shaw & Co.

Handbook of Sales Management, by S. Roland Hall. New York: McGraw-Hill Book Company.

What a Salesman Should Know About Advertising, by J. C. Aspley. Chicago: The Dartnell Company.

Scientific Space Selection. Chicago: Audit Bureau of Circulations.

Advertising by Motion Pictures, by E. A. Dinch. Cincinnati: Standard Publishing Company.

Selling Advertising Space, by J. E. Chasnoff. New York: Ronald Press Company.

Newspaper Cooperation, Merchandising & Promotion, by R. E. Smith. Indianapolis: The Author.

Specialty Advertising, by H. S. Bunting. Chicago: Novelty News Company.

Travelling Publicity Campaigns, by M. S. Routzahn. New York: Russell Sage Foundation.

Crystallizing Public Opinion, by E. T. Bernays. New York: Boni & Liveright.

Publicity, by Wilder & Buell. New York: Ronald Press Company.

Getting the Most out of Business, by E. St. Elmo Lewis. New York: Ronald Press Company.

The Advertising Index, by Rubin Jaffe. Los Angeles: Los Angeles Advertising Club.

# APPENDIX
## OF
# USEFUL TABLES

Recommended Widths for Type Lines

Words to the Inch (Approximate)

Recommended Paper Sizes for Booklets and Catalogues

Recommended Paper Sizes for Unstitched Circulars

Standard Envelope Sizes

## RECOMMENDED WIDTHS FOR TYPE LINES

| If Your Copy Is Set in | Set in the Lines Between |
|---|---|
| 6 point | 7 to 10 picas wide |
| 8 point | 9 to 13 " " |
| 10 point | 13 to 16 " " |
| 11 point | 13 to 18 " " |
| 12 point | 14 to 21 " " |
| 14 point | 18 to 24 " " |
| 18 point | 20 to 34 " " |

## WORDS TO THE INCH (APPROXIMATE)

| IF SET IN | WORDS PER SQUARE INCH | | WORDS IN 1 INCH | 13-EM COLUMN |
|---|---|---|---|---|
| | Solid | Leaded | Solid | Leaded |
| 6 Point | 47 | 34 | 102 | 74 |
| 8 Point | 32 | 23 | 70 | 50 |
| 9 Point | 28 | 25 | 61 | 46 |
| 10 Point | 21 | 16 | 46 | 35 |
| 11 Point | 17 | 14 | 37 | 30 |
| 12 Point | 14 | 13 | 30 | 24 |
| 14 Point | 11 | 9 | 24 | 20 |
| 18 Point | 7 | 6 | 15 | 13 |

## RECOMMENDED PAPER SIZES FOR BOOKLETS AND CATALOGUES

| This Page Size | In the Following Number of Pages | Cuts Economically Out of These Sheet Sizes |
|---|---|---|
| 3 x 6 | 4, 8, 16, 24, 48 | 25 x 38—38 x 50 |
| 4 x 9 | 4, 6, 8, 16, 24, 48 | 25 x 38—38 x 50 |
| $4\frac{1}{2}$ x 6 | 4, 8, 16, 32, 64 | 25 x 38—38 x 50 |
| 6 x $9\frac{1}{8}$ | 4, 8, 16, 32 | 25 x 38—38 x 50 |
| $9\frac{1}{4}$ x $12\frac{1}{8}$ | 4, 8, 16, 32 | 25 x 38—38 x 50 |
| $3\frac{1}{2}$ x $6\frac{3}{8}$ | 4, 8, 16, 24, 48 | $30\frac{1}{2}$ x 41—41 x 61 |
| 5 x $7\frac{1}{4}$ | 4, 8, 16, 32, 64 | $30\frac{1}{2}$ x 41—41 x 61 |
| $7\frac{3}{8}$ x $9\frac{7}{8}$ | 4, 8, 16, 32 | $30\frac{1}{2}$ x 41—41 x 61 |
| 10 x $14\frac{7}{8}$ | 4, 8, 16 | $30\frac{1}{2}$ x 41—41 x 61 |
| $3\frac{3}{4}$ x $5\frac{1}{8}$ | 4, 8, 16, 32, 64 | 32 x 44—44 x 64 |
| $3\frac{3}{4}$ x $6\frac{7}{8}$ | 4, 8, 16, 24, 48 | 32 x 44—44 x 64 |
| $5\frac{1}{4}$ x $7\frac{5}{8}$ | 4, 8, 16, 32, 64 | 32 x 44—44 x 64 |
| $7\frac{1}{2}$ x $10\frac{5}{8}$ | 4, 8, 16, 32 | 32 x 44—44 x 64 |
| $10\frac{3}{4}$ x $15\frac{5}{8}$ | 4, 8, 16 | 32 x 44—44 x 64 |

## RECOMMENDED PAPER SIZES FOR UNSTITCHED CIRCULARS

| This Page Size | In the Following Number of Pages | Cuts Economically Out of These Sheet Sizes |
|---|---|---|
| $3\frac{1}{8}$ x $6\frac{1}{4}$ | 4, 6, 8, 12, 16, 24 | 25 x 38—38 x 50 |
| $4\frac{1}{8}$ x $9\frac{1}{2}$ | 4, 6, 12, 16, 24 | 25 x 38—38 x 50 |
| $4\frac{3}{4}$ x $6\frac{1}{4}$ | 4, 8, 16, 32 | 25 x 38—38 x 50 |
| $6\frac{1}{4}$ x $9\frac{1}{2}$ | 4, 8, 16, 32 | 25 x 38—38 x 50 |
| $9\frac{1}{2}$ x $12\frac{1}{2}$ | 4, 8, 16, 32 | 25 x 38—38 x 50 |
| $3\frac{3}{4}$ x $6\frac{3}{4}$ | 4, 6, 8, 12, 16, 24 | $30\frac{1}{2}$ x 41—41 x 61 |
| $5\frac{1}{8}$ x $7\frac{5}{8}$ | 4, 8, 16, 32 | $30\frac{1}{2}$ x 41—41 x 61 |
| $7\frac{5}{8}$ x $10\frac{1}{4}$ | 4, 8, 16, 32 | $30\frac{1}{2}$ x 41—41 x 61 |
| $10\frac{1}{4}$ x $15\frac{1}{4}$ | 4, 8, 16 | $30\frac{1}{2}$ x 41—41 x 61 |
| 4 x $5\frac{1}{2}$ | 4, 8, 16 | 32 x 44—44 x 64 |
| 4 x $7\frac{1}{4}$ | 4, 8, 16, 24 | 32 x 44—44 x 64 |
| $5\frac{1}{2}$ x 8 | 4, 8, 16, 32 | 32 x 44—44 x 64 |
| 8 x 11 | 4, 8, 16, 32 | 32 x 44—44 x 64 |
| 11 x16 | 4, 8, 16 | 32 x 44—44 x 64 |

## STANDARD ENVELOPE SIZES

| Commercial | | Legal | |
|---|---|---|---|
| *Number* | *Size in Inches* | *Number* | *Size in Inches* |
| 3 | 2⅝ x 4¾ | 9 | 3⅞ x 8⅞ |
| 4 | 2⅞ x 5¼ | 10 | 4⅛ x 9½ |
| 5 | 3⅛ x 5½ | 11 | 4½ x 10⅜ |
| 6 | 3⅜ x 6 | 12 | 4¾ x 11 |
| 6¼ | 3½ x 6 | | |
| 6¾ | 3⅝ x 6½ | | |

| Baronial | |
|---|---|
| 4 | 3⅝ x 4 11/16 |
| 5 | 4⅛ x 5⅛ |
| 6 | 5 x 6 |

# INDEX

# INDEX

529

# Titles in This Series

**9.**
C. Samuel Craig and Avijit Ghosh, editors. The Development of Media Models in Advertising: An Anthology of Classic Articles. 1985

**10.**
C. Samuel Craig and Brian Sternthal, editors. Repetition Effects Over the Years: An Anthology of Classic Articles. 1985

**11.**
John K. Crippen. Successful Direct-Mail Methods. 1936

**12.**
Ernest Dichter. The Strategy of Desire. 1960

**13.**
Ben Duffy. Advertising Media and Markets. 1939

**14.**
Warren Benson Dygert. Radio as an Advertising Medium. 1939

**15.**
Francis Reed Eldridge. Advertising and Selling Abroad. 1930

**16.**
J. George Frederick, editor. Masters of Advertising Copy: Principles and Practice of Copy Writing According to its Leading Practitioners. 1925

**17.**
George French. Advertising: The Social and Economic Problem. 1915

**18.**
Max A. Geller. Advertising at the Crossroads: Federal Regulation vs. Voluntary Controls. 1952

**19.**
Avijit Ghosh and C. Samuel Craig. The Relationship of Advertising Expenditures to Sales: An Anthology of Classic Articles. 1985

**20.**
Albert E. Haase. The Advertising Appropriation, How to Determine It and How to Administer It. 1931

**21.**
S. Roland Hall. The Advertising Handbook, 1921

**22.**
S. Roland Hall. Retail Advertising and Selling. 1924

**23.**
Harry Levi Hollingworth. Advertising and Selling: Principles of Appeal and Response. 1913

**24.**
Floyd Y. Keeler and Albert E. Haase. The Advertising Agency, Procedure and Practice. 1927

**25.**
H. J. Kenner. The Fight for Truth in Advertising. 1936

**26.**
Otto Kleppner. Advertising Procedure. 1925

**27.**
Harden Bryant Leachman. The Early Advertising Scene. 1949

**28.**
E. St. Elmo Lewis. Financial Advertising, for Commercial and Savings Banks, Trust, Title Insurance, and Safe Deposit Companies, Investment Houses. 1908

**29.**
R. Bigelow Lockwood. Industrial Advertising Copy. 1929

**30.**
D. B. Lucas and C. E. Benson. Psychology for Advertisers. 1930

**31.**
Darrell B. Lucas and Steuart H. Britt. Measuring Advertising Effectiveness. 1963

**32.**
Papers of the American Association of Advertising Agencies. 1927

**33.**
Printer's Ink. Fifty Years 1888–1938. 1938

**34.**
Jason Rogers. Building Newspaper Advertising. 1919

**35.**
George Presbury Rowell. Forty Years an Advertising Agent, 1865–1905. 1906

**36.**
Walter Dill Scott. The Theory of Advertising: A Simple Exposition of the Principles of Psychology in Their Relation to Successful Advertising. 1903

**37.**
Daniel Starch. Principles of Advertising. 1923

**38.**
Harry Tipper, George Burton Hotchkiss, Harry L. Hollingworth, and Frank Alvah Parsons. Advertising, Its Principles and Practices. 1915

**39.**
Roland S. Vaile. Economics of Advertising. 1927

**40.**
Helen Woodward. Through Many Windows. 1926